SOMEBODY ELSE'S CHILDREN

SOMEBODY ELSE'S CHILDREN

THE COURTS,
THE KIDS, AND
THE STRUGGLE TO SAVE
AMERICA'S TROUBLED FAMILIES

John Hubner and Jill Wolfson

Authors Choice Press
New York Lincoln Shanghai

Somebody Else's Children
The Courts, The Kids, and The Struggle
to Save America's Troubled Families

Authors Choice Press
an imprint of iUniverse, Inc.

For information address:
iUniverse, Inc.
2021 Pine Lake Road, Suite 100
Lincoln, NE 68512
www.iuniverse.com

Originally published by Crown Publishers, Inc.

ISBN: 0-595-30078-2

Printed in the United States of America

For our children,
Alexander Sam and Gwendolyn Sarah.

And in memory of Don Sagatun-Edwards, 1979–1996. Thank you.

PROLOGUE

The Authors in Court

THE FUTURES OF OUR OWN CHILDREN WERE NOT AT STAKE; ALEX AND Gwen were across town, happily chasing school friends around the playground. We were appearing at a hearing in juvenile court because our book was on the line.

The juvenile justice system is really two separate systems: the "dependency," or "child welfare" branch, whose purpose is to protect children who have been neglected or abused physically, sexually, or emotionally; and the "delinquency" branch, charged with determining if a minor has broken the law and how he or she should be punished and rehabilitated.

This system is a complex web of individuals bound together by esoteric laws and mind-boggling funding structures. Investigators check out charges of abuse, and an army of social workers provides services. Separate sets of attorneys guard the legal rights of parents and of children; a third set guards the legal rights of the social workers. Volunteer advocates, who often know the children better than the professionals, sometimes appear in court to push the system to do what it is supposed to do. Therapists help families understand and control violence. An industry of "rehabs" works with alcohol and drug problems. Foster parents take over when a family falls apart. Children who have suffered serious psychological damage are placed in residential care facilities that routinely cost $7,000 a month.

In delinquency proceedings, district attorneys press charges against minors, who are represented by private counsel or public defenders. Probation officers check out family histories, and psychologists put kids through a battery of tests. Counselors at youth ranches try to instill discipline and a sense of responsibility. Minors who run from ranches or commit serious crimes are often sent to "youth authorities," "training schools," or "youth correctional facilities," which are, in fact, prisons for youth. In California, the Youth Authority costs $30,100 per year per ward.

What sets juvenile justice apart from the rest of the legal system is that it is wrapped deep in a cocoon of confidentiality, and, like everything about the system, the cocoon is purported to be in the best interests of children. But the system—and the public and often the children themselves—pay a heavy price for confidentiality.

Inside the system, confidentiality means that few people—the judge, perhaps an advocate—have access to the full and complete records of any family or any child. Attorneys are prohibited from asking certain questions, and in turn they prohibit certain things from going into the record; social workers are barred from reading certain records; therapists are not permitted to share their insights with foster parents.

Outside the system, confidentiality has contributed to making juvenile court the least understood, least explored branch of the American legal system. Journalists have long complained that they cannot cover the system in any on-going, comprehensive way because no one will talk to them except in the most vague generalities. While there have been several excellent television documentaries and books, often by system insiders, mainstream journalists frequently ignore the system until there is a catastrophe—a child dies in foster care, and under the law no one is permitted to explain why the baby was taken from her biological parents. A child is returned to parents who have a history of violence; the child ends up dead, and again, no one is permitted to talk. No one puts these calamities into perspective.

Attorneys can talk to journalists only with all the telling details obliterated; social workers who have worked with a family for years and years cannot even hint to a reporter that they are furious at the way the case has been handled; psychologists go on about diagnostic criteria, but they cannot divulge the events that transform dry clinicalese into a portrait of a family struggling for its existence.

It was our idea to shed light on this system by following children and families through the shelters and the courts, the foster homes and the juvenile halls, along the way explaining the law, deciphering how the system worked, or how it didn't work, in a number of specific cases, examined over a long period of time. We also wanted to give voice to people who are so rarely heard. We have all read disturbing things about the quality of foster care, but what is the reality of life for a sixteen-year-old who has been raised in twenty foster homes? What words does an eight-year-old use to describe being caught in the middle of a vicious divorce? How does a fifteen-year-old explain why he committed a murder? And so much more.

John Hubner is a former probation officer at the Cook County Juvenile Court in Chicago. His long interest in the system led him to profile Judge Leonard P. Edwards, the presiding judge of the Santa Clara County (California) Juvenile Court, for the Sunday magazine of the *San Jose Mercury News* in 1988. Jill Wolfson has been a feature writer, an editor, and a columnist at the *Mercury News* for fifteen years. Her interest in juvenile justice grew out of her writing on women, families, and children.

In the summer of 1993, we laid out our ideas for Judge Edwards: California is the perfect place to x-ray the juvenile justice system. One eighth of the country's children live in this state. The racial mix in Santa Clara County is what America will look like in the next century—Hispanic, Vietnamese, Portuguese, black, white, Chinese. The economic strata goes from the very poor to the superrich, and the youth problems that plague New York, Chicago, Los Angeles—and, increasingly, small towns and rural areas—are all here: abused children, gangs, teenage pregnancy, kids without homes, kids without a future. It is a setting that accurately reflects what is taking place with children and families around the country.

"Sure. Do it. You've got to do it," the judge said when we had finished our pitch.

There was, of course, the "small" matter of confidentiality. The insiders who have written books have usually gotten around the confidentiality issue by basing their work on their first-hand experience. On rare occasion, a judge has given a reporter controlled access to a specific case. But at this point, we did not know what cases we wanted to write about, or who we even needed to talk to.

"If we are going to give a full picture of the system, we need to understand the system from the inside out," we told the judge. "The only way to do that is to be able to wander through it. We'd like to be able to read a wide variety of case files, talk to as many workers and families in the system as we can. We need to be free to hear different viewpoints. And everyone needs to feel free to talk to us."

"Let me think about that one," the judge said. "When the time comes, we'll deal with it."

When the time came, the judge did something that had never been done in California—or, as far as he knew, in the U.S. He issued a broad judicial order that opened the cocoon of both the dependency and delinquency branches of the system: "Good Cause Appearing, John Hubner and Jill Wolfson shall be permitted to have access to all information relating to children and families under investigation by the Department of Family and Children's Services ("the Department"), or under the protection of the Department. Such access shall include records, interviews with social workers, and (if they are willing) interviews with children and families.

"John Hubner and Jill Wolfson shall also be permitted to have access to all information relating to children and families under investigation by the Probation Department or under supervision by the Probation Department. . . ."

The first impulse of a sealed-off system, whether it is the bloodstream or the juvenile court, is to reject intruders. There was nothing mean-spirited about this; people were just doing their jobs. A deputy DA who had worked with Judge Edwards for years called to say that he didn't think the judge could issue such an order. He was all for the book—the work he did and the children he represented should not exist in a shadowland—he just didn't think that the book could be done legally. Somebody would surely file a writ and take the order up to the appeals court and stop the book cold.

Social workers, trained in confidentiality since college, were incredulous when the court order landed on their desks. They grilled their supervisors and called the judge to say that they were all for the book—they felt that no one understood the legal and moral boundaries they worked under and that resulted in their having been scapegoated in the press for years. They would love to talk about specific cases—but were they reading the order correctly? Could they really use names and details? Could they really open their files to these outsiders?

The public defender was also all for the book. The parents he represented were always portrayed as the bad guys; they had never had a voice. But he was furious with the judge's order, and, in many ways, his concerns were justifiable. Social workers had no right to open his clients' files without their permission. The judge was throwing confidentiality out the window! How could he do that without consulting anyone?

For weeks, meetings with representatives from every part of the far-flung system were held in Judge Edwards's chambers. The judge pointed out that the order letting us wander unrestrained through the system also bound us to confidentiality—"Such access shall be permitted on the condition that [the writers] not disclose to anyone any information that would identify any child or parent. . . ."

Here is how it would work: After reading dozens of cases and interviewing hundreds of people, the writers would select the individual cases they wanted to include in the book. The judge would then bring the parents and children into court, along with their attorneys and social workers and any other interested parties. At this hearing, anyone who had objections would be heard.

And now, after more than a year of research, here we were, in court, seeking to open our first case for publication. Judge Edwards's small courtroom was packed with system insiders—the DA, the public defender, the attorney representing the Department of Family and Children's Services; representatives from Court Appointed Special Advocates (CASA); and attorneys who had become advocates of the book. Everyone was curious to see what the judge would do.

"Item number one on your morning calendar, the case of Kimberly Beyer, a hearing on confidentiality," announced Judge Edwards's court officer.

Kimberly Beyer* [When a name has been changed an asterisk appears at the first mention. In these cases, names of family members have also been changed.] is a five-year-old at the center of a sexual abuse case. The judge asked us if we were prepared to make a few small concessions: would we change her name, disguise some minor descriptions of the family, and camouflage the father's occupation in order to conceal the family's identity from people who might know them?

We would.

"The writers have discussed with you the changes they are prepared to make? You have discussed this with each other, and with your attorney?" the judge asked Ron and Sandy Beyer, the child's parents, who were seated at the rear of the court. The parents said that they had.

"You agree to these conditions?" the judge asked. The parents said that they did.

The judge turned to two attorneys who were sitting next to each other at the U-shaped table below the bench. One was a deputy county attorney who was representing the social worker from the Department in this case. The other was the deputy district attorney who was representing the child.

"We have discussed this at length," the deputy DA said. "When Kimberly turns eighteen and decides she wants to tell her story, she can tell it then. The records in this case have been sealed and should remain sealed."

"Just a minute, Judge!" said the private attorney who was representing the parents. "That is a ridiculous assertion! Kimmy has two very fine parents who are sitting right here. They are perfectly capable of speaking for her. If you need reasons why this story should be told, ask them!"

And so it went. We were trying to take notes, but midway through we looked at each other and realized that we were both completely lost. Parents had described to us how powerless they felt when the court took control of their children. A book is certainly not a child, but we were getting an invaluable lesson. This was a taste of what it must have been like to have the fate of something we considered ours—the book—in the hands of strangers who acted as if it were theirs.

Unlike a majority of parents who come before the court, we knew how the system worked. We knew that the court is much like a drama and that everyone has his role to play. We knew the players personally and had mastered the jargon; we spoke English and were college educated. Yet, we had only a vague idea of what was going on.

Somehow, our book had vanished, buried in legal minutiae. One attorney requested a continuance because the grandparents had not been "noticed," meaning that they had not been formally notified of the court hearing. Another said that a continuance was necessary, but not in order to notice the grandparents. First, the grandparents' attorney had to be noticed so that he could decide if the grandparents had to be noticed. We hadn't even interviewed the grandparents. What did they have to do with this case?

An attorney who had told us in the hallway that she could not wait to read the book was now on her feet, attacking it. "It's the precedent that concerns me, Your Honor. Once you let the press in, you can't keep them out. You're opening the door for every tabloid that issues a press card!"

The argument wound up where it had started, with the classic battle between the rights of the child—"A five-year-old cannot decide whether or not she wants to be written about"—and the rights of parents to make decisions for their children. The case was continued, and we ended up in the hallway, our heads spinning.

At another hearing two weeks later, the judge made his ruling. "As long as there are no 'identifiers'—specific facts that reveal the identity of the minor or any adult who wishes to be concealed, I'm going to open this case to publication," Judge Edwards said. "Confidentiality does not mean secrecy. The public has a right to know the full story of what we do here. When we make mistakes, they need to know why. When we do something right, they should know about that, too."

Similar hearings were held on every case you will read about in this book.

•　•　•

With the mountain of material we had gathered, how did we finally settle upon the stories that make up this book?

A lot of the writing on the juvenile justice system tends to focus on sensational stories that are used by authors with an agenda to make one or two hard-hitting points. We, too, could have shaped our material to make any political argument we chose: Does the child welfare system endanger children by leaving them with abusive or neglectful parents? It certainly does, and we had cases to prove it. Is the opposite also true? Does the system unfairly pluck children away from parents only because of poverty and physical disabilities? We had those cases, as well.

Does the court release delinquents with nothing more than a lecture from the judge? Do those delinquents go out and commit more serious crimes? We had plenty of cases that could make that point. We also had plenty of cases that made the opposite point: judges lock up kids who, with the right supervision and opportunities, could be living meaningful, productive lives.

We could have written a book that was nothing but system success stories: drug-abusing parents who turned their lives around so that they could raise their children; gang members who turned into promising young citizens.

Writers are naturally attracted to such high drama, but we found ourselves in a remarkable situation. Ultimately, we decided to bypass extraordinary drama for the ordinary drama that more accurately reflects the day-to-day workings of the system. We decided upon stories that are not "special," that do not stand out, that do not represent any kind of legal breakthroughs. Each case we selected is no more or no less compelling than the case that came before it on the judge's calendar that day. The child born addicted to drugs, the teenager who was raised by the system, the member of a gang—these are everyday cases in juvenile court. That is what makes these "ordinary" cases so extraordinary.

Woven together, they create a tapestry that reveals how intricate the juvenile justice system is and how interconnected are the problems facing America, how there are no easy answers, no silver bullets for child abuse and domestic violence, foster care, drugs, teen pregnancy, and gang wars.

Those are the journalistic reasons for the stories we have selected. There are, of course, more personal reasons. Anyone who witnesses the hopes, the frustrations, and the pain of families and children ends up being moved, over and over again. Simply put, these are stories that just got to us.

When we started our research, we were insistent upon publishing real names whenever possible. But in cases where the court ruled that names and identities must be changed, we found—to our own surprise—that we agreed. Slightly altering identities costs the reader nothing. It took great courage for these people to relive their pasts. There is no reason why they and their children should have to relive them forever.

There are no composite figures. Names of attorneys, social workers, and others who work with children have not been changed. The events depicted are based on interviews, court reports, and social service and probation records. In some cases, events unfolded when we were present.

We urge the reader to turn to the supporting material appearing at the end of the book, especially the historical notes. If we are going to learn to care for somebody else's children, we have much to learn from the mistakes and successes of the past.

SOMEBODY ELSE'S CHILDREN

1

DEPENDENCY COURT, 8:30 A.M.

IN THE EARLY 1950s, SAN JOSE, CALIFORNIA, AT THE BOTTOM OF SAN Francisco Bay, was an agricultural town with a population of 95,000 that was known as the prune capital of the country. As the electronics explosion hit in the 1960s and roared throughout the 1970s, San Jose, the largest city in Santa Clara County, grew faster than any city in the U.S. Spurred by the success of high-tech giants like IBM, Apple Computer, and Hewlett-Packard, the area continued to boom throughout the 1980s. Today, Santa Clara County has a population of 1.5 million, with a diverse ethnic mix, and is the largest county in Northern California. San Jose ranks as the eleventh largest city in the country, only a notch behind Detroit. The estimated population of 880,000 surpasses that of San Francisco by more than 100,000.

Now known as the capital of Silicon Valley, San Jose does not have San Francisco's startling beauty and world-class culture, its sense of fun and of the absurd. Like Phoenix or Houston, San Jose is a Sunbelt boomtown trying desperately to develop a character of its own. The city's redevelopment agency has poured hundreds of millions of dollars into revitalizing the downtown with some success, but San Jose remains at heart a mall town. On the city map, eye-catching canary yellow blots mark the major shopping centers.

One of the few old buildings in San Jose and the most majestic structure downtown is the Santa Clara County Superior Court. Built in 1867 to lure the state legislature and lovingly restored in 1994, the courthouse faces the small park where Robert Kennedy gave his last speech in 1968. Its stone facade is painted a rich butterscotch and is set off by huge oak-framed windows and cream-colored Corinthian columns that soar to an ornate frieze high above the steep front steps. The courtrooms inside resemble opulent Victorian drawing rooms, a testament to the importance society places on the kind of law practiced here. There are elegant wainscoting, meticulously restored filigree, and impressive chandeliers. Judges' chambers have the leather furniture of private men's clubs.

This stately building is, of course, *not* where Judge Leonard P. Edwards, presiding judge of the Juvenile Court, reports to work each morning. Superior Court is reserved for high-profile and high-paying cases like homicide and tax evasion. Families and children are shuttled off to the Santa Clara County Dependency Court, a boxy two-story structure painted a flat, dreary oatmeal color. No towering columns guard the entrance to the building; over the door, there is a blue cloth awning that is beginning to fade in the intense sun. The name of the court is not chiseled in marble, as it is in the frieze of the Superior Court building; plain metal letters are riveted onto the plaster and announce not the name of the court but "Santa Clara County Court Annex."

The annex is the setting for dependency, or child welfare, proceedings. Here, judges and often lesser judicial officers make decisions that have unfathomable ramifications: First, they decide if children have been abused physically, sexually, or emotionally, and if so, they then determine the fate of these children. Are they to be separated from the only world they have ever known—their families—and placed into the potentially impersonal world of foster care, maybe for the rest of their childhood? Are they to remain in the care of parents who, despite safeguards put into place, still have the potential of inflicting the most deadly wounds?

What dependency court lacks in stature, it makes up in emotional charge and danger. It is a rare social worker, attorney, or judge who does not have a story to tell about an obsessed mother who phones ten times a day to swear that she never beat her daughter or about anonymous death threats that arrive in the morning mail. A few years ago, a father who had lost custody of a child burst into the annex armed with a .357 magnum. He shot and wounded three bailiffs before he himself was wounded. In a wall near the courtrooms, there are still bullet-sized indentations that plaster did not completely cover up.

Episodes like that are one reason there is a line snaking up the block by the annex every weekday morning at 8:30. Parents with children squirming in their arms and children who dart in and out of the line, social workers who keep shifting the stacks of files in their arms, attorneys in dark suits who are buzzing through court reports, and an occasional judge wait while two deputy sheriffs rummage through purses, attaché cases, and diaper bags to check for weapons. Everyone must also pass through a metal detector that buzzes when someone forgets to cover a belt buckle or overlooks the stray dime wedged deep in a pocket.

By 9 A.M., the upstairs waiting area usually looks as if an invisible wave has come crashing down, leaving in its wake a multitude of tangled lives. The people here have all been struggling and living in chaos. What happens in court this day will go a long way toward determining what happens in the rest of their lives. On this particular morning, in the waiting area for Judge Edwards's Courtroom #42, a little boy and an elderly woman, obviously his grandmother, were sitting on the same padded chair and gently rocking each other. In the row behind them, a girl, maybe six, methodically ripped apart a magazine while her mother stared into space. Standing nearby, an attorney kept jabbing his index finger at the thick manila envelope he was carrying while a mother and a father, their eyes dull with sorrow, listened silently. Their son, a handsome ten-year-old, looked at the ceiling, as if none of this was happening.

In the back row sat a young woman in her midteens with eyes the color of opal and the chalky yet luminous skin that only Rossetti has captured in paint. Her chin-length hair was colored as black as shoe polish, as were her nails. To amuse herself, she was biting them off and making a game out of how close to the wall she could spit them. She radiated a hostility so visceral that, even in a crowded waiting room, the chairs around her remained empty. Her name was Jenny Langdon*.

"How many times have I had to come to court? I don't know. Probably the first time was when my dad sliced up his arms with a razor. I was only like a little kid, like four, but I can still see all that blood squirting everywhere. He was crazy to do something like that. My mother was crazy, too. That's when the social workers first came for me.

"You know what they do when they come? The social workers beat around the bush with the little kids. They say: 'Oh, we are just going to take you away for a little while. You'll see mommy and daddy again, don't worry.' They lie to you so they can keep you. It really didn't dawn on me until I got older that I was never going to see mommy and daddy again."

Child welfare workers say that there is always at least *one* on their caseload at any particular time, a person they usually describe in medical terms: a headache, a pain in the neck, a heartbreaker, a walking wound. This person is either nowhere to be found or she is phoning five or ten times a day, crying, pleading, and threatening. She lies. She misses court appearances. The social worker bends over backward to get her a good foster home; she blows out of it in a week. Every encounter leaves the social worker emotionally drained and questioning her own sanity.

During her twelve years in the child welfare system, Jenny has been the *one* for a series of social workers, in addition to a string of attorneys, foster parents, counselors, therapists, and judges. The past two years of her life have been particularly rocky; Jenny has been in and out of six different foster homes and has landed in the Children's Shelter at least a dozen times. She dropped out of school, went back to school, and dropped out again. Her love life consisted mostly of hanging out with boyfriends who smacked her around. Four months ago, she was picked up by the police at midnight in a park with a known drug dealer. She has had one abortion. And now, although she was not yet showing, Jenny was pregnant again.

"My heart breaks when I think of that girl. Jenny is what I call triple-cursed," one of her former social workers explains. "She has been abused; she has been in the system all her life. And, she is just beautiful."

On this particular day, Jenny was scheduled for another "dispositional" hearing. In layman's terms, this meant that, once again, she had blown out of a foster home and been picked up by the police and taken to the Children's Shelter, where she was now living. Her social worker needed the judge's approval to place her in yet another foster home. For once, Jenny did not have the usual endless wait. A court officer stuck his head in the waiting room door and said that they were ready for her case. Jenny had dressed up for the hearing in the skirt and tailored blouse that her court-appointed special advocate had bought for her on a recent shopping trip. The new clothes made Jenny look taller, more slender, and certainly more mature than she did in her usual baggy jeans and flannel shirt.

· · ·

Judge Edwards's small, utilitarian courtroom does not reflect the stature of the man who has been called "California's strongest voice for children" and who is the recipient of the award the American Bar Association gives to the country's outstanding juvenile judge. He is the first and only chair of the Juvenile Court Judges of California, an organization that he believes will give juvenile judges around the state the power that comes from cohesiveness, the prestige that can get things done for children in the legal community and in the community at large.

Since the first juvenile court was inaugurated in 1899 in Chicago, there has never been any political power or prestige in working there. In the legal community, "Juvie" is often perceived as not even a real court, but rather a "social institution with legal trimmings." Attorneys and judges-to-be get that message from their first days in law school; juvenile law is rarely taught as part of the core curriculum and is perceived as "an exotic course, one which will not lead to employment."

It stands to reason, then, that lawyers with any ambition and judges with the most exacting minds have always gotten out of "Kiddie Court" as fast as they can in order to move on to the civil and criminal courts, where lawsuits and felony charges generate big legal fees and the publicity they create assures that future cases will bring even higher fees and greater career advancement.

Emotional burnout, too, is a fact of life here, even among the most dedicated and selfless. Veteran child welfare workers talk longingly about getting a license in counseling, going into private practice, and treating nice, "normal" neurotics. Foster parents are dropping out in droves. A prosecutor takes one look at the color pictures of an eight-month-old who was scalded by his mother and tells himself, "This is my last case in juvenile. I can't take this anymore."

With his credentials, Judge Edwards could have moved up the judicial ladder long ago. He could have gone into private practice and turned his skills and connections into $500,000 a year. He could have followed his father to Washington, D.C. Congressman Don Edwards was one of the last great liberals, a towering figure in the U.S. House of Representatives for thirty-two years, where he opposed the Vietnam War, championed civil rights, and was chairman of the judiciary subcommittee that oversees the operations of the FBI. When he retired in 1994, his son Len could have used the family name and resources it commanded to run for his seat. He would have won.

But Judge Edwards has chosen to remain in this remote corner of the legal solar system. During his fourteen years on the bench, he has helped build the Santa Clara County court into what is generally recognized as one of the best systems in the country.

Juvenile court judges traditionally confine their role to the courtroom. They make decisions and leave it to the other parts of the system—the social workers, the probation officers, the drug counselors—to enforce those decisions. Edwards's role extends far beyond the bench. He is a community activist and a cheerleader for children at large. He has promoted and organized programs to get children inoculated and to keep weapons out of their schools. Call his courtroom early in the morning and the judge answers the phone—he almost always arrives before his bailiff or court officer. At noon and at the end of the afternoon session, there is always a thick stack of phone messages waiting in his chambers.

His reputation stretches nationally and internationally, where he has become a sort of butterfly of the juvenile justice scene, flying to Chicago to help overhaul a social services system that has collapsed, to Montana to introduce a program he has started in California, to Miami to examine a program that may work back in California, to Brazil to help reform a child welfare system that currently leaves millions of children on the streets. With his wife, Inger Sagatun, who holds a Ph.D. in sociology, Edwards has published *Child Abuse and the Legal System*, a book that is emerging as the definitive text on the subject.

With all this, the question most often asked about the judge is "Why is Len Edwards still over there in Juvie?"

The judge has always found the question slightly amusing, because to him the answer is so obvious: "This court is society's means of holding ourselves accountable for the next generation," the judge says. "It is the arena where politics, economics, and morality intersect; where everything that Americans care passionately about yet seem incapable of agreeing upon—the family, individual rights, the role of government, taxes, welfare, crime, punishment, and rehabilitation—are embodied in society's most vulnerable members, its children. Working in the system is a chance to help keep hatred and violence from being passed on from one generation to the next, to keep violence from spilling out of the home and into the schools and streets.

"What can be more important than that?" the judge asks.

In his early fifties, Judge Edwards combs his brown hair low over his forehead, the same way he did when he was a law student at the University of Chicago and a civil rights volunteer in the early 1960s. There is a photograph of him from that era, sitting in a chair in a sharecropper's yard in Mississippi, looking as boyish as a first baseman on an American

Legion team. It is a photo from footage that ran over and over on *The CBS Evening News with Walter Cronkite.*

Thirty years later, Judge Edwards still has the same blue eyes, even white teeth, and earnest expression that had made him an unwitting poster boy for the Mississippi summer. At times, Judge Edwards seems almost too Pollyannaish to be true. No one who spends so much time off the bench trying to maneuver within a political system that all too often is indifferent to children can stay this upbeat, this energetic. No one who sees the pain he does day in and day out on the bench can stay this enthusiastic. But, in fact, he does.

·   ·   ·

Jenny Langdon came bouncing into Judge Edwards's courtroom and dropped into a seat next to her court-appointed attorney at the horseshoe-shaped table beneath the bench. "Good morning, Jenny," the judge said, smiling. "You're looking well."

"Thanks, Judge," Jenny replied. During the walk from the waiting room, she seemed to have transformed herself from a sullen, hostile teenager into a polite, ebullient, attractive young woman.

The judge glanced down as he thumbed through a report he had read carefully the night before. "I see here that you are back at the shelter again. And that you are expecting a child." The judge turned to the social worker: "We are working very quickly to find a more suitable home, aren't we?" It was more a statement than a question.

"That's right," the social worker replied. "We will have a placement in a day or so. It has just been very difficult to find a place where Jenny will stay without running."

The judge focused on Jenny. "I understand that you were not very happy at your last foster home."

"They were on me all the time! I'm not a baby. I'm going to be a mother. I don't like it when people tell me what to do," Jenny blurted out.

"I can understand that. You are almost seventeen. My son is nineteen and he sure doesn't like being told what to do, no teenager does. But this is very important now that you are pregnant. You need a stable environment. You need to eat and sleep properly."

"I can do everything right," Jenny said with great confidence.

"I know you can. It has been hard for you over the past few years, but you have a very good social worker now. She really wants to help you. But you have to try, too."

"Oh, I will," Jenny agreed. "Everything is going to change."

An attorney who appears often in Judge Edwards's court describes the judge's style as "breakneck," moving from hearing to hearing with barely a pause. It is a tempo well suited to a schedule so jammed that Judge Edwards typically holds at least fifteen hearings before lunch.

In a single day, the judge may preside over two "detention hearings," where he places children in protective custody; three "jurisdictional hearings," where, if he determines that the children have suffered abuse or neglect, he will make them dependents of the court; several "dispositional hearings," where he places children with relatives or in foster care. In that same day, the judge will have several "six- and twelve-month reviews," where he checks on how children who have been taken from their parents are faring and what progress the parents—or parent—are making toward getting their children returned. The juxtaposition can be emotionally boggling: Just before lunch, amid sadness and deep hostility, the judge terminates parental rights and frees a child for adoption. After lunch, amid joy and some trepidation, the judge returns a child to his parents.

But somehow, while moving at this breakneck pace, Judge Edwards manages to create the illusion that he is moving slowly and calmly, and he is almost chatty. The judge leaned slightly forward and smiled at Jenny again. "Yes, you are going to be a mother," he said. "Now, you have the best reason in the world to change."

The judge's eyes darted over to Jenny's attorney. He pointed an index finger, as if cuing a soloist. "Anything to add for the record?"

"No, Your Honor."

He swung his black leather swivel chair to face the social worker on the opposite side of the table. Again, he pointed.

"No, Your Honor," she said.

Adult legal proceedings traditionally end with the striking of a gavel, a strong acoustical symbol that the law is the final determiner of right and wrong. Child welfare hearings are not supposed to be about establishing guilt and innocence or about meting out justice. They are supposed to be about protecting children and helping families. So, there is no gavel, in theory, no need for a show of power. Yet, Jenny's hearing needed a con-

clusion. There was a feeling of something left hanging, som
said.

"That's it?" Jenny said, looking around. "I can go now?"

Her attorney nodded, and Jenny practically skipped out of the courtroom. When the door closed, the social worker let out a sigh. "Maybe
this time, with a baby coming, she'll stay put," she said.

Judge Edwards held up his right hand. He crossed two fingers, a motion as clear in meaning as the sound of a gavel striking wood.

*Jenny been in & out of 6
F. H.
    ↳ Preg. 2x
        ↳ keep 2nd
    ↳ Children's Shelter 12^tx
    ↳ no School
    ↳ bad b.f.s

*Judge Len Edwards best
in juvie courts
    ↳ Long family his. of
      judicial power
    ↳ International status
    ↳ Book w/ wife
    ↳ Strong child advocate

2

DEPENDENCY COURT: THE LAW

SINCE 1980, WHAT HAPPENS TO A CHILD WHO COMES INTO THE CHILD welfare system has been determined in large measure by a set of complex federal and state regulations. Public Law 96-272—the Adoption Assistance and Child Welfare Act—was a legal response to the miserable condition of children who were being raised in the foster care system.

In the late 1970s, the media showed the nation what people on the inside had long known: far too often, far from protecting the children under its care, the state abused them. Newspaper and television accounts documented the scandals: thousands of children were wasting away in soulless institutions where, at best, they were languishing and, at worst, they were being sexually assaulted and physically abused. No one knew how many foster children there were, where they were, how long they had been in foster homes, or how many homes they had been in.

Native Americans and blacks were accusing child welfare departments across the country of cultural genocide, charging that their children were being legally kidnapped simply because they were poor, Native American, or black and left to drift through a netherworld of foster homes, going "from one placement to another, with no long-term plan for their future and little likelihood that they would ever enjoy a stable, family-like placement."

Social policy at that time actually discouraged the development of significant relationships between foster children and foster parents. If they became too emotionally attached, that was considered reason enough to move the child into a new home. Acting under enormous political and economic pressure to reduce the number of foster children, the U.S. Congress established a new set of policies and procedures. Most significantly, the 1980 act took power away from individual social workers and child welfare departments and gave that power to the juvenile court. Social workers and dependency court judges must now follow three key polices when deciding the fate of children.

FAMILY PRESERVATION prevents the removal of children from their families unless it is absolutely necessary. In essence, child welfare agencies are now legally charged with keeping children in their families whenever possible. They do this by providing "up-front," or "family preservation," services: Does the family need financial aid? Does a mother need to move into a new apartment, away from the boyfriend who abused her and her children? Does a father need parenting classes to learn to put his children in "time-out" rather than hitting them?

FAMILY REUNIFICATION is the policy by which, if a child is in immediate danger and has to be removed, the agency is charged with trying to place the child with a relative before putting him or her in a stranger's home or in a shelter. Then, the agency must make "reasonable efforts" to help get the child safely back home again. A social worker establishes a "reunification plan" and makes services available. For instance, addicted parents must complete a drug program and prove that they can put their child's needs before their own. Abusive parents must go into therapy and show that they have learned to control their violence.

PERMANENCY PLANNING addresses the physical and psychological needs of children. To prevent them from drifting from foster home to foster home, it limits the time the parents have to complete reunification. When a child is not returned home after twelve to eighteen months, reunification services are terminated and a permanent plan for that child must be established. He or she must be transferred to a long-term foster home, a guardianship, or an adoptive family, "the most family-like and stable setting available, with adoption being the placement of first choice."

Last, to make sure that children who have been placed into long-term out-of-home care do not get lost in the system, the child welfare department must review their status and present a report to the court on a regular basis. Is the placement still suitable? Does the child appear to be thriving?

Since 1980, all of these policies are supposed to be carried out under the watchful eye of the court, with its full regalia of judges, clerks, court officers, court procedures, and continuances. Almost everything done on behalf of a child requires a hearing. Children have legal representation. Parents have attorneys. The social workers have an attorney. What this means is that everyone spends a lot of time in court.

． ． ．

"Number eleven on your morning calendar, Your Honor. The matter of Nicky Delgato*," the court officer announced. "This is scheduled for a jurisdictional hearing."

For the record, a lawyer representing the Department of Family and Children's Services introduced herself; she also introduced the social worker from the Dependency Investigation Unit who was sitting beside her. Next, the deputy district attorney who was representing Nicky, a newborn, introduced himself. The court-appointed attorney representing the parents also introduced himself.

"Good morning, Mrs. Delgato. And good morning, Mr. Delgato," Judge Edwards said, making sure that he and Nicky's father made eye contact. So many fathers walk away from their families or are too ashamed to set foot in dependency court; when a father does appear, the judge makes a special point of acknowledging him. "And good morning to you," the judge said, turning to the Delgatos' attorney. "I didn't mean to save you for last."

"That's okay, Judge. Just as long as I'm not last on your calendar," the attorney joked. The cliché "time is money" was made for attorneys and, like every lawyer who practices in dependency court, this one hates it that the court is the legal system's version of the Department of Motor Vehicles: If you don't get there on time, you lose your place on the calendar. Get there on time and you can count on waiting an hour or two, usually more.

The judge surveyed the tables beneath the bench and nodded to his court officer. "I see we're all here. Shall we begin?"

To Judge Edwards, part of the role of a juvenile court judge is to be a teacher. He cannot control how a parent will react to court proceedings. But he can try to make sure that the parent understands those proceedings. The judge began by reviewing the case aloud, looking up from the file to see if the parents were following.

Steven and Phoebe Delgato were the parents of Nicky, a baby boy who tested positive for drugs at birth. As required by law, the hospital duly reported the results of the drug scan to the Department. The Department then dispatched a dependency investigator (DI), who, as required, completed her investigation within forty-eight hours. Based on what she had learned in Nicky's case, the social worker filed a petition seeking to make the infant a dependent child under Section 300 of the California Welfare and Institutions Code. A petition is the dependency court's equivalent of the charges that are filed in criminal courts. The Department alleges that certain events have taken place and urges the court to take action.

A day after the DI filed the petition, Judge Edwards presided over a detention hearing and made the obvious decision: Nicky would remain in protective custody in the Neonatal Intensive Care Unit (NICU) until today's jurisdictional hearing. This hearing is pivotal and was the reason Nicky's parents and their attorney were in court.

If Nicky's parents accept the allegations in the petition, the court will take custody of their child and they may never get him back. If Nicky's parents contest the allegations, the case will proceed to trial before a judge—there are no juries in juvenile court. Trials in dependency court—where every mistake a parent has ever made can be presented as evidence—can quickly turn ugly.

Until recently in California and other states, an infant who tested positive was likely to be made a dependent child. Judges decided that since his parents had not protected him in utero they could not protect him at home. Now, more and more women who give birth to "drug babies" take their babies home and go into treatment.

But Nicky's petition alleged that his parents should not take him home. Under Section 300(b) of the California code, it was alleged that Nicky had suffered serious physical harm as a result of his mother's drug abuse; in addition, it was alleged that, because Nicky's parents had been in and out of jail, they were unable to provide a home for the child. Further, the petition alleged that there was a substantial risk Nicky would be further abused or neglected since four years earlier Phoebe had lost a daughter to the system because of chronic drug use.

After Judge Edwards finished reading the petition, he asked the parents if they understood the allegations. Steven, a handsome man with a head of rich black hair and a powerful upper body, and Phoebe, a small woman with delicate features, nodded solemnly.

"Do you understand that if I find they are true, the court will take control of your son? Do you understand that?" the judge asked. He was not smiling now.

More solemn nods.

The judge asked the Delgatos' attorney if he was prepared to proceed, and the attorney rose to his feet: "The allegations in this petition are without foundation and we ask that this matter be set for trial."

Showing no trace of emotion, the lawyers and the social worker reached for their calendars. The fact that the dependency system is grounded on individual rights—the child has rights, the parents have rights, the Department has the right to investigate and make recommendations—makes it inevitable that some cases will be scheduled for trial. Dates were set for discovery, the sharing of documents between the Delgatos' attorney and the attorney for the Department. A date was set for the trial, and the parents left the courtroom, holding hands.

• • •

While the Delgatos were in Judge Edwards's courtroom, their newborn son was in the NICU at Valley Medical Center. The tubes in his throat and the IV running into a tiny vein on the back of his hand were silent testimony to the devastating effects cocaine and alcohol have in the womb.

When researchers give a pregnant lamb a shot of cocaine, her blood pressure soars. The lamb soon metabolizes the drug and passes it out in her urine, and her blood pressure returns to normal. Not so for the lamb's fetus. An hour after the injection, when the mother's blood pressure has stabilized, the fetus's is still sky-high. The mother can metabolize cocaine; the fetus cannot break the drug down. The mother can pass the drug out through her urine; the fetus urinates into the amniotic fluid, and the cocaine keeps getting recycled.

In the womb the massive constriction of the blood vessels that cocaine causes can shut off the blood supply to the placenta. This can cause the placenta to hemorrhage, and if the bleeding is severe enough, the placenta, the baby's life-support system, may separate from the mother, triggering a premature birth.

The damage cocaine causes in utero can also be more gradual and subtle. If a pregnant woman keeps using cocaine, the blood vessels in her placenta keep closing. The blood flowing to the fetus keeps getting choked off, and the fetus does not get enough oxygen. Oxygen deprivation causes fetal distress, which produces uterine contractions that can also trigger premature birth.

If anything, the effects of alcohol are even worse. There is no placental barrier to alcohol. When a 125-pound pregnant woman has five drinks, her 2-pound fetus has five drinks. It is as simple as that.

Alcohol has the potential of wrecking the development of every cell line there is, from the eyes—children born with fetal alcohol syndrome (FAS), or fetal alcohol effects, tend to have very small eyes—to fat and bone cells—children with FAS are short and skinny and have unusually small heads—to nerve and brain cells. The average IQ of a child born with FAS is sixty-five, but low test scores only begin to tell the story. Such children often suffer from seizures, hyperactivity, and attention deficit. One of the most tragic legacies is the child's permanent "immaturity"—an inability to make cause-effect connections or to "think ahead."

Like most substance abusers, especially women, Phoebe was as emotionally addicted to her lifestyle as she was physically addicted to the chemicals she put into her body. Along with abusing drugs and alcohol, she had also smoked heavily when she was carrying Nicky. She had eaten only when it occurred to her, stopping at a fast-food restaurant to dunk chocolate doughnuts into coffee she had laced with packet after packet of sugar. She lived where she could and slept when she could. She had gotten no prenatal care.

In medical literature, attempts are made to distinguish between fetal damage that is directly attributable to the drugs and the damage that is indirectly caused by a chaotic lifestyle. But this demarcation did not matter to Nicky; to him, causes were academic. From the moment he was born, nine weeks premature with a cyst on the right side of his brain that would require surgery to remove, Nicky was condemned to living out effects.

Being born so prematurely meant that Nicky was as unprepared for life on earth as an astronaut would be if he had been dropped on the surface of the moon without a space suit. He had been whisked from the delivery room to the NICU, a miniature version of a newborn, so much smaller, so much more fragile. His skin was red and almost translucent, the color of a freshly filleted bass.

Asleep, Nicky was so inert that he looked dead. It was as if he were conserving every ounce of energy for the battles ahead. There was one oddly jarring thing: the little covers he wore to shield his eyes from the light looked like a miniature version of the sleeping masks starlets wore in 1930s movies. After several days of being alive, he had yet to see the world.

Nicky had been placed into a high-tech womb, a miracle of modern medicine, full of monitors and meters, computers and respirators, beeps and hums. Without it, the three-pound four-ounce baby would be dead. In 1963, President John F. Kennedy's son Patrick was born one month early and weighed five pounds. The power of the White House and the best doctors in the country had kept him alive only twenty-four hours. Today, babies who weigh under two pounds routinely survive.

Nicky was born without an ounce of fat on his tiny body. Subcutaneous fat is not manufactured until well into the fetus's third trimester; Nicky would have died of hypothermia without the heat monitor that was attached to his abdomen. The monitor picked up changes in his body temperature and triggered a warmer, which turned itself on and off automatically.

Other high-tech computerized systems monitored Nicky's heartbeats, his respiratory activity, and the percentage of oxygen in his blood. Dehydration is not a problem in the womb, where the fetus is surrounded by amniotic fluid and receives liquid nutrition through the placenta. In the NICU, fluids evaporate quickly through a baby's soft, smooth skin and must constantly be replaced. The fluids Nicky received through the vein on the back of his hand were made in the hospital pharmacy, specifically for him. An Apple computer that was updated and reprogrammed several times a day generated a recipe and fed Nicky the precise amounts he needed.

In the womb, a fetus is an amphibian and the lung does not breathe: instead, the lung secretes fluid into the amniotic sac. In the NICU, a ventilator with a tube running into his lungs breathed for Nicky. A ventilator is a costly and complex device, with multiple backup computer systems. Such advanced medical equipment is one reason it costs $2,000 a day, or more, to keep a premature baby alive.

For Ron Cohen, the head of the NICU, the horror is not just that babies like Nicky are born prematurely with serious medical and physical problems. What tortures the doctor is the fact that the damage drugs and alcohol wreak in the womb are absolutely, positively, 100 percent preventable. "The world is running around being lunatics over Alar on apples and malathion sprayed on fruit trees and God knows what in our water and maybe, maybe, maybe these things cause cancer," the doctor says. "There is zero evidence to suggest that any of that is having any significant impact on us.

"Alcohol is the number one environmental cause of a birth defect. It is the number one preventable cause of mental retardation and teradigity, a medical word that means 'a cause of developmental malformations.' "

Dr. Cohen and his miracle machines had saved Nicky from a death that would have been certain only a decade or so earlier. But what kind of life would he lead? Would he end up being raised in the system, costing taxpayers hundreds of thousands of dollars? Did he face a future where, if he managed to reach his peak potential, he might be able to hold down a job at McDonald's?

Nicky was a wild card. Only time would tell.

3

KIDS WHO WAIT

The Santa Clara County Social Services Agency is looking for a long-term foster home for Charles, a handsome, soft-spoken 14-year-old.

Despite a difficult childhood, Charles gets along well with adults and is popular with his peers. He and his older brother were adopted after experiencing severe physical abuse by their birth parents. Since the divorce of his adopted parents, Charles has lived in several group homes and has had to deal with feelings of abandonment and the lack of a stable family environment.

Because of his previous inconsistent attendance at school, he will need an educational assessment and, possibly, some special assistance. He is currently enrolled in school and enjoys his art classes greatly.

San Jose Mercury News
April 30, 1995

FOSTER CARE AND ADOPTION HAVE TRADITIONALLY BEEN PROMOTED BY publicity campaigns that paint a sunny picture of the joys of opening one's heart and home to a disadvantaged, yet essentially ordinary, child who needs only a home and caring parents in order to thrive. Newspapers around the country run columns similar to "Kids Who Wait," which appears regularly in the *San Jose Mercury News*. Modeled on another newspaper tradition—the pet of the week—the intent of these features is certainly touching. What could be more humane than finding homes for children who desperately need them?

But the columns' upbeat language only hints at who these children are, what they have been through, and what kind of care and commitment they may require. Being "soft-spoken" and having to "deal with feelings of abandonment" can mean a child who is seriously depressed. Needing "educational assessment" can mean that a sixteen-year-old is reading at a third-grade level.

Certainly, there are children who require nothing more demanding than simple kindness and a foster parent with an open heart. But over the past decade and a half, the kind of child needing long-term care has changed dramatically and consists of more Jenny Langdons and Nicky Delgatos, more "disturbed children . . . who require some degree of specialized care."

A whole lexicon of adjectives has attached itself to these children—"severely troubled," "extraordinarily needy," and "unattached." Professionals refer to "special needs kids," an elliptical way of lumping together every child who does not fit the stereotype of a "normal" child. The category encompasses a "medically fragile" newborn like Nicky who is hooked up to a respirator, a child with dyslexia, and children who have been sexually molested and who need three or more therapy sessions a week. Often, the unavoidable act of becoming a teenager with teenage problems lands a foster care child in this category.

The influx of special needs children into foster care is a side effect of the 1980 act and the social policy of reunification. In theory, the law was designed to cut down on the number of children needing substitute care and to move those who enter the system out of it as quickly as possible. By providing services to their families, children who would have once become foster kids because of poverty or simple neglect, in theory, are now able to remain at home.

To the foster care system, the act has meant that children who are the most seriously abused or neglected—thus, those who exhibit the most serious physical, emotional, psychological, and/or developmental damage—are the children least likely to be candidates for family reunification or adoption. Instead, these are the children most likely to become permanent foster care or group home placements.

However, the 1980 act by itself is not responsible for the changing face of foster care. During the past two decades, the country has been hit by high unemployment, increasing use of addictive street drugs, lack of affordable housing, surges in teenage pregnancy, homelessness, AIDS, and HIV infection. The Reagan-Bush administrations have also left a legacy of indiscriminate and massive social service reductions. The effects of cutbacks in prenatal and infant care are now being felt in the formidable physical and emotional problems of the fifteen-year-old children who populate foster care.

The result is that now there are more—not fewer—children needing substitute care and that there are fewer "little angels" and many more difficult, disturbed, and medically fragile children who are not quite so easy to love.

There are also fewer foster parents available to care for them. According to the National Foster Parents Association, the number of homes available has dropped dramatically from 137,000 in 1984 to about 100,000 in 1992.

Lois Raap is an activist in Santa Clara County's Foster Parent Association. With her husband, Peter, she has been a foster parent for twenty-five years; for the last ten years, the Raaps have specialized in the tiny victims of the AIDS plague. The couple has taken in a dozen HIV-positive newborns, nursed them, taught them to walk and to talk, and read to them, until the children were too weak to move, to listen—until the children, some of them almost school-aged, died in their arms.

Foster parents, Lois Raap complains, are being asked to do more and more with less and less. Like most adults who work with children, foster parents have the curious distinction of being both deified and underpaid. They are supposed to be saints who take in children for purely altruistic reasons. The fear seems to be that, if foster care paid more than survival wages, people would get into it only for the money. California's foster parents have not received a "raise" in at least six years.

"I know that there are some foster parents who just squeeze as many children as they can into their homes for the money. I know that many just give nominal care, but to say that most foster parents are in it for the money? That's not what I have seen," Raap says. "The money they pay you can't begin to cover the special needs of these children—the extra medical care, the special equipment.

"In my own cases, I've had to fight tooth and nail to get what I need for the kids—for instance, going to the Rotary Club to beg for money for plane tickets to Washington so one of the babies could be treated with a new protocol. . . . Social services did give us money for memorial services to bury the children though. They did do that much."

But money, Raap says, is not even the primary frustration. While foster children have gotten more demanding, so have the legal and bureaucratic pressures placed on those who care for them. Foster parents face any number of legal liabilities. For instance, babies born addicted to drugs have a high mortality rate, and their foster parents risk being sued for inadequate care. Foster parents have also been included in lawsuits by parents charging that child welfare departments improperly removed their children from their homes.

Most disturbing though are how policies that were designed to protect children now cast suspicion upon foster parents. Social workers, Raap says, "approach us as potential abusers and potential molesters." In recent years, allegations of child abuse against foster parents have increased, making it very difficult to discipline children in their care and all but impossible to live a normal life.

"There are some absolute horror stories," Raap says. "I know one older lady who had been a foster parent for twenty-seven years with no complaints against her. One of the children told her biological mother that the foster mom had shut the car door on her leg. The biological mom pressed charges, and the Department swooped down. She hardly had a chance to defend herself. Here was a woman with a great heart, but something small comes along, a fluke happens, and they just wipe out a decent foster home. It's no surprise that so many foster parents are saying: I can't afford this kind of risk. Who needs it?"

So what happens, as more and more foster homes close and more and more children need them? The theory of supply and demand kicks in. Foster parents can pick and choose among children. They can select those who are the easiest, the ones least likely to make problems and cause foster parents to lose their licenses.

The result is that an unofficial caste system has developed, one that has nothing to do with the needs of children. It is ironic that little girls—destroyed at birth in some civilizations, little more than chattel in others—are the Brahmins of foster care, the most requested by foster families. This is not because girls are more in need of family stability or more inherently valued but because they are perceived to be more flexible, more docile, less troublesome than little boys.

Toddlers are also high on the most-requested list. They sleep through the night and give their temporary parents a smile-for-smile return on their emotional investment.

Way down—somewhere along with AIDS babies and minority twin boys with histories of arson—come teenagers, any teenager. The Department pays extra for housing an adolescent, but, not surprisingly, they remain the untouchables of the system. Especially a pregnant teenager. Especially a pregnant teenager like Jenny Langdon, who has piled up an impressive reputation for running away, sexually acting out, and turning a household upside down.

· · ·

Jenny's social worker finally managed to find her a new foster home, and Jenny managed to stay put for several months. It wasn't a particularly bad place; it was just more of the same. "Nobody ever asked me what would make me happy and feel at home," she says. "The foster mother always points out my bed and recites the house rules that I didn't get any say in making. What gets me is when the foster mother and the social worker stand around talking about me, like I'm not even there. 'Be careful of Jenny, she is going to test you. Don't give her an inch. Watch out for her temper!'

"At every foster home I've ever been in, the message was clear: 'This is somebody else's house. There are five other kids out there waiting to get in. Mess up and you are gone.' "

When Jenny had had enough, she handled things her way: she broke her 10 P.M. curfew, told her foster mother to go fuck herself, trashed her room, and then dug her nails into her cheeks and dragged them down, leaving five angry-looking red lines on each side of her face. "If I have to stay in this house one more minute," she screamed, "I'm gonna kill your real kids' rabbit!"

Afraid of what she might do, Jenny's latest foster mother silently retreated into the kitchen and stayed out of her way. No one, Jenny least of all, could separate how much of her rage was genuine and how much was a performance. For while she was yelling and cursing, she was neatly putting her makeup into its plastic container and tossing everything else she wanted into a backpack. Minutes later, without saying a word, Jenny stormed out of her room and slammed the front door behind her.

The foster mother immediately called Jenny's social worker: "That's it! She is not coming back here! This is not working!"

The social worker sighed; Jenny was now seven months pregnant and had been told repeatedly how vital it was that she be settled in a home when the baby arrived. If Jenny were out on the streets or living in the Children's Shelter, there was a strong possibility that the court would intercede and the newborn would be taken from her and placed in protective custody in an Emergency Shelter Home. But that had not been enough to keep Jenny from slamming the door.

So once again the social worker would have to go through the drill: notify Jenny's attorney, issue a warrant to pick up Jenny, start scrambling to find her another foster home, plan for yet another court hearing. The paperwork would add another minichapter to Jenny's social service record, a massive four-volume work in progress that constituted her biography.

Even the most straightforward dependency case is a towering stack of documents. At minimum, there is the original petition, a jurisdictional report, a reunification plan that lays out what the parents have to do in order to get their children back, and a services documentation log that sometimes lists point by point, phone call by phone call, what the social worker is doing to help the parents meet their requirements.

Added to that are still more papers: court orders, court addenda and notices of court continuances, family histories, contracts for the foster family, placement orders and, often, detailed psychological evaluations of the children and their parents. That is for a "simple" case.

Jenny's colossal file opens on the first day of her life. The county hospital, Valley Medical Center, made a social service referral on Jenny's mother regarding "the questionable ability of Nora Langdon to care for the new infant. . . . The mother is retarded . . . unable to tell time, make change or read." The father "has serious emotional problems."

An intake worker came out to assess the situation and to decide whether or not the family needed to be in the system: Did they need services? Did the newborn need to be removed from the family and placed under the protection of the court? According to the file, the matter was "settled at intake." What this boiled down to was that, after a cursory interview, three-day-old Jenny was sent home with her parents "as the parents appeared to have a good supply of all necessities for a newborn."

Jenny was born in the late 1970s, right after Ronald Reagan was governor of California. One of the governor's most publicized acts was the deinstitutionalization of the developmentally disabled and mentally ill. The Reagan administration closed many large state hospitals, and the governor spoke eloquently about the humanity of integrating these people into our communities. But the Reagan administration did not provide the funding to set up, staff, license, and monitor the halfway houses, the educational facilities, and the network of community support services that were supposed to care for all of these former inmates. Like baby Jenny's parents, they wandered downtown streets in cities like San Jose. The only help given to Jenny's "retarded" mother and a father with "a long history of psychiatric problems" was a referral to a public health nurse.

A year later, Jenny's mother reported to social services that she believed her young daughter had been molested by her husband. There was no proof of abuse, and, again, the matter was "settled at intake." Jenny was left with her parents.

When Jenny was three and her mother was six months pregnant with her second child, Nora again called Child Protective Services, this time to report that her husband was abusive and that her home was filthy. The home was indeed filthy, but again there was no proof of abuse. The social worker offered homemaker services and some child care, but the parents, mentally unstable and terrified of strangers, refused to let the homemaker in the door. Once again, the matter was "settled at intake."

The next incident in Jenny's file occurred when she was four and "apparently witnessed" her father's suicide attempt. Her father had called Jenny and her little sister into the bathroom. When they arrived, they found their father standing in the bathtub, a knife raised to his wrists. He started slashing. Jenny described to social workers how she had tried to cover her sister's eyes so that the younger child would not see all the blood. The two children stood numbly as their father ran around the apartment and out the front door, finally fainting on the pavement from loss of blood.

While their father was hospitalized in the psychiatric ward of Valley Medical Center, Jenny and her sister were taken to the Children's Shelter, where social workers pieced together the details of Jenny's first four years on earth. Her days had been filled with "terrible lashings" by her mother, who would suddenly "go crazy"—yelling threats to people who were not there, claiming that Jenny was not her child, hitting the children with high heels and coat hangers. Jenny described being locked in closets and cowering under the kitchen sink with her sister, trying to stay out of the way while their parents fought.

Often, lost in their own mental torment, Jenny's parents would forget to feed her. Jenny would try scavenging for food, but when nothing could be found, she would whine, then cry.

"I remember this one time when my daddy was very angry with my mommy," Jenny told a social worker. "He kept screaming at her, 'Why don't you feed your fucking kid?' Mommy yelled back and they started throwing things at each other."

One of her mother's weapons—a loaf of bread—flew out of the plastic wrapper, and slices of white bread fluttered to the floor. Jenny scooted out of her hiding place under the table on hands and knees and started stuffing bread into her mouth, "thankful that in the middle of her parents' fight, she had at least gotten something to eat," the social worker noted in her report. In a masterpiece of vague understatement, Jenny, at age four and a half, was diagnosed in a social service report "as needing out-of-home stimulation."

From this point, Jenny's social service and court records began growing an inch in thickness for every inch she grew in height. Now, her latest social worker was back to square one: she had to begin figuring out where next to place this dilemma who kept creating dilemmas, this terribly troubled, beautiful young woman.

. . .

Meanwhile, Jenny was headed to a bus that would get her to one of her sanctuaries, the familiar intersection of First and Santa Clara in downtown San Jose. The bus stop there is a central point for lines that radiate to every corner of the county, north to high-tech firms like Hewlett-Packard, south to Gilroy, known as the garlic capital of the world. The corner is a connection point in a larger sense as well.

As usual, Jehovah's Witnesses were there, dressed up in ties and long overcoats. But when the bus doors opened, Jenny stepped out onto a corner that really belonged to teenagers, an almost old-fashioned, disappearing kind of street corner, now that middle-class teenagers prefer the safety and comfort of malls. There were boys, many of them gang members or gang wanna-bes, never cracking a smile, and girls in their black lipstick, always smiling. There were runaways like Jenny and kids who were playing at running away. Some of them had their backs pressed against the marble facade of the former Bank of America, one of the oldest and tallest buildings in town. Others kept walking up and down the street, looking almost as if they were picketing the place.

A young woman, her blond hair streaked with purple, let out a shriek that seemed too loud to have come from her small frame. She rushed up to Jenny, and they wrapped their arms around each other and rocked from side to side. "Girl! Look at that belly!"

Vicky was one of the few constants in Jenny's life, a friend she had known "almost forever." At the Children's Shelter, Jenny and Vicky became close whispering late into the night, sharing war stories about bad foster homes and how they had put something over on a social worker. By the time they were thirteen, they were a notorious duo, infamous among group home counselors, social workers, and the police who would pick them up after their many runs from the shelter. "A lot of people call us 'The Twins,' " Jenny says proudly. "But usually, we say that we are cousins."

Jenny told Vicky that this was probably her "final adventure," her last time living on the streets. Now that she was going to be a mother, she had to grow up. Without a comment, Vicky nodded seriously, then held out her newest possession, a beeper. Suddenly, Jenny's pregnancy was no longer the big news. The two friends huddled together, bouncing with nervous energy, to examine the present from Vicky's boyfriend.

At eighteen, Vicky had already "graduated" out of the system and was crashing in a former bar on South First Street that had been condemned and boarded up. All she and Jenny had to do was to panhandle enough money to buy a blanket and a towel at the Community Thrift Shop down the street. Even in Jenny's condition, crawling through a window was no problem. Everyone was staying there.

Jenny and Vicky spent the next few days hitting up people for money, talking, laughing, thinking up names for the new baby, taking in the downtown smells of diesel fumes mingling with the scent of roasted chicken from a nearby Mexican rotisserie. "When kids think about the fall, the cool weather, I suppose they think about going back to school," Jenny says. "Me, I think about jumping the fence at the shelter, being on the run, just kicking it on the streets and seeing what will happen next."

The inevitable happened late one afternoon. A police officer who knew Jenny by sight happened to drive by in a squad car. He pulled to the curb, shook his head in mock annoyance, and pointed to the backseat. Jenny shrugged, yelled good-bye to Vicky, and got in. Tired and bloated, Jenny ended her "final" adventure the way she ended all her oth-

ers, pretending to listen to a cop's lecture—"Don't you know hc
gerous it is for you out there!"

Sitting in the backseat, her face pressed against the window, she was
driven through downtown, past the new arena where the Sharks played
hockey, past the upscale restaurants and the small shops run by the Vietnamese who had flocked to San Jose after Saigon fell, and back to the
Eastside and the place that was the closest thing she had ever had to a
home, the Children's Shelter.

✻ Jenny's home life before
foster care was unpredictable.
→ father would be abusive
towards mother & sexually
assult Jenny
→ no evidence

✻ Jenny's mom called child care
services when she was 3, wasn't
removed from home until she was
4

✻ Jenny met up with her best
friend from foster care and did
one last heighst with her, then
went back to the child's Shelter

4

NICKY:
LOVE AT FIRST SIGHT

THE NICU MEDICAL WONDERLAND CAN REPLICATE THE WOMB, BUT IT cannot accelerate what happens there. Inside the womb or out, pregnancy takes forty weeks. So Nicky, who was born nine weeks prematurely, spent nine weeks in the NICU before being placed in an Emergency Shelter Home (ESH), a temporary foster home. This ESH was run by Sharon Ruprecht, a public health nurse who specializes in caring for children with special needs.

Ruprecht is a middle-aged woman with a high, almost squeaky voice who has four grown children of her own. She radiates the calmness and quiet confidence of someone who has found her calling in life. Her career as a foster parent began on a summer evening eight years earlier, when she took two of her children to the Santa Clara County Fair. She had always known she could care for kids who were not her own, but her husband wanted no part of being a foster parent. When they divorced, she automatically assumed that a single parent could not be a foster parent. That night at the fair, she went up to a social services booth and was thrilled when a woman told her that, of course, a single parent could qualify.

Ruprecht's first foster child, Joey, arrived when he was nine months old, already seriously delayed, with a cleft palate and a bad heart, the result, in large measure, of the cocaine and alcohol his mother had used throughout her pregnancy. He was still being fed through a tube because his mother had not breast-fed or taught him to take a bottle. She had taped his feeding tubes to his crib and left him alone for hours. Ruprecht vividly recalls the painstaking process of teaching him to take a bottle: "It would take an hour or two every time I fed him. Joey would suck and then rest, suck and rest again.

"One evening, I had given him a bath, bundled him up in warm jammies and was sitting in a chair, holding him close and feeding him his bottle when he gave me an amazed look that said, 'My God! Have I gone to heaven? I didn't know life could be like this!' I will always remember that night. It was like he was saying, 'Thank you, God!' "

That was an epiphany for Ruprecht, the moment when she made up her mind to adopt the child. Nothing anyone said or did could dissuade her once her mind was set. Not the doctors who warned her that Joey might not make it through the major heart surgery that he required; not her daughters and friends who wondered aloud if she was crazy to start over with bottles and diapers at her age; and, especially, not Joey's biological father, who marched up to her in court one day and threatened, "If this adoption goes through, I'm going to hunt you down and kill you."

The court battle was long and grueling, but in the end Ruprecht prevailed. For the past eight years, she and Joey, now a rail-thin boy—"forty pounds soaking wet"—with pale blond hair, have been mother and son. His developmental disabilities are formidable. Joey did not walk until he was three and a half; even now, he has to struggle to string together more than a few words at a time. What adults first notice and take delight in is Joey's affectionate nature, the way he flings himself upon a stranger without any shyness or self-consciousness. Love without boundaries is Joey's blessing—and his curse.

"It's part of the retardation of never growing up, of always remaining a child, of always having that simple need of being hugged," Ruprecht explains. "The concept of stranger just doesn't exist for him, and that's one of my greatest fears. How will he discriminate between who is a good person and who is not a good person?"

While raising Joey, Ruprecht has also taken in nearly fifty other medically fragile children—usually no more than two at a time. The homes on the street where she lives have a cookie-cutter feel and a two-car garage in the front, as if the automobile got the pick of the rooms. The street itself is so broad and bland and has such a comfortable feel that it is hard to believe this is the setting where scores of babies like Joey and Nicky have shrieked their way through the effects of addiction.

Inside, there is a nursery with a string of Peter Rabbits bouncing along on the wallpaper and a mobile twirling slowly over a crib. But no mobile was hanging over the Nature's Cradle, a large, square bassinet on a pedestal, where Nicky had just fallen asleep. A randomly moving object would drive Nicky into spasms of rage.

The Nature's Cradle is designed to soothe premature babies by replicating the womb. A mechanism in the pedestal produces the sound of a heartbeat and simulates the motion of a mother's womb. A hood keeps out light. Nicky's head was nestled in an indentation in a bolster. To prevent his arms and legs from flailing, he was swaddled in a snug "burrito wrap" and tucked between two cylindrical foam bolsters that a Velcro strap kept close to his body.

Except for being especially tiny, the four-and-a-half-pound boy sleeping in the cradle now looked normal in every way. Nicky was an exceptionally beautiful infant: his head was covered with rich black hair, and his features were perfect. But this little bundle held rage and pain that few people will ever fathom. Parents who have cared for a colicky newborn whose cries were knives that pierced their sleep night after night, who kept dragging themselves out of bed until they went stumbling through their days in a semipsychotic state, can only begin to understand Ruprecht's day with Nicky.

Eight hours earlier, Nicky had woken up crying. When Ruprecht picked him up, he arched his back, went stiff as a board, and kept on screaming as only a newborn can. His entire body, from his curled toes to his clinched fists to his furrowed brow, was locked in fury.

Like a veteran magician working to an impossible crowd, Ruprecht tried every trick in her repertoire. She held him flat against her chest, her palm firmly against the top of his head, trying to mimic his snug position in the womb. Nicky kept screaming. She sat in a rocking chair and cooed nursery rhymes, rocking slowly at first, then more rapidly. It didn't work. She paced from room to room, went from inside the house to the patio outside, hoping a change in environment, something in the light, something in the temperature, anything, would cause Nicky to stop.

Nothing had. Nicky had howled for eight straight hours. Ruprecht's ears rang as if she had stood too close to a jet engine. Finally, with no warning and certainly not because Ruprecht had done something magical, Nicky gasped for breath several times, went limp, and fell asleep. It was as if angels had arrived to drive away the demons and unfurl his brow, open his clenched fists. Now he was a portrait of peace, sound asleep in the Nature's Cradle.

It had been a maddening day, and Ruprecht was exhausted. All of the babies who had passed through her home had required vast amounts of patience, skill, and love, but none had been as oppressive as Nicky. Every day had been a replica of this one: if Nicky was awake, Nicky was screaming. But now, finally, a quiet had settled over the house. Ruprecht was in the kitchen, making a cup of tea for Claire Kenney*, her closest friend. After a day like this one, a simple thing like talking to an adult was elevated to a rare pleasure. That was something both women could appreciate, since both led lives that revolved around the endless needs of children.

Kenney, too, is middle-aged with biological children of her own, two daughters about to enter their teens. She is a tall, angular woman with brown, curly hair, big glasses, and a narrow face. She runs a day care center out of her home and is an activist member of the local school board. Some years earlier, Kenney had decided that she wanted to care for special needs kids in her day care center and had filled out the necessary applications, taken the courses, and remodeled part of her home. That is how she met Ruprecht. Five days a week, a specially equipped van owned and operated by the Department collects the children Ruprecht is caring for and drops them at Kenney's house, where they spend the afternoon.

While the tea was brewing, Kenney said very little, lost in thought as she stared into her teacup. "Sharon," she said finally. "Greg and I have talked it over. We want to adopt Nicky."

Ruprecht was dumbfounded. To begin with, Nicky was not even up for adoption. His parents had not even submitted to the petition; the trial had been postponed again and again. Who could tell how long Nicky's case would stretch on? Who knew what would happen? Dozens of children had passed through Ruprecht's home; many had been returned to their families. Claire knew all that. Why had she jumped to the conclusion that Nicky would be available? And why, Ruprecht wondered, did Claire want Nicky, of all children? Claire had a big heart and knew how to care for special needs kids, but she had them only a few hours every afternoon. Then they left and she went on with the rest of her life.

Did Claire and her husband have any idea of what living with Nicky twenty-four hours a day would be like? Of what Nicky would do to their relationship? Of the special schooling and the special doctors he would need? Had they thought about how such a baby, such a child, and then such a teenager would sap their time and patience? How he would radically alter the lives of their own daughters?

"I can understand you wanting to adopt, but why this child?" Ruprecht finally asked. "We can find you a better one!"

Ruprecht is something of a hallowed figure in child welfare circles. When social workers are desperate to place a child that no one else will take, they call Sharon. Once, when Judge Edwards heard her name mentioned, he said, "If there was ever a candidate for a job floating on a cloud, playing a trumpet, it's Sharon." Ruprecht's remark about Nicky was so unlike her that Kenney did not have to stop herself from lashing out with a question like "How could you of all people label one child as being better than another?" Instead, she just smiled.

"I don't have words for what happened," Kenney said. "I fell in love the first time I ever saw him. So did Greg. He's just so beautiful, so precious."

Ruprecht listened without comment as Claire recited a litany of Nicky's virtues: He's a fighter, a survivor. He is so charming, so bright, all you have to do is look in his eyes and see that. "He's so perfect," Claire concluded.

"He's far from perfect," Ruprecht replied.

"Well, he's perfect for us," Kenney said. "In fact, Greg and I were saying last night they'll probably never let us have him. He's too cute for us."

Ruprecht did not argue. She knew that Claire would be politely deaf to any of her warnings about the limits of love. Sharon, of all people, understood something about having all of your common sense wiped away by this glorious, irrational feeling for a child.

. . .

After her long battle to adopt Joey, Ruprecht emerged keenly aware that adoptions are not set up ad hoc between friends. Her advice to Claire was to go by the book. Otherwise, it might look as if they were conspiring to kidnap Nicky, legally. Both women independently called Mary Agnes King, Nicky's caseworker, to inform her that the Kenneys were interested in the little boy.

What infuriates Ruprecht about the system is that going by the book often means doing more for parents than for children. From her perspective—an understandable perspective coming from someone who spends her days rocking and feeding and caring for very difficult, very vulnerable children—that is exactly what the policy of reunification mandates. Many ESH mothers try never to lay eyes on the parents who produce the babies in their care. The desire to shake them by the shoulders and say, "You should go to hell for what you have done!" is just too great.

Ruprecht no longer walks around seething with that kind of outrage; she has seen too much of humanity not to understand that these parents, too, have been victims of someone, at some time in their lives. The stories they tell of their pasts are often so lurid that she has to turn away and cringe. Yet, they have a simplicity, an eternal naïveté, that makes Ruprecht feel for them. "So many women out there are giving birth who desperately need to be loved themselves," she says. "They are as needy as their babies."

But that is her whole point. As much compassion as she has for these mothers, she knows who they are. She knows how much their babies require, and she is absolutely convinced that the vast majority will never be capable of raising a child with so many needs. "The system is terribly naïve when it comes to parents," Ruprecht says. "You can throw resources at some of them forever and you'll never reach them. What is a parenting class going to do for them? They're too far gone. It's pouring money down a dark hole."

And yet like the system she condemns, Ruprecht has resolved to always give parents a chance, even if for her it means giving them a chance not to succeed but to fail, to realize on their own that they cannot be parents.

That was her mind-set the day she took Nicky to Clover House to meet his mother and father for the first time. Years ago, when Ruprecht first started as a foster parent, visits took place in the lobby of a social services building, a setting so loud, chaotic, and degrading that it was nicknamed "The Zoo." Now, they are held in Clover House, a former tract house that is painted light brown with a dark brown trim. The idea is to make the setting as much like a home as possible, so that families can feel as comfortable as possible.

While Nicky's case was pending trial, Judge Edwards ordered that his parents could see him once a week for an hour. Following the established protocol, Ruprecht brought Nicky in through a side entrance. His parents walked through the front door—an arrangement that has always irked Ruprecht. Nevertheless, the first thing she did was to tell a counselor that she would be glad to meet Nicky's parents and give them a detailed report on his progress.

Clover House counselors are usually in their twenties and have recently earned a B.A. in psychology or counseling. They hover about in the hallway, monitoring several visits at a time, trying futilely to be as unobtrusive as possible as they record their impressions in short reports: "The mother was on time... The father did not look the baby in the eye.... There were lots of hugs and kisses when the visit concluded." These reports are written for the most part by novices operating under the most artificial conditions imaginable. The counselors do not have to appear in court to defend their observations, but the reports, which can be overly subjective, become part of the social services record. They may heavily influence a judge who is about to make the final decision on where to place a child.

The counselor came back with word that Nicky's parents were eager to meet his foster mother, and Ruprecht carried the baby into what looked like the living room of an average family home—couches, a carpet, toys that were freshly washed. Nicky's father jumped up and came quickly toward them.

"Here's my little guy!" Steven Delgato cooed, taking Nicky from Ruprecht. "You're daddy's little guy, aren't you? Hey, look here, look what I got for you. Show him, Mommy!"

Nicky's mother, Phoebe, was, as always, dressed in a short skirt and beret, making her, at age twenty-six, look so girlish that bartenders still carded her. She approached her husband and handed him a white paper bag. Inside was a miniature San Francisco 49ers jersey with the number 16 and the name "Montana" on the back. Steven placed the little jersey under Nicky's chin, and Nicky, to Ruprecht's amazement, smiled. Ordinarily, a strange face, a touch he didn't like, or any alteration in the routine they had established over the last few weeks triggered a screaming fit that lasted for hours. And yet, here Nicky was, grinning up at his father, waiting to see what would happen next.

It was enough to make Ruprecht question her own prejudices. "I've always been convinced that biological ties mean nothing," Ruprecht would say later, "but if you ever wanted to make a case for them, this was it. It was like there was a magical bond between this father and son."

"He looks like me, he looks just like me. I can't get over it," Steven kept repeating.

Nicky had inherited his father's dark green, almond-shaped eyes, which in Steven's thirty-four years had been trained to dart around and quickly size up his surroundings. Steven is handsome in an urban sort of way, the kind of man who always seems to be posing, wearing a shirt one size too small so that it strains across his muscular upper body. Steven has a thick black mustache and a grin that is, at once, vain and charming.

Steven had in fact survived on his charm. The son of abusive, alcoholic parents from Boston's North End, Steven was seven when he and his three brothers and sisters were placed in separate foster homes. By his early teens, Steven had lost all track of his siblings. Bouncing from placement to placement had taught Steven an invaluable lesson that foster children who are not as bright and not as resourceful fail to learn: First impressions matter most. Make people feel good and they will want to believe you. When they ask where you got your tattoos, tell them a good story about how you were a crazy young kid in the merchant marines, and they'll go for it. Say you developed your physique in Gold's Gym and they'll nod with approval. There is no percentage in telling the truth, nothing to be gained by saying, "My upper body? I got it lifting in San Quentin when I was doing a two-year bit for car theft."

Steven had come to Clover House prepared to put one over on the social worker types, but there was no need to. For the first time in Steven's life, he felt something he had always faked before. Daintily, he ran his index finger down the smooth slope of Nicky's nose, traced the shape of the rosebud mouth, and explored the crevices of the baby's miraculous, perfect ears. "This is my son. He's a miniature version of me!" Steven said to no one in particular.

Phoebe, too, seemed infatuated by Nicky, though obviously more self-conscious about it. When Steven finally handed him over, she took a moment to look around the room, then cuddled Nicky in her arms and began whispering baby talk. She and Steven had been through some tough times, but that was all behind them now. She was going to clean up, and so was Steven. Together, they would get Nicky out of the clutches of the court and be a real family.

When the Clover House counselor monitoring the visit announced that the hour was up, Steven handed Nicky to Sharon Ruprecht. Tears were actually streaming down his face. "I know you'll take good care of him; I'm glad he's with you," Steven told the foster mother. "But he's our son and we'll jump through whatever hoops the judge wants us to to get him back."

Steven's sincerity deeply impressed the Clover House counselor, who made a note of it for the record. "Did you ever see a father bond with a child like that?" he asked Ruprecht. "It was beautiful! I really think they have a chance to make it."

Ruprecht nodded but did not say anything. It was obvious that her friend Claire was not the only one who had fallen in love with the beautiful curly-haired baby. Judge Edwards had this case. Ruprecht has known and worked with him for years and thought as highly of the judge as he did of her. She also thought that he was like the system, "fundamentally naïve when it comes to biological parents. He really believes that, when confronted with a choice between changing their behavior and losing their children, most parents will opt to change."

Phoebe and Steven did indeed have a chance to get Nicky back, and that worried Ruprecht.

5

JENNY: THE
CHILDREN'S SHELTER

A MONTH HAD PASSED SINCE JENNY LANGDON RAN AWAY FROM HER foster home, and she was still in the Children's Shelter. Her social worker was not having any luck finding a foster home for her and the baby, when it arrived. But no one was panicking; there was still another month before her due date.

It was bedtime now for the youngest children on a mild winter evening, but it could have been any night, any season. The only thing different was a big Christmas tree in the main room, freshly cut and glittering with tinsel. Come Christmas morning, there would be toys and clothing under the tree, donations from fire companies and civic groups. But for now the presents were for display only, beautifully wrapped empty boxes.

"There's no place like the shelter for the holidays," Jenny said, jerking her head in the direction of the tree. "I always keep it in the back of my mind to try to get here for Christmas. There's always a big pile of shit and they let you take anything you want."

Earlier that day, a half-dozen new intakes had been processed into a facility that was built to house forty-two children but that now typically held close to ninety. Four of the new children were immediately placed on "special watch": one had suicidal ideation, another a history of assault, a third a history of sexually acting out and of arson. To help curb his violent outbursts, a fourth child was on heavy psychotropic medication.

In the playground that afternoon, there had been a fistfight between two fifteen-year-olds with gang affiliations, the thirteenth assault registered in the shelter in less than two months. A counselor had jumped in, and no one had been seriously hurt. Somehow, the shelter clinic had managed to miss the head lice on one of the new girls, and now the entire dorm was infested. Every sheet and every blanket on every bed had to be changed. A week ago, it was scabies.

Around 7:30, the two women counselors on nursery duty, looking tired and drawn, began putting the babies to sleep. As usual, to maximize space, the cribs were lined up like little boxcars around the perimeter of the nursery. In each one, a tiny face that was supposed to be drifting off to sleep was peeking out from behind bars. The counselors walked from crib to crib, checking diapers, tucking in blankets, and guiding thumbs into mouths, patting and rubbing backs, saying "night-night" in a whisper. From somewhere in the room came the sound of a soprano voice singing nursery rhymes on a scratchy, worn-out tape: "Jack and Jill went up the hill. . . . And when the bough breaks. . . ."

For a blessed moment all was silent. Then, from a crib, a toddler with a full hip-to-ankle cast on his right leg started crying, tears the size of dimes spilling down his face. That was the end of sleep in the nursery. An eighteen-month-old girl, her hair in a skimpy ponytail and the right side of her face swollen and bruised, hurled her stuffed bear to the floor and let out a long, shrill screech. Two days earlier, she had been rushed to the hospital after being beaten by her father.

Another child used his spidery thin arms to pull himself to a standing position and rest his chin along the crib guardrail. He didn't make a sound. Although he weighed no more than ten pounds, the weight of an average three-month-old, he looked like a little old man in miniature. Police brought him to the shelter after the boy's mother abandoned him in the filthy motel room where they had been living. The first assumption was that the tiny boy might have the fast-aging disease, progeria, because he so resembled the newspaper pictures of those children, as shriveled as dried-apple dolls, shaking hands with Mickey Mouse at Disneyland.

But doctors ruled that out, as they ruled out malnutrition and a half-dozen other physiological problems. For the moment, the boy's diagnosis was "failure to thrive," a catchall term used to mean that an infant has gotten so little human warmth and comfort, so little of what his soul craves, that he has somehow willed himself to stop growing.

It is easy to understand why the nursery is the room in the shelter that the women's club volunteers and the firemen who come dressed as Santa and his elves remember long after their Christmas gifts have been opened. The children in this room are so huggable; their physical wounds are unforgettable and hint at other, more terrible wounds that cannot be seen. This room is proof that life can be unspeakably horrid before you even learn your name.

In the dorm room next door, older children, elementary–school age boys and girls, sweaty and dirty faced from a day of play, were also getting ready for bed. By age seven or eight, many are already Shelter veterans who fall quickly into silent, straight lines when shower time is announced. Counselors say that they can always spot the first-timers, the children who have not yet bounced among relatives, foster homes, and institutions, and have thus yet to learn how to "get with the program." They dawdle and wander out of line; they goof around; they cry; they tickle the child in front of them, forgetting that such "inappropriate behavior" is one of many things that can lose them TV privileges. Rules are a necessary part of any institution, especially one bound by a catalog of federal, state, and county child welfare codes. But as one counselor said wistfully, "You can tell the first-timers here because, unlike the others, they still have their childhood spark."

As the evening progressed, teenagers began drifting out of the senior units to hang around the Christmas tree in the main room of the shelter. Strolling the perimeter was a handsome, sweet-faced fifteen-year-old with slicked-back hair, a boy who had been beaten by his father for most of his childhood. His left arm was draped protectively around the shoulders of a gloomy-looking girl: "Why can everyone find love but me?" she was asking him.

For the most part, though, the teenagers in the room that evening looked neither huggable nor vulnerable. They were sullen and edgy, as if waiting for someone to say the wrong word. A trio of teenage boys, longtime foster kids, their heads shaved, huddled together, making plans to run from the shelter that night to hook up with their gang.

Jenny was sitting on a couch, her swollen legs propped up on a table, when she felt a spasm in her lower back, then a rolling pain across her abdomen. She yelled for a counselor: "My baby's coming!"

The counselor told her to stay where she was and rest. She was jumping to conclusions. Moments later, though, Jenny's water broke and a puddle lay by her feet. The hospital was called. "I told you! I know these things! I'm going to be a mother. Mothers know," Jenny kept repeating as two counselors helped her into the ambulance that rushed her to Valley Medical Center.

Only later did it dawn on Jenny that she had followed a family tradition: "I found out that my grandmother had been a foster kid and she had given up my mother. And then, my mother was a foster kid, too, and when she was pregnant with me, she was living at this same shelter. That was really trippy."

• • •

Valley Medical Center (VMC) is a glistening white, seven-story building on the edge of Interstate 280, the eight-lane freeway that bisects San Jose on its way south from San Francisco. Like county hospitals everywhere, it is charged with treating the elderly and indigent. Waiting rooms, lined with the kind of molded plastic chairs that no one is ever comfortable in, are typically loud and crowded.

But the irony is that the constant noise and chaos is what makes a county hospital like VMC the place to go if you have been in a car wreck or are about to deliver a premature baby. Expertise in emergency medicine is honed by performing the same lifesaving heroics over and over under the most impossible circumstances. At VMC, which has one of the finest emergency clinics in the San Francisco Bay Area, doctors and nurses attend to more accident victims, more gunshot wounds, more crisis labors in a week than community hospitals in tree-filled suburbs get in months. Its OB-GYN and pediatrics departments are affiliated with prestigious Stanford Hospital, twenty miles up the freeway in Palo Alto.

It was here that Jenny delivered a girl. "I decided to name her Lisa because I just always liked that name," she explains. Lee Ann Osterdock, Jenny's court-appointed child advocate, arrived a few minutes after the baby. Osterdock was an emotional wreck. Considering the way Jenny had been living, so many things could have gone wrong with the baby. "I had never known Jenny to have a drug problem, but who knew for sure?" Osterdock says. "She had been on the run for weeks. She had dodged most of her prenatal appointments. Who knew if she had been drinking? Had she had anything more nutritious than hot dogs and Cokes?"

But Lisa, to everyone's relief, was born perfect and was not even premature, as had been suspected. Jenny had just lost track of her menstrual cycle. Lisa was a full-term seven-pounder with good color, excellent reflexes and muscle tone, and a first-rate set of lungs. The labor had been a snap, even though Jenny had not taken Lamaze training. When Osterdock arrived, Lisa was in Jenny's arms and the new mother was "looking as if she had been out for walk. Her hair hadn't even gotten messed up."

Jenny had been around babies before, in the shelter and in a couple of foster homes, but she had never really studied one so closely. She had not been prepared for how small Lisa was, how her hands looked like wiggling little starfish. There was no doubt whom Lisa resembled. Jenny looked down at her daughter's dark hair, broad forehead, and flattened nose and could not wait until Bobby saw his daughter.

• • •

"I met Bobby about a year before Lisa was born," Jenny recalls. "It was really a trip. I was on the run from the shelter and there was word out that some guy was talking shit about my friend Vicky. I called the guy and told him, 'What the fuck do you mean, talking shit to my friend?' He got all 'Fuck you, too.' Later, I went to my friend's house, and he was there and he said to me: 'Wow. I should have known! Are you fine! Bitches with an attitude are always fine!' "

Bobby was not much to look at, kind of scrawny and plain, but the way he studied her with frank admiration made Jenny feel appreciated. Not just for her looks, but for everything that she had been endlessly criticized for—her tyrannical temper, her wildness, her arrogance. Here was someone who seemed to understand and did not want to change her.

Jenny and Bobby quickly became inseparable. They ran the streets and stayed up talking all night. They took vows: No head games. No tripping each other out on jealousy. "The first time he started talking all that lovely shit, I did what I usually do: I pushed him away and held my hands over my ears," she says. "Kissing and being touched made me feel, like, all cold and stiff. I get this kind of a spaced-out feeling like I'm on the roof looking down at myself."

After awhile, Jenny finally trusted Bobby enough to explain why she behaved that way. She had been molested in foster homes and had horrible flashbacks. Sometimes, they would arise in nightmares, but more often they would surface during sex. One night, she confessed something else: she might act tough, but she walked around terrified that one day, she was going to become crazy like her mother, all alone, wandering around downtown, screaming at walls and barking like a dog.

It was a big moment. Bobby told her that nothing like that would ever happen to her because he would not let it happen. He was going to stay with her forever.

That vow lasted a few months, just long enough for Jenny to get pregnant. She had spotted him talking to one of his old girlfriends, so, to get even, she started talking to lots and lots of guys. Bobby's worst crime was that he started lecturing her—about how insecure she was, about how stupid she was to pick fights with him for no reason, about how she never considered other people's feelings. Bobby, Jenny would later explain matter-of-factly, really got on her nerves. "He kept trippin' on me, like some social worker."

This was Jenny's pattern, one that Osterdock knew only too well: She starts out vulnerable and sympathetic, so obviously aching for love and attention. You think that you are getting close to her, breaking through, but suddenly, without warning, a suit of armor goes on. Her face hardens. Her muscles tighten. For no reason you can fathom, you have become an enemy to be driven from her life. "One time soon after we met, I took her to Taco Bell and told her to order anything she wanted," Osterdock says. "It was horrible. I went and found us a table and she was standing in line when she just flipped out. 'Fuck this!' she started screaming. 'I hate the fucking food in these places!'"

It took Osterdock months to get Jenny to talk about it, and when Jenny did, she blurted out, "I never ordered in no restaurant before." Jenny had been raised in a system where some adult was always in charge, always making the decisions. Somebody had always ordered for her; someone else had always paid the bill whenever she had eaten in a restaurant with a set of foster parents or kids from a group home. Worst of all, Jenny could not read the menu. "There were all these little kids in front of me in line who were acting cool," she told Osterdock. "They knew how to do it. I felt stupid."

After that explanation, Osterdock was more committed than ever to staying with Jenny. Bobby, on the other hand, had not been too difficult to push away. Jenny's attitude—the very thing that originally attracted him—became too much. Months before Lisa was born, he had started going with a young woman named Melinda.

But that was all in the past now. With Lisa here, Jenny was sure that everything would change. For the first time, things would start going right in her life. She had it all pictured: Bobby and his mother would rush in and see her there, Bobby's daughter asleep beside her. In that instant, Bobby would be sorry that he had broken up with her, that he had suggested naming their baby Melinda. He would see how Lisa had already changed Jenny, how responsible she had become. She couldn't wait to tell him that for a whole month, all of recorded history to Jenny, she had not taken off from the shelter.

She had also made plans. "I'm going to read to Lisa the way my own mother never read to me. I'm gonna teach her all about computers as soon as I learn about them. I'm going to do fun stuff with her, like take her to McDonald's and let her play in those ball things," Jenny said. "And I won't let other kids hit her or nothin'. I know I'll be a good mother because she isn't going to get around me the way I got around my foster parents. I know all the tricks. I'll stop her from that shit."

And when Lisa got old enough, Jenny planned on starting her own foster home, "in a big house with seven rooms." She wouldn't care if she made any money. She would spend it all on the kids. Buy them clothes and give them the things they didn't have. "The only kids I won't let in are the pyros, who try to set things on fire every single minute," Jenny explained.

If Bobby did not want to be part of this, that would be OK. Jenny would raise Lisa herself. The important thing was that Jenny was going to break what she had come to think of as "my family curse." Perfect Lisa with the pitch black hair "was never, never going to become a foster care kid."

✗ Jenny ran away again
around christmas
↳ came back one night

✗ Jenny's water broke & she had
baby Lisa
↳ learn about Bobby, Lisa's
dad

✗ Jenny starts to plan how to raise
Lisa
↳ would be nice if Bobby came
back but okay if not

6

JENNY: VALLEY MEDICAL CENTER

TWO DAYS AFTER LISA'S BIRTH, JENNY STOPPED WAITING FOR BOBBY. He had called all excited and said that he and his mother were on their way to see the "new granddaughter," but Bobby had never shown up. Now Jenny was sitting up in her hospital bed, a pillow tucked behind her head, her eyes fixed resolutely on one of the soap operas that were like an anchor in her life. No matter what, she could count on these characters being there every day at the same time.

People kept coming in and out of Jenny's room—nurses, doctors, the hospital social worker, one of her former foster moms, and Lee Ann Osterdock—but Jenny pointedly ignored them all. They kept pacing and circling around her, talking to each other in worried whispers. It was making Jenny angry that they were treating her like she had a disease instead of a brand new baby.

The light had started fading when a nurse brought in Lisa for her early evening feeding. Jenny reached out and took the baby, but she refused to meet the nurse's eyes. Osterdock could sense the tension in Jenny's body and recognized the look on her face, a slit-eyed aggressiveness that meant her sword and shield were up. "Here, let me help you," Osterdock said gently.

"I don't need help," Jenny snapped back.

With everyone watching, Jenny slipped her left breast out of her nightgown and tried to stick the nipple in the baby's mouth, but the baby still wasn't doing it right. The greedy little mouth, the wet tongue flickering on her skin felt strange and embarrassing. "Everyone was staring at me," she recalls. "They kept acting like it was my fault that the baby wouldn't eat right."

This was the way Jenny had felt around adults for as long as she could remember: all her life, she had been scrutinized by social workers and attorneys, studied by foster parents who were waiting for her to screw up, observed by therapists as if she were a bug under a microscope. "I decided they could all find another show to watch," she said later. Abruptly, she yanked Lisa from her breast, placed the baby on the bed beside her, and went back to staring at the TV. The adults glanced at each other, then quickly looked away.

Osterdock sat down on a chair and pressed her hand against her temple. She had a headache. She had had it for two days, ever since Lisa was born.

There are some people who, due to some combination of intelligence, economics and social class, temperament and luck have lives that follow a smooth and predictable course. A fastidious woman, Osterdock has certainly faced the uncertainties and calamities that come with modern life—earthquakes, traffic accidents, deaths in the family, the stresses that accompany even the best marriage. But for the most part, the world has behaved more or less rationally for Osterdock. She teaches pharmacology and has a lovely mountain home with a pool surrounded by coastal oaks and towering redwoods. As a mother, she applied a solid child-rearing philosophy—be a good role model and the child will learn—and her daughter and son sailed safely through adolescence. She has been married for thirty years and claims never to have had a fight.

"Among family and friends, I'm famous for my patience," she says. "I don't lose my temper—period."

When Osterdock's children went off to college, she found herself "wanting to do something instead of sitting around and saying that the country's problems are too big and there's nothing I can do about them. A lawyer friend suggested I look into becoming a child advocate. I knew I couldn't save everyone, but I could make a stab at trying to make a difference in one person's life."

Osterdock and a dozen other volunteers went through twenty-five hours of training to become Court Appointed Special Advocates (CASA). A district attorney described his job protecting children's rights, and a public defender talked about protecting the parents' rights. Osterdock received a crash course in the fundamental dynamics of child abuse, and an instructor taught the volunteers how to testify and how to stand up under cross-examination.

CASA started in Seattle in 1977 and quickly spread to all fifty states.

In most places, advocates monitor a child's case on paper, but in Santa Clara County they often become the one consistent figure in a dependent child's life, someone who goes to court with them, someone who takes them out to a movie, someone who helps them move from one foster home to another, someone who knows them better than their busy social workers or attorneys with bulging caseloads could ever hope to. Someone who, ideally, is as close to a parent as these kids are likely to get.

After finishing the course and being sworn in, Osterdock read through a dozen files before settling on Jenny. She was struck, as everyone is, with the number of haunting episodes that had occurred in the life of someone so young. Perhaps nothing was more haunting than this: name after name appeared in the file—foster parents, attorneys, social workers, a potential adoptive mother—and then disappeared, their absence haunting Jenny's file like ghosts.

The CASA training had tried to prepare Osterdock for what she was getting into. Jenny was one thing; but no amount of training, no raft of personal experience that Osterdock could cling to, could have prepared her to work in a system she found "crazy, totally irrational. I couldn't believe it."

"Jenny was essentially a prisoner," Osterdock explains. "Any change of plans, any seemingly innocuous request, required a court order. And getting a court order meant involving judges, attorneys, court clerks, social workers, the entire ungainly system with its endless paperwork, continuances, clogged calendars, interagency politics, and bureaucratic procedures. I don't know how many times I've been told over the years: 'I know this would be best for the child, but we can't do it legally.' Right or wrong, whether the rules make sense or not, whether they benefit Jenny or not, they have to be followed."

Which is why Osterdock's head had been pounding ever since Lisa was born. The Department was holding its ground. If someone did not find Jenny a foster home, she would be released from the hospital and returned alone to the shelter. Since the shelter was not "appropriate" for Lisa, a social worker would take the baby into "protective custody" and place her with strangers in an Emergency Shelter Home. Osterdock knew that it could take weeks, perhaps months, of phone calls, reports, and court hearings to reunite Jenny with Lisa.

The shelter might not be appropriate for a newborn, but how appropriate was it to separate a mother from her baby during this crucial bonding time? How was Jenny going to get comfortable holding her baby? How was Jenny going to nurse? Her milk would dry up, the baby would get used to formula, and Jenny would never learn to breast-feed.

"I wasn't naive enough to think that having a baby was suddenly going to transform Jenny into a levelheaded, responsible mother," Osterdock said later. "But I thought that giving birth to Lisa—that being part of the natural cycle of things for the first time in her life—could touch Jenny in a way that nobody, myself included, had ever been able to touch her. She deserved a chance to bond with her baby, to begin learning what it means to truly connect to another human being. And how was she going to do that if the Department came in and separated them?"

Unfortunately, Lisa came into the world on a Friday night, when Jenny's social worker had already left for vacation. The social worker's voice mail left callers general instructions: "If this is an emergency and you need to talk to someone immediately, hang up and call the OD, the Officer of the Day." The OD connected Osterdock with a supervisor, but the supervisor did not know much about the case and did not want to step on anybody's toes. Osterdock then called the shelter, hoping to persuade a supervisor to bend a few rules and let Jenny and Lisa stay there until a more permanent home could be arranged. The supervisor said that it could not be done. Nobody there had the authority to make that kind of decision.

Lee Ann—the person Jenny was closest to in the world—could not take her and her baby home, even for a few days. Her home wasn't li-censed, and she would be stepping across another strictly drawn legal line. Advocates are not to move children into their homes. Finally, in desperation Osterdock cornered the hospital administrator in the hall and pleaded Jenny's case. "Let her stay one more night," she begged. "Give me another twenty-four hours to find a place that will take them both."

It could not be done.

"She told me that it would be against hospital policy," Osterdock said later. "She said that there was no drug addiction, no jaundice, no medical reason why the baby and the mother should be allowed to remain in the hospital one more night."

The woman who was famous for never losing her temper finally lost it and yelled at the administrator: "Tell Medi-Cal that Lisa has a hangnail or something! Give this mother and her baby a chance to bond!"

.   .   .

What is this mysterious event called bonding? What is it that children need in order to feel connected to other human beings, to feel that the world is a relatively safe and loving place? How do they get what they need, and what happens when they don't get it?

Nowhere are these questions more crucial than in the child welfare system. It is an easy decision to remove a child from her home when her life is in danger. But often, the call is not so clear-cut. It is then that social workers, attorneys, and judges face the awesome task of determining what, beyond the bare necessities of physical survival, children require in order to become full citizens of the human community.

Bonding, or attachment theory, attempts to answer that question. It pinpoints a critical period in childhood when emotional bonds are supposedly formed and warns that, if the attachment process is disrupted or never started, the child suffers disastrous, often irreversible, developmental damage. It explains why, so often, the abused child grows up to be the abuser and why some people seem incapable of ever understanding anyone's needs but their own.

Recent medical research has given bonding theory a firm physiological foundation by showing that neglect, separation, abuse and stress can profoundly effect an infant's actual brain biochemistry, with possible lifelong consquences on growth and mental abilities.

In the history of psychology, bonding theory is a relative latecomer. As recently as the 1950s and 1960s, during the apogee of behaviorism, young children's needs were seen as being essentially physical and uncomplicated. Infants were said to cling to their mothers mostly as a function of feeding, a way of satisfying their innate biological requirement for food and oral gratification. Behaviorist theory held that infants cry not primarily to be held or cuddled or to be gazed at with loving eyes. They are demanding the nipple, and as long as they get it, their needs are being met.

Parents were advised to ignore the almost mystical sensation that some describe, that their week-old child is "falling in love" with them, wooing them, smiling only at their voice. The baby's cry—her so-called infatuation with mother or father—is only her way of controlling the lunch wagon. The smile is only gas. From this notion came an influx of "modern" child-rearing advice from experts who endorsed a hands-off policy and warned parents—particularly "overindulgent" mothers—against following their well-meant but misguided intuition. Don't pick up an infant whenever she cries; it will just reinforce the behavior and create a crybaby. Too much cuddling and too much responsiveness will lead to spoiling.

The child welfare policies of the era also reflected this prevailing psychological theory. If infants' needs were mostly physical, anyone could provide them. If the parents were not adequately providing food, shelter, and clothing, it made sense to take the children away from those parents and place them in institutions or foster homes. It should not matter how long they stayed or how often they were moved from place to place, as long as they had three square meals a day.

In the midst of this behaviorist-dominated atmosphere, Harry Harlow, an animal-learning theorist, became intrigued by the earlier work of psychoanalyst René Spitz, who had studied infants in foundling homes. These babies had received adequate food and water, but were often left in their cribs for prolonged periods of time. Their cries were certainly not "reinforced." A rotating crew of aides picked them up only to be changed and fed on a strict schedule that did not allow for rocking, cuddling, and playing.

Today's proponents of a return to orphanages and large-scale children's institutions—even well-run ones—should view the film that Spitz made of the foundlings. As behaviorist theory would have predicted, these babies did, indeed, cry a lot less than the "average" baby. In fact, they completely stopped crying and babbling altogether. They never learned to talk.

By the end of their second year, the once healthy foundlings had deteriorated to the mental level of imbeciles and showed no response to the appearance of a human figure. Child psychologist Selma Fraiberg, author of *Every Child's Birthright: In Defense of Mothering*, writes, "The motion picture made of these mute, solemn children, lying stuporous in their cribs, is one of the little-known horror films of our time."

From these studies, Harlow posed the questions: If infants have only physiological needs, what happened to these foundlings? Why did they wither away? Why did some of them actually die when deprived of human contact? In 1958, Harlow experimented with rhesus monkeys in a study that every Psych 101 student has since read about. Two newborn monkeys were separated from their mothers, put into a cage, and "raised" by two surrogate mothers, both of which were constructed of wire mesh and equipped with nipples so that they could provide their babies with food. The only difference between these two foster moms was that one was covered with a piece of soft terry cloth.

The hypothesis was that if baby monkeys sought only the basics of food and water, they should cling equally to both monkey moms. But Harlow discovered that even when the "uncovered" monkey mother was the only one providing food, the offspring clearly favored the soft, cuddly mother, rushing to it when frightened, huddling next to it in sleep, and using it as a base for exploration.

Harlow concluded that infants—infant monkeys, at least—crave warmth and body contact. Without the closeness of a mother, as he showed in later experiments, baby monkeys grew up into aberrations of their species, strangely self-absorbed and eschewing contact with other monkeys. It was as if depriving them of a mother had deprived them of their "monkeyhood." In a scene that echoes that of institutionalized children, the monkeys sat staring into space or circled their cages as if in a trance. Some of them chewed or tore at their own skin until it bled. At the age of sexual maturity, these monkeys showed no desire to copulate. In one experiment, one of the mother-deprived "foster" monkeys was impregnated by a "normal" male. Rather than caring for her offspring, the mother ignored them or tried to kill them.

Monkeys are not human beings, but the British psychoanalyst John Bowlby, drawing both from studies of children's institutions and ethology, took the scientific leap: a human infant also needs early and consistent maternal contact. In fact, the infant's every act—crying, sucking, clinging, cooing, smiling—is biologically designed to keep his mother close, not just for food but also for the child's innate need to feel safety and intimacy with another human being.

For it is in early infancy, Bowlby concluded, that mother and child "bond" to each other by creating a reciprocal language of love. A smile elicits a smile, and a cry brings soft words and an embrace, over and over, a thousand times. In a mirror of adult romance, separation is unbearably painful for both, then almost unbearably blissful when they are reunited.

Originally, bonding theory emphasized the mother-child bond, but it later was expanded to include any consistent, devoted primary caregiver. Through this crucial person at this crucial time, the child learns to trust and to feel cherished by the world. She learns to put aside self-desires and to redirect aggressive behavior in the interest of another human being. As Fraiberg has written, "In every act of love in mature life, there is a prologue which originated in the first year of life."

Bowlby is now recognized as the father of what has become known as "attachment theory," which burst upon the general public in the late 1970s and laid the foundations for the boom in natural childbirth, special hospital birthing rooms where music is played, and the revival of breast-feeding—what a writer in the *The New Republic* snidely dubbed "The cult of happy childbirth—one of those typically American mixtures of Rousseauian naturalism and scientific authority."

The immediate popular appeal of attachment theory rests in a very romantic and appealing notion with ramifications for all of society. We can "control" a child's future—for example, increase IQ points and eliminate bothersome neurotic tendencies—by making sure that the first few years of life—indeed, some have said, the first few minutes of life—go absolutely right.

And if bonding goes poorly, the consequences—in varying degrees of severity—are what Fraiberg has called "the diseases of nonattachment . . . the incapacity of the person to form human bonds . . . characterized by . . . no joy, no grief, no guilt, and no remorse."

Proponents of this theory point to some very compelling studies. In one, two-year-old children who are described as "insecurely" attached already lack self-reliance and the enthusiasm for challenges shown by their peers. By age five, they are already the troublemakers at school, fighting with peers, refusing to participate, sulking, alone and unhappy on the playground.

Of course, any psychological theory that simplifies all human behavior into direct cause and effect is bound to be criticized. Academics say that some of the most-cited bonding studies are rife with methodological errors and unexamined assumptions. Attachment theory has been attacked by feminists for its overemphasis on the mother's role and for its reactionary "family-oriented" ideology that makes women feel guilty for being in the workplace. It has been ridiculed by psychoanalysts for offering a simpleminded view of humanity that overlooks such pivotal events as childhood illnesses and sibling rivalry.

Common sense alone says that to ascribe all future psychological pathology and success to a few early years is absurd. Genetic character traits, economic status and social class, educational level, on-going parenting, and societal values obviously have a lot to do with how a child turns out.

But in the child welfare system, bonding theory is not a feminist ideological debate over whether new mothers should nurse their newborns or should nurse their careers. It is not the middle-class worries about whether full-time childcare hampers an infant's future chances of getting accepted at Stanford. It is a theory that must be put into constant practice:

When are biological parents meeting a child's "minimal physical and emotional needs" and where is the line when society is compelled to step in?

If we leave a child in a troubled family, what can we do to encourage bonding with parents who, due to their own miserable childhoods, may lack this supposedly "instinctive" behavior?

If we remove the child, what kind of out-of-home care can we possibly put in the place of parents who, despite being abusive and neglectful, are still mommy and daddy?

For children like Jenny and her daughter, Lisa, bonding offers the possibility of emotional survival, of breaking a chain that has been passed down for generations.

• • •

"Do we need to call a security guard? Do you think Jenny could get violent?"

There was an uncomfortable silence as Lee Ann Osterdock stood in the hall outside Jenny's hospital room and pondered the social worker's questions. Osterdock did not want to answer them. She wanted answers to her own questions: Why couldn't anyone in this convoluted system figure out a way to keep Jenny and Lisa together? Why does the law keep people from doing what is obviously right?

But Osterdock had learned how useless it would be to pose such questions. The social worker was not particularly cold and unsympathetic. She was simply powerless, like so many others Osterdock had tried to work with. The Department was not paying her to debate policies and procedures, but to carry them out as efficiently as possible. The hospital said that Jenny had to leave. The Department said that Lisa must go to an Emergency Shelter Home. The social worker was just being professional.

"You told her this is temporary, right?" the worker asked Osterdock. "You told her that we would find them a home together as soon as possible? She heard all that?"

The advocate nodded yes, but she understood that Jenny would never believe anything a social worker told her. That was why Osterdock did not know how Jenny would react when a stranger walked in and demanded that she turn over her own daughter. Jenny "went off" all the time; she threatened and created huge scenes, but through the years, foster parents and therapists had remarked upon the fact that Jenny had never physically attacked anyone. "I suspect it was because Jenny didn't feel safe enough to hit anyone," Osterdock theorizes. "She was stopped by the memory of being hit back twice as hard."

But could Osterdock be sure? Could she swear that Jenny would not pick up Lisa and throw her across the room? "Let's get a guard," she told the social worker. "Truthfully, if someone tried to take my baby away from me, you would have had to call a guard, too."

Osterdock returned to Jenny's room first, followed a few minutes later by the social worker and a hospital security guard. It was obvious that Jenny knew what was about to happen. She had Lisa locked in her arms, jaw clinched, scowling like a samurai, her eyes fixed on the baby. Osterdock sat next to her, rubbing her tenderly on the arm. "Things will go better if the social worker sees how mature you can be, how you are willing to put the baby's well-being first," Osterdock whispered. "Don't fight this. Don't hurt anyone."

As the social worker approached, Jenny let out a scream and tightened her grip on Lisa. She started to sob. Gently but firmly, Osterdock and the social worker pried open Jenny's fingers one by one. Her whole body was shaking, but her hands remained open, as taut as claws. The social worker lifted Lisa away from her mother, turned and silently left the room with the guard. Osterdock placed one arm around Jenny's shoulders and pulled her closer.

"You did so good. You did so good," Osterdock kept whispering. "You didn't hurt anyone. You didn't hurt Lisa. I am so proud of you."

..nother person might have embraced Osterdock, broken down and gone limp with sorrow. But Jenny, for the first time in their three-year relationship, hit her advocate, first a light open-handed slap on the shoulder, then slightly harder, then harder still on the arm and on the back.

Osterdock did not move away. She sat on the bed, shaken, numbed from the past two days, and made no attempt to stop Jenny. "That's OK. Be angry at me. Be as mad as you want," Osterdock kept saying. "You have every right to be mad."

Jenny and Lisa were Seperated within 12 hrs by Jenny had to leave the hospital and Lisa was put into a seperate home

7

NICKY: THE HEARING

MONTHS HAD PASSED AND THE TRIAL IN THE CASE OF NICKY DELGATO had still not been held. Child welfare law mandates that all cases move with dispatch, but the dependency system is such an intricate engine that a small malfunction can jam the gears and stop things cold. On one of the days the trial was scheduled, the Delgatos' attorney was stuck in a criminal trial that had lasted longer than anticipated and the case had to be continued. On another date, the deputy district attorney who represented Nicky was out sick and the case was continued again.

Families in crisis generate so much friction that trials often melt away like snow under a hot sun. A father determined to fight allegations that he has a drinking problem wakes up with no memory of the past three days and decides to check into a rehab facility. Parents walk into the lobby convinced that they have a valid case until they catch a glimpse of the social worker carrying a stack of files. The parents know what is in those files and what will be presented in court. After hurried whispers, they hunt for their attorney and say, "We've decided not to go through with this." Other parents get so intimidated by the social workers and formal court process that they just cave in and decide not to fight the system.

Before the Delgato case could be heard, Steven and Phoebe were arrested for being drunk and disorderly and spent two weeks in the county jail. After that, their attorney explained to them that there was no sense in going to trial for Nicky. Judge Edwards would never award them custody. They had a better chance of getting Nicky back if they accepted reunification services.

On the day of the hearing, the case was called, and as soon as the formalities were completed, the Delgatos' attorney stood and said, "Judge, we are going to submit to the petition." Mary Agnes King, Nicky's social worker, permitted herself a small sigh of relief. A heavy-set woman with short gray hair, she had spent hours interviewing Steven and Phoebe, reading records, and delving into their backgrounds in preparation for the trial. King can be tough when she has to be but, like a majority of her colleagues, does not relish going to court. "I did not become a social worker to take the stand and defend my work—and sometimes my character—against the attacks of an attorney," she says.

In general, social workers consider the attorneys who represent parents to be gladiators who have lost sight of the fact that the court is there to do what is best for children and families. They believe all attorneys care about is winning, and to win, they cross-examine social workers and demand that every terrible thing the parents have done to themselves and their children go on the record. "How can a social worker ever work with parents after that has happened?" King asks. "How can the social worker ever win the trust of a child who has sat in court and listened to her drag out all the dirt she knows on the child's parents?"

Judge Edwards made certain that the parents understood that submitting the petition to the court was the dependency court's equivalent of a guilty plea in criminal court. They were waiving their rights to a trial, to see and hear witnesses, to remain silent, and to testify. When the Delgatos acknowledged that they understood, the judge made Nicky a dependent child of the court and removed him from his parents' care and control.

"If you are not successful in reunifying with Nicky during the next twelve to eighteen months, I will have to establish a permanent plan for him," the judge explained. "That could mean long-term care with a relative or in a foster home, a guardianship, or the termination of your parental rights and an adoption by another family.

"Please," the judge went on, "don't let this happen. Follow the reunification plan that Mrs. King has written so that you can be reunified with your son."

Each reunification plan is supposed to be unique, tailored to the needs of a specific individual and specific family. But the reality is they are all pretty much the same. Parents who have physically abused their children enter therapy and are sent to parenting classes. Parents like Steven and Phoebe who have substance abuse problems must complete drug programs. Both would also have to submit to regular urine analysis. Both would have to successfully complete a twelve-week parent education class and establish a stable address.

The judge turned to the deputy district attorney who was paging through the case file. The courtroom was silent as he lifted a page, scanned it, and lifted another. When he looked up, the DA noted that, according to the record, Phoebe Delgato was a registered narcotics offender, with six convictions on drug and alcohol charges. (In California, narcotics offenders, like sex offenders, must register with the police.) Steven Delgato's lengthy record included arrests on drug charges, plus five arrests for driving under the influence of controlled substances.

"Nicky would best be served if all efforts were made to find a residential drug treatment facility for both parents," the DA said. The judge nodded and instructed the social worker to search for a residential placement.

"Meetings between the parents and the child will continue at Clover House?" asked the DA.

"Judge, if I may interject?" asked the Delgatos' attorney. "Except for a two-week period when the parents were in custody, they have not missed a visit. They love their little boy, judge. They would like to see him more frequently than once a week."

"We'll increase the visits to two a week, two hours each," Judge Edwards said, looking at the parents. "I want you to know your son. I want you to see him grow." The judge then asked his clerk to select a date for the six-month review hearing, and everyone in the courtroom got out their calendars. After a date had been agreed upon, the judge spent a moment thinking about what he was going to say.

"You know, we're very lucky," the judge told Steven and Phoebe. "A few years ago, we would have lost Nicky. Today, because the equipment is so sophisticated, doctors were able to save him." The judge paused. It was an actor's touch, something he has developed over the years.

"Drugs almost claimed your son's life," he continued. "Think about that for a moment. Your behavior almost cost us your son. If you go back to drugs, they will cost you your chance to raise him. And that will be terrible. Nicky is the most important job you will ever have."

There was silence when the judge finished. Then Steven blurted out, "We're gonna do our best, Judge."

The judge nodded solemnly. "I know you will," he said.

• • •

Claire and Greg Kenney were approved to become the Fost-Adopt parents of Nicky Delgato. As the name implies, Fost-Adopt is a way the dependency system can hedge its bets on a very young child. If the reunification efforts succeed, Nicky will be returned to his parents, and a system dedicated to finding as permanent a placement as possible will have kept him in a single, stable home. If Phoebe and Steven fail reunification, the Kenneys will immediately become eligible to adopt Nicky. The trial period will be over, the bonds will be established, a judge will simply make the relationship permanent.

King, the social worker, scheduled a visit with the prospective parents. In preparation for that meeting, Claire scrubbed the house and Greg came home early from his job as a software developer and did what an engineer does only on the rarest of occasions: he put on a tie.

Claire and Greg were nervous when they shook hands with King and stiff during the small talk that typically precedes an important meeting. But before long, the Kenneys found themselves relaxing, in large part because they found themselves liking the social worker.

King had earned a master's degree in social work (MSW) at Boston College in 1967 and had worked for several years before taking time off to have a baby. She went back to work and then quit to have a second child and had spent more than a dozen years away from her profession. When she returned in 1990, she was struck by how much higher and more professional the Department's standards had become. Ninety-six percent of the Department's 296 social workers now had MSWs, a figure without equal around the country. Every day in the office, there were announcements over the loudspeaker system about a seminar on the cultural issues of one of Santa Clara County's many ethnic groups. Other seminars tackled hot-button issues: sensitivity training on gays and lesbians, the concerns of foster parents, how to write court reports, children and psychotropic medication.

But the image of social workers had not changed much during the time King was raising her daughters. At best, social workers are seen as do-gooders in Birkenstocks, victims of a soft heart and a fuzzy education. At worst, they are viewed as vicious and power hungry, insensitive to the very families they are being paid to serve.

The problems go deeper than mere image, as they do in child-welfare departments around the country. In Santa Clara County, a 1992 grand jury report—while conceding that the Department had "made more progress within the last two years than it had made in the previous twenty years," blasted it for everything from "removing too many children unnecessarily from their homes, especially minority children," to "not placing children with relatives" to "operating as if it is accountable to no one." The Fost-Adopt program received a particularly low mark for having a "conflict of interest."

"The Grand Jury heard from staff members and others outside the Department that the Department puts too much money into 'back-end' services, i.e., therapists and attorneys, and not enough money into 'front-end' or basic services. The county does not receive as much in federal funds for front-end services, which would help solve the problems causing family inadequacies. In other words, the Agency benefits, financially, from placing children in foster homes."

Overall, even in one of the nation's best child-welfare agencies, the grand jury "did not see clear and convincing evidence that the foster care system operates with the best interest of the child in mind. It did find that the interest of the child often took a back seat to the interest of others."

"The report raised another important issue that really hit home with me," King says. "It accused adoption workers of doing what workers across the country have been doing for decades: withholding the psychosocial and medical history of a child from adoptive parents. That was a holdover from the old days."

In those days, "good adoptive parents" did *not* ask for crucial information about a child. Good adoptive parents were willing to take a child without knowing anything about her or her family history. Good adoptive parents did not shop for a child as if they were buying a car. They opened their hearts and took a child, as is.

Not coincidentally, this "take-her-as-is" policy was a blessing for social workers, who are always under tremendous pressure to close cases. Workers introduced adoptive parents to a beautiful baby and watched while they fell in love, without ever mentioning that there was a good chance the child had suffered brain damage or that both birth parents had a history of schizophrenia. This is no longer Department policy or even within the confines of the law, but, according to the grand jury, there are still workers in the adoption unit who "forget" to pass on vital information. The result can be adoption "disruptions"—parents "return" the child to the Department before the adoption is final—or adoption "disillusionments"—parents essentially "divorce" their adopted child.

"I think the move toward sharing all available information is a major breakthrough," King says. "It allows potential adoptive parents to soul-search before making such a momentous decision. It allows them to be honest. Inevitably, some have told me that they cannot raise a child who will never be like themselves. That is much better than having them come back five years later at their wits' end, ready to terminate the adoption.

"I've found that you can't predict what the reaction will be," King continues. "Some couples have told me, 'We can't deal with a child born drug-addicted, but a history of mental illness doesn't scare us.' Other couples have said exactly the opposite."

Sharing information also allows adoptive parents to prepare for what might be coming. A family King worked with adopted a child whose mother suffered from a crippling bipolar disorder. The parents did extensive research. If signs of the illness surfaced, they would be on top of it.

Nicky's case was unique for King because, instead of telling prospective Fost-Adopt parents about a child, they were telling her about Nicky. Claire was bubbling over with the details of Nicky's terrible ear infections—doctors had warned that he would be prone to them—and Nicky's eating habits.

"You understand that reunification is going on?" King asked. It was a gentle way to point out that, as deeply in love as Claire was, Nicky was not her baby. Greg saw where King was leading. As an engineer, he was used to dealing with a reality that was defined by mathematics. He took a breath and asked the big question. King's answer would establish the parameters of their hopes over the next eighteen months.

"Realistically, what are our chances of adopting Nicky?" he asked.

King told the Kenneys that, in general, most families who have their children removed and undergo reunification are successful in Santa Clara County. The children are returned, and the family never again appears in court. "However, given the drug history of the parents, you realistically have a fifty-fifty chance," King said. "But, I have to tell you, the odds don't really matter. If you are the ones who end up giving a child you love back to his parents, it is going to hurt."

The Kenneys were silent, absorbing the information. "We just want what's best for Nicky," Claire said finally.

King leaned forward on the couch. "You have to understand, my job isn't necessarily to pick the best parents for Nicky," she said. "My job is to reunify Nicky with his parents. If that can be done safely, that's probably what's best for the child."

"We can't just be his caregivers! We love him!" Claire snapped.

"I don't want you to be caretakers; I want you to love him," King replied. After a moment, she added, "I also want you to be ready to give him up." There was another silence.

"Fost-Adopt is crazy," Greg said finally. "We get to take care of Nicky; we feel good about that. But we're going to feel guilty, too. We're going to be rooting against his parents."

●　●　●

The notation in Nicky's file was the same one that appears in the files of so many children: "Goal: Reunification." In everyday language, this meant, help Steven and Phoebe get their lives together so that they can take their son home. That is the law. Not long ago, this federal policy was seen as the so-called answer to the "problem." Reunification was one of those rare political measures that was greeted with optimism from all corners of the political spectrum.

Children's rights advocates applauded reunification because the philosophy was sensitive to children's psychological needs and promised to keep more kids out of institutions and foster homes; parents' rights groups favored reunification because it recognized that troubled families have strengths as well as weaknesses. Liberals considered reunification enlightened because it recognized the political and economic causes of child abuse and neglect. The way to stop neglect and abuse was not to blame the poor and punish them by removing their children; the way to stop abuse and neglect was to relieve the pressures of poverty by providing housekeeping assistance, transportation, child care, housing allowances, job training, and drug counseling and by providing parenting classes and therapy that would teach parents the skills and insights their own parents never taught them.

Political conservatives also embraced reunification. The law promised to respect the tradition of the family and to keep government interference at a minimum. And, not incidentally, conservatives embraced reunification because it was a lot cheaper than out-of-home care. If paying for a housekeeper for six months, putting $800 down on a new apartment for a family, and paying for parenting classes at the local YWCA would get three children off the child welfare payroll, conservatives were all for it.

But reunification did not turn out to be a miracle cure. It did not stop the flow of children into foster care; for a variety of reasons, the number has actually grown. Today, reunification is being vilified as intensely as it was once embraced, from inside and outside the system, from all points of the political spectrum. Fiscal conservatives are demanding to know why we are continuing to "shower" parents like the Delgatos with millions of dollars worth of housing allowances, drug programs, and anger-management classes—when there are selfless people like the Kenneys willing to raise Nicky with their own resources.

But more disturbing than fiscal concerns are the horror stories of what has happened to children under reunification, stories so grotesque that just the minimal facts are unbearably painful to read. One such story caused outrage in Santa Clara County. Four-month-old Jory Daniels suffered a fractured skull and bruises when his father went into a rage and beat him. The Department removed the child and placed him—not with strangers in a foster home, not in an institution, but with his grandparents. The social workers went by the "reunification" book: whenever possible, the child should be placed with the closest relative. Jory's case was closed. The reunification was "successful."

At age five, Jory starved to death in his family's apartment, "his body weighing nineteen pounds on the April day that coroner's officers lifted his cold body from the living room floor. . . . His five little years were five years of hell."

Opponents of reunification cite the number of children who have died in their parents' care—at least 1,300 in 1993, almost half of whom had previously come to the attention of welfare agencies. Even onetime proponents of family reunification, like Cook County (Illinois) Public Guardian Patrick Murphy, are arguing that aggressive family reunification "has gone too far" in keeping children with parents who have no ability and no intention of ever changing. As one social worker in the Santa Clara County Department puts it: "The only time I get congratulated is when I reunify a family or when I don't remove the children in the first place. You get rewarded here for not digging too deeply."

. . .

Should we be risking the lives of children by leaving them with dead-end, dangerous families?

Should we be "bribing" parents with services when any decent parent would walk over hot coals to protect and nurture their child?

Should we postpone a child's being adopted on the minuscule chance that a drug-abusing mother and father will turn their lives around?

Should we be supporting a "naive and myopic" ideology that, as Murphy claims, "returns children to drugged-up, noninvolved or abusive parents whose only relationship to parenthood is a sex act nine months before the birth of a child"?

The answers would appear to be obvious. Basic human instinct says that we should rescue these children and remove them from their parents as quickly and as permanently as possible. That will solve the problem.

But if we look into the past, if we follow the waves of history, with its shifting social policies and swells of surefire solutions, we come away with a different picture. We see that raising somebody else's children has similarities to raising our own. Nothing is obvious; nothing is simple. If we think that any one policy, any one solution, is going to make the problems disappear, we are wrong. When it comes to raising children, there are no perfect answers.

8

CHILDREN, FAMILIES, AND THE LAW

The history of childhood is a nightmare
from which we have only recently begun to awaken.

LLOYD DE MAUSE
The History of Childhood

WHEN THE CHARITY WORKER FOUND MARY ELLEN IN 1875, THE
child was ten years old, sick and malnourished, covered with welts and
bruises. The worker was married to a New York City financier who
rubbed shoulders with Cornelius Vanderbilt and Peter Cooper. But despite her connections, the worker could find no judge or agency who was
willing to remove the child from her stepmother. Desperate, she turned
to Henry Bergh, a member of her social circle, who was president of the
Society for the Prevention of Cruelty to Animals.

One version of the legendary story says that the SPCA brought the
case to court, arguing that Mary Ellen, as a member of the animal kingdom, had the same rights to protection as an abused dog. This remarkable assertion that a child had a right to be protected, that a parent could
be hauled into court for something he or she had done in the kingdom
of the home, filled the courtroom with reporters, who watched as the
judge placed Mary Ellen in a temporary home and sentenced the stepmother to one year of hard labor.

Mary Ellen's case gave birth to the Society for the Prevention of Cruelty to Children, the first organization in history dedicated to protecting

children from violence inflicted by family members. By the turn of the century, there was a branch in every state.

But for each supporter and volunteer, the SPCC also attracted a skeptic who raised questions that are much the same questions asked about today's child welfare system. At what point does society step in to help children? What form does this help take? The labor press saw the SPCC as "not much better than a fraud," well-to-do philanthropists who were busy supposedly saving children while ignoring the evils of child labor in factories. The organization only stepped in if children were causing trouble on the streets, not if they were quietly being beaten in their own homes, and certainly not if they were making money for adults.

The SPCC was accused not only of doing too little but also of doing too much. Critics on the other end charged that "The Cruelty"—as it came to be nicknamed—was led by wild-eyed radicals who, if you let them in the door, would destroy that building block of civilization, the family. To counter these charges, Bergh went out of his way to make sure everyone knew that The Cruelty would intervene only in the most desperate circumstances. "A good wholesome flogging," Bergh said reassuringly, is appropriate for "disobedient children."

But, added a lawyer for the SPCC, "Children have some rights."

Looked at historically, the lawyer's tepid assertion was actually revolutionary. Despite the Bill of Rights and the freedoms it assures the individual, nowhere in the Constitution are children awarded specific rights. To the founders, the reason children had no rights was obvious: the family had always been, and would always be, a law unto itself. In this sense, the Constitution was a reflection of English common law, in which women and children—and the mentally ill—had no standing, no personal or legal rights, a precedent that went back at least as far as the Roman Empire, where the paterfamilias had the power of life and death over his children.

From ancient times, the law has always feared to tread upon the "bond of blood." The father has always been free to use his human assets as he saw fit. In antiquity, assets he could not use were abandoned at the edge of marketplaces. In early Christian Europe, children were left at the church door. That the early Christian canons did not dispatch these parents to the lower confines of hell is a reflection of how deep-seated was the belief that God gave a parent the right to do with his children as he saw fit. Throughout the Middle Ages and into eighteenth- and ninteenth-century Britain, children remained valuable commodities who could be sold for adoption or sent out to beg or prostitute themselves.

The Puritans, who brought the idea of the family to the New World, conceived of it as more than an economic engine. It was also spiritually sacrosanct, a version in miniature of the ideal community, "a little commonwealth, at least a lively representation thereof . . . a schoole wherein men are fitted to greater matters in Church or commonwealth."

Like everything else in Puritan society, the relationship between parents and children was defined by duty to the larger community. The children did not have separate rights, but the mother and father had a duty to raise God-fearing children, to educate them in His ways, and to provide "reasonable provision for their future usefulness and happiness in life" by training their offspring for their carefully defined futures as farmers, ministers, or merchants.

If a child transgressed, the parents were expected to "beat the devil out of him." In Massachusetts, the Body of Liberties that became law in 1641 made the cursing and striking of a parent a "capital crime." But the Puritans, harsh though they were, realized that there was a place beyond which corporal punishment did not instruct, that a father could inflict "unnatural severitie." In the unusual instance when Colonial authorities found a home situation to be truly degenerate, when "the morals, or safety, or interest of the children required it," the courts could take a child from the home he had been born into and place him elsewhere.

The legal doctrine that allowed Puritan authorities to intervene in the private life of a family was *parens patriae*—"the state is the ultimate parent of every child." *Parens patriae* was based on the Elizabethan Poor Laws, which gave noblemen the right to apprentice children of parents who, they had decided, were not capable of "keeping or maintaining their children." In effect, the state was willing to be the "ultimate parent" as long as its children could be turned into indentured servants.

While America was a homogeneous, agrarian society, *parens patriae* existed for the most part in law books, used only on rare occasions. This changed in the nineteenth century, after the "huddled masses" had descended upon the United States. The country's first urban reformers turned *parens patriae* into the legal equivalent of the hammer in Vulcan's hand, a tool that could be used to reshape society. In doing so, they laid the foundation for the modern juvenile justice system.

Nothing in New York City today compares to the filth, disease, crime, and overcrowding that reformers witnessed on the Lower East Side in the nineteenth century. Even Charles Dickens, who had seen the poverty of London, was impressed. "All that is loathsome, drooping and decayed is here," Dickens wrote after visiting the Five Points District.

A crime wave that had begun after the Civil War and gone roaring through the so-called gay '90s had made American cities deadlier than the frontier had ever been. A prudent man carried a revolver when he ventured onto the streets of New York. The most disturbing of the "criminal element" were the ruthless urchins who roamed the streets in packs, descending on grocery stores like a plague of locusts, stripping men of their wallets and women of their jewelry. In New York they called themselves the Dead Rabbits, the Molasses Gang, and the Bowery Boys, and a cop did not set foot on their turf alone.

To the reformers, the adults living in the slums were beyond redemption, members of "the Perishing and Dangerous Classes." But the children darting through the crowded streets, the wild and undisciplined "Street Arabs," could be saved. More important, society could be saved from them.

The Child Savers were heavily influenced by the Enlightenment and the ideas of John Locke. The children of immigrants were born no different than their own children: both were *tabula rasa*, empty slates. What a child could become was largely a matter of the impressions that were recorded on that slate.

In New York City in 1825, the Society for the Reformation of Juvenile Delinquents opened the first institution dedicated solely to serving young lawbreakers by finding them work in the trades, where they could develop skills that would propel them into the middle classes. Instead, the superintendent in this "re-form" school contracted out his captive workforce to small manufacturers, where they performed the same task day after day. Their wages went to the superintendent, just as the wages of indentured children had ended up in the pockets of the Elizabethans who had "rescued" them.

As is often the case when an institution fails, the blame did not fall on the greedy superintendent as heavily as it did on the boys the institution was created to protect. They were rebellious; they ran away; they displayed no gratitude for what the reformers were doing for them; they had no appreciation for the value of hard work. It was concluded that the boys in the New York institution had been too old to begin anew. They had arrived thoroughly corrupted by their environments. To succeed, the reformers had to go after younger children with cleaner slates.

The agents of the Children's Aid Society, founded in New York in 1853 by Charles Loring Brace, combed the breeding grounds of the "Dangerous Classes," first for young orphans, then for any child who, in the eyes of the CAS, needed to be rescued from a dismal future. Brace was convinced that salvation lay in hard work. Girls captured by CAS agents for the "crime" of being sexually active were sent to industrial schools, where they spent their days sewing. Boys were put to work selling papers on the street. Believing that he was turning wayward boys into sound little capitalists, Brace established the Newsboys Lodging House and charged them six cents a week to stay there. If a newsboy ran short of pennies, Brace lent him money—and charged interest.

But like the boys in the first reform school, these children were always running away back to their homes. Clearly, the reformers decided, poor children were too susceptible to remain in the corrupting city. The next solution was an elaborate network of farm families. Children were plucked from the slums, loaded onto "orphan trains," and placed with God-fearing farmers in need of extra hands. There, in their newly adoptive homes, they breathed fresh, clean air, and as part of their "rescue" they were often worked half to death.

In his own time, Brace was hailed as a great rescuer, the savior of thousands of children who otherwise would have succumbed to poverty, drunkenness, and crime. Today, he stands as the social equivalent of a crude nineteenth-century surgeon. Brace and his agents made no attempt to differentiate between children whose parents were truly abusive and children who had poor but loving families. They failed to see that kinship, security, and community, the values they believed only the middle class possessed, could flourish in the same environment that rats did.

In truth, the CAS did not exist to aid children who had been abused and neglected; it was there to rid the city of "Street Arabs." And somehow, there were just as many "Street Arabs" running around New York as there had been before the CAS used the doctrine of *parens patriae* to carry out thousands of legal kidnappings.

· · ·

The SPCC and the CAS were harbingers of an unprecedented period of social reform in the late nineteenth century that came to be known as the Progressive Era. Around the country, crusaders, convinced that they could build a better society, were going into slums with a sense of providence and optimism.

In Chicago, Jane Addams and a new school of charity workers established Hull House, a settlement house where "well-educated, upper-class men and women lived for the purpose of up-lifting [the poor] morally, intellectually and physically." Muckracking journalists were printing stories of human degradation and bringing the call for reform to millions of readers. A growing body of ministers—proponents of the Social Gospel—were struggling to arouse public concerns and the consciences of their parishioners.

In a courtroom in Denver, Judge Benjamin Lindsey watched a parade of boys come before him for sentencing, most of them rail-thin children of immigrants. Lindsey was a compassionate man who believed in the dignity of the individual. As a boy, the judge had been so hopelessly poor that he had attempted suicide. Still, except for the occasional kind word, he could express no sympathy and exercise no leniency toward the miserable lads who came into his courtroom. He could not allow sobs from the miscreants and anguished pleas from their mothers to move him. It was the judge's duty to sentence boys and lock them up in the same cells as the professional safecrackers, the prostitutes, and the muggers who split the skulls of downtown businessmen.

One day, the judge went to examine the living conditions of one of the boys, a coal thief, who had appeared before him. The father was in bed, dying of lead poisoning, the result of years spent working in a smelter. The company had no health plan, and workers' compensation did not exist; the family was penniless. The small room was so cold that Lindsey could see his breath. The boy's theft had been a desperate attempt to put coal in the stove. Judge Lindsey left the tenement struggling with the same profound questions that judges and settlement workers in a dozen cities were asking: Is this a bad boy? What creates a bad boy? Does he pose such a threat that we must lock him away? What can we do to change bad boys into good boys?

The answer was the creation of the first juvenile court, in Chicago, in 1899. True to the idealism of the Progressive Era, the new courts were going to do what no society had ever done: control behavior in families by holding parents and children accountable.

The new courts were the first in the world to be designed specifically for children. Children brought in because they had been abused or neglected or had committed a crime would have no contact with hardened adult criminals. To protect the identities of children and their parents, and to assure that no stigma followed them as a result of appearing in court, hearings and records would be kept confidential. Because the court was there to rehabilitate rather than to punish, the hearings would deliberately be informal. And because the judge was *parens patriae* come to life, a kindly, all-knowing father figure who was there to act in the best interests of the child, there was no need to extend to children the legal rights that adults have in criminal court. A child did not need the right to be represented by an attorney, to be formally charged, to have his case decided by a jury, to confront and cross-examine witnesses, or to remain silent.

These were revolutionary ideas, a true historic breakthrough. But despite all of the well-intended laws—and all too often because of them— the state still made a lousy parent.

The juvenile justice movement burned hot for a few years and then, like so many other movements—the temperance movement, campaigns against poverty, feminism—it slid into a long period of apathy. As the years went by, it became clear that in juvenile court children got "the worst of both worlds." In one of its rare decisions regarding children, the U.S. Supreme Court ruled that in juvenile court a minor "received inadequate due process and inadequate care and treatment."

In the first half of this century, *parens patriae* in the form of the juvenile court was, at best, an absentee parent and, at worst, an abusive one. Without due process, children who had committed minor crimes that would bring only a fine and a suspended sentence in adult court were sent to training schools where they spent years being "rehabilitated" in conditions that were often more Dickensian than those in state prisons.

Without due process, social workers were answerable only to themselves. A worker who found parents charming or convincing was free to drop an abuse case after doing a cursory investigation. Another worker could capriciously whisk children away from families because the parents were poor or minorities, were physically disabled, or had low IQs. The system was as blind to a child's psychological well-being as the old CAS. A child who had loving parents could be in wonderful psychological health in a home that appeared absolutely deplorable to an outsider, particularly if the outsider happened to be a member of the middle class.

Reform began in a most unlikely place: the organ of the medical establishment, the *Journal of the American Medical Association*. In 1961, *JAMA* published "The Battered Child Syndrome," by C. Henry Kempe, a pediatrician at the University of Colorado School of Medicine. In this landmark article, Dr. Kempe gave the world a medical diagnosis for child abuse, describing the physical evidence—children who have arms wrenched from sockets, subdural hematomas, fractures of the long bones—and the accompanying psychological phenomena: "A marked discrepancy between clinical findings and historical data as supplied by the parents is a major diagnostic feature."

Social workers had long been investigating cases of children who had suffered fractures and were covered with welts. A father would explain that the child had taken a terrible fall down a flight of stairs. A child, even a maimed child, was not considered a reliable witness. The worker had to have an adult witness. Without that, abuse was all but impossible to prove in court. The worker ended up recording her impressions in the case file, hoping that this would not be the child who would haunt her for the rest of her life.

Now a physician had come forward with scientific evidence, hard evidence that could be used in court to prove that a child had been abused, even after the wounds had healed. An inexhaustible lobbyist, Kempe argued that to stop the cycle of abuse doctors had to do more than treat small victims: they had to report cases so that the legal system could intervene.

In 1963, Kempe formed a group of pediatricians who convinced the U.S. Children's Bureau to draft model legislation on child abuse. No piece of legislation has ever swept through the country faster. By 1966, all fifty states had passed laws mandating that doctors and health workers report suspected cases of beatings, sexual abuse, malnourishment, and neglect.

The fear of a lawsuit that all too often cripples physicians' best instincts was banished by giving doctors immunity for reporting cases of suspected abuse. Another finding also motivated doctors: In a civil case centered in San Jose, the California Supreme Court held that a child could sue a physician after the doctor had not reported her injuries and had returned her to her family.

Cases came pouring into the courts through the channel that Kempe had opened. Historically, the system had always been filled with somebody else's kids, the children of the poor, minorities, the mentally unstable. These new cases flew in the face of our romanticized vision of the family as a Garden of Eden for children. For the first time ever, "ideal" families were showing up in the courts. Bankers, school principals, and physicians were being convicted of abusing their children.

The nation was forced into the painful conclusion that, for many, childhood was a nightmare. To protect children, the ramparts of the family, that "little commonwealth," had to be breached. New laws were passed, creating new mandated reporters—teachers, day care workers, therapists, anyone who worked with children. For the first time, over the strenuous objections of defense attorneys, children were taken seriously as witnesses—and more cases came flooding in.

The U.S. Congress held hearings and in 1974 passed the Federal Child Abuse Prevention and Treatment Act, putting the federal government in the child abuse business. States that did not tighten their reporting laws did not receive federal funding to fight abuse. More cases of physical—and now sexual—abuse came flooding in.

The system could not handle the deluge and the public scrutiny. The whole thing came crashing down in the 1970s, when a series of horrendous foster care scandals aroused national outrage and, once again, the attention of Congress. Civil libertarians and others screamed that the system was out of control, that in the haste to ferret out abuse the rights of children and families were being trampled. Conservatives saw that hundreds of millions of dollars were being poured into this sorry system and questioned what taxpayers were getting for their money.

• • •

The result was the creation of the act of 1980, which was based on the hard-learned dual lessons of history: Families are not necessarily a safe haven where David and Ricky and the Beaver are surrounded with love. The levels of abuse and neglect in this country are far greater than even experts in the field had realized. But plucking children out of their homes is no solution either. It has never been a solution. Throughout history, the state, no matter how well-meaning, has proven over and over that it is a rotten parent.

When Judge Edwards first came on the bench, he had routinely ordered that children remain in the Children's Shelter while a social worker completed a report. Separating a child from his parents would show the parents how serious these proceedings were, and two or three days in the shelter would not hurt the child. But when the judge visited, he saw children who were exhibiting signs of shock. "I realized then that removal from a parent is a terrible event for a child," the judge says. "They found themselves in a new world of strangers, and they had the terrible fears of not knowing where their parents and brothers and sisters and other loved ones might be. I regularly come across children who have been removed for a weekend and then return home to suffer from months of nightmares. They refuse to be out of the presence of their mothers."

Long, painful experience has also taught the judge that long-term, out-of-home placement is no more of a panacea today than it was in the Progressive Era. He has presided over cases in which children have been raped, beaten, starved, and badly neglected in foster homes. The media reports the worst of these cases. What it doesn't report are the garden variety cases, in which children drift because foster parents move, have a child of their own, or decide that they really don't like a particular child.

"The juvenile court, however well resourced, can only be effective in assisting children in a limited number of areas surrounding a child's growth," says Judge Edwards, a national spokesman for reunification. "The touchstone of our response to children must be the family. The same family which was in part responsible for the plight of the child often contains within it the solution for that child's best chance. By family, I mean grandparents, siblings, aunts and uncles, more if possible. They must be given the first opportunity to solve the problem, for they have the greatest incentive to reach a resolution."

However, despite the common perception, reunification does not mean that children are supposed to be kept at home at any cost. The law is a balancing act that supports families and also protects children from their parents and the system. "The act is a finely tuned instrument; we've just got to start using it," Judge Edwards explains. "Some judges never bother to learn the law, and others simply ignore it, operating as if it did not exist. Many jurisdictions don't have the resources to make it work. We are not showering families with resources; we never have."

A Santa Clara County task force concurred that even one of the best systems in the country has "serious gaps in services." A January 1996 report from the California Department of Social Services says that the situation is the same or worse throughout the state: "Currently, very few families receive ongoing services when a child is returned home. Many counties do not have enough money for follow-up services."

All of this has led Judge Edwards to believe that "the biological family really is the best engine we've developed for raising children and we should support it." At the same time, the judge has no illusions about couples like the Delgatos. He has terminated parental rights in hundreds of cases similar to theirs. Still, he did not order reunification services for the Delgatos just to go through the motions and comply with the law.

"Many parents love their children, but their lives are so chaotic and their troubles so crippling, they cannot raise them," the judge says. "The services are costly and time-consuming, but, in the long run, they are worth it. If we can help them get control of their lives, if we can teach them how to be parents, they can be parents in ways that an institution or foster parents never can. Parents who make it through reunification are more likely to stay with their children through the long haul. They are a lot less likely to bail out in the teenage years, when so many foster parents do."

All this is well and good, but what about "bad parents"? Why should the courts waste taxpayers' money trying to turn lifelong druggies like Steven and Phoebe Delgato into responsible parents?

Judge Edwards answers, "We really don't know who the truly 'bad' parents are until we give them a chance to fail or succeed. Don't we need time to examine the strengths and weaknesses of a family before we terminate? Don't we need to be able to say to ourselves that we have done everything possible to help this family before we do something as traumatic as taking away their children?

"We simply do not know on the first day or the first week or even the first month which families will be reunified and which will not."

9

JENNY: THE
DEPARTMENT

HULL HOUSE, OPENED BY JANE ADDAMS MORE THAN 100 YEARS AGO, was right in the middle of a ghetto teeming with Greek, Italian, and German immigrants. Addams had been influenced by the settlement house movement in England and believed that to help the poor it was first necessary to establish trust and intimacy. From today's perspective, Addams' settlement workers—the forerunners of today's social workers—may seem as patronizing and moralistic as missionaries sallying forth into a heathen land. Symbolically renouncing their social position, they believed that their mere presence would raise the cultural, moral, and intellectual level of the community.

By walking the same streets and shopping in the same shops, the settlement workers soon recognized that poor people had a vital culture of their own and strengths that could be used to better their community. Their neighbors came, tentatively at first, some out of curiosity and others for relief and diversion from their own crowded homes. Eventually Hull House, always bustling and always open, became the heart of the neighborhood.

Like living beings, institutions evolve, and the Department in Silicon Valley has adapted itself to its own unique surroundings. Social workers informally refer to this descendant of Hull House as "Technology," named for its address on Technology Drive. The building itself is a sprawling, low-slung structure made from tilt-up slabs of concrete that is indistinguishable from other buildings in this high-tech industrial park near the airport. There is little landscaping but plenty of parking.

Inside, at the center of the 147,000-square-foot area is the Atrium, a circular common area with comfortable couches, tables, and chairs and the kind of huge potted plants usually found in upscale restaurants. On clear days, sun floods in through skylights. Except for Department supervisors, none of the workers have offices. Chest-high partitions covered with gray nappy fabric separate their workstations. This huge space is obviously designed to be democratic. There are few walls and few doors, which is supposed to make the room conducive to intra-office communication. But it also means that there are no focal points, not even windows. Walking into Technology is like walking into a huge maze.

There is one other notable designer touch: the rows of workstations are named for the county's thoroughfares. But since the "roads" bear little or no relationship to the real world, they don't make the infrastructure any easier to navigate. The cute street signs—Montague Expressway, Bird Avenue—give the place the air of a theme park.

Technology, with its top-notch security system and on-site cafeteria, has its defenders. Some consider the building a symbol that the county truly values the work that is done there. As one Department supervisor puts it: "This place is a safe haven and a refuge. You can't do this kind of emotional work day in and day out without having a comfortable place to go for relief."

Others, many of them social workers, ironically agree that the building does indeed say it all: To them, Technology is a symbol that priorities are all screwed up, that child welfare departments have all but abandoned the original vision of social work. They believe that social workers should be out in the community, like the old settlement workers, not sitting in air-conditioned comfort next to twelve-foot-tall potted banana plants. They wonder how social workers can get to know parents when the parents have to travel so far to get there, sometimes transfer buses three times, to see their workers.

The fact is, today's social workers have evolved into "case managers," who spend much of their day indoors, trying to stay ahead of an avalanche of paperwork and coordinating resources and services by telephone. This way, they can manage dozens of cases at any one time. They may also go months without seeing a particular client in person.

In a world where dress is fairly predictable—comfortable print dresses and sensible shoes in the field, conservative suits in court—the dependency investigator sitting at an "intersection" at the far end of the office cuts quite a figure. At age fifty and the mother of three grown children, one of them adopted, Sallie Bearden has a rail-thin build that she maintains by snacking on nothing and accents by wearing skirts, an ankle bracelet, and spike heels. Bearden talks with her hands, and each finger sports a silver ring with a tinkling charm, so that she always seems to be jingling.

As a young girl, Bearden was "just the ugliest thing," always slouched over, as adolescents who are too tall tend to be. She is making up for that now. "I take a lot of criticism," she says good-naturedly. "I remember one grandmother taking a horrified look at me and saying, 'No way am I going to turn over my granddaughter to some biker chick.' "

One of Bearden's coworkers fondly calls her "Sal Gal," a fitting nickname for someone with big, auburn hair, like that of a country singer. Others in the dependency system refer to her—sometimes with admiration and sometimes not—as the "Removal Queen." Everyone agrees that Bearden is a devoted social worker who puts in ten to twelve hours a day. She genuinely cares about the families on her caseload. She is also tenacious. The word is that, when Sallie gets a case, she wins. The children will be removed from the family and, more often than not, they will not go home again.

Bearden's job puts her at the front end of a system that operates under the same management philosophy Henry Ford used to mass-produce the Model T. The damaged families who come into the Department to be "fixed" find themselves on an assembly line of sorts, passed from one "specialist" to another: emergency response worker, family preservation worker, family maintenance worker, foster care intake specialist, adoption specialist—to name just a few.

As a dependency investigator (DI), Bearden in essence is the specialist who decides whether or not the family will continue down the line. After a child has been taken into protective custody by police or an emergency response worker, the DI has forty-eight hours to sort out the facts: Has the child indeed been abused or neglected? What safeguards can be put into place that would allow the child to return home? If the DI decides that the child is in danger and cannot return home, she writes and files a petition with the court asking the judge to make the child a dependent. The judge makes the final decision, but a judge hears dozens of cases each day and is heavily influenced by the DI.

These reports generally make dull reading, which is surprising, considering that they are full of tragedies and that a family's future is at stake. For instance, a social worker describes incest with a toddler as "definite evidence of prior penetrating vaginal trauma." There is a reason social workers use this flat, objective language. In academic and legal circles, sociology and social work in particular have been ridiculed as a "soft" discipline, more art than science, not as quantifiable or authentic as a "hard" science. Social worker reports that are concise, clinical, and dispassionate seem more "scientific," more suited to the legal setting of a courtroom.

In this world of boilerplate, Bearden is the Department's Thackeray. Once she gets a case, she immediately delves into the back files. She not only interviews children and parents but also tracks down neighbors, teachers, and relatives, who are often—to put it mildly—not eager to get involved. The result is a report that Bearden uses to "lecture and teach the court about bonding, about child development, about family dynamics, about all the things that they might not see on the surface." Her reports sometimes start with a table of contents and end with an index. In between are fifty or more exhaustively detailed pages in which families are dissected, intrigues revealed, and motivations laid bare. A typical line from a Bearden report may read, "Each day that little Carol experiences her mother's unpredictability is another day that unseen, but very real, emotional damage begins to take its toll."

Bearden makes no apologies for her relentless digging. Tacked to the partition above her desk is a montage of photographs: infants swaddled in blankets and held by beaming foster parents, toddlers with goofy grins being hugged by adoptive mothers and fathers, children in party dresses blowing out birthday candles—each of whom has an unspeakable history. This is Bearden's Shrine of the Children with Happy Endings, the ones she got out "in time, before they are three and four and the damage is so great that they have no chance of ever learning to bond.

"I'm not on a mission. It isn't that I am against giving parents every opportunity. I believe in reunification. I believe that there are many families who can change when given help. I just don't get those so-called simple cases—the first-time referrals, the cases where services are readily accepted and children can be sent safely home," she explains. "Actually, those cases bore me. I prefer the ones that drive other social workers up the wall."

So when Bearden was assigned Lisa's case and Jenny's thick stack of disorganized files landed on her desk, she was in her element.

Over time, so many hands had gone through Jenny's records that the papers were no longer in chronological order. Bearden opened the most current file to find a psychological report done when Jenny was thirteen; the examiner had labeled her "angry and oppositional." Bearden turned the page, and Jenny was suddenly "a healthy and creative 5-year-old who loves showing adults her art work." She flipped to the next page and Jenny became a teenager again, fifteen years old, "crying daily and talking about not wanting to live and not deserving to live."

The files followed the crazy logic of a dream. Bearden's task, as usual, was to find the flesh-and-blood person in this maze of psychiatric evaluations, names, dates, and sketchy accounts of traumatic past events. Her task was to turn this chaos into the answers to some very specific questions: How would Jenny's past affect her ability to be a mother to Lisa? Could Jenny be counted on to feed and bathe her, to protect her from harm, to give Lisa the basic emotional stability that newborns require?

The phone on Bearden's desk rang. A professional-sounding voice introduced herself as Lee Ann Osterdock, Jenny's child advocate. Osterdock immediately launched into the same frustrated speech that she had given to Jenny's social worker, several supervisors, and the counselor at the shelter: It was inhumane to separate a mother and a newborn. If only someone had the sense to bend a few rules.

Bearden assured Osterdock that she was very concerned about disrupting a mother from bonding with her child. But she had just gotten the case minutes ago, and it would take her some time to sort things out. Not surprised by one more delay, Osterdock said that she would call back tomorrow and hung up. Bearden jotted down a note: She respected most of the advocates she had worked with, and this one obviously was deeply involved. It was a point in Jenny's favor that she had Osterdock in her life, a mother figure who could offer parenting guidance and support. That obviously would benefit Lisa.

Bearden returned to Jenny's files, and the more she read, the more disheartened she became. Jenny had been exactly the kind of child that Bearden would have fought desperately to remove as soon as she was born. She was saddened yet not surprised to learn that even after her father's suicide attempt Jenny and her sister were returned home. Life did not really change for Jenny and her sister until a year later, and only then because their schizophrenic mother begged a social worker to take the girls away. At age six, Jenny and her sister were finally placed in an Emergency Shelter Home and made dependents of the court.

Bearden's phone rang again. It was the physician at the shelter calling about Jenny. For the past few months, he had been monitoring her pregnancy and had experienced her temper firsthand. "Do you think she might harm the baby? Is her temper that out of control?" Bearden asked.

Knowing that what he said would wind up in her court report, the physician weighed his words. "She's a very volatile young lady," he said finally. "Truthfully, I am very concerned about her ability to parent."

Bearden was about to thank the physician and hang up when his professional demeanor evaporated and he went on a tirade against the Department: "Of course Jenny has no parenting skills! How could she with the Department standing in her way? Everything will be fine once Jenny starts breast-feeding."

Bearden certainly believed in the importance of bonding; she based so many of her decisions upon the need for a baby to connect with another human being. But the doctor's interpretation was so naive. Bonding does not happen overnight. Nursing is not a miracle that guarantees anything, even with an "ordinary" mother. Jenny clearly had a lot of other issues.

The physician did not relent. Before hanging up, he told Bearden that if she stood in the way of Jenny's breast-feeding, the Department would "have the failure of this family on its conscience."

As soon as she hung up, the supervisor who had assigned Lisa's case to Bearden walked up and said: "You better call Jenny's attorney. She wants to kill you." Bearden took a deep breath and called the attorney, known for her aggressiveness, who must have been waiting because she answered immediately and went on the attack: "This is unconscionable! You do something to rectify this situation immediately, or we are going to sue the Department for stopping the bonding process!"

Bearden made a feeble attempt at trying to reason, but then gave up and just let the attorney go on. What was happening? Why all this hostility over a case that had just landed on her desk?

For the next few hours, Bearden continued to sort through Jenny's files. In the end, she came away thinking that the file was a kind of antifamily album. When parents put together a record of a child's early years, they fill the book with successes: the gymnastics award, the excellent report cards, the photos of the first bluegill. Jenny's file was page after page of failure: The foster home that failed because seven-year-old Jenny reported that the foster mother had been "hitting her with a coat hanger on the neck and buttocks"; the foster home that failed beca eight-year-old Jenny "was showing marked sexualized behavior and had been observed humping the dog."

Where had such a young girl learned such provocative behavior? A therapist discovered that one of Jenny's early foster homes had been the biggest failure of all: "The foster parent's son had been involved in sexual activity, including acts of penetration, with both Jenny and her sister." When the foster mother found out what was going on, she punished the girls by whipping them with a belt.

During these years, Jenny's parents were supposed to be receiving re-unification services to learn to be better parents. Instead, they were in and out of the psychiatric unit of Valley Medical Center. Months went by without Jenny seeing them. The only thing in life she could count on was that wherever she went her little sister went too.

And then, she too was gone. When Jenny was eight and a half, she and her sister were sent to separate foster homes, never to see each other again. Jenny "severely regressed." There were more temper tantrums, more sexualized behavior. Everywhere she went, Jenny carried the only photo she had of her sister—a Polaroid of a naked toddler, her face turned away from the camera. "This is my sister," she still tells everyone proudly.

Jenny was first made a dependent of the court in the same year the 1980 act became law. The act was designed to get children like Jenny back home safely or to free them for adoption, all within eighteen months. Yet, it was not until 1985, when Jenny was already ten years old, a system veteran and well past the cute and cuddly stage, that her parents finally signed relinquishment papers. This meant that Jenny could now be adopted.

There was one attempt. A single woman took Jenny into her home and started adoption proceedings. But the aggressive, obnoxious, de-pressed, extremely needy, sexualized girl heading hard into adolescence proved to be too much. Jenny was sent to a group home, and from then on she proved to be too much for everyone.

When Bearden finally closed the file, she understood why people were so adamant that this obviously troubled young woman should be given every chance to raise her daughter. "Everyone in the system felt guilty," Bearden says. "Everyone wanted desperately to do something good for Jenny because the system had already done so much bad."

NICKY AND JENNY: THE PROGNOSES

Nicky at Twelve Months

WHEN NICKY FIRST MOVED IN WITH THE KENNEYS, CLAIRE BEGAN A journal in which she recorded the events of his life. The entries are remarkable for being evenhanded, testimony that Claire considered it a privilege to care for such a nerve-racking child. When Nicky had a bad night, there was no indication of stress or second-guessing. Claire simply wrote, "Terrible night. Nicky was screaming and was totally inconsolable," and she noted that she and Greg had traded two-hour shifts, walking the shrieking baby through darkened rooms. When Nicky had a good day, there was no false hope. Simply a notation: "Has been in a great mood. Introduced sweet potatoes for dinner today. Ate the whole jar."

Claire told everyone that if Nicky never settled down it wouldn't matter, for they loved him as he was. As Nicky approached his first birthday, Claire began to notice little things about him, things that only somebody who was around him twenty-four hours a day would be aware of. For instance, he was so cute when he was trying to crawl, the way he would struggle, then plop down and roll over onto the shag carpet. His antics made everyone smile, but Claire knew that by this age her daughters were already tearing across the living room floor.

Claire's understanding of premature babies who had been exposed to drugs was heavily influenced by Sharon Ruprecht. Sharon, of course, was not a scientist who had conducted statistically accurate surveys and compared the results to a control group. But she was an extremely perceptive woman who knew what children were all about. She had stayed in touch with a majority of the fifty or so children who had been in her Emergency Shelter Home and had discovered that when they reached school age every child she had cared for, every child who was adopted or returned to his parents or placed in long-term foster care, had been diagnosed as having a learning disability.

Claire knew what her friend believed: that babies who graduated from the Neonatal Intensive Care Unit might look perfectly normal, but that it all depended on how one defined perfectly normal. "Just because they are not retarded or do not have cerebral palsy does not mean they got away scot-free," Ruprecht has said. "I don't believe there are any children who have been drug- and alcohol-exposed who get away scot-free. Trust me, they don't."

For that reason, Claire tried to prepare herself for the reality of what might be coming. She did not want to be one of those mothers who, out of fear, ignored the obvious. Claire held the spoon she was using to feed Nicky in front of him and waited to see if he would grab it. He didn't. She clearly remembered her daughters doing that before they turned one. The right side of Nicky's body seemed weaker than the left. Claire placed a bracelet on Nicky's right wrist, and he barely noticed it. When she put the bracelet on his left wrist, Nicky kept rubbing and pulling on it.

So when the day came to take Nicky to Valley Medical Center to get the results of the developmental tests the experts had run, Claire had a pretty good idea of what to expect. She had concluded that Nicky was delayed. She knew that small delays at twelve months are significant because, as time went by, the gap between Nicky and a normal child would increase. Still, Claire was hoping that she was wrong. She was not an expert, and maybe she had missed something. Perhaps the months she had spent loving Nicky were transforming him; perhaps a miracle was occurring before her eyes.

The physical therapist who had been working with Nicky led Claire into a cramped office and had her place Nicky on an examining table. The therapist tried to hand Nicky an object. Nicky swung at it but did not come close to grasping it. The therapist explained that the response indicated a delay in Nicky's motor development, evidence that drugs and alcohol had done residual damage to the nervous system.

The therapist tickled the bottom of one of Nicky's feet. Nicky didn't jump or act irritated. Instead, a tremor went through his leg. This meant that there was a hypertonicity, a stiffness, in his legs. The brain was sending the muscles in Nicky's legs continuous signals to tighten, more evidence that drugs had assaulted his nervous system.

Next the therapist placed a toy next to Nicky. Even though he appeared to be right-handed, Nicky twisted around so that he could pick the toy up with his left hand. The therapist explained that this was probably the result of the surgery that had been done at eight months to remove a benign cyst on the right side of Nicky's brain. To remove the cyst, the surgeons had cut into brain tissue. "He appears to be hypersensitive," the therapist said, and Claire had to smile at the understatement. "Does he get upset if someone looks at him in a way he thinks is wrong? When a stranger enters a room or someone moves too quickly, does he scream in terror?"

Claire told the therapist about the Sunday in church when a friend came up and said hello and Nicky's screams filled the chapel, about the time she took him to a band concert in the park and the crash of the cymbals set him off. The therapist explained that this behavior was also related to drugs and alcohol. Nicky's nervous system was maturing very slowly. He was still responding to stimuli like a newborn.

The physical therapist patted Nicky's back. Claire knew that he was waiting for her to ask the questions. "How bad is it?" she asked. "Can he catch up?"

"Well, those are loaded questions," the therapist replied. "It depends. On a lot of things."

• • •

In the 1980s, the "drug babies" that were flooding NICUs were portrayed as being damaged beyond medicine and the power of love, with IQs that ranked with Down's syndrome children and an inner rage that made parenting impossible. The early statistics and initial studies released during that time painted a picture of children without futures. Nothing would ever work with these children. Providing early medical intervention or special schooling or stable homes was pouring money and effort into a black hole.

The consensus, promoted by fiscal conservatives and the media, was that these were genuinely lost children, a "bio-underclass, a generation of physically damaged cocaine babies whose biological inferiority is stamped at birth." As infants, they were already clogging the foster care system and the hospitals. Soon, they would overload the school system and the juvenile halls. As adults, they would fill up the psychiatric wards, the soup kitchens, the welfare rolls, the prisons.

This "diagnosis" scared off countless adoptive and foster parents. Who had the emotional strength to give and give and never, ever get anything in return? The grim forecast also led to economic and moral questions about the validity of NICUs, questions that are still echoing today. Yes, all this high-tech wizardry is impressive, but does it make sense to keep children alive who have so many medical problems that they will be a drain on society their entire lives? How can we ethically save the life of a newborn, but then sentence him to an existence that is barely human?

When Ron Cohen of Valley Medical Center's NICU hears these criticisms, he explodes with indignation: "That every child who has been exposed to drugs, that every child who is born prematurely ends up with chronic disabilities is a common, persistent, false impression. The vast majority of the roughly five hundred babies a year that pass through my unit will live relatively normal lives once they leave here."

Standing by a window in the NICU that is crowded with baby pictures, the doctor looks as proud as a new father. The two-year-old with the golden curls, the little boy in a great floppy hat, the child thrilled to be sitting on top of a baby slide are all NICU graduates. What *is* a crime, Dr. Cohen says, sweeping his hand to indicate the high-tech equipment, "is that taxpayers will pay for all this. But they won't pay for prenatal care to keep kids out of here."

Day after day, Dr. Cohen is witness to the fact that the United States is a Third World country when it comes to prenatal care—babies born here are less likely to celebrate their first birthday than are children born in twenty-one other countries—largely because little or no prenatal care is available to poor women, in particular to poor teenage mothers. Sex education in this country is limited and often inadequate. Poor women generally know very little about sex and even less about embryology. They have no idea what is going on in the womb and little idea of how to take care of themselves. If they drink when they are pregnant, it may not be because they are careless or self-destructive. No one may ever have told them that there is no placental barrier to alcohol. Or that there is such a thing as a placenta.

"I'm running a kind of *M*A*S*H* unit here," Dr. Cohen says. "That's the reason I think we're actually better in the United States at saving sick premies than our colleagues in a country like Sweden. We are better because we produce so many more sick babies than they do in Sweden."

But Dr. Cohen insists that he is not running a salvaging plant for babies who have been devastated in the womb. "I would estimate that probably 10 kids a year end up with significant problems down the line. Of course, that is not a lot of consolation to the people who are raising those 10 children. But we need to look at the statistics. Ten out of 500. It is not fair to stigmatize the other 490 as babies who have no futures."

Sharon Ruprecht may argue that Dr. Cohen's figures are inflated by his optimism, that he never sees the children who spend their lives in institutions, never sees the subtle and not-so-subtle damage as his "graduates" go out into the world. But these two experts on children agree on something else: In both their experiences, these children are not unreachable; they are not black holes. The abuse that these children endured in the womb can be ameliorated in some degree by their upbringing, education, and health care.

That is what the therapist who examined Nicky explained to Claire: "Who knows what is ahead for Nicky. Much will depend on the quality of his care and the strength of his character. We're going to have you start working with someone twice a week. The first task will be to get him to sit up." Claire was suddenly overcome with how wonderful Nicky was and with the immensity of the battles he would have to fight. "I don't know about the other things," she said, "but you can put a check on the plus side under care. As long as he's with us, this little boy will get the best care there is."

Jenny: The Assessment

Three days after Jenny was taken back to the shelter and her three-day-old daughter, Lisa, was placed in an Emergency Shelter Home, mother and daughter were together again in a foster home that Jenny's advocate and her attorney had worked together to find. When Sallie Bearden arrived to do an initial check on Lisa, she congratulated Jenny on being reunited with her baby. Jenny didn't bother to reply. This woman with the short skirt and all the makeup was going to be her last social worker, and this was her final foster home. In only a few more months, she would turn eighteen. No more social workers, no more foster parents, no more court hearings, no more telling her where to live; just she and Lisa making decisions for themselves.

Jenny sat on the living room couch where Lisa was asleep, snug in a blanket. She lit a cigarette and kept shifting it from hand to hand. Sitting in a nearby chair, Bearden noted that the foster home was at least clean. Ideally, she would have preferred that Jenny be with a young or middle-aged woman who had an abundance of time, energy, and patience. But this foster mother was a very religious woman in her late sixties who had set ideas of right and wrong. Her decision to become a foster parent came from deep pro-life convictions. If she was going to live according to her beliefs, she felt that she should open her home to the brave but unfortunate teenage girls who had decided not to abort. She figured that her advanced age would be no problem since she would not be caring for the newborns; the new mothers would handle the diapering and feeding themselves.

When Jenny moved in, two other teenage moms who had spent much of their lives in foster care were already living there. The foster mother was dumbfounded to find that the young women were neither guilt ridden nor grateful to have a roof over their heads. They kept sneaking out at night to be with their boyfriends.

"How are you doing here in the house? Are you getting along with everyone?" Bearden asked.

"Yeah," Jenny replied. Bearden turned her attention to Lisa. "The baby looks wonderful, so healthy and clean. She's adorable."

"I love my baby," Jenny said, perking up. "I hate everyone in the world except her. She's the only one who listens to me."

"I can see you love her," Bearden said. "Tell me about what's going on in your life."

For the next hour, Jenny lit cigarettes and detailed every plan she had for when she turned eighteen. The big news was that Jenny had gotten over Bobby and had a new boyfriend, someone really good-looking, really smart, and really good for her. Down the hallway, the telephone rang, and in the middle of a sentence Jenny bounded out of the room, yelling "That's him" over her shoulder.

Ten minutes passed; Lisa began to stir and was soon crying. Bearden picked her up and walked with her and tried rocking her, but the piercing screams could be heard all over the house. The foster mother yelled for Jenny; she yelled again, but Jenny did not return. When she did arrive, it was apparent that the phone call had not gone well.

"He's really tripping on me," Jenny said, pacing the living room. When Bearden held out the red-faced and howling Lisa, Jenny grabbed the baby and sat on the couch.

"He's not going to get away with this," she said.

"I think Lisa's hungry," Bearden suggested.

Jenny lifted up her blouse and jammed Lisa under it. The phone rang: "It's him again."

Jenny jumped up, then looked down at the wiggling bulge under her shirt, as if surprised to find Lisa there. Glaring, Jenny said: "You little piggy. All you do is eat." Then she yelled, "Get this fucking kid off my fucking nipple," loud enough for the whole house to hear.

• • •

Driving back to Technology, Bearden had two thoughts: The first was that she really felt for this young woman. There was no way a person could know her story and not think that life was terribly cruel, life was unfair. But the second, and overriding, thought was that "having sympathy and empathy for Jenny did not mean that I thought she could be out there on her own, parenting a child."

Bearden had seen it all before. Right now, all that was required of Jenny was to change a diaper and give a few kisses and perfect little Lisa would usually respond in a perfect way. But what would happen when Lisa needed much more than little kisses? When Lisa was no longer always good and perfect? When Lisa was no longer like a teddy bear that her mother could clutch for emotional comfort?

Bearden decided that she could not sit back and allow Jenny to create another Jenny. That afternoon, the "Removal Queen" started to build her case.

Nicky: Building the Case

At her workstation a few "streets" away from where Sallie Bearden sat, Mary Agnes King was adding a report from Clover House to the Nicky Delgato file. A counselor had received a phone call from an anonymous male voice: "Phoebe Delgato shoots up before she visits. Look a neck; there are track marks on it."

King knew that it was Steven who had made the call; who else could it be? He also had been writing letters. The last one she had received said, "Phoebe is doing things I just can't turn my back on. I don't think she should be allowed around our son. I feel like a rat, but the old rules don't apply."

King had rules of her own, and they definitely did apply. If a father or mother worked with her to reunite with their children, King did everything she could to help them get their children back. But if King concluded that a parent was going through the motions or playing games with the system, she became their opponent. The social worker kept very detailed records, carefully logging every missed visit at Clover House, every program a parent failed to complete. When she got up in court and read from the record, the record spoke for itself.

The file King was compiling in the Delgato case was beginning to speak against the parents. At first, Steven and Phoebe had not missed a visit at Clover House. They were warm and caring with Nicky, especially Steven, who was very loving. But then the couple started missing visits with no explanation; several times Steven called at the last minute to say that he couldn't get there because his car had broken down.

Most disturbing, Steven had dropped out of a drug program and had tested positive for amphetamines. He had spent a month in jail and had now entered another drug program. After his phone call to Clover House, King ordinarily would have had Phoebe tested right away. But Phoebe was about to start in an outpatient treatment program, and she would then be entering a residential program. Both programs were first-rate. If Phoebe was using, she would get help.

[handwritten notes:]

* Jenny & Lisa found a home together
* Jenny has new boyfriend
  ↳ might spend more time about him then baby
* Jenny might get Lisa taken away

11

PHOEBE:
THE DRUG REHAB

OF ALL THE MYTHS OF MOTHERHOOD, NONE IS SO WELL ENTRENCHED as this: through some combination of hormones and mystical bonding, pregnancy makes a sinner into a saint, a bottomless vessel of altruism and self-sacrifice. Living in the world, we know that pregnancy does not automatically turn bad traits into good ones; if it did, there would be no mothers who smoke, lose their tempers, get depressed, and overeat. And yet, we persist in thinking that pregnancy should be enough to break the toughest habit of all: drug and alcohol abuse. We revile pregnant women who do not immediately break free from an addiction that is not only physical but also emotional, spiritual, economic, and sociological.

Even among other drug users, there is something taboo about a woman who is not suddenly transformed by pregnancy. One pregnant heroin user talks of wearing baggy clothes when going out to score because her drug dealer, who felt no qualms about selling to elementary–school-age children, drew the line at supplying a pregnant woman.

Since the days of the "War on Drugs," there have been many attempts to turn the public's revulsion into public policy. Proposals have been floated to ship pregnant cocaine addicts to boot camps, where their babies would be born drug-free. Pregnant women using drugs and women giving birth to addicted babies have faced criminal prosecution on such controversial charges as "fetal abuse" and "delivery of drugs to minors."

Not surprisingly, the zeal to punish and intern pregnant women has not, in any way, been matched by a willingness to cultivate more permanent and humane solutions. Historically, there has been little support and very little funding for serious drug treatment for women. Until recently, most drug rehab programs would not admit pregnant women because bureaucrats had fears of attorneys descending with lawsuits.

What would happen to a fetus exposed to methadone? What if a woman went into premature labor while detoxing?

Like much of the rest of the country in the mid-1980s, Santa Clara County did not have a drug treatment program that was designed for women, nothing that acknowledged that women addicts—especially those who are pregnant and parenting—are very different from men. What little treatment was available was developed for a distinct part of the population—white, upper- and middle-class male alcoholics who could afford to leave the kids at home with their wives while they checked into rehabilitation centers that were covered by private insurance.

Often, these men were bosses at work and leaders in the community. They had never been forced to look into a mirror until they checked into a treatment center and someone said, "You are worthless and a drunk. You are destroying your family." Treatment based on confrontation works with well-heeled men, but it ignores the reality that women addicts are often poor, with little education. In most cases, they have always been dependent on someone else, usually the men they live with, usually men who are addicts, pimps, or dealers. These women have spent most of their lives being reminded that they are worthless. What they need is to look in the mirror and see someone who is a valuable, productive human being, someone who is capable of getting off drugs.

In 1987, Anthony Puentes, the director of medical services for the county's drug treatment programs, became alarmed by statistics that mirrored the rest of the country: 15 percent of women giving birth had exposed their fetuses to alcohol and other drugs. Jailing these women would not make a dent in the problem. What we have been doing, Puentes reasoned, is denying treatment to the very people who need it most, at the time they need it most. That was the beginning of the county's outpatient Perinatal Substance Abuse Program (PSAP) that Phoebe Delgato, Nicky's mother, entered on a muggy July afternoon.

PSAP is tucked away in a shabby temporary building that sits across a parking lot from Valley Medical Center. At 12:30 on a Thursday, a flurry of children and women with diaper bags began arriving. The weather was enough to make drivers in air-conditioned cars irritable; it was exhausting if a woman was pregnant and bloated or had just suffered through an hour-long bus ride with sweat-drenched, whining children. Phoebe, however, looked pert and healthy, her signature beret perched on her head. Standing outside, a few women enrolled in the program stood on tiptoes to kiss their boyfriends good-bye and headed to the bathroom for the routine urine test. Two others with round bellies leaned against a rail, puffing on cigarettes, chewing gum, and talking in a mad rush about children, husbands, and rotten landlords. One of the counselors stuck her head out of the door and yelled: "Group! Let's go, ladies."

A few minutes later, Phoebe joined fifteen other women around a rectangular table in a small, stuffy room. On the wall in front of them was a colorful, cheery-looking poster with the grimmest of messages: "Alcohol can cause mental retardation." Despite the heat, a small air conditioner in the window had not been turned on. Everyone reluctantly agreed that it was too loud to talk over, and to talk was why they were here.

The rules for the support group were simple and firm: What is said here stays here. Don't interrupt. Don't preach. Don't give advice unless you are asked for it. Don't pit one speaker against another. The whole idea is to allow each woman a chance to do what she so rarely gets a chance to do—to talk without the furtiveness that rules the lives of most addicts, to speak honestly with no fear of criticism, with no fear of arrest, with no boyfriend telling her to shut up or a bunch of kids demanding her attention. In the center of the table, as if on an altar, sat an unopened box of Kleenex.

The session was run by two counselors who were complementary in a Mutt and Jeff kind of way. Myrna, compact and bouncy, always seemed to be hugging someone. Monica, tall and stately, wore soft, flowing clothes and spoke in a slow, precise whisper: "Ladies, we have a little exercise to get us started today."

Myrna walked around the table and handed each woman a mimeographed sheet of paper titled "Life Stress Measure"—a list of thirty-three "life events" with a numerical value assigned to each. If the women had been regular readers of women's magazines or the lifestyle section of any daily newspaper, they would have instantly recognized this test. The list begins with "death of a spouse (or partner)," which rates 100 stress points, and slides down the anxiety scale to "minor violations of the law," at a mere 11 points. Scattered between are experiences that the majority of the population pray will never happen: "marital separation" (65 points), "fired at work" (47 points), "outstanding debts" (28 points).

"For the most part, these women believe the same myth that nonaddicts, people on the outside of this world, believe," Myrna explained later. "They think that the problem is drugs and only drugs. They think that all they have to do is kick and everything will be beautiful. They need to understand that, after they stop using drugs, all their problems are still there. There are still money problems, still education problems, still housing problems. Many have legal situations, and those are still there. If they don't accept this, if they don't start working on all areas of their lives, they might stop using drugs for awhile. But they will start using again."

The questions asked about the test emphasized Myrna's point. One woman wondered: "It has 'jail term' listed. Does that mean that I get credit if I went to jail, or do I get points for my husband being in jail?" Another raised her hand and asked: "What about living in the homeless shelter? Does that count as a 'change in residence?'" Another wanted to know: "Why isn't trying to kick heroin listed? That's stress." The woman next to her suggested a solution: "I put kicking heroin under 'change in social activities'—18 points—because I don't see my dealer like I used to."

That got a knowing laugh, and soon the women were shouting out their point totals, auction-style: 367! 459! Can anyone beat 689? In the women's magazine version, there is a scoring key at the end of the test that reads something like this—"200 points and over: Whew! Phone the closest beauty spa and sign yourself up for a week of total pampering." The undisputed winner at PSAP had 832 points!

"Ladies, what these numbers tell you is that there is not one woman here for whom life is not a day-to-day struggle," Myrna said. "Now, let's continue the way we usually do—by going around the table and stating our first name, our drug of choice, how long we have been clean. And then, say something about how you are feeling right now, this very moment." Myrna turned to a willowy blond in her late twenties who was sitting to her right. "Bonnie, can you start?"

"My name is Bonnie," she began. "My drug of choice is heroin, but I've never been choosy. Right now, I feel very overwhelmed by all the stuff that's going on in my life. But I'm staying clean through it all. I've been clean for one year, four months, and eighteen days. I'm about to graduate from this program. My daughters are healthy, and for all that I feel very blessed."

PSAP drug counselors try hard not to play favorites. The women around the table have been pitted against other women for most of their lives, vying for money, for drugs, for men, for a trace of recognition from the outside world. Each woman in the program needs to be encouraged to do the best she can, not made to feel like a failure because someone else is doing better. But the reality is that people who work with addicts do not get a lot of rewards that are either immediate or permanent. That was why Myrna's face lit up as Bonnie was speaking.

"Some of you have known Bonnie for awhile now, but I'd like to tell you a story about her. I don't think she'll mind. When Bonnie first came here, she already had two daughters who had been born drug-positive. She was pregnant again and still using. Her track record was horrible; she had dropped out of I don't know how many other programs. I don't often feel so pessimistic, but I thought to myself, 'Here is one young lady who is never, ever, ever going to make it.' Bonnie, thanks for proving everyone wrong."

Newcomers to a drug program often spend their first few meetings silent and detached, as if their real self had drifted, unseen, out of the room. Many, in flat voices, deny that they even have a problem: "The cops made a mistake, that's all." In contrast, Phoebe Delgato sat perched in her chair with the twitchy alertness of a small bird at dawn. "I just need to say something," she said, waving her hand to be called on. "I just want to say that hearing stories like Bonnie's gives me so much encouragement. Thank you, Bonnie, for everything."

"Would you like to introduce yourself next?" Myrna asked.

"Sure. I'm Phoebe," she said, her eyes darting around the table for approval. With no hesitation, Phoebe admitted her longtime addiction ("I started with marijuana and a big bottle of Drambuie when I was twelve") and told of her drug of choice ("Junk, but I'm just like Bonnie. I've done it all."). She told how she already had had one child taken away and placed for adoption, and now she was in danger of losing another. "But right now, I've been straight about four days and I've never felt so terrific. We want our son back; that would make my husband real happy, so he's behind me on this. I've messed up a lot, but this time, I just know I'm going to make it, just like Bonnie did."

For Bonnie, who had sat through so many of these sessions, this group ritual of stating name and drug of choice had become as familiar as an old song and, in many ways, as comforting. For in every refrain—in the women's histories, in their desperate hopes and paralyzing fears, in their attempts to bullshit the counselors, in this woman Phoebe's desperate desire to please at any cost—Bonnie recognized herself.

When counselors explain recovery, they draw a V-shaped curve as a visual aid. Before an addict can get serious, she must slide down the left side of the V, passing through a series of stages—guilt, blackouts, excuses, moves from town to town, loss of willpower, tremors, drinking with inferiors, impaired thinking, arrests—and being shorn of everything that makes life worth living—job, possessions, friends, health, spouse, children, self-respect, freedom. Only when she has sunk to the very pit of the V and all her alibis have been exhausted can she begin the climb up the other side. Only then does authentic recovery begin.

Bonnie's journey from San Francisco's Tenderloin district, where she grew up, to a drug program in San Jose was not far in miles, but her real journey—from being an abused child of a prostitute to prostituting herself, from running away from foster homes to almost losing her own girls, from being a lost cause to a cause for hope—was long and hard. "The bottom point is different for everyone. It's like a mystery. I don't understand why I had to put myself and my children in every fucked-up situation imaginable," Bonnie recalls. "I look back and it's like looking at a different person."

Bonnie did not hit bottom when she was jailed on heroin charges. She did not hit bottom when, an hour before the C-section that would save her baby's life, Bonnie snuck into the hospital bathroom and shot up. "Nothing got to me until a nurse lead me into the newborn room and pointed out my little baby. She told me that they were going to take her away from me and put her in foster care. My baby had all these tubes in her. I started shaking and crying. I said out loud, 'God, she doesn't have to be perfect or normal. Just make her as perfect and normal as possible and let her live through this. If she does, I vow to try everything and anything not to use again.'"

Epiphanies, the religious say, are gifts from the angels that instantly evaporate unless we mortals draw sustenance from them. Bonnie immediately went on methadone, checked herself into a residential program, detoxed, succeeded in reunification, and had her daughter returned. Just when she thought her problems were over, Bonnie faced the painful truth of being sober: life is hard. She had four young children, no job, no education, no money. "When I was high all the time, parenting was a snap. I didn't hear all the noise; I didn't see any problems. I didn't worry about how I was going to pay for stuff," Bonnie says. "But sober, I feel the full brunt of life and, wow, I'm on edge all the time. I'm finally feeling what it means to be a parent. And it's rough.

"Like a lot of the women here, I started using drugs in my teens and that's when I stopped learning. I didn't know how to write a check, heat up a bottle, get somewhere on time, clean a bathroom, give my kids a birthday party. When I first got sober, I was like that guy in the fairy tale, the one who went to sleep and then woke up. I stayed the same, but the world went on without me."

It seemed clear to Bonnie that this new woman Phoebe, so glib and euphoric, did not even know that she was still asleep.

•   •   •

Beneath Phoebe's cheery exterior, psychologists saw someone who was angry at the world, who did not form lasting relationships, who lacked empathy. In Phoebe's social services file, there was a psychological evaluation that diagnosed her as "an antisocial personality, angry and irresponsible type; [with a] borderline personality disorder."

Compared with Bonnie's, Phoebe's childhood was idyllic. Her hometown, Los Gatos, twelve miles from downtown San Jose in the foothills, is small and chic, full of boutiques and restaurants. The public high school has a statewide reputation for excellence; a "fixer-upper" house can cost $300,000. Of course, no family is perfect: Phoebe's father worked too much and drank too much; her mother escaped into the role of "good wife" and was emotionally distant. But Phoebe never lacked for anything that money could buy; she was neither abused nor treated cruelly. The same parents raised two other daughters, both of whom were athletes in high school and who are now married to nice young men. Why did Phoebe, the youngest, turn to drugs?

That is always the question when a child who "has everything" goes bad. It is a puzzle that occupies every arena of human thought, from biochemistry to psychology to religion. Is such a person born with some genetic glitch? Does she bear the brunt of deep, dark family secrets? Is she working off karma from a past existence? After much analysis and handwringing by Phoebe's family, drug counselors, and social workers, the only conclusion that anyone seems to have reached is that Phoebe simply got lost.

From an early age, she was always just there: not as good a student as her two older sisters, but certainly not dumb; not as popular, but more complex, had anyone bothered to notice. Phoebe preferred being alone, but it wasn't the comfortable solitude of the class brain who gets caught up in the excitement of her own mind. In elementary school, Phoebe was listless and detached, as if life were a movie she did not find particularly engaging. Until the day she turned twelve. Everything changed on that day. To celebrate her birthday, Phoebe smoked her first marijuana and shared a bottle of Drambuie with three older girls. Somehow, a fight started. Phoebe charged one of the girls, and the girl hit her. Intoxicated, Phoebe fell, and her head hit the sidewalk. The next day, she had a seizure; doctors speculated that she had suffered a hemorrhage that had slightly paralyzed the right side of her body.

Before the stroke, Phoebe felt alone and different. Now, she was an outcast who walked with a limp and had a slightly misshapen face. She refused to go to school. She would not take her medications. She would, however, take any and all drugs that came her way. San Jose was the PCP capital of the United States in the mid-1970s, and angel dust became Phoebe's favorite drug. She would disappear from home for days at a time and return spent and disoriented. For awhile, her mother tried locking Phoebe in her room and letting her out only when she was home to watch her. But Phoebe opened her window and jumped onto the limb of a ginkgo tree and ran away. It was a risky move, and it scared her parents. After that, they let her come and go pretty much as she pleased. They had taken her to doctors and psychologists and put her in a special program at school. They could not think of what else to do.

At age seventeen, Phoebe left home for good. Every couple of years, she did a short stretch in the county jail and a few weeks in a rehab. It was in one of those programs that she met Steven. He was the guy who dominated every group, the guy who had his pick of the women, and he chose her.

"Phoebe was such a sweet person, and so very dependent," recalls Sharon Ruprecht. "Steven was so important to her. She loved him so much. She had something that she never thought she'd have, this gorgeous guy that other women really wanted. And Steven? He liked Phoebe's girlish looks and short skirts. He also liked the Social Security check she received every month for disability. The check paid the rent and bought the groceries and left Steven free to do the things he had always done."

. . .

No one knows why Phoebe drove into the parking lot of the strip mall.

A place had opened in a residential drug treatment program, and she was due to check in early the next morning. Perhaps she went to the mall to buy new clothes.

No one knows what triggered a seizure that was similar to the one Phoebe had suffered on the day after her twelfth birthday. She may have gone on one last drug binge. She may have bought drugs that had been cut with a poison. She may have been trying to detox.

What is known is that for the twelve hours Phoebe was alone in the car she was continually racked by convulsions and muscle spasms. When a security guard finally found her, he called an ambulance and Phoebe was rushed down a freeway to a nearby hospital. It was too late.

Mary Agnes King called Phoebe's parents as soon as she was notified. "Oh my God! It's Phoebe! It's Phoebe! She's dead!" Phoebe's mother screamed. Then she gathered herself and listened to the details. "A seizure!" she shouted. "That was her problem all along! I knew it had to be that!"

Phoebe's parents refused to have an autopsy performed. In their daughter's death, they had finally found a satisfying answer for her life. It was not their fault; there was nothing more they could have done. A seizure was why one of their daughters had gone wrong and why she had died. There was no sense in looking beyond that.

12

JENNY AND NICKY: BUILDING A CASE

Jenny

A VOICE MADE ITS WAY INTO JENNY'S SLEEP. SOMEONE WAS TELLING her to wake up, but she was exhausted. Early every morning, she had been getting up, dressing herself and her baby, taking a bus to school, staying awake through school, feeding the baby, changing the baby, bathing the baby. Jenny groaned loudly and pushed away the hand that was shaking her shoulder. "Your kid's crying. Get up!"

Jenny squinted open an eye. Disoriented, she forgot where she was. Then, as the irritated face of a counselor came into focus, she remembered. The old lady had given up and closed her foster home, and Jenny was back in the shelter, sleeping in the senior girls' dorm. Lisa was asleep in a crib that had been set up in the doctor's office.

"Your kid's hungry. Don't you care?" the counselor accused. Jenny was about to roll over when she suddenly remembered the "conspiracy." Everything she did and everything she did not do were being reported. The shelter was full of Sallie Bearden's spies. With that in mind, Jenny pulled herself out of bed. Still groggy, she got a bottle, picked up Lisa, and began walking her around the main room. In the quiet, the baby's screams sounded like a car alarm and made Jenny feel so tense that she too wanted to scream. But that was exactly what the conspiracy wanted her to do. So Jenny controlled herself. Slowly, she kept walking, patting Lisa's back, until the baby gave a final cry and started sucking.

The next day, Lee Ann Osterdock came to visit Jenny and found her in a rage. "Everyone is out to get me," Jenny insisted. "There *is* a conspiracy. I am *not* crazy! First, the counselors tell me to ask for help with the baby whenever I need it," she said. "But then, when I do ask for help, they write a report saying I can't handle the baby on my own. A couple days ago, they all got together and started criticizing me for forgetting to burp the baby. They put that in a report, too. Then, the next day, they wrote another report: I was burping the baby too much.

"And last night! Last night is the proof. I did everything right, but that was not good enough. Go ask," Jenny urged Osterdock.

In Jenny's file, there was indeed a report written by the night counselor: "The only time Jenny seems to spend a lot of time with the baby is when the main room is closed at night. She seems to want to have an excuse not to be in her unit when she is supposed to be."

Osterdock was incensed. "I know the system has problems, but I didn't think they would intentionally try to sabotage Jenny's chances to raise Lisa. But what else could I think? First they report her for not getting up with the baby; then they report her *for* getting up. They were saying that Jenny was paranoid, but that would mean that she was imagining the whole thing. These people were supposed to be helping her, but it became increasingly clear to me that they were out to get her."

•　•　•

Most children have someone who has known them over a long period of time and can take the many facets of their life and fit them together into a cohesive picture. But the life of a "systems" child like Jenny has a "Rashomon" quality. Isolated by the laws of confidentiality, she can never be fully known. People in the system know only the part of Jenny that they have been assigned to fix. One social worker knows the Jenny who was molested, and another knows the runaway Jenny who needs a foster home. Her therapist knows the angry Jenny of the Rorschach test. The counselor at the shelter knows the unpredictable Jenny who was forever threatening to beat her up. Often, these people are prohibited by law from talking to each other. The counselor cannot read Jenny's mental health evaluation. The therapist who wrote the evaluation often cannot get information about Jenny from the counselor.

Jenny's attorney and her advocate saw her as an unfortunate teenager with a new baby who was doing as well as she could under trying circumstances. She was obviously caring for and nurturing Lisa; at the baby's four-month checkup, she weighed in the 90th percentile.

Sallie Bearden, however, was just as vehement in her version of the "truth" about Jenny. From her perspective, Lisa weighed in the 90th percentile not because she was thriving but because Jenny ignored her and allowed her to suck on a bottle for hours at a time. A public health nurse noted that Lisa was already showing signs of becoming "very guarded."

Over the next few months, as Jenny approached her eighteenth birthday, Bearden continued interviewing Jenny's teachers and counselors. She was not orchestrating a conspiracy, Bearden insists; her job was to talk to everyone. She was slowly, tenaciously gathering evidence that she frankly hoped would add up to enough to have Lisa declared a dependent. Some workers would move on after calling a teen parenting teacher once to get a read on how a mother was doing. Bearden called every few days and in the process compiled a list of events that, to her, said everything:

"Jenny brought the baby to school in dirty, soiled blankets that needed immediate washing."

"Jenny screamed, 'I'll leave the baby if I don't get my hair spray!'"

"Jenny leaves half-finished bottles of milk under Lisa's crib. On one occasion, the milk had become curdled but Jenny tried to give it to her anyway."

Jenny's attorney and her advocate were livid at the way Bearden was gathering her so-called evidence. Bearden was doing what social workers are often accused of doing: taking things out of context, embellishing events to fit her agenda. "What new mother doesn't make mistakes, especially if she is tracked twenty-four hours a day?" Osterdock asks.

In a criminal or civil suit, the kind of hearsay evidence that Bearden was ferreting out could not be admitted. Evidence that was admitted would be subjected to intense cross-examination. A good trial attorney would get the public health nurse on the stand and take her apart: "Exactly what does a 'guarded' four-month-old look like? On what basis were you able to make such a definitive statement?" But in a dependency hearing, subjective accounts that "are often no better than over-the-fence gossip" can be presented as proof of neglect or abuse and put into a permanent record. A public health nurse goes on the record unchallenged, as if she were the nation's leading expert on "guarded" newborns. A counselor at the shelter can say whatever she wants without Jenny having a chance to respond, "Wait, she's been my enemy for years."

The day that Jenny's attorney bumped into Bearden outside Judge

Edwards' courtroom, she stood nose to nose with the social worker: "If the Department tries to make Jenny's baby a dependent on this flimsy evidence, I will immediately take it to trial. It will never, in a million years, stand up."

Later, a pensive Bearden explained: "She was right about that. There was no one specific incident that I could point to and say: 'There! That is clear proof of abuse.' But that is exactly my point. Jenny was never alone with the baby long enough for that to happen. And in a few more weeks, when she turned eighteen, she would be completely on her own. To me, that was a scary thought."

Nicky: Building a Case

Two weeks after Phoebe's death, Steven Delgato failed a drug test and landed back in the county jail. While there, he enrolled in a drug program and emerged as the star pupil. The instructor was so impressed that he wrote Mary Agnes King a letter—at Steven's urging.

"I want to tell you that I am very reluctant to write letters for individuals who are incarcerated," the instructor began. "However, in the case of Mr. Delgato, I am happy to make an exception. Rarely do I work with an individual who is ready 'to go to any lengths' for his recovery. From the first time I met this man, his honesty, willingness and open-mindedness [were] displayed as a role model for others. Steven knows that unless he addresses the chemical dependency issue, all the other areas of his life, most particularly the reunification with his son, will be jeopardized. It is my feeling that Steven's feet are firmly on the road to recovery."

King was not impressed. She had gotten letters like this from drug counselors before and had called to tell them she thought they were being conned. Says King: "It's supposed to be the other way around. Drug counselors are the ones who are supposed to be streetwise, the ones telling social workers they're naïve."

When Steven was released from jail, he went directly into a residential program. It was a move that put Nicky's life on hold once more. Reunification had been going on for a year. If Steven had not been visiting Nicky, if he had not made any efforts toward kicking drugs, King could have gone in at the twelve-month review and recommended that Steven's parental rights be terminated. But as long as Steven was in a residential rehab, working toward recovery, the law gave him six more months to prove that he could raise Nicky.

. . .

Nicky's breathing sounded labored as Claire approached the crib, and she wondered if he was coming down with a bad cold. Moving closer, she heard a deep gurgling sound, as if Nicky were drowning. Suddenly, his head started rolling and jerking. "Greg! Nicky is having a seizure!" Claire shouted.

"Get him in the car!" Greg yelled.

"He's going to die!" Claire screamed.

On the road, there was nothing that Claire could do but hold the thrashing, semiconscious child and whisper his name, say over and over that she was there, and tell him what Claire herself did not believe, that everything was going to be all right. Greg ran two lights before careening into the semicircular drive in front of the emergency room. Barefoot, Claire raced in with Nicky.

The doctor immediately put him on oxygen and ran an IV. It took three doses of intravenous Valium to slow the seizure. A medical team did lab work and performed an EEG before wheeling Nicky away for a CAT scan. The emergency room doctor went off to call the neurologist who had performed the surgery to remove the cyst from Nicky's brain.

Four hours later, the doctor came into the waiting room and told Claire and Greg that they could take Nicky home. In all probability the seizure had been caused by scar tissue that had formed around a shunt that had been inserted when the cyst was removed. As the scar tissue grew, it put pressure on the brain. Nicky would have to take phenobarbital for the next two to three years.

The doctor said that more seizures were coming. Claire could deal with that. What she could not deal with was the anger and resentment that had been unleashed that night. She had been patient up until the seizure. But now she kept asking herself how much longer she would have to wait until Nicky was really her son. Nicky's father had been in and out of at least three programs in the year that reunification had been going on. Why wouldn't the system face it: he would never be able to raise Nicky. How many times did he have to fail? No matter what he did, the system kept giving him every consideration.

Claire finally poured out her frustrations in a letter to Mary Agnes

King that began, "I am concerned and very confused." Visits at Clover House were always scheduled to accommodate Steven's schedule in rehab, something "We all pay for when Nicky gets home." The visits wrecked Nicky's nap and messed up Claire's day care center. He arrived home fatigued, clingy, and fussy; any little thing sent him into a rage. But no one bothered to ask about that. Claire went on about how Steven sometimes forgot to give Nicky his bottle or to change him, small indicators of what was really bothering her: Claire felt that she had earned the right to be Nicky's mother. "I was haunted by stories I read in the paper about children who were taken from loving adoptive parents and sent back to a biological parent," Claire says. "I stayed awake nights, worrying that the same thing would happen to me."

Claire never did send the four-page letter she wrote to King. As much as Claire liked and trusted her, Mary Agnes was still the system, and you could never tell what the system might do. She was not about to put anything in the record that could conceivably jeopardize her chance to adopt Nicky. She stapled the letter into Nicky's journal, where it remained, unopened.

13

JENNY AND NICKY: CROSSING THE LINE

In child welfare hearings, the cases that are the hardest to listen to are the easiest to decide.

"If a child has been molested repeatedly or badly beaten, the answer is always, 'Get her out of that home as fast as possible!'" Judge Edwards says. "If parents have missed every court hearing, have violated every court order and never returned a social worker's call, have never even signed up for a parenting class and never visited their child, it is an easy decision for me to stop reunification services and sever parental rights. But the majority of decisions I make are not so obvious."

There are a lot of "bad" parents out there, mothers who endlessly scream at their children, fathers who use children to satisfy their own narcissistic needs. When does society in the form of the court say, "This is more than just a run-of-the-mill bad parent?" When is it decided that this is an abusive, neglectful parent and that the court must step in?

This line separating the merely bad from the legally negligent is as fluid as the boundaries in eastern Europe. What is harsh but "acceptable" discipline in one ethnic community constitutes abuse in another. A child's squalid living conditions may constitute "neglect" in one part of the country; in another, they may be the status quo, and are therefore acceptable. Even within the same child welfare department, if two social workers with the same budget and the same legal guidelines look at the same family, one social worker will see hope, the other, hopelessness.

What determines where the line ultimately gets drawn is an Indra's net of cultural and personal forces—the political climate; the amount of money in the social services budget; the racial and economic makeup of a community; the child-rearing philosophy that is in vogue at the time;

the personal beliefs and professional biases of the people with power: the social workers, the district attorneys, the judges.

If Judge Edwards were to apply the standards of his own home to neglect cases in which children arrive in his court with rat bites, if he used the love and care he and his wife Inger have given their sons as a measure in abuse cases in which children come into his court with broken bones, his job would be simple: he would take children from their parents in almost every case. But that is not his job. In each case, his job is to determine the line of demarcation: When "bad" parenting crosses the line into abuse; when "trying hard" is not trying hard enough. "The basic question always comes back to 'Can a parent protect this child?' " says Judge Edwards. "Determining this fine line between yes and no is what dependency court is all about."

Jenny

On a warm spring day in April, the young mothers and babies in Jenny's teen parenting program went on a field trip, then stopped off for a late afternoon snack in a shopping mall. Jenny was in a particularly foul mood, cursing her teachers and snapping at her classmates.

A fifteen-year-old named Gloria*, who was also in foster care, sat down next to her. Ever since Jenny had entered the program, Gloria had been upset by Jenny's mood swings and her rough handling of Lisa. Once, she had seen Jenny shake the infant in anger and had reported the incident to a teacher, who told Gloria that Jenny needed more kindness and more understanding because she had never seen how "real" parents behave. The teacher suggested that Gloria take Jenny under her wing and help her learn to be a better mother. Gloria took the suggestion to heart; she was the only daughter of two alcoholics and was used to being the responsible and grown-up one in the family.

At the restaurant, Gloria noticed that the louder Jenny talked, the fussier Lisa became. She was probably hungry, too. But before Gloria had a chance to suggest feeding Lisa, Jenny exploded. "Here, you little bitch," she shouted at the baby. "I'll give you something to cry about!" Gloria saw Jenny rip open a packet of salt, pour it into her hand, and force the grains into Lisa's mouth. A few moments later, Lisa threw up all over the table.

"Get me some water so I can clean the puke off me!" Jenny demanded. Dutifully, Gloria scampered off, and when she returned with the water, "I saw poor little Lisa on the table in her own throw-up. I figured that Jenny just kind of dumped her there." A minute later, Jenny stormed out of the restaurant with Lisa.

The following day—a little more than a month before Jenny would turn eighteen—two child abuse referrals arrived on Sallie Bearden's desk. One was from the director of the teen parenting program that Jenny attended. The other was from Gloria's foster mother, another mandated reporter. Gloria had agonized over whether or not to tell what she had seen. "But I finally decided that Jenny needed help so that she would not hurt her baby," she said. Both reports referred to the "salt incident."

Jenny denied that the incident had ever taken place. Lisa, she said, had simply thrown up formula. She swore to Bearden that she would "never, ever put salt in my daughter's mouth." She claimed that Gloria and the other kids at the school were trying to get her kicked out of the program. "They are trying to make me think that I am crazy, just like my mother." As Bearden was writing down everything Jenny said, she knew this was it. This was the line. She now had enough to take Jenny and Lisa to court.

Nicky

Mary Agnes King knew that it was Steven Delgato as soon as she picked up the phone. The chaos in the background, the sound of shouts bouncing off cement and catcalls ringing off steel, could only be coming from jail. A few days earlier, a plainclothes officer had spotted Steven driving erratically through a known drug area and had pulled him over. When the officer asked his name, Steven's speech was slow and drawn. Since Steven was on parole, the officer was able to search the pickup truck. In the glove compartment, he came up with three hypodermic needles, a bottle of rubbing alcohol, cotton swabs, and a tarlike substance that turned out to be heroin.

Since his arrest, Steven had been calling King several times a day to discuss relinquishing his parental rights. He liked the idea of making the decision himself rather than having the judge make it for him, but he was having difficulty accepting that this would be the last decision he would ever make for Nicky. King found Steven, as usual, "to be a confounding mixture of naïveté—he asked, 'If we go to trial, do you think the judge will be mad at me?'—and manipulation—he hinted that he might relinquish Nicky if it would help at the sentencing for his latest drug arrest."

Finally, he told King that he wanted to see Nicky one more time and to meet the people who were going to raise him. "I need to know who they are. It'll make what I have to do easier."

Claire and Greg agreed to bring Nicky to the visit, and a week later they found themselves with King in the basement of the Santa Clara County Jail. They were buzzed through a door with bullet-proof glass, then followed a deputy down a long row of steel doors with narrow slots at eye level. The deputy stopped, opened a door, and motioned them in. Steven rose to introduce himself, shook hands, and thanked the Kenneys for coming. Nicky, who a year earlier had not been able to sit up unassisted, buzzed around the room a couple of times and then went straight onto the lap of Steven, who blinked back tears.

"I have another child; he's five," Steven told the Kenneys. "Once a year, I go up to Golden Gate Park and watch him play. It's never bothered me not being part of his life. I can't say why. I've never felt love for him like I do Nicky."

"Nicky's a very special child," Claire agreed.

"I tried harder to get my life straight than I ever did," Steven said. "I came close, but to tell you the truth, if I had gotten Nicky, I'm not sure I could have taken care of him."

The Kenneys were silent for a moment and then began telling Steven about Nicky. When they finished, Steven told them about his life. There was an uncomfortable pause when he finished. Greg asked if there was anything Steven would like them to tell Nicky when he was old enough to understand.

"I've got a letter here for when you think the little guy's ready," Steven said. "And, I want to give you this." Steven opened a manila envelope. "His mother would want him to have these," he said, and he took out Phoebe's ring, two snapshots of her, and the bulletin from her funeral. "Well, I guess that's it. I guess that's all. Except once a year, could you send me a letter and a picture?"

The Kenneys hesitated. "They'll send it to me, and I'll forward it along to you," King assured him.

Steven stood up and said good-bye to the adults. Nicky had gotten bored with all the talk and was running circles around a small table. Steven hunched over like a linebacker and intercepted Nicky, lifted him, and held him, squirming and giggling, high over his head. Then, Steven gently returned Nicky to earth, nodded to the deputy, and, without once looking back, returned to his cell.

• • •

Three days later, Steven signed the relinquishment papers. The next day, he revoked them. The case would have to go to trial.

On the afternoon of the final hearing, everyone gathered in Judge Edwards's small courtroom. Up to this point, the focus had been reunification. Now, the focus shifted to determining the best option for the child. Lawyers for the Department submitted the record King had compiled and a psychologist's report and asked that parental rights be terminated. Steven's attorney argued that recovering from a lifelong addiction was an arduous battle and that Steven was definitely making progress. To support that, the attorney submitted two letters from counselors, both of which stated that Steven was as motivated as anyone they had ever worked with.

"I know I can make it if I just get more time," Steven told Judge Edwards.

"The reports from the counselors are encouraging, but Nicky can't wait for you to get your life together," the judge said. "He has needs that must be met now. I am adopting the recommendation of the Social Services Department. Parental rights are terminated. Nicky is a candidate for adoption."

For almost eighteen months, Claire had been waiting, begging, praying for this moment. With a few words from the judge, her prayers were answered. But at the same time, Claire was surprised at the sadness she felt when she saw Steven slumped in his chair, unable to get up. Was it his fault that he could not raise Nicky? Claire had wanted Nicky so badly, but she had not wanted to cause this kind of pain. But at least Steven had been given a chance; at least he got that.

In the hallway, Claire thanked King: "The system worked, and not just because we got custody. All the hoops we had to jump through, all the money that's been spent on services, it's all worth it. I can give Nicky's parents a human face. I can tell him that they loved him to their greatest capacity. To give a child that, it's all been worth it."

Jenny: Back in Court

On a morning in early May, Sallie Bearden entered the courtroom on skinny heels, pressing under her arm a twenty-page dissertation with a heavily supported thesis: Jenny is a dangerous parent. The attorneys and the advocates, mother, and child had already assumed their posts. On the bench was a formidable-looking judge with a reputation for speaking her mind. Earlier that week, word had filtered down to Bearden that the judge was feeling the same as the other adults who had closed rank around Jenny. Bearden had been too tough on Jenny, a victim of the system. The judge was emphatic: "We need to give this young woman every chance."

"In my ideal scenario, I wanted the judge to place Lisa into foster care and to order Jenny reunification services to help her mature and learn to be a mother," Bearden explains. "A year or two in the life of a teenage mom can make all the difference in the world. I thought she might have a chance that way."

But now, even with the salt incident as her trump card, Bearden knew that she could not convince this judge to take such drastic measures. The petition that Bearden presented to the court requested the "mildest" form of dependency for Lisa: The baby would not be physically separated from her mother; she would be "permitted to remain in the home of her parent under the care, custody and control" of the Department.

As the judge read Bearden's recommendations aloud, Jenny and her attorney, their heads bowed close together, followed along on their copy of the petition: Jenny was to participate in a parenting group for teens and was to "refrain from cursing, shouting and loud displays of anger while Lisa is in the same room." She was to "consistently participate in individual counseling" and must cooperate with a public health nurse. As soon as a new foster home was found, Jenny was to "provide a stable home environment for her daughter by remaining in their newest foster home for at least a three-month minimum time period."

The judge declared Lisa a dependent child and then quickly tried to reassure Jenny: "This court knows how you feel about the Department. No one is going to take away your child—not even for a day—without a direct order from me. Please do not look upon this ruling as punishment. Please take it as an opportunity to get some services that will make your life and Lisa's life easier, better."

But Jenny could not be reassured; the system was a monster that lived on a steady stream of lives. She could tick off the names of a dozen teenage moms whose children had already been sacrificed. "The system calls it help," Jenny says. "I call it fucking with my life."

● ● ●

Lisa was no longer on Sallie Bearden's caseload. After dependency was declared, Lisa traveled further down the Department's assembly line to a new social worker. Jenny did not return the new social worker's calls. Jenny also refused to attend the teen parenting program: "It's such bullshit. Half the stuff they teach me, I already know because I'm a mother. The other half, I don't believe."

It was the same story in another program that helped prepare teenage foster children for the inevitable day when the system cast them into the real world. Jenny would have nothing to do with classes on finding a job, applying for an apartment, or cooking on a budget. "I've had their help all my life and it was worthless. Look at me! The only thing I want, they won't give me. And that's to be left alone."

One morning, Jenny tossed Lisa's diapers and two changes of clothing into a suitcase and left her final foster home without even throwing one of her infamous scenes. On the momentous day Jenny turned eighteen and was cut free from the system, she was nowhere to be found. Rumor had it that she and Lisa were living with her newest boyfriend. Yet another scenario had her in a run-down motel room with another young mother.

A few weeks into her eighteenth year, Jenny, the new adult, was rushed to Valley Medical Center, so badly beaten by her latest boyfriend that she was barely conscious. The system was no longer responsible for Jenny; now it had to decide what to do with Lisa.

● ● ●

The chambers of the judge were packed with attorneys, advocates, and a supervising social worker from the Department. In the center of the tableau was Jenny, her face bruised, her lower lip stitched with little X's. Baby Lisa in a flowered sunsuit was in her arms, looking the picture of health. "Jenny, this is a really terrible situation," the judge began. "You have been showing a lot of bad judgment in how you are living your life."

"I know I made a mistake with this boyfriend," Jenny said. "But I'm finished with him. He's no good for me, and he's no good for my daughter."

Jenny's attorney stated her case: "My client should not be punished because she is a victim of a bad domestic relationship. She protected her baby. After fourteen years, the Department has no right forcing itself into Jenny's life any longer. If the Department has evidence that Lisa is being abused or neglected, let them present it."

The judge turned to the Department supervisor: "What are your thoughts on this?"

There was an irony to this question, for, like coworkers on tandem career tracks, Jenny and this particular supervisor shared a long, tangled history. Long ago, when Jenny was not much older than Lisa was now, it was this same social worker who had rapped on the door of Jenny's home, saw toddler Jenny playing under a table, and offered her mother housekeeping and child care help. "This is an impossible situation, a real catch-22," the supervisor began. "We cannot assure the safety of this baby without services in place. But Jenny is not a cooperative client. She will not accept what we offer."

"What are you suggesting then?"

The supervisor thought for a moment. "There are only two choices. If Lisa is going to remain a dependent, we will have to take her into protective custody and order Jenny to go through reunification. Or, we have to dismiss this case and send them out into the world."

The judge paused, then asked, "Would you be willing to say that on the record?" The supervisor did not hesitate. "I would."

When they entered the courtroom, the supervisor was aching to speak the truth in her heart: Every family struggles to make sense of an offspring who goes awry, and Jenny's "family"—the Department—was no different. Over the years, the theory had always been that "we could have saved her if. . . ."

If she had been removed from her parents earlier. If she had gotten good foster care. If she had gotten the right psychological treatment. If she had been kept with her sister. If we had been tougher. Kinder. If we had done more. If we had done less. But when the judge went on the record, the supervisor went by the book.

"Lisa appears to be physically OK. There are no signs of abuse or neglect. There is no clear-cut evidence that this mother is not bonding with her child. This mother does not use drugs. Therefore, the Department cannot write a petition asking the court to remove Lisa from her mother's custody."

The judge surveyed the courtroom and said the words Jenny had been waiting her entire childhood to hear: "Case dismissed."

14

THE SEXUAL ABUSE
MONSTER

ONE RAINY MORNING IN FEBRUARY, JUDGE EDWARDS HAD THREE SEX-
ual abuse cases in a row, an occurrence that was not particularly unusual.
The cases were heartbreaking, which also was not unusual. "Children are
defenseless, and in this world terrible things happen to the defenseless,"
the judge told a visitor who was shaken by what he had seen. "Judge,"
the visitor asked, "is our society falling apart? Or are we finally confronting a monster that's been hiding in the closet."

"We're confronting the monster," Judge Edwards replied.

Until the early 1960s, the sexual abuse of children was believed to be
restricted to deviants lurking deep in the bowels of a city and to inbred
families hidden in mountain hollows. In 1955, a study estimated that
there was only one incest victim for every million people. Today, approximately 14 percent of substantiated abuse cases indicate sexual abuse.

Suddenly, the sexual abuse of children was a hot topic for researchers
and the media. In 1979, a survey of college students reported that 19
percent of the women and 9 percent of the men surveyed had been sexually abused as children. In 1985, a *Times-Mirror* survey interviewed two
thousand adults; 27 percent of the women and 16 percent of the men
claimed that they had been sexually abused as children. Things got so
surreal that it became almost fashionable for celebrities to confess to
being victims: television star Roseanne and La Toya Jackson alleged that
their fathers had done unspeakable things to them when they were girls.
Oprah Winfrey told a congressional panel that she had been abused by a
cousin. The press was full of horrific stories of mass sexual abuse, the
most sensational being the McMartin Preschool case in Manhattan
Beach, California, in which Raymond Buckey and Patricia McMartin

Buckey were charged with subjecting hundreds of children to satanic sexual abuse.

Back in the 1950s, the comedian Lenny Bruce performed a routine about his mother and aunt walking around Brooklyn with big black purses, on the alert to bring those purses crashing down on the perverts who were lurking behind bushes. By the mid-1980s, child abusers had taken the place of the perverts who haunted Bruce's relatives. The attitude was that they were everywhere and that every child was in danger. Men who taught elementary school, the kindly bachelor down the street, priests, Boy Scout leaders, and soccer coaches—all were now suspects.

The law reflected the fear. State after state toughened child abuse reporting laws. The federal Child Abuse Prevention Training Act of 1984 funded classes that explored physical and sexual abuse in the schools, heightening awareness still further. Expert witnesses—psychologists, social workers, physicians—began taking the stand to answer questions a small victim could not.

And for the first time, juvenile courts began taking children seriously as witnesses. For centuries, for the most part, young children had been unable to testify against adults who had abused them because, in the eyes of the law, they were too young to understand the nature of an oath, too young to answer the question "Do you swear to tell the truth, the whole truth and nothing but the truth?" They were considered incompetent witnesses because children have a different sense of time than adults, who measure time by clock and calendar. (Think back to how the week before Christmas could seem like an eternity.) Unless an event had occurred on a big day, like a birthday, the feeling was that children could not accurately answer an investigator's most basic questions: What day did it happen? What time did it happen?

There was another reason children were so rarely put on the stand. The Sixth Amendment gives defendants the right to confront their accusers in court—"In all criminal prosecutions, the accused shall enjoy the right . . . to be confronted with the witnesses against him. . . ." It is a crucial right—Sir Walter Raleigh, for example, was put to death solely on the basis of signed affidavits; no person ever took the stand to testify against him.

But the Sixth Amendment also places children who have been molested in a terrible position. Imagine in how many thousands of cases of sexual abuse no action was taken because a mother did not want to put her three-year-old daughter through the ordeal of testifying against an uncle or, worse, against her father.

This ancient bias against children as witnesses started to fade when case law and clinical studies demonstrated that age does not automatically discount children as witnesses. A child's sense of time does not automatically deter her from understanding what she is doing when she takes an oath, does not intrinsically interfere with her ability to describe what has happened to her. Like adult witnesses, children can be either competent or incompetent; like adult witnesses, their reliability should be assessed case by case.

States have now passed legislation allowing children to testify on videotape or on closed-circuit television. (Electronic testimony is still generally inadmissible in adult trials because it violates a defendant's Sixth Amendment right to confront his or her accuser.) In cases like that of Malinda S. in California, state supreme courts have reaffirmed that juvenile court judges can accept hearsay evidence from children who are involved in abuse cases.

Great strides have been made in bringing the sexual abuse monster out in the open; no one wants it hidden away. But there are critics who charge that the hysteria it has produced has created the modern equivalent of a witch-hunt. The defendants in the McMartin Preschool case were acquitted after a trial that lasted months and cost Los Angeles County $15 million. Their supporters took out full-page newspaper ads under the banner headline, SALEM, MASSACHUSETTS, 1692. MANHATTAN BEACH, 1985.

All around the county, parents who have lost children to the system and believe that they have been wrongly accused of abusing those children are joining volunteer organizations like VOCAL (Victims of Child Abuse Laws). In Santa Clara County, the spokesman for such a group, the Coalition of Concerned Parents, calls the system a "septic tank" and complains that it doesn't take much to "start the nightmare. Someone—anyone!—can phone in an anonymous report and the next thing you know there is a social worker at your door, taking away your child."

The problem, say legal scholars like Douglas J. Besharov, is that child abuse laws are so vague and open-ended; they are the legal equivalent of a trawler, hauling in cases the system should never catch. Besharov estimates that 65 percent of all abuse cases reported to child welfare departments are based on erroneous information. "Besides being a massive violation of parental rights," Besharov writes, "the flood of unfounded reports is overwhelming the limited resources of child protection agencies, so that they are increasingly unable to protect children in real danger."

Reports of children being sexually abused do keep flooding into the system—nationally, between 1979 and 1986, there was a 60 percent jump in the number of calls to social service offices reporting suspected physical and sexual abuse, with another 30 percent rise from 1986 to 1991. A fair percentage of these calls do turn out to be unfounded, but people who work with abused children say that this is something that goes with the turf.

"For the first time in history, our society has decided to take the abuse of children seriously," Judge Edwards says. "That means looking into every case, in much the same way that a mother listens to a five-year-old's complaints about an aching stomach or a sore throat. Usually, there is nothing wrong. But there is always the chance that the five-year-old isn't just tired and whiny; she is really sick."

In Santa Clara County, the Child Abuse and Neglect Center receives 120 to 140 calls every day, coming from M.D.'s, school principals, and concerned next-door neighbors. The social workers who staff the center's hot line do what child abuse hot line staffers do in cities across the country: perform on-the-spot triage. When it appears that someone is calling to get even with a neighbor or when a child does not appear to be in immediate danger—about 40 percent of the total—the calls are treated as nonemergencies. The hot line worker steers the caller toward available resources like family counseling, and the case goes no further.

The other 60 percent are referred to the Emergency Response Center, where a social worker is assigned to do an investigation. In a vast majority of cases, workers do not end up filing a petition that brings a child into dependency court for two basic reasons: Either there was scant or no evidence of abuse or the evidence was not legally sound enough to bring the case before a judge. The social worker then does pretty much what the hot line workers do: drops the case or refers the family to counseling or parenting classes and ends the investigation.

In 1993, Emergency Response Center social workers filed petitions in only 7 percent of the abuse and neglect cases they investigated. One of those cases was a three-and-a-half-year-old girl named Kimberly Beyer*.

. . .

A bubbly little girl with crystal blue eyes and a pug nose, Kimberly headed straight for the corner of her pediatrician's office, where a plastic log cabin was overflowing with dolls, toys, and picture books. Kimberly had recently suffered through a bout of meningitis and, after so many checkups, she had developed favorite friends among the stuffed animals.

Kimberly's mother radiated the same good cheer as her daughter. In her late thirties, Sandy Beyer had the kind of life most people would envy: three wonderful children, a caring husband, a good-paying job as a personnel director, friends she had kept since grade school.

Kimberly had been complaining to her mother that her stomach hurt. When she mentioned that it hurt to urinate, Sandy thought, "Uh-oh, she could have a bladder infection; I'd better have her looked at." She called the office and was told that David Safir, the family pediatrician who always cared for Kimberly and her two older brothers, was on vacation, and so Sandy made an appointment with one of the partners.

The pediatrician who examined Kimberly checked for evidence of a urinary infection and then gave Sandy a querying look. "Something is not right here," the pediatrician said. "There's a notch in Kimberly's hymen. It's probably nothing to be concerned about, but it should be looked at. Could you bring Kimberly back tomorrow? There's a physician in the practice who has experience in examining children who may have sustained a genital injury."

Sandy's hands began to tremble. "What about right now?" she asked. "Can you do anything right now? What about an X ray?"

The pediatrician assured her that there was no cause for immediate concern. Tomorrow would be fine. "I'll have her here the first thing in the morning!" Sandy promised.

The Beyer family lives in a section of San Jose known as Almaden Valley, once a golden land of orchards and vineyards, now a setting for bloated track homes on mazelike streets with names like Royalwood and Queenswood. Sandy was surprised to find herself parking her station wagon in the driveway of her mock-Tudor two-story home. She had no memory of how she had gotten there. "I took one look at her and knew something was terribly wrong," her husband Ron recalls. "My first thought was, 'Oh God, somebody died!' "

When Sandy told Ron about the visit to the doctor, he jumped to the same conclusion his wife had reached on the way home: What if something had happened at Kimberly's day care center? But the more the couple discussed the possibility, the more difficulty they had believing it.

Like many parents dependent on two incomes, the Beyers had been wary and felt a bit guilty when they first put their children in day care. The paper was full of frightening stories about sexual abuse; Sandy had also been haunted by articles in which child psychologists warned that day care was no substitute for a stay-at-home mother. So Ron and Sandy had been extremely diligent and checked out a half-dozen places before finding Irene. Irene ran her center out of her home and never took in more than four children. She had cared for the Beyers' sons, eight-year-old Richard and seven-year-old Tim, when they were preschoolers. The kids adored her, and she was practically a member of the family.

The Beyers are something of an anomaly in Silicon Valley, where so many people come from someplace else. Ron and Sandy are both California natives; they grew up in Cupertino, once a village surrounded by orchards, now the home of Apple Computer. And while many emigrants move to California to put as many miles as possible between themselves and their families, Ron and Sandy are very close to both sets of parents. Sandy called them that evening to tell them about Kimberly. From her mother-in-law, she learned that Ron's sister and a cousin had been born with abnormal hymens. It wasn't anything serious, just an irregular fold in the labial tissue. Perhaps this genetic glitch explained the bump the pediatrician had discovered.

Heredity gave them something to hold onto, a theory that could explain the unexplainable, but that was all it was—a theory. In bed that night, the couple tried to develop other theories. "We came up with the time Kimberly started screaming in the backyard; the edge of the swing hit her right in the vagina," Sandy says. "There was also the day the children were jumping on the beanbag chair and Kimberly landed right on her brother Richard's bare foot."

The next morning, as Sandy was getting Kimberly dressed, she explained that the doctor needed to do some more tests. At the office, when the nurse finally called her name, Kimberly went bouncing back to an examining room. The physician discovered a small tear in Kimberly's hymen. It was microscopic, only a few millimeters long, so small only a trained eye would spot it. But since the physician was a mandated reporter, she was required by law to report her findings. The Child Protective Services branch of the Department would see that Kimberly was examined by a specialist skilled in the use of a photocolposcope, a combination camera and magnifying device used to examine the ano-genital area.

Sandy gathered Kimberly in her arms and held her tight, although not as tight as she wanted to. She pictured some kind of exotic instrument probing her little girl and repressed a shudder. She did not want Kimberly to think anything out of the ordinary was taking place. "The sooner we get her to a specialist, the better," Sandy told the physician. "We've got to find out what happened!"

• • •

Of the ninety minutes it takes to do a colposcopic examination, approximately eighty-seven are devoted to preparing a child psychologically. Children who have been sexually abused, especially those abused by a family member, have been made to feel utterly powerless by an authority figure who has crossed a boundary that should never be approached. Having a strange and frightening figure in a white coat probe the area where a child may have been violated perpetuates this sense of powerlessness, a feeling that can deepen into despair and a sense of worthlessness.

For all these reasons, David Kerns, chairman of pediatrics at Valley Medical Center, who established the Child Abuse Diagnostic Center there in 1985, has developed techniques to give children the feeling of being in control of the exam. A serious, soft-spoken man who is emerging as a national expert on child abuse, Kerns trains the physician's assistants who perform the exams. The doctor personally studies each case and examines the colposcopic pictures, and he writes the reports that go to the Department.

The assistant assigned to the Beyers introduced herself, then immediately asked, "Kimberly, I'm going to need your help today. Will you help me? I want to be sure I won't hurt you. I don't think I will. But if anything should happen to hurt, will you be sure and tell me?"

Kimberly was curled up in her mother's lap, her head resting on Sandy's chest. She nodded. "That's great, Kimberly!" the examiner said.

"I'm not going to be putting anything inside you. I'm not going to be poking at you or anything. All I'll be doing is taking some pictures. But if anything does hurt, even a little, I'm real glad you'll be telling me."

The physician's assistant showed Kimberly several gowns and asked which color she would like to wear. Would Kimberly like to change in the bathroom or the examining room? Would she like to leave her socks on or take them off? Where would she like her mother to sit when she was on the examining table?

Sandy helped Kimberly pick a pale yellow gown, and when they returned to the examining room, Sandy blurted out, "Before you begin, there's something you should know." She told the physician's assistant about the genetic glitch and the slightly irregular hymens on her husband's side of the family. The examiner nodded and wrote the information down, then had Kimberly take a seat on the table.

First, she was going to do a general physical exam. But how would Kimberly like to help her examine a doll? She would? OK, which ear should they begin with?

When Kimberly and the physician's assistant had completed the physical exam on the doll, the assistant showed her the colposcope, focusing the bright light on the back of her hand and allowing Kimberly to look through the "binoculars" to see how big the hairs and follicles had become. Together, Kimberly and the physician's assistant examined the pelvic area of the doll. Then the examiner said, "Now, it's your turn, Kimberly!"

Kimberly did everything she was asked, and the exam went smoothly. "That didn't hurt a bit!" Kimberly announced when it was over. Sandy got Kimberly dressed and out of Valley Medical Center as quickly as she could. "The people who worked there were obviously very competent, but a little girl should never have to go through the procedure that Kimmy did," Sandy says.

15

KIMBERLY: THE INVESTIGATION

THE FOLLOWING DAY, A SOCIAL WORKER CAME TO THE BEYERS'S HOME.
A polite man in his mid-twenties, he asked Ron and Sandy if they
thought that Kimberly had been injured and, if she had, how it had happened. He sat down on the floor and asked Kimberly if she knew the
difference between good touching and bad touching. Two days later, the
social worker called Sandy at work. The colposcope pictures and a report
had come in from Valley Medical Center. The physical evidence showed
that Kimberly had suffered definite vaginal trauma.

Sandy's nerves were already strained; hearing the blunt statement
pushed them to their limit. "Could you hold on a minute, please?" she
asked. She got up from her desk, closed her office door, and started sobbing. She managed to pull herself together, but when she got back to the
phone, her whole body was shaking. She took a couple of deep breaths
and asked what would happen next.

The social worker wanted to know if she was willing to bring Kimberly downtown to the Child Interview Center for a few more questions.
"Of course I am," Sandy replied. The social worker said that he would
call right back with the time of the appointment. Sandy began speed-dialing. Ron, an aeronautical engineer who worked in electronic warfare, was away from his desk in a meeting. Her parents were not at
home. Her in-laws did not answer. She got her sister's answering machine. She called Ron's favorite uncle, a lieutenant in the San Jose Police
Department, hoping that he could tell her what was going to happen.
The lieutenant was in the field and unavailable.

The social worker called back with the news that he had scheduled an
appointment in an hour. "You are bringing Kimberly alone, aren't you?"
he asked.

"No, I'm sure I'll reach my husband and he will want to be there. I'm so upset, I don't even know if I can drive," Sandy replied.

"We prefer that only one parent accompany the child," the social worker said.

Sandy started to cry. "Look," she said, "next to telling me my daughter has cancer, you've just told me the worst news a mother can hear. I need my husband there."

"We really prefer only one parent," the social worker repeated. A terrifying thought hit Sandy. "Are you going to take my baby away?" she blurted out.

"Absolutely not," the social worker replied.

When Sandy arrived with Kimberly at the address the social worker had given her, Ron and Janice, Sandy's younger sister, were waiting in the parking lot. They entered a door marked "Child Interview Center" and found four plainclothes police officers in the lobby. One of them, Sergeant Marv Lewis, of the Sexual Assault Unit, stepped forward and said that he would be interviewing Kimberly. A well-built middle-aged man, Lewis ushered the family into a small waiting room. A respected police officer in a department that has a reputation as being one of the best big city police departments in the country, Sergeant Lewis helped develop the protocol for the Multi-Disciplinary Interview (MDI) Team in Santa Clara County.

A few years ago, a child like Kimberly at the center of a sexual abuse case would have been interviewed over and over again. Two or three different police officers would have taken statements; a district attorney would have interviewed her several times; two or three different social workers would have conducted interviews. MDI teams developed out of the desire to cut down on the staggering number of times children had to repeat their stories. Instead of multiple interviews, a team of representatives from different branches of the system discusses the case and agrees on the questions to be asked.

While Sergeant Lewis was conducting the interview, the rest of the team would be observing behind a one-way mirror. The team in Kimberly's case consisted of the emergency response social worker who had visited the Beyers' home; Charlotte Ketterer, a dependency investigator who had thirty years' experience and would be deciding whether or not to file a dependency petition in the case; and a deputy district attorney. If Kimberly named the perpetrator and the evidence she presented was convincing, the deputy DA could file criminal charges.

The Beyers were led to a waiting room, and in order to make Kimberly comfortable, Sergeant Lewis made three trips in and out of the room. The first time, he brought Kimberly a teddy bear. The second time, he brought her a fruit drink. When he came back the third time, Sergeant Lewis told Kimberly that he had a special room where he talked to children. Would Kimberly like to see the room? The sergeant did not have to work all that hard. Kimberly was always ready to make a new friend, always ready for a new adventure. The sergeant took her hand, and as her parents watched, she went skipping off down the hall.

In the special room, Kimberly sat at a pint-sized table, and the sergeant sat on the floor nearby. The sergeant asked how she liked the pictures on the wall. Then he asked where she lived and who she lived with. Where she went to day care and who her friends were. The sergeant pointed to a stuffed animal and asked, "What color is that horse over there?"

"Pink and white," Kimberly replied.

Could she find the color green? Kimberly pointed to the dinosaur on her shirt and said, "Dino baby is green!"

The sergeant had Kimberly count to five. Then he produced a box of Kleenex and a ballpoint pen. He had Kimberly put the pen on top of the box, beside the box, and at the end of the box. "Can you put the pen inside the box?"

Kimberly stuck the pen in the box.

"Can you put the pen a little ways inside the box?" Kimberly put the end of the pen in the box.

Next the sergeant placed a line drawing on the table. The girl in the drawing had the exaggerated features of a doll—large eyes and big lips. Except for the bows in her pigtails, she was naked. Sergeant Lewis asked Kimberly to circle the child's nose, mouth, arms, and hands. When she had done that, he asked if Kimberly knew where the private parts were. Kimberly nodded and drew a heavy circle around the vaginal area. Then she circled the nipples. "What part is that?" the sergeant asked. "Boobies," Kimberly replied.

"Kimberly, has anyone ever touched your private parts?"

Kimberly said no.

The sergeant made small talk and came back to the question: Had anyone ever hurt her in her private part?

Kimberly said that her brother Richard had put his finger in her private part.

"Did it hurt when he did that?" the sergeant asked. Kimberly said that it did.

"Was anyone else there when he did that?"

Kimberly seemed to become tense. She rambled a bit before saying that her daddy had seen Richard do it. Her daddy had said that if she told about it someone would get into trouble.

Had her father ever touched her privates?

"With a washcloth when he gives me a bath," Kimberly replied.

Had he ever hurt her privates when he touched her? Had he ever tried to place anything inside her privates? Kimberly said no, but she seemed apprehensive.

Had anyone at her day care center ever touched Kimberly's privates? Kimberly said no.

Kimberly was tiring and began asking for her mother. Sergeant Lewis took her back to the waiting room, assured her family that he would be back in a moment, and returned to the interview room.

Some cases are difficult for the MDI team to call. The physical evidence is inconclusive, or a child clams up tight or keeps contradicting herself. This case was not one of them. Kimberly had clearly been molested. She had named a suspect. It happened at home, and the father appeared to be trying to cover it up. The MDI team unanimously agreed that Kimberly "would be in jeopardy if she was allowed to return to [her home]." Kimberly was going to the Children's Shelter.

．　　．　　．

After the interview, Kimberly asked to go to the bathroom and, while walking her there, Sandy passed a detective carrying a car seat. "It didn't hit me until we were in the rest room: the car seat was for Kimmy," Sandy says. Rushing back to the waiting room, Sandy closed the door and leaned against it, as if they were cornered.

"Ron, something is going on," Sandy said evenly, trying not to alarm Kimberly. "There is a man out there with a car seat."

Ron is a stocky man, with a powerful chest and muscular arms, the perfect build for a catcher, which he had been on the high school base-ball team. He has a reputation for having a cool head, a trait that serves him well in his work. Emotions have no role when you are trying to fig-ure out how to jam a signal the enemy is sending to jam your radar. But now, the man whose favorite saying was "Let's keep things in focus" felt horribly out of focus. A part of him was thinking, "This can't be happen-ing! They can't take Kimberly! I've got to do something!" Another part was saying, "Anything I do will only make things worse. My God, what can I do?"

Janice saw the anguish in her brother-in-law's eyes and said, "Wait right here, I'm going to find out what's going on." She opened the door to find two detectives in the hallway. "Please step back into the room; someone will be with you in a moment," one of them said.

When Sergeant Lewis opened the door, the two plainclothes officers were standing behind him. "We've made a decision to place Kimberly in protective custody," the sergeant announced.

"Does that mean what I think it does?" Sandy asked. "You are going to take our baby away from us?"

"That's right, Mrs. Beyer. We have decided it is in Kimberly's best in-terest to remove her from her home."

"You haven't even talked to us! What could a three-and-a-half-year-old child have told you that would cause this to happen?" Ron yelled.

"I'm sorry, I can't discuss this," the sergeant replied. "Someone will be calling you in the morning."

Ron was holding Kimberly. He and Sandy started weeping, and Kim-berly's eyes were darting from her mother to her father. "Don't take my parents away! Don't take my parents away!" she began shrieking.

"Please, don't make this any harder on yourselves or on Kimberly," Sergeant Lewis said.

Ron walked closer to the sergeant. "This is the United States of America. Don't we have any rights? Aren't we innocent until proven guilty?"

"Someone will be calling in the morning," the sergeant repeated. "You can discuss that then."

"Please don't take my parents away! Please don't take my parents away!" Kimberly kept screaming.

Sandy was hysterical. "Officer, please, please don't take my baby from me!" she pleaded. "Take me with you. Handcuff me to her. Handcuff me to her bed! Just please don't take my baby from me!"

A detective stepped into the room and took Kimberly out of her father's arms. Kimberly shrieked and thrust her arms out, begging her mother and father to rescue her. Sergeant Lewis asked Janice to come with Kimberly. Janice looked at Ron and Sandy for a moment, then took Kimberly from the detective and followed the sergeant out the door. Ron and Sandy tried to follow, but the two detectives blocked the exit.

"Please, please let me take Kimmy home," Janice pleaded as she carried the screaming child to a police car that was waiting outside at the curb.

"I'm sorry, we don't have that option at the present time," the sergeant replied.

Janice managed to get the kicking and screaming child into the car seat. When the door closed and the car drove away, Kimmy was pressing her palms against the window, as if trying to push out the glass. Janice would see Kimmy doing that in her nightmares for months to come.

• • •

When disaster hits, some people slip into a semicatatonic state and hide. Others bury themselves in ceaseless activity—the widow who oversees every detail of her husband's funeral, the neighbor who is everywhere helping everyone after the earthquake. Ron and Sandy left the Child Interview Center talking about the thousand things that they had to do: call Dr. Safir ("Maybe he could intervene"); call Ron's uncle, the police lieutenant ("There must be something he can do"); call a lawyer friend of Ron's ("Maybe he can recommend a lawyer who will storm into court with a writ—or whatever those things are called—and get Kimmy back").

But first, they had to race across town to the Little League Park and pick up the boys. Ron was the team coach, and they were already more than two hours late; the game was long since over. On the way, they needed to figure out what to tell Richard and Tim.

Sandy was getting into the front seat when she glanced back and saw Kimmy's car seat sitting where Kimberly always demanded to sit—in the middle, between her brothers. Sandy started sobbing. Ron waited a few moments, then drove out of the parking lot and merged with the flow of traffic. In a few minutes, they reached the ballpark, and the boys were banging on Ron's window almost before the car stopped.

Richard has sharp brown eyes and light brown hair that is cut short, except for one long strand that curls down his neck. He is smart and very intense, very vocal. Whatever emotion he feels at the moment, he expresses forcefully. "Where were you guys? How come you missed our game?" Richard demanded as his father zipped down the electric window.

"Get in, both of you," Ron said as he opened a back door.

"But dad—" Richard said.

"Just get in!" Ron interrupted.

"Where's Kimmy? Kimmy's not here!" Richard asked.

"She's fine; she just got sick," Ron said.

Ron was hoping that somehow this would all be worked out in a day or two and he would never have to tell the boys the truth. Saying that Kimmy was sick was lame; he knew that, but it was the only thing he could come up with.

"Sick? You wouldn't leave her alone if she was sick. And why's mommy crying? Something is wrong!" Richard insisted.

"Well, something is wrong," Ron admitted, "but we're working on it."

"Working on what? You haven't even told us what's wrong!" Richard yelled.

"And I'm not going to!" Ron yelled back. "Do you understand that? Your sister is alright. She's not home, but she will be home soon. Until then, Mommy and I need your help. You can start by not asking any more questions."

The phone was ringing when they walked in the door. Janice had called the family; now the family was calling. Ron spoke to Sandy's parents, and they were there in half an hour to take the boys. Richard did not ask any more questions, but he must have overheard a phone conversation or two because that night, when his grandfather was putting the boys to bed, Richard said, "Grandpa, if the police come tonight to take us like they did Kimmy, will you hide us?"

• • •

In general, the only people who give the child welfare system much thought are the people who work in it or the people who are going through it. To the safe, secure, happy middle class, the Ron and Sandy

Beyers of the world, the system remains as obscure as an emerging country in Africa. If the dependency court had ever previously caught their attention, Ron and Sandy would have dismissed it as a place that dealt with *them*, the poor and the wretched, the drug addicts and the sickos who burned children and let them starve. Who could understand parents who did such horrible things to children? Ron and Sandy, their family and friends, everyone they knew, were part of the great, vast *us*, who loved and were devoted to their children.

But now, Sandy and Ron found themselves cast among the *them*. It was 1 A.M., and they were slumped in armchairs, still wearing the same clothes, wondering how this could have happened to people who had never done anything wrong. Growing up in the 1960s, Ron had never let his hair grow, and neither he nor Sandy had even experimented with dope. They had nothing to hide. That was one reason Sandy had been so willing to cooperate with social workers and the police.

"The work we do is classified, and we're both regularly subjected to background investigations and polygraph tests," Sandy says. "It never bothered us, and we were never able to understand people who asked, 'Don't you think that is a terrible intrusion?' We believed that investigators have to delve into the private lives of people who work in defense."

Now that same government had invaded their home and taken their baby, and taken her without even talking to them. So when the phone rang, Ron and Sandy froze, paralyzed by the same thought: nobody would be calling at this hour unless something had happened to Kimmy!

It was Dr. Safir, Kimberly's pediatrician, who had returned from vacation and was stunned when his answering service informed him that Kimberly had been taken to the Children's Shelter. The doctor had been in private practice nineteen years and had come "to consider Sandy and Ron two of the most honest, deliberate, straightforward parents in my practice."

Dr. Safir explained that he had called the partner in his practice who had examined Kimberly and learned that the tear in her hymen was tiny, only four or five millimeters long. In sexual abuse cases involving children, suspicion falls first upon the closest adult male. Here, the physical evidence ruled out Ron—the tear was too small to have been made by an adult penis—or even by an adult's little finger.

Dr. Safir was adamant that he did not agree with the report produced by the Child Abuse Diagnostic Center. Dr. Kerns believed that an injury such as Kimberly's could only have occurred through a deliberate attempt at penetration. "I have no doubt that it could have occurred accidentally," Dr. Safir told the Beyers. "She might have fallen at day care, cried for a while, and forgotten all about it by the time she got home."

But Dr. Safir was not calling at 1 A.M. to contest Dr. Kerns's report. He had called the Children's Shelter earlier that evening and explained that Kimberly Beyer was his patient. He wanted to come to the shelter and examine her, thinking that "if I could just hold her, it would be better for her." That was out of the question. Kimberly was in protective custody.

"She's not in protective custody from me," Dr. Safir replied to the shelter counselor. "I'm her pediatrician. I've examined children at the shelter before."

"I am not going to have this conversation with you!" the counselor said and hung up.

Dr. Safir—and there is a grassroots movement that agrees with him—believes that zealots are making decisions about the sexual abuse of children, that too many innocent injuries are diagnosed as sexual assaults. "Why didn't the investigators talk to me? If I had told them, 'This father has given me the creeps from the beginning, [and] I'm plenty worried,' that would have given the case a context. That was what troubled me the most: there was no context for taking Kimberly. As far as I was concerned, the possibility that sexual assault had occurred in the Beyers' home approached absolute zero."

Over the coming months there would be many long late-night conversations with Dr. Safir. It was during this first one that the battle lines were drawn. In this country, history has been essentially gentle to white, middle-class people like the Beyers. Storm troopers have never destroyed their churches; a local despot has never driven them off their land. It is difficult to come up with anything that delivers the radical message that power can be capricious, that power must be opposed, but the system does this when it takes a child from parents who believe they have done nothing wrong.

"With Dr. Safir as our ally, we were going to fight this every step of the way," Sandy says.

16

KIMBERLY:
IN THE SYSTEM

It was a Saturday, Kimberly's second day away, when Charlotte Ketterer, the dependency investigator on the case, arrived at the Beyers' home. The day before, Sandy had spoken to Ketterer on the phone and found her to be singularly unhelpful. "She wouldn't tell me anything except that Kimmy was doing fine. I know it's against the law for her to give out information, but she was so cold, just reeking of judgment. It was like I was a criminal for asking about my own child." Had it not been for the Beyers' parish priest, who called to say that he had learned "through channels" that Kimberly was out of the Children's Shelter and in a "very nice" Emergency Shelter Home, the Beyers would have had no idea what was happening to their daughter.

Ron asked Ketterer to sit down. The gray-haired social worker sat on the edge of a couch, her back rigid, and surveyed the living room with the cold eye of a New England schoolmarm. "I am here to do an investigation," Ketterer announced.

"Fine. Then do you mind if I tape-record our conversation?" Sandy replied, producing a cassette player, just as she and Ron had rehearsed. Ketterer looked surprised and annoyed. "No one has ever asked to use one of those," she said.

"I'm not trying to be hostile or anything," Sandy explained. "I'm just trying to stick up for my rights."

"I don't want to get into a conversation about rights. Let's proceed with the investigation," Ketterer said. Sandy turned on the tape recorder.

"May I have your Social Security numbers, please?" Ketterer asked.

"No," said Sandy. "No," said Ron.

"No?" asked Ketterer, taken aback. Asking for Social Security numbers was the most routine of requests. The Department used them to check arrest records.

"We will be retaining legal counsel," Ron said. "When our lawyer says it is OK to give you the numbers, we'll give them to you."

There was a long silence. Ketterer reached into her briefcase for a copy of the colposcopic examination. "Let me turn to the report written by Dr. David Kerns at Valley Medical Center. It is important that you understand Dr. Kerns is very careful in stating his findings."

Ketterer explained that Dr. Kerns was acutely cognizant of the powerful legal and social consequences his examinations could produce. He therefore tended to be conservative in his medical diagnoses, using phrases like "suggestive of sexual abuse" or "indicative of possible sexual abuse" in only about 10 to 20 percent of his examinations. His most typical finding, in 70 to 80 percent of the reports he issued, was that there was "no indication of trauma." Dr. Kerns used the phrase "injuries that are consistent with sexual abuse" only when the physical evidence was overwhelming and he had ruled out other causes.

The social worker fixed her gaze on Sandy and Ron. "In Kimberly's case, Dr. Kerns concluded there is 'definitive evidence of hymenal penetration,'" Ketterer said. After pausing to let the words sink in, she asked, "Do you have any explanation for how your daughter could have sustained this trauma?"

Ron and Sandy stared at the ceiling. They had promised each other that they were not going to ask or answer any questions, but they wanted in the worst way to tell the social worker that Dr. Kerns wasn't the only expert out there; Dr. Safir, for one, was convinced that Kimmy's injury was accidental. They were eager to know if Kimmy could be examined by another expert. Finally, Sandy couldn't stop herself. She informed Ketterer that there were things about this case that were unique. For one thing, there was a genetic glitch in the women on Ron's side of the family.

"Other than volunteering that, we feel we can't answer any questions until we have consulted an attorney," Ron said after giving Sandy a quick look of warning.

Without a word, Ketterer put away Dr. Kerns's report and there was another uncomfortable pause. To the Beyers, she was an inquisitor, a living archetype of a system that had torn apart their family. "She was there to get something on us," Sandy would say later. "From the moment I produced the tape recorder, she did not like me. From then on, she would come into my house, sit in the chair in the corner of my living room, watch my family, and take notes. She was very prosecutorial."

From the days of "The Cruelty," social workers have been accused of being "inquisitors." As often as not, the families they "serve" view them as representatives of an occupying power. At the other extreme, cops refer to them as "cupcakes" or "marshmallows." As with all public servants, their stature has sunk lower during an era when Americans distrust and are angry with government. The public approval rating for social workers is down there among journalists and politicians.

Stereotypes tend to be unfair, but often they are wrapped around a germ of truth. Give people too much power and they will misuse it. The grand jury that looked into the Department in Santa Clara County concluded that all too often social workers are racially biased and insensitive to class and cultural issues. "Grievances pour into my office," says the ombudsperson who handles complaints for the Department. "People tell me that their social worker is rude and arrogant, insensitive to their family systems, to their lives, to their role as parents. The bottom line is that people feel that the social worker doesn't respect them. I see it myself when I try to point out problems. Some social workers get defensive and are rude to me. To me! And I work with them. I have power."

But to say that all social workers are alike is to disregard human nature. The differences between individual caseworkers are as vast as the disparity in professional skills between a reporter who covers NASA for the *New York Times* and a reporter on the astrology beat for the *Midnight Globe*. Some social workers are naturally warm and empathetic; others, like Ketterer, are detached and analytic. Among her coworkers, Ketterer has a reputation for being tense and uncommunicative, but no one calls her vindictive or inefficient.

Like all social workers, Ketterer was working within legal parameters. The county's medical expert had found evidence of sexual trauma, so she had to investigate the Beyer family. And she had a gut instinct that something was very, very wrong. Ketterer was instructed not to tell Ron and Sandy that she had sat behind the one-way mirror when Sergeant

Marv Lewis interviewed Kimberly—there was a police investigation going on. She did not tell them that she had found Kimberly completely credible and that Kimberly had given the MDI team a suspect—her brother Richard—and reason to believe that the father knew what had happened.

In her long career, Ketterer had worked with hundreds of parents who were terrified of losing their child and were willing to do anything to get her back. That cooperative attitude—even in the most troubled families—told the social worker that they, at least, were facing their problems and were ready to try to change. But the Beyers were sitting there with a tape recorder and an attitude that said they were hiding something. Why else would they be so hostile and defensive?

· · ·

Unlike many of the families who feel that they are being run over by the system, the Beyers had the money, education, and connections to do something. On Sunday afternoon, Ron and Sandy retained Albie Jachimowicz, a private attorney, to help fight their battle. They chose well, for Jachimowicz had long experience in dependency court. Looking at Ron, the first thing he said was, "In cases like this, suspicion falls first on the closest male." It was therefore decided that Jachimowicz would represent Ron and that the Beyers would retain a second attorney to represent Sandy.

"Most of the cases I've seen, somebody did something wrong to a child," Jachimowicz said later. "The Department may go about the investigation wrong, people may ask leading questions that contaminate a case, but their hearts are in the right place. They are honestly trying to find out what happened. The Beyer case was unique. The Department was dead wrong on that one. By pushing a case when there is no case, the system cheapens itself and calls into question the work it does on valid cases."

Monday morning, Ketterer arrived at the Beyer home for a second interview. Jachimowicz had advised Ron and Sandy that, in the long run, it was best to cooperate with the social worker. After disposing of the mundane details—dates of birth, Social Security numbers—Ketterer asked if they were now prepared to discuss their thoughts on how Kimberly was injured. Ron and Sandy nodded yes.

"We agree 100 percent with our pediatrician, Dr. Safir, who believes the injury was accidental," Sandy said. "The only other possibility is the genetic glitch."

Ron told about the day Kimberly had come in crying from the backyard, saying that the swing had hit her. He also mentioned the afternoon that Kimberly had jumped from the stairs onto a beanbag chair and had landed on Richard's foot. But he explained that the incident could not have caused Kimberly's injury because she had been wearing Pampers.

Instead of alleviating Ketterer's suspicions, these well-thought-out explanations actually increased them. Experience had taught her that parents who have sexually abused a child try to minimize and deflect blame. That was precisely what the Beyers seemed to be doing. The social worker had already contacted Dr. Kerns about the supposed genetic glitch. The doctor said that nowhere in the literature was there a report linking the kind of tear Kimberly had suffered to a genetic deformity. Perhaps the Beyers had concocted this story with their parents. Perhaps a pattern of sexual abuse ran through the extended family, as it often does.

Over the weekend, the police had given Ketterer clearance to go into the details of Sergeant Lewis's interview. Without comment, she reached into her briefcase and pulled out a transcript. "Did you know there is a suspect in this case?" Ketterer asked. "Kimberly named her brother Richard as the one who abused her. To your knowledge, has Richard ever hurt Kimberly?"

Ron's head started spinning; Sandy felt "like a horse kicked me in the stomach." "Are you going after *all* our children? Is that what you are doing here?" Ron asked, leaning toward Ketterer. Ignoring him, she asked again, "To your knowledge, has Richard ever hurt Kimberly?"

"Other than what I already told you about the beanbag chair, no, I have no knowledge that happened," Ron replied.

The physical evidence may have ruled out the father as a suspect, but that did not place him above Ketterer's suspicions. Many children who sexually assault other children have themselves been molested. Where else could eight-year-old Richard have gotten such ideas? Had the father molested the son?

"Kimberly told Sergeant Lewis that her daddy was there when it happened," Ketterer said evenly, making it clear that she was presenting the facts. "Kimberly stated that her daddy had told her not to say anything or someone would get into trouble."

In even the happiest of marriages there are always small suspicions lurking somewhere below the surface. Trust usually keeps these fears buried until something happens to open the floodgates. "For a split second, I thought, 'What if they're right?' " Sandy recalls. "I searched myself for any evidence—feelings, hunches, anything the children had ever said, anything I had seen—that might suggest that Ron was not the man I had loved and shared my life with all these years. I'm glad I asked myself those questions, because as soon as I did, I knew for a certainty that Ron could never harm Kimmy. My husband is a good man."

Meanwhile, Ron was near tears. "Sandy," he said in a half-whisper, "if Kimmy told the sergeant that, then I must be a suspect. If I'm the reason Kimmy can't come home, I'll move out. I'll stay with my parents until this is over."

"You'll go nowhere," Sandy said, reaching out to pat her husband's hand.

"Kimberly did not say you touched her, Mr. Beyer," Ketterer said. "The sergeant specifically asked her about that. Her reply was, 'Only in the bath, with a washcloth.' "

Ron's mind went back to the many nights he had bathed Kimmy, and for the first time something in this horrible mess made sense. "I know what happened!" he said. "There's been times when Kimmy is in the bathtub that I've said, 'Kimmy, your privates are for you only. No one should see or touch them but me and mommy and Dr. Safir. If anyone else ever touches your privates, you tell us and that person will get into trouble.'

"That's what happened!" Ron continued. "Kimmy got it backwards! She's only three and a half, for God's sake! She didn't mean to say, 'Don't tell or someone will get into trouble.' She meant, 'Tell and someone *will* get into trouble.' "

To Ketterer, this was all part of the pattern. She presented evidence; the parents found a way to deny it. The tear in Kimberly's hymen was not a result of innocent play; it was the result of a sexual assault. The sooner the parents admitted that, the sooner they could all sit down and figure out what needed to be done to help Kimberly and to get the family back together again.

"You are in denial," Ketterer told Ron and Sandy. "You are not willing to accept that your daughter has been injured. You are not willing to accept the possibility that your son may have injured her. You are trying to protect your son at the expense of your daughter."

"You are putting us in a double bind!" Ron shouted. "If we say we don't believe Kimmy was sexually assaulted, you say we're in denial. But if we don't believe it—and damn it, we don't!—how can we say we do?"

Like the first interview, the second ended in stony silence.

17

KIMBERLY:
THE HEARING

THE LAW SAYS THAT A DETENTION HEARING MUST BE HELD WITHIN seventy-two hours after a child is taken into protective custody. Kimberly was taken to the Children's Shelter late on a Thursday afternoon. The court's clock does not tick on weekends, and so it was not until the following Tuesday, six days after Kimberly was removed from her parents, that Ron and Sandy appeared in court. Charlotte Ketterer had filed a Section 300(d) petition, alleging that the Beyers had "failed to protect the[ir] child adequately from sexual abuse and the parents knew or reasonably should have known that the child was in danger of sexual abuse."

Commissioner Christine McCarthy was assigned the case. A middle-aged woman with a round face and a cordial manner, she prides herself on being relaxed and creating a family-like atmosphere in her courtroom, courtesies that were lost on the Beyers. They were basket cases and felt as disoriented as if they had landed in a foreign country. The cool, rational deportment of the county attorney representing the Department, of the DA representing Kimberly, and of the Beyers's attorney, Albie Jachimowicz, was a world away from the emotions that were seething inside Ron and Sandy. The attorneys seemed to be speaking English, words like "motion" and "recommendation" kept flying past, but Ron and Sandy could not follow what was going on. Almost before they knew it, they found themselves back in the corridor, asking Jachimowicz if it were really true—could Kimberly really come home?

She could indeed. Kimberly would be transferred back to the Children's Shelter, where her parents could pick her up later that afternoon. Ketterer had recommended that the child be allowed to return home—

but only under certain strict conditions. Kimberly was not to be left alone with her brothers or any adult male—even her grandfathers.

Ron and Sandy hurried off to get ready for Kimberly's return, in their joy ignoring the fact that this was only the beginning of the case. Jachimowicz and Mike Clark, the county attorney who represented the Department in Commissioner McCarthy's courtroom, knew better. They huddled in the corridor.

"Mike, you and I have worked on a lot of cases together," Jachimowicz began. Clark, who has a reputation for being one of the most thorough attorneys practicing in dependency court, nodded yes. "Mike, in my experience, 80 to 90 percent of the petitions that are filed should be filed. Eighty to 90 percent of the time, there is something going on in a child's life that is very wrong. The court has got to get involved." Again, Clark nodded in agreement.

"Mike, this is not one of those cases. This family is your family, Mike. It's my family. This father is you, Mike. He's me. The Department has made a mistake on this one. Don't make it any worse than it already is. Dismiss the petition; let them go on with their lives."

"I can't do that," Clark replied. "The child told the police her brother digitally raped her. She said her father knew about it and told her not to say anything."

When lawyers plea-bargain in criminal courts, prosecutors agree to lesser charges and the amount of time served in exchange for the defense attorneys' agreement to plead their clients guilty. What was going on in the hallway was the dependency court's equivalent: both attorneys were looking for a resolution that would assure the safety of the child and, at the same time, minimize the system's impact on the child and the family.

"Here's how we could settle this case without taking it to trial," Clark said. "We've got to sustain the petition. The parents have to agree that the facts as presented are true. If they do that, the only remaining question will be what kind of services the family will require."

There are attorneys who have never read the child welfare code and have only the vaguest idea of how dependency court operates but who, nonetheless, show up from time to time to represent parents. Such an attorney would have no idea what Clark was talking about. But Jachimowicz knew Clark, and he knew the law. If Richard or someone else had sexually assaulted Kimberly, if Ron or Sandy or both parents knew about it and were trying to cover it up, the deal Clark was offering was great.

The Department's attorney was essentially saying, "Let us help you get the services you need to heal your family, and the court will get out of your lives."

But if Kimberly's injury was truly accidental, if Richard was innocent and Ron and Sandy were telling the truth, the offer was an outrage. To get free of the system, the parents would have to admit to something that they did not believe had ever happened. Richard and Kimberly and probably Tim would have to attend therapy sessions they did not need. Ron and Sandy would have to go to parenting classes and sit in the same room with parents who really had abused their children.

"I'll talk to my clients and get back to you," Jachimowicz told Clark.

• • •

"No! No way! No deals!" Ron Beyer told his attorney. "They can't come in and destroy us and then expect us to roll over. They started this fight; let them try to finish it."

The Beyers were sitting at a table in the legal library in Jachimowicz's office. The thick, light brown volumes with the red squares on the spines and the gold lettering gave the room a solemn feel, but Jachimowicz's language was closer to the street than the courtroom. The case had an easy way and a hard way. The easy way was to go along with the system, to agree that the facts as stated in the petition were true and let the attorney try to talk Clark into the least intrusive form of Department services. In six months, the Beyers could begin to forget this had ever happened.

The hard way, Jachimowicz explained, was to take the case to trial. The trial would be long, and Ron and Sandy would both be put on the stand and asked embarrassing questions. A trial could cost from $15,000 to $20,000 in legal fees, and, Jachimowicz warned, they could end up losing.

"I don't care what the odds are; we can't admit to things we haven't done," Sandy said. "Somebody has to hold them accountable." Ron pulled out his checkbook, wrote a check for $3,000, and handed it to Jachimowicz. He had cashed in part of his 401(k) retirement fund; he would cash in the rest on an as-needed basis.

It would seem logical that a majority of the cases that come to trial in dependency court would involve middle- or upper-middle-class families. They do not qualify for a public defender and must hire private attorneys, who may be eager to take on the system—and generate fees. But, in fact, the reverse is true: cases involving families from the higher social strata *rarely* come to trial *because* the family has financial resources. An attorney who is representing a well-to-do family and knows what he is doing will walk into dependency court having already done the Department's work far better than the Department could with its overloaded social workers and underfunded services. Typically, the attorney will submit a service plan that is far more extensive than anything the Department can afford. Typically, a judge will accept the plan, thankful that something is being done and that, in this case, the taxpayers do not have to pick up the bill.

But Ron and Sandy were not interested in playing ball. They wanted to march into court and tell Commissioner McCarthy that the system that had taken Kimberly away "for her own protection" had returned her with nasty black-and-blue welts on her forehead. Kimberly's explanation was that she had banged her head against a wall in the Emergency Shelter Home, and when Sandy asked, "Accidentally?" Kimberly had replied, "No, on purpose." When Dr. Safir examined the child, he confirmed what the parents already knew: "What we have here is a little girl with a severe case of separation anxiety."

"The effects of them taking Kimmy away were terrible," Ron remembers. "At home, she wouldn't get off her mother's lap. If I got up to leave a room, she'd appear at my side and take my hand. Every time we passed a McDonald's, we'd have the same damn conversation."

" 'Mommy,' Kimmy would say, 'the lady in the house where I stayed wouldn't let me have a Happy Meal.' "

" 'Happy Meals are something special that a mom or dad buys,' Sandy would say, and then Kimmy would start with . . . 'Mom, how come they took me? Are they going to take me again? Are they going to take my brothers?' "

The Beyers wanted the court to see firsthand how it had inflicted damage, not just on Kimberly but on their entire family. They wanted the court to feel the anguish when they had to ask their eight-year-old if he had ever hurt his little sister, if he had ever put his finger in her vagina. Richard's eyes had widened and became blurry. He dropped his head and covered his eyes. "How . . . could . . . they . . . think that?" he asked. Then he raced across the room and buried his head in his mother's lap. "I love Kimmy."

Ron and Sandy wanted a chance to tell the court that they believed their son, would believe him until their dying days. They wanted to tell Commissioner McCarthy how truly kafkaesque this system that she ruled over could become, how their boys were having terrible nightmares and acting like fugitives in their own home.

"If the kids wanted to watch Nickelodeon, I had to be there, sitting on the couch with them," Sandy says. "It was a court order. Even her grandfathers couldn't spend time alone with her. We were terrified that we'd slip up and that Charlotte Ketterer would catch Kimmy alone with her brothers and use that against us in court."

Their in-laws knew what they were going through, but the Beyers told none of their friends, even the friends they had grown up with and had shared everything with, from a first kiss to the birth of a firstborn. "We knew that, guilty or not guilty, the charges would change people's perception of us," Ron says.

In Ron, all this stress turned to rage, and, like a child, he sometimes directed his rage at Sandy, the person he felt most safe with. "It's all your fault!" Ron would suddenly yell. "If you hadn't taken her to the doctor, this never would have happened. You always drag the kids in for the least little thing! Look where it got us!"

This was why the Beyers wanted a trial—to show everyone in court what the system had done to their family.

• • •

As a young woman, Christine McCarthy spent time training to be a Maryknoll nun; she is now a divorced mother raising a teenage son and daughter. The commissioner has been on the bench ten years and is well respected throughout the system. In almost every one of her cases, the attorneys stipulate that she be a judge pro tem for the duration of the proceedings, at which point her decisions take on the same legal weight as the rulings of a judge.

McCarthy believes that it is usually much more effective to settle a case than to take it to trial. "Settling a case, you get beyond the personalities of the lawyers who are fighting each other and get down to what a case is really about. You get everyone to buy in," she explains. "In a trial, I sometimes feel as if I'm baby-sitting personalities. People say nasty things about each other and then everybody turns to me, like I'm a mother who's supposed to settle an argument between the children."

The trial in the Kimberly Beyer case lasted nine afternoons, and Commissioner McCarthy must have indeed felt like a mother. There are no juries in dependency court. The idea is that the professionals who assemble in the courtroom are a kind of family, acting in the best interests of the child. The matriarchal or patriarchal figure on the bench keeps everyone focused and in the end decides what actions should be taken. The family metaphor, unfortunately, sometimes applies too well. A trial, like an unhappy family gathering for Thanksgiving dinner, often degenerates into petty bickering and name-calling, an endless questioning of veracity and hidden motives. When Sergeant Marv Lewis took the stand, the Beyers were hoping that their attorneys would discredit him. The sergeant had not tape-recorded his interview with Kimberly and had taken only sketchy notes. Had the sergeant relied on his memory and paraphrased Kimberly when he wrote his report? The sergeant testified that he had gone back and dictated his report immediately after the interview. The only drama in the sergeant's testimony occurred when one of the Beyers's attorneys asked if there was an ongoing investigation of Richard.

"There is not," the sergeant replied. The interview with the boy had been inconclusive; Richard had talked about the incident with his foot and had denied hurting his sister. The DA had instructed the sergeant not to pursue a case against the boy.

Ron and Sandy clasped hands under the table and squeezed tightly. Richard, at least, was in the clear.

When Charlotte Ketterer took the stand, the Beyers's attorneys attacked her for the prosecutorial way she handled the case. Mike Clark, the attorney for the Department, just as vigorously defended her. Ron and Sandy thought that they were going to relish seeing Ketterer get what she had coming, but they did not. All the trial seemed to be doing was recycling the pain.

Ron and Sandy were just as deflated when it came time for them to testify. They had envisioned themselves telling their story in a seamless narrative, creating a powerful portrait of a family that had been wrongly accused and badly abused. It didn't happen. Clark kept objecting, breaking the flow. He questioned their motives, subtly suggesting that, instead of telling the truth, they were unwilling to face the truth.

At one point, Leslie Packer, a clinical psychologist who had evaluated Kimberly, took the stand. An expert in child abuse, Dr. Packer testified that Kimberly was "a delightful and essentially intact preschooler . . . [who] portrayed a rich and supportive family life in her projective play. . . . The types of themes that emerged in test results were of parents feeding and nurturing their children. There were no sexualized preoccupations or themes in Kimberly's test findings, no positive findings of a sexualized, traumatized, or victimized child. . . ."

Finally, as trials so often do in dependency court, this one ended not with a bang but a whimper. Commissioner McCarthy did what cannot be done in a criminal trial: she basically declared the proceedings a draw, saying that she found both sides to have presented a case true to their beliefs.

Technically, the evidence supported the petition. Case law and appellate court rulings say that when there is physical evidence of sexual trauma and the parents cannot account for how it happened the court must take some action—even if, as the Beyers claimed, the trauma must have been accidental. But Commissioner McCarthy also did not discount testimony like Dr. Safir's and Dr. Packer's. All indications were that the Beyers were truly a loving, nurturing family.

Therefore, with the Department's consent, the commissioner placed the Beyer family on informal supervision. If the Beyers got therapy for Kimberly and the boys, the case would be closed in six months. Clark was pleased with the decision.

"The system worked in this case," Clark insists. "These cases are terribly difficult. We may never know what happened to Kimberly, or who did it, but we can't just turn our backs. If it was the brother, the research is clear that sibling molestation can have a devastating impact on the cognitive and emotional development of a child. We wanted to get the family connected with appropriate mental health intervention so they could deal with their issues. Sometimes, the only way for that to happen is to go through a trial."

As for the Beyers, they could have gotten the same ruling months earlier and saved themselves thousands of dollars. Still, to Ron and Sandy, the money was well spent. They would have mortgaged their house to hear Commissioner McCarthy describe them as a loving family.

But that was not enough. Most couples who endure a trial walk out vowing to never even drive down the street and look at the dingy court building again. Ron and Sandy walked out holding hands, resolutely making eye contact with every attorney, every social worker, every bailiff they passed.

"We had decided that, no matter how the trial came out, we were going to file a lawsuit against the Department," Sandy says. "We didn't care what it cost or how long it took; we were going to do whatever we could to make sure these people cannot just walk in and destroy a family!"

18

THE CUSTODY BATTLE:
HIS VERSION

IMMEDIATELY AFTER WORK ON A SATURDAY AFTERNOON, DENNIS Wright*, a lanky, well-muscled man with a handsome head of hair, parked his truck in front of his sister's house and got out to pick up his eight-year-old son, Brian. Since his divorce six years earlier, Dennis had court-ordered custody of the boy every other weekend, and on those Saturdays he woke up early and drove all the way to Modesto to pick him up. Over the years, his ex-wife, Debbie, had succeeded in putting emotional distance between Brian and Dennis. Now he suspected that she had moved a hundred miles away—not to cut her living expenses, as she claimed—but to put physical distance between father and son.

For Dennis, two weekends a month were not nearly enough for the kind of football-tossing, fishing buddy dad he had always envisioned being. Recently, the time he spent with Brian had gotten even tighter. His boss at the air-conditioning company where Dennis was employed as a technician had told him that if he could not work overtime on Saturdays he should start looking for another position.

That was out of the question. Dennis could not afford to give up the seniority and benefits that came with his job. Even working forty plus hours a week, he was still struggling to pay bills. There were Brian's child support payments, of course, but it was the legal fees that were still bleeding him white. During the divorce, Dennis and Debbie had wrangled over every shared possession: the lawn mower, the car, and, of course, that most precious possession of all, Brian.

"I can afford only a small apartment for myself," Dennis complains. "I figure that, by now, I've bought my attorney a beach condo with an ocean view."

The Saturday situation was far from ideal, but Dennis's sister Karen made things easier by agreeing to watch Brian until late afternoon. She had a comfortable, kid-friendly house with lots of toys, and her children were always eager to play. Karen loved Brian and tried to make him feel welcome, but the boy always complained bitterly when his father dropped him off: "You shouldn't work now. You're supposed to be with me!"

Every visit, Dennis managed to placate his son, but every visit, he felt a pang of guilt knowing that Brian was absolutely right. Trying to make his son as well as himself feel better, Dennis always rubbed Brian's sandy-colored hair and promised, "All Saturday night and all day Sunday will be our time, just the two of us together." Dennis was walking across his sister's lawn thinking about the video that he and Brian would rent that night when the front door opened and Karen came rushing out. She took Dennis by the arm and turned him away from the house.

"Something's happened," she said.

This news was not unexpected. Brian is a big, boisterous kid—"First he crawled, then he ran, then, finally, he learned to walk," his father says. Physically, he takes after his mother, husky and very strong. As a toddler, Brian played too rough for most kids his age. Now mothers and teachers were always complaining that the eight-year-old hurt someone, and Karen inevitably had some new atrocity to report: Brian lost his temper and threw blocks at a neighborhood kid; Brian hit one of his cousins.

It was clear to Dennis that Debbie was far too lenient with the boy. Instead of disciplining him as a mother should, she acted as if they were friends the same age. She cried on his shoulder about her money problems and her love life. Worst of all, Debbie filled Brian's head with garbage about how Dennis had abandoned the family and how Dennis could never be trusted. If Dennis made even the smallest suggestion about Brian's upbringing, Debbie would pounce: "He's fine! You have no right to complain about how I'm raising him!"

Dennis wanted to believe what Debbie believed, that Brian was just "all boy," but he had been a boy himself—one with a short fuse—and what he was seeing in Brian transcended typical little boy mischief. Brian was starting to steal, not just loose coins left on a dresser, but five dollar bills right out of Dennis's wallet. And when Dennis called him on it, Brian lied his head off.

At playgrounds and at his sister's house, Dennis watched other boys roughhousing and noticed that whenever Brian joined in good times deteriorated into shouting, punches, and kicks. The other children only pretended to be at war; when the battle ended, they were friends again. In Brian's play, there was a real viciousness. "Even I had to give up playing football with him," Dennis says. "He would plow into me and start hitting me if he didn't catch the ball."

Now Dennis was worried that Brian had attacked one of his younger cousins with the same fury. He asked his sister, "Who did he get into it with this time?" Karen did not remove her hand from her brother's arm. "It's not the usual stuff. It's worse," she said. "He keeps hitting himself on the head. An hour or so ago, he started stuttering. His body is twitching in these jerky movements. Dennis, he even peed in his pants. I'm scared."

Behind them, Brian burst through the screen door. "Let's go, Dad. Go! Now!" Before Dennis had a chance to open his mouth, Brian was pulling at his sleeve. "Leave. Now. Leave," he stuttered. Brian jumped and grabbed at his father, motioning that he wanted to be picked up and carried, as Dennis had carried him as a toddler. "Up, up!" he kept repeating. When Dennis tried asking him questions, Brian sank to the cement and wrapped both arms around his father's legs. He was sobbing too hard to speak.

"It was as if Brian had short-circuited," Dennis remembers. He and his sister looked helplessly at each other, then agreed that the best thing would be for Dennis to take him home. Maybe when Brian calmed down, he could explain what was going on.

Dennis managed to get Brian into the truck and buckled up. As soon as they pulled away, Brian's body went slack and he stared blankly into space. Gently, Dennis helped the boy out of the car and into his apartment. It was then that Brian suddenly turned into someone his father didn't recognize. With almost superhuman strength, Brian pushed his father aside and began slamming himself into walls and furniture. Dennis was terrified that Brian might throw himself against a mirror or against a glass window. For a few seconds, he managed to get the boy pinned down on the floor, but Brian quickly broke loose.

"Tell me what is going on," Dennis kept pleading. "Let me help you." Finally, Brian calmed down enough to force out a few words: "I'm afraid to go home. Wade is there." With that, Brian curled himself into a fetal position on the couch and would say no more.

Dennis had a long list of worries, and Wade was at the top. For her second husband and a stepfather for their son, Debbie had chosen a real loser. Wade had served time for burglary and was a heavy drinker. "I never saw him with a shirt on his back or without a drink in his hand," Dennis says. "I know he had guns in the house, too. Now, I have nothing against a man owning guns—I have a couple of shotguns for hunting myself—but Wade has handguns and a mean temper, and that made me nervous."

Several times when Dennis went to collect Brian, Wade had answered the door and said that, he didn't care if it was Dennis's weekend, Brian wasn't going anywhere. Then he slammed the door in Dennis's face. Once, Dennis kept pounding, and Wade finally threw open the door and came out with his fists up. They wound up throwing punches in the front yard while Debbie screamed and Brian hid behind a tree. Neighbors called the police, and it took two officers to get the men apart.

The police did not seem to care who was at fault. "That was when I started writing everything down," Dennis says. In a file labeled "Journal Record," he began to meticulously record the date and time of every phone call between himself and Debbie, every threat that Wade made, every promise to have Brian ready at such and such a time that was not fulfilled. Dennis started having a police officer—"a civil standby"—accompany him when he picked up his son.

After the pickup, Dennis's visits with his son always followed a predictable pattern. "At first, Brian would be so hyper that I would have to tell him to sit in the back so I could drive," Dennis says. But at the Altamont Pass, as the truck began the climb up the mountain range out of the Central Valley and the tule fog began to lift, a change always came over Brian. "I could count on it," Dennis recalls. "Everything in him would go whoosh!—like all the tension of the whole week was being released. I guess to him that pass was the place where he was leaving everything behind."

It was at that point that Brian always climbed back into the front seat and started rambling on about school and his comic books. But these were topics that Brian could discuss with anyone. So eventually, the conversation rolled around to the one subject that Brian and Dennis alone shared: their hatred of Debbie's husband, Wade. Taking aim at this mutual target was an instant and sure way to reestablish intimacy.

"Are you worried about that creep, Brian?" Dennis always asked. "If he ever lays a hand on you, you just tell me, OK?"

At that, Brian always nodded and moved closer to his father. "Wade's always bragging about how he's going to kick your butt again, Dad. But I told him, Dad, I told him that he wasn't gonna do that because then he'd have to fight me too. We could do that, right Dad? We could beat him. Wade's not as big as you, right? You'd probably win, huh Dad? With me on your side, we'd win for sure." Dennis always smiled and took one arm off the wheel and put it on the boy's shoulder: "I appreciate your concern, son. But I can take care of myself. It's you I'm worried about."

After exchanges like that, the two weeks that Brian and Dennis had been apart were erased and the weekend began. But this time, lying on the couch and curled up like a baby, Brian could not be reassured.

"Your mom can protect you against that dickhead," Dennis said.

"But Mom isn't always there," Brian said. "And he's mean to her, too. She's been talking that if Wade doesn't change we're gonna move back with Grandma."

A warning bell went off in Dennis's head. As he helped Brian remove his 49ers T-shirt and put on his pajamas, Dennis carefully checked the boy for bruises or burn marks, but he found nothing more than ordinary playground scratches. Spent and exhausted, Brian finally fell asleep, but two hours later he was awake, sobbing, and begging to be cuddled. The pattern continued throughout the night and into the next day. Twice, the eight-year-old wet the bed. He would not eat anything, not even a Big Mac, which was something he never refused.

By late afternoon, a few hours before he was supposed to be on the road taking Brian home, Dennis knew that he had to make a decision. Something was definitely wrong. He had found no marks, but what did he know about child abuse? What if Brian had been beaten or molested? Another terrible thought crossed Dennis's mind. What if Wade really had done something to the boy? What if Debbie tried to protect Wade by twisting things around so that Dennis somehow got blamed for it? He would not put that past her; she would do anything to make Dennis's life more miserable.

"I decided that I should have someone official check things out,"

Dennis says. "I had learned to put everything in writing. That way, I would show that I had nothing to hide. Everything would be on the record."

Knowing what he did about the system, Dennis could not believe that he was even considering walking into the door of a government agency of his own free will. In the years since he and Debbie had split up, Dennis felt as if he had spent most of his waking hours untangling himself not just from the marriage but also from the system that was supposed to help them. All Dennis had ever wanted was what was legally his: a few hours a month with his son. But to get it, he had to scream at mediators who always seemed to take Debbie's distorted version of the truth, slam his fist on the desks of court clerks who misfiled his paperwork, and listen to know-it-all bureaucrats lecture him about following the proper procedure.

"When it came to the divorce, I figured the system had stacked the deck against me, against men in general," Dennis says in retrospect. "But this was a child, and I figured the system would really want to help him. So, I took a deep breath and put my feelings aside. I heard about Child Protective Services, and I thought, 'OK, this is where you go when a child needs protecting.'"

. . .

Seven days a week, twenty-four hours a day, the Child Protective Services (CPS) hot line is open for calls. A high school principal, a mandated reporter, phones about one of her tenth graders. She claims that, to prevent the girl from dating, her father beat her and locked her in a closet for days. The father is an immigrant and comes from a country where strict discipline and protection is regarded as a measure of his love for her. But the principal wondered aloud whether the girl was telling the truth, or whether she was retaliating against her family for their old-world ways.

Another caller says, "I don't want to give out my name, but this lady in the same apartment building lets her kids run around in filthy diapers. I just know that she is abusing them, too! You should put those kids in the shelter."

It is out of the question, both practically and legally, for CPS to conduct a full-blown investigation of every allegation, so it falls to the intake worker—traditionally one of the least-trained and lowest paid people in child welfare work—to listen to the anonymous voice on the other end of the line and to make a monumental decision: Is there reason to think that the immigrant father crossed the often fine line between his "right" to discipline his daughter and abuse of her? Are the filthy diapers a symptom of more dangerous neglect and abuse? Or did the call possibly come from someone who has a personal vendetta against the mother?

Since most allegations of child abuse are phoned into the CPS hot line, it was unusual for a father to walk into the unadorned portable trailer on the grounds of the Children's Shelter, hand in hand with his child. Dennis told Brian to take a seat while he talked to the lady in charge. The social worker wanted the whole story from the beginning, so Dennis sketched it all: his bitter divorce, the terrible fights over visitation, his ex-wife's schemes to keep Dennis and Brian apart. "She has always made me out as the bad guy," he told the worker. "But it looks like it's his stepfather he needs protection from."

The worker listened, then told Dennis that she needed to talk to the boy alone. Taking Brian by the hand, she led him into a small private room.

In the days when child welfare work was a calling, workers were wildly subjective, relying mostly on gut instincts, including the dark side of those instincts: personal prejudices, racism, gender bias, religious zealotry. As social work has struggled to transform itself into a profession, there have been countless attempts to standardize assessments of children, to develop objective criteria that use psychological exams, charts, graphs, and grids.

The worker who listened to Dennis's allegations and then to Brian's story followed the rules of the Department's "Decision-Making Grid." First she answered the procedural questions: Can we locate the child? Is there an open case in the Department files? Does the allegation meet the legal definition of abuse? Is there an in-family perpetrator? Then she plotted the responses on a grid that would determine the proper course of action. When she and Brian emerged from the interview room, the worker's mouth was set in a hard, straight line.

"There does seem to be some substance to the accusation," she told Dennis. "Brian said that he showed his stepfather his report card and that his stepfather became really angry and tied him to a chair. Then his stepfather got a leather belt and hit him several times across the chest and groin area."

Dennis came off his seat, a mass of clashing emotions: sadness for what his son had lived with, guilt for not acting sooner on his instincts, rage at Wade for hurting the boy and at Debbie for not protecting him. "That settles it," Dennis said. "He can't go back home then. I'll keep him with me."

"I am not in a position to advise you to do that," the social worker said.

"Why not? I'm his father."

"Legally, you only have custody for a few more hours. If you don't return him, legally it's kidnapping."

"Let's go, Dad," Brian said, pulling at his father's shirt. "You promised that after I talked to the lady we would leave."

"Miss, what are you telling me?"

CPS workers say that they make every attempt "to go by the grid," to view every allegation of abuse, from whatever source, as objectively as possible. But when a case comes to them from Divorce Court, it is the rare CPS worker who does not wonder if one parent is using an allegation of child abuse to retaliate against the other. First the worker assured Dennis that she did not believe Brian was in enough immediate danger to warrant the trauma of removing him from his home. Then she made another point: Dennis and his ex-wife were obviously involved in a long-standing custody battle, and unfortunately in those situations there tend to be some false claims of child abuse. One parent may be trying to get back at the other. Sometimes children themselves embellish an incident. Sorting out the truth can get very complicated. Whenever possible, the Department prefers to move a little slower in these kinds of cases in order not to inflict any more emotional damage on the child.

The worker suggested that Dennis return Brian to his mother at the scheduled time. Proper procedure dictated that abuse be reported in the county where it allegedly took place. Dennis could report the matter to the police there, or the worker would notify CPS in Modesto. They would determine whether or not the matter needed further investigation.

If Dennis had learned anything from his years of fighting Debbie in court, it was to say "yes miss" and "no sir" to the people in charge. He had been exceedingly polite and soft-spoken, which made his sudden explosion all the more startling: "Are you accusing my son of lying? Are you accusing me of getting him to make this up?"

The social worker stiffened. If Dennis did not want to take her advice, he had two other options: He could, on his own, ignore the visitation order and keep the child with him. Or he could leave the child at the shelter and let the Department look into the matter. Within seventy-two hours, Brian would be released or a hearing would be scheduled.

"Look at the double bind they were putting me in," Dennis said later. "I could 'kidnap' my child and maybe even lose all future rights to visitation. I could return him to an environment that, in my eyes, was obviously abusive. Or, I could dump him in a strange place where he didn't know anyone. That was my reward for trying to protect my son."

Dennis faced Brian, who was holding tightly onto his father's arm. He wanted to explain to the boy that this was the law, the way the system worked, the way it had to be. He could not find words to explain all this, so he simply said, "Son, I think the safest thing for both you and me is, I am going to have to leave you here."

"You lied!" Brian started shouting. "You lied!"

"I promise. By Tuesday, this will all be worked out. You will come live with me or maybe with Grandma. Maybe you can go home to Mom. But, trust me, son, Wade won't bother you anymore. And I promise, I'll never leave you again."

Brian began clawing at his father's leg. When a counselor tried to pry him away, Brian swung wildly. Then he threw himself backward onto the floor; his legs went up, and he started peddling furiously. The counselor stepped back so that he wouldn't get kicked and motioned for Dennis to leave.

As Dennis walked out into the sunshine, all he could think of was that this was Debbie's fault. Everything from the beginning had been her fault. "I couldn't sleep," Dennis says, recalling that night. "I was pacing around the apartment and had serious notions about killing her. I wanted to kill her for putting the boy through this."

19

THE CUSTODY BATTLE: HER VERSION

A HUNDRED MILES AWAY IN MODESTO, DEBBIE WAS SITTING ON THE living room floor, playing peekaboo with her infant daughter, Tammy. Debbie is an attractive woman in a tomboyish way, with deep dimples and brown eyes, which kept darting to the clock. As always, Dennis was late. The court order specifically said that Brian was to be home by 6 P.M. on Sunday evening. It was already after 7. It was just like Dennis not to care that Brian had school the next day and that it always took hours to calm him down and get him to sleep after visits with his father.

One of the many things that had once attracted Debbie to Dennis was his "smooth way of talking. . . . He's the strong, silent type, but when he does talk, he always sounds so educated," Debbie says. "A lot of guys just talk trash all the time, but Dennis has a good handle on the English language. Little did I know he would use it to bullshit me." Any minute now, Dennis was going to pull in with some lame excuse about the traffic out of San Jose or the fog on the Altamont Pass or about how he and Brian were having such a great time that they got a late start.

It was all garbage. Dennis didn't care about Brian. He missed support payments. He missed visits. He didn't care that Brian was messing up in school. The only reason Dennis even bothered to take his son was because "it was a way to stay in my life and inflict misery," Debbie says. "He was still jealous. He still loved me."

Debbie knew exactly what took place on these so-called great visits. On Sunday nights, the second Dennis drove out of sight, Brian always snuggled up close to his mother and gave her a complete rundown of the weekend. The pattern was always the same: At exactly 8 A.M. on his Saturday mornings, Dennis showed up at the door, visitation orders in hand, stone-faced and cold, not even mumbling a hello. Behind him, terrifying Brian, there was always a cop in tow. Then Brian would run and hide, refusing to go with his father. Dennis and the officer would have to hunt for the boy, whom they usually found hiding in a tree or cowering under the bed. Then they had to drag him screaming and kicking into the car. On the whole ride back to San Jose, Dennis pumped his son for information about Debbie and Wade. Did Wade drink? When he drank, did he get drunk? How drunk? What did he act like when he was drunk? Did he yell? Did Debbie yell back? Did the police ever come? Did Wade have any girlfriends? Did Wade ever do anything real bad, like maybe hit Debbie?

"You should hear what Dad says now, Mom," Brian would always report. "He says that the next time he comes and Wade answers the door, he's gonna beat Wade up. You won't be able to stop him." During the drive to San Jose, Dennis asked only a few halfhearted questions about Brian himself: "School okay? You okay?" Then he would dump Brian at Karen's with a "Sorry, kid, but I have to work today."

Debbie knew that Karen used to do a lot of drugs and was now some kind of religious fanatic, which explained why Brian despised staying with his aunt. Not only did she dote on her own children, but she also spent the whole day bombarding Brian with "God stuff" and telling him what a rotten mother Debbie was. The high point of every "great weekend" was when Dennis finally got around to picking up his son late on Saturday evening. Did he toss around a football like a father is supposed to do? No, he took Brian to some party, got drunk, and ignored him. Or, even worse, Dennis would humiliate Brian just as he had humiliated Debbie during so much of their marriage.

After one visit, Brian told his mother, "I woke up to go to the bathroom and Dad started teasing me about this little rip in my underwear. He grabbed me and ripped them even more, in front of all his friends, even his new girlfriend. They all started whistling and cheering and stuff. Then, he screamed, 'Get back to bed.' He wouldn't even let me go to the bathroom or get a drink."

Stories like that drove Debbie crazy. She threw up her arms and told her son, "That's your father all right. He treats everyone like a dog, even his own son."

So when the phone finally rang at 7:15, Debbie thought, "Well, here comes the latest lie." But instead of Dennis, there was a woman's voice asking to speak to Brian's mother: "I'm from the Santa Clara County Children's Shelter," she said after Debbie identified herself. "I'm calling to inform you that your son won't be coming home tonight."

"What? What do you mean? Is he hurt?" Debbie stammered.

"No, he's fine. I'm a counselor and I've seen him," the voice assured her. "But there's an allegation of abuse that will have to be investigated."

Debbie's mind raced and then settled on the usual suspect, Dennis. Maybe Dennis was drinking and there was an accident and Brian was really hurt. Maybe he had lost his famous temper and actually hit Brian. Debbie sounded hysterical, but she didn't care: "This is my ex-husband's fault. He's violent. He has guns. He doesn't live here. I won't let him near Brian ever again. Can I come pick him up? He must be terrified. He's a really sensitive boy."

The voice on the other end waited until Debbie ran out of words: "I'm sorry, but your son can't come home. The problem is not your ex-husband. Brian is claiming that his stepfather abused him, that he tied him up in a chair, then beat him with a belt."

"That's a lie," Debbie shrieked, but then, instantly and with some embarrassment, she recalled the incident. "Well, not exactly a lie. My husband did tie him up, but it was part of a game, a cowboys and Indians thing. Brian had seen some kids playing it and asked his stepfather to do it. Sometimes my husband is just a grown-up kid. He teases Brian a lot, but he never hits the boy."

"I know this is hard. You have my sympathy, but there will need to be an investigation," the counselor said. "He may be released, or there may be a court hearing. A social worker will contact you on Monday."

When Debbie hung up, she held her baby daughter close to her. "My heart felt like it was ripped out and my whole world had ended," she recalls. Unable to sleep much that night, Debbie, like her ex-husband a hundred miles away, paced the house. "This is all Dennis's doing. Everything that has ever gone wrong is Dennis's fault. He must have bribed or threatened Brian to get him to say these things.

"That night, I wanted to kill Dennis, to put an end to this miserable relationship once and for all," Debbie says. "I thought to myself: 'If I kill him, I'll get sent to jail. My life will be over. But who cares? At least Brian will finally be free of him.'"

. . .

Real-life relationships rarely resemble melodrama, with clear-cut villains and unblemished heroines. Yet, it is human nature to try to simplify life by putting good guys in white hats and bad guys in black, by declaring someone a winner and another a loser, by labeling one a good parent and the other a bad parent.

There is not much about their life together that Dennis and Debbie can agree upon, except for one fact: after their champagne wedding brunch in a Reno hotel, it all went downhill. Trying to sort out their conflicting accusations, their years of charges and countercharges, the minutiae of who did what to whom would be a daunting, crazy-making task for an adult investigator. And yet, that was exactly what their young son Brian, "the love of their lives," was forced to spend his childhood struggling to do.

When Brian was with Debbie—the center of his universe—he tried desperately to see and support his mother's view of the world: She was the good parent, the victim. She believed that Dennis was all bad, so his dad had to be bad.

When Brian was with Dennis—the center of his universe—he tried desperately to see and support his father's view of the world: He was the good parent, the victim. He believed that Debbie was all bad, so his mother had to be bad.

Brian's dilemma was that he loved them both and depended on both. As a child grows, one of his most important psychological tasks is to begin seeing and accepting his parents for who they truly are: complex human beings who are sometimes gentle and kind, sometimes angry, selfish, and stubborn. But in the bitter black-and-white world that Brian's parents had created, that was impossible. Brian was trapped in an emotional civil war and forced into the role of a double agent who keeps switching loyalties. Like all spies, Brian paid a terrible emotional price.

To explain the bind, therapists do not use espionage metaphors; they apply geometry. Imagine an equilateral triangle with the boy at the apex and his parents at each corner. The baseline connecting the divorced parents is thin and broken, a symbol of their negative, malicious association. But the lines binding child to mother and child to father are thick and dark. They symbolize the force with which each parent is striving to enlist the child's sympathy or support against the other. This "emotional incest" blurs the generational lines and totally disregards the child's developmental needs. Family therapy pioneer Jay Haley explains "triangulation" this way: "In almost every instance of emotional disturbance, you find this simple, sad, common story: two parents are emotionally estranged from each other, and in their terrible aloneness, they overinvolve their children in their emotional distress."

There was no sane way that an eight-year-old could please both his masters. Developmentally, children can "freely love more than one adult only if the individuals in question feel positively toward one another." Therapists have a lot of technical jargon to explain what happens to children like Brian who have been "triangulated." Brian became "extremely hostile, going on the attack in both passive and aggressive ways." He "incorporated punishing critical parents," which means that he saw himself as bad to the core and blamed himself for every family fight, every problem, and every failure.

But the preciseness of geometry only hints at the inner chaos that overwhelmed Brian the weekend his father took him to the Children's Shelter. As soon as Dennis walked away, Brian began tearing the place apart. He threatened to beat up anyone who even glanced at him. He refused to take a shower, brush his teeth, or change his underwear. He jumped on furniture, pushed over a bookcase, and shoved smaller children out of his way. In the cafeteria, he threw Jell-O across the room.

When a counselor in the junior boys' dorm refused to give him an extra snack, Brian screamed, "You suck!" and picked up the stuffed giraffe the shelter staff had given him for comfort and threw it at the counselor's head. The counselor ducked, and in the second he took his eye off the boy Brian charged. He knocked the counselor onto the floor and began beating on him. It took two grown men to get the eighty-five-pound boy down on his bed and to restrain his arms behind his back.

Later that evening, after Brian had calmed down, the counselor he attacked took him into the main room to talk. Brian threw himself on the sofa and turned away from the counselor. His bulk and the belligerent look on his face made him seem a lot older than eight. "What's going on?" the counselor asked.

"Leave me the fuck alone. Get away from me or I'll beat you up again," Brian said. The counselor considered walking away, but he knew kids and he knew that, despite Brian's words, being alone was the last thing he wanted. They just sat there, not saying a word, not even looking at each other. Several minutes passed, and then the counselor took a chance. "You're angry, aren't you?" he asked.

Brian didn't answer. "I can't blame you. You haven't had an easy time, have you?" Still, Brian didn't say anything.

"Are you scared? Sometimes kids get scared that no one will ever come and get them out of here. They think they are going to be here forever." With that, the boy who looked like a tough adolescent disintegrated into what he was: a frightened child only three years out of kindergarten. He moved over to the counselor's lap and practically curled up.

"I don't want to hurt either of my parents," he said. "I love them. But every time I say something good about one, the other gets angry with me. I don't want them to stop loving me when I tell them things. I'm too young for this. I just want to live in peace and quiet."

20

CHILDREN, CUSTODY, AND THE LAW

IN THE LATE 1960s, A PERIOD OF SOCIAL AND ECONOMIC CHANGE rivaling that of the Progressive Era, California became the first state to establish no-fault divorce. "This was a significant break with the American tradition of treating marriage as a religious state, breakable only by some fault that went to the heart of the moral/religious contract made between two parties," explains Judge Edwards.

True to the radical mind-set of the time, this same 1969 statute, California's Family Law Act, led the nation in revamping child custody laws, which, like divorce and marriage, had been ruled by economics and religion since antiquity. Puritan society, for instance, was labor-intensive, and the notion of a father losing rights to his child, especially her services and wages, was as unthinkable as his being ordered to pay child support. In the extremely rare case of divorce, even a "prudent, discreet and virtuous woman" would lose her child to a husband who was a notorious adulterer. This assumption of paternal authority was justified in the same way that Puritans justified everything else: common law was a reflection of the Divine Plan.

Later, during the industrial revolution, as fathers left homes and farms for jobs in factories, mothers remained at the hearth and functioned primarily as caregivers for children. It was economics that placed women in this role; it was an emerging social philosophy—the new "religion" of the time—that kept them there. "Natural law" imbued these stay-at-home mothers with a set of moral standards that were seen as superior to that of men. Since women were "naturally" refined creatures with gentle temperaments, they were obviously better suited than men to raise the next generation.

The courts of the time began to reject common law for this more modern and higher natural law. By the 1920s, "maternal presumption" was as firmly set in judicial code and practice as paternal presumption had once been. Unless a mother was determined to be unfit (unforgivable transgressions were adultery and deserting one's husband), the judge awarded her custody. (It is not surprising that the shift of custody to mothers coincided with a period when children were losing their value as economic assets and becoming expensive luxuries.)

At first, this shift to maternal presumption did not have a dramatic impact on families, since the divorce rate was low and child custody cases mostly involved orphans. But as the twentieth century progressed, the number of cases exploded, the product of a skyrocketing divorce rate. In the late 1960s, divorce joined with feminism and economic necessity to bring more mothers into the workplace. Between 1970 and 1985, the number of women with an outside job with children under three went from 27 to more than 50 percent. As the legal system looked at this phenomenon of more and more working mothers, it saw fewer and fewer reasons to continue judicial preference in their favor. At the same time, a growing father's rights movement was calling for the same thing as the feminists: Equal treatment of men and women before the law; equal rights to custody for both parents.

The path to "gender neutrality" was paved by California's Family Law Act. Custody decisions and practices were no longer supposed to be biased by gender, religion, or economics. Today, all states offer some form of legal innovations that are, in theory, designed to be "in the best interest of the child."

In several states, including California, mediation is mandatory in contested custody proceedings. The idea is to keep volatile issues out of the cold, legalistic setting of a courtroom and to allow parents to meet in a more informal setting and try to agree on a settlement that works for everyone. Custody laws around the country now stress liberal visitation rights for the noncustodial parent. California's Family Law Act says, "The public policy of this state is to assure minor children of frequent and continuing contact with both partners after the parents have separated or dissolved their marriage."

Gender-neutral custody was taken to its logical conclusion in 1979 when California enacted the country's first joint custody statute. Currently, forty-three states have similar statutes that advocate joint custody as either an option or a preference; no state bars the arrangement. In the ideal scenario, joint custody allows children to receive care and affection from both their parents. It also benefits the adults, and ultimately the children, by eliminating the emotional and financial burden of single parenting.

All of these modern laws and practices were designed to remedy centuries of inequities between men and women and centuries of overlooking a child's psychological needs during an obviously traumatic event. They were meant to simplify a complicated procedure. In many, many divorces, that is exactly what they do.

However, what is "in the best interest of the child" is often elusive and subtle. These same laws can be manipulated by vengeful and embittered adults; they can easily backfire on the children they are supposed to help. There are fathers who demand joint custody and visits not because they want the responsibility and experience of caring for their child but because they want to get back at their ex-wives or want to avoid child support payments. Visits with a child can be a way of continuing to harass and abuse a former spouse.

There are mothers who use visits as a weapon to control their ex-husbands. They threaten: "If you don't increase your child support payments, I won't let you see the kid. If you don't pay more, I'll move and you'll never see him again."

All too often, the court misuses joint custody by ordering it as a last resort. When divorcing parents can't agree upon anything at all—Who gets the car? Who takes the children on holidays?—the system throws up its hands in frustration and orders, "Split everything, even your time with the children, right down the middle."

To placate these warring parents, the child is forced into a rigid, stressful schedule of back-and-forth visits that are completely out of sync with the child's own developmental needs, the child's own social schedule, and the child's desires about where he wants to live. "Loyalty conflicts are common and normal under such conditions and may have devastating consequences by destroying the child's positive relationship to both parents," write the authors of *Beyond the Best Interests of the Child*, a pivotal book on children and the legal system.

In the bleakest of cases, the divorce may be final on paper, but joint custody and enforced visitations allow the battles to continue for years. A full-blown divorce industry, with its battalion of lawyers, mediators, therapists, and financial advisers, has sprung up to reap the spoils of family strife. The bewildered child drifts between two homes, two styles of discipline, two worldviews, and two conflicting opinions about who is causing all the misery. The child is deprived of any stability, any emotional relief, any sense of closure.

Together, the parents and the legal system join forces to do what King Solomon in his wisdom threatened, but never intended, to do: they split a boy like Brian in half.

• • •

The morning of the detention hearing, Debbie and her mother were anxiously awaiting their turn in Judge Edwards's courtroom. Both the investigating social worker and Debbie's public defender had several other cases, so they were not able to meet until midmorning. There were only a few small conference rooms, and they were filled, so the only way to talk was to huddle in a corner by the staircase.

Debbie attempted to convince the social worker that Brian should come home with her, that she was perfectly capable of protecting him, that she always put Brian's needs first. Debbie firmly believed that Wade had not beaten the boy, but she understood that the court would want him out of the house before Brian could go home. That had already been taken care of. After a huge argument that weekend, Debbie told Wade to pack up and move out.

"The marriage had been falling apart anyway—Wade was drinking too much; it was an instant replay of Dennis," Debbie explained later. "Wade told me that he hadn't done anything wrong to Brian and he wasn't about to jump through hoops—go to court, parenting class, and stuff—for a kid who wasn't even his. That blew me away. I thought he understood how much I love Brian. I thought we were in this together. I should have known."

The worker told Debbie that taking Brian home was out of the question. She was pleasant but direct: Brian's accusations against his stepfather were serious, and he also said that Debbie did not protect him. The worker had filed a formal petition with the court on Brian's behalf under Section 300(c), "The minor is suffering serious emotional damage . . . evidenced by severe anxiety, depression, withdrawal or untoward aggressive behavior toward self or others, as a result of the conduct of the parent or guardian."

"He is a very disturbed child," the worker told Debbie. "I'm not sure exactly how much of what he told me is the truth. But obviously, something has happened to him. We need to get this boy some help."

Most likely, the case would be transferred to the Department in Modesto, and Brian would be moved into the Children's Shelter there until the next scheduled hearing. Given the typical backlog, that could take two weeks, during which Brian would be with strangers and Debbie would see him only occasionally during arranged visits.

However, there was another possibility. If Debbie would agree with the social worker's recommendations and permit Brian to be placed with Debbie's mother, the case would remain in Santa Clara County. He would not have to go back to the shelter; he could live at his grandmother's until the next hearing. The social worker had already checked out the house, and it seemed fine. Brian himself had told the worker that he really liked staying there.

The worker finished speaking, but Debbie's mind was stuck back at the first part of her suggestion. "You mean you want me to give up custody?" Debbie asked, looking at her attorney in a panic. "I've fought my ex-husband tooth and nail for years to get custody."

"It's not giving up custody. This is only temporary, and it would certainly make things less traumatic for Brian," the social worker said. "Think about it. He would be living at Grandma's instead of at the shelter."

"And if he was at his grandma's, I could see him?" Debbie asked. The social worker explained that the judge would probably grant visits. Debbie could even move into her mother's home and see Brian every day. Debbie and her attorney conferred, but she did not have to think about it for long before she agreed.

"Brian is my world," she explained later. "He has been through everything with me—more than anyone else has, for sure. Brian has been through my battles with his father, through all my boyfriends, all our moves, all our ups and downs. In the end, it has always been Brian and me hanging in there together, taking care of each other. And that's the way it's going to stay."

• • •

At the detention hearing, Judge Edwards did what the social worker had predicted: he gave Brian's grandmother temporary custody of the boy, then set a date for a jurisdictional hearing in two weeks, where

Brian could be declared a dependent. If that happened, a more detailed plan for Brian and his parents would be established.

On the day of the jurisdictional hearing, Dennis Wright was walking toward the courtroom, trying to convince himself that everything was going to work out alright. This was not Divorce Court. There were different judges here, a whole new cast of characters. They would certainly recognize that he was the good guy, the one who was trying to keep his son safe.

Experts who study how humans think speculate that our experiences are the building blocks of our mind, just as cells are the building blocks of our body. Try as we may to come into a situation fresh and unbiased, we cannot help but understand it through the filter of our past. As soon as Dennis rounded the corner, he saw Debbie and the social worker gabbing like old friends, and that triggered old resentments. Debbie's lies and sob stories had always convinced the mediators and judges that she, much more than Dennis, had Brian's best interests at heart.

As Dennis passed them, he noticed that the social worker did not look away from Debbie to acknowledge his presence. "That gave me strange vibes," Dennis said later. "Especially after the conversation I had had with her the day before." Dennis had been expecting the worker to call, but he had not anticipated the kinds of questions she asked, questions that "in my opinion, overstepped her bounds." Did Dennis drink? How much? How often? Did he own weapons? Where did he keep these guns? What did he use them for? Had he ever hit his son? Had he ever threatened him? Had he ever threatened his ex-wife?

Dennis's first instinct had been to demand to know what these questions had to do with Brian being tied to a chair by his stepfather. But instead, he reminded himself that it was best to play by their rules, to kowtow if necessary. The only thing that demanding information had ever gotten him was a reputation for being unwilling to cooperate. So Dennis answered the social worker's questions directly and honestly. He had nothing to hide. Yes, he drank on occasion, but it was Debbie and Wade who were the big boozers. Yes, he had guns for hunting. Yes, he had threatened his wife, but not as much as she had threatened him. Dennis kept trying to bring up the subject of Wade, who, after all, was the problem here. But the social worker did not seem at all interested, and that confused and irritated him.

Dennis's confidence was shaken further when he walked into the courtroom and saw Brian, who was sitting at the far end of the table next to his attorney. The boy looked quickly away from his father. "I couldn't blame him for being pissed," Dennis recalls. "I kept whispering 'psst' to get his attention. I wanted to give him a thumbs-up that said, 'See, I didn't let you down. I told you I would be back for you.' But when Brian refused to look up, that really made me nervous. He was acting as if it was me, not Wade, who was responsible for this whole thing."

The private attorney that Dennis hired was already seated at the table and motioned for his client to join him. The day before, the investigating social worker had submitted an updated petition, which Dennis had yet to see. His attorney handed him a copy. "You better look through this," the attorney said. "You aren't going to like what you see."

Dennis turned to the "reasons for the hearing" and found what he expected. The petition alleged that "said minor has been the victim of inappropriate discipline in that he was tied to a chair by his stepfather and beaten." But when Dennis read the next allegation, he was stunned. The new petition also charged—and Dennis had to read it three times to believe it—that "minor states he does not want visitation with his father as father drinks to excess and has put a gun to his head to gain information about the stepfather."

"What!" Dennis shouted aloud. His lawyer patted him on the shoulder and told him to calm down. Just then, Judge Edwards took the bench. "But this isn't true," Dennis said in a loud voice, rising to his feet and looking around the courtroom. His attorney jumped up and lowered Dennis back into his seat.

The court officer announced the case and introduced everyone in the courtroom. "Good morning, Brian," the judge said, smiling broadly at the boy. But when he turned to face Debbie and Dennis, the smile was gone. "Good morning. I want to explain what is happening here today. A petition has been filed on behalf of your son, Brian. A petition is a legal paper which says that something has happened in your son's life which makes it necessary for the court to step in to protect him. If I find this petition to be true, it will give me the power to decide where your son will live, perhaps permanently. You must understand that this is a very serious legal proceeding having to do with the future care and control of your child. I will read the petition to you now unless you tell me that you have read it and understand it."

When the judge turned in Dennis's direction, his attorney started to speak, but Dennis beat him to it. "This is all lies, Judge! I never put a gun to his head! I would never do such a thing. When did he say this happened?"

"Mr. Wright, you need to calm down," Judge Edwards said evenly. "You have an attorney, and you will have your chance to speak."

"Oh, this is just great. Here we go again. I'm the bad guy, as usual."

"Mr. Wright, I'm warning you. I don't want to have to ask the bailiff to escort you out of the courtroom."

"Your Honor. We could solve this right now," Dennis continued, ignoring the admonition. "Someone put my boy up to saying these things. Ask him. Ask him right now while I'm sitting here whether I put a gun to his head."

Judge Edwards was not about to put an eight-year-old on the spot by asking him to speak in court against his father. The judge turned instead to the deputy district attorney who was representing the boy. The attorney leaned over and said something to Brian, who shook his head no. The attorney then addressed the bench: "My client has nothing to say other than what is already in the petition."

"I will never forget that moment for as long as I live," Dennis recalls. "Every eye in the courtroom was focused on me. Every eye but Brian's."

21

BRIAN:
THE PSYCHOLOGICAL
EVALUATION

In the end, Dennis submitted to the petition, but only after the line "father denies the substance of the minor's allegations" had been added. After declaring Brian a dependent, Judge Edwards set a date for the next hearing, at which time a plan for Brian's immediate future and a reunification plan for his parents would be presented. In the interim, Brian and both his parents were to be psychologically evaluated by a court-appointed therapist.

When it comes to children and families, judges have always turned to some immutable "higher truth" on which to base their decisions. The Puritans were following divine law by giving the children to their father; the natural law of the Enlightenment gave them to the mother.

But in modern law, decisions are not to be based on gender or racial stereotypes, on economics, or on the sanctity of the biological family. They are to be based on more flexible and more humane principles. In dependency hearings, the question is, Is this parent a "detriment" to this child? In custody hearings, the question is, What is in the best interest of the child?

"The 'best interest' standard does not mean that anyone—a neighbor or a friend can say, 'Come live with me,' and have a court change custody," Judge Edwards explains. "Under the law, a parent has a higher status, a greater right to a child than a nonparent. This is a societal value which provides some legal glue for keeping families together. To remove a child from a parent, the court must find that it would be detrimental to have the child remain with the parent.

"But, once that finding is made," the judge says, pausing for emphasis, "then the best interest standard determines who will get custody."

But when exactly is a parent a "detriment" to a child? What exactly does "in the best interest of the child" mean? With the old order of religion and economics theoretically displaced, another standard is needed on which to base these decisions.

Starting in the early 1970s, the social sciences rushed in to fill the vacuum. Psychology was heralded as the missing tool, a rational science that could chart, graph, and predict human behavior. Legislators who were rewriting foster care ordinances began referring to the "empirical evidence" of child-parent bonding studies. In drafting reunification law, they cited child development experts like Jean Piaget, and, in particular, they referred repeatedly to a slender book that was published in 1973, *Beyond the Best Interests of the Child.*

The authors—the legendary Yale University law professor Joseph Goldstein; Anna Freud, the great psychoanalyst and child development specialist; and Albert J. Solnit, professor of pediatrics and psychiatry at Yale—admonish the legal system in an Olympian manner. Our laws, while purporting to safeguard children, have never been written specifically for children. It has always been adults making laws that best suit adults, laws that are deemed fair and reasonable by adult standards. If society is truly going to act in a child's best interest, social policy and the courts that carry it out must be in accord with the inner world of the child.

Children, the authors emphasize, are not adults in miniature. They have unique psychological and developmental needs that the legal system has failed to recognize. The book introduced the legal community to the concept of "a child's sense of time." To Goldstein and his colleagues, a separation of any duration must be treated as the crisis it is for the child. A child has a "marked intolerance for postponement of gratification or frustration, and an intense sensitivity to the length of separations. . . . The younger the child, the shorter is the interval before a leave-taking will be experienced as a permanent loss accompanied by feelings of helplessness and profound deprivation."

The authors also introduced attorneys and judges to the notion of the "psychological parent," the one adult in a child's life—not necessarily a blood relative—with whom that child is most closely connected. Adults who have witnessed pregnancy and the birth process feel strongly possessive of their biological children. But young children, who are "emotionally unaware of the events leading to their birth," could not care less about something as abstract as blood ties. What registers in their hearts and minds "are the day-to-day interchanges with the adults who take care of them and who, on the strength of these, become the parent figures (the 'psychological parent') to whom they are attached."

Beyond the Best Interests of the Child provided the language for the emerging "psychological" era of juvenile and family law. In divorce mediation, the moderator is often as versed in psychology as in legal procedure. In child welfare departments, case workers are returning to school for courses and advanced degrees in family therapy. Some of the more progressive courts are doing what Judge Edwards says is still not "politically acceptable"—awarding custody of a dependent child to his "psychological parent."

"Biology still rules over psychology and sociology, so, for the most part, the psychological parent—the child's stepmother, his parent's partner in a gay relationship, his day care provider, a close neighbor—all take a secondary role and in some cases are not even allowed inside the courtroom," Judge Edwards explains. "It's a continuing struggle."

The outsiders who do have standing in courtrooms are "expert witnesses." In custody battles, therapists routinely testify as to whether the mother or the father is the child's psychological parent. Authorities on sexual abuse testify to the child's "hidden" symptoms of incest. In dependency hearings, psychological evaluators, armed with a battery of tests, assess the strength of the parent-child bond. They appraise a parent's capacity to change. They recommend whether or not a child should be removed from the home. As a result, the style and diction of many courtrooms have changed. In some settings, especially one with a reputation for being "psychologically oriented," as Judge Edwards's court is, the word "relationship" is heard as frequently as the word "rights."

"I am a little wary of saying that I am running a 'psychologically oriented' court because it sounds as if I might be caught up in psychobabble, which I'm not. We have a very sophisticated system," Judge Edwards explains. "So many of the children who are under court supervision, maybe half of them, are emotionally damaged. It is helpful to get a handle on their needs and to have a professional make therapeutic recommendations to the court."

If there is one consistent pattern in the history of the juvenile court, it is this: every reform that moves to help children also stomps on somebody's rights. There are those, like the public defender who was assigned to represent Debbie, who are convinced that psychology has taken precedence over the law.

An outspoken man with a florid complexion, Howard Siegel has for years been expressing outrage over the power granted to "so-called expert witnesses who claim to be able to predict future human behavior." Because a person behaved a certain way in the past, because his family of origin behaved a certain way, because he saw a certain pattern on an inkblot test, "these experts think the course of his life is set. Physicists don't even talk that way about atoms anymore. How can an imprecise science like psychology claim to predict something as mysterious, as utterly unpredictable, as human behavior?

"We have in large measure attributed super powers to these so-called experts," Siegel concludes. "Many of them are fine when it comes to therapy, counseling, and helping people work out their problems. But when they come into court with their litany of derogatory labels—'borderline personality,' 'narcissistic tendencies'—and those labels enter the court record as if they were gospel, it is not only wrong, it's fraudulent."

• • •

However, Howard Siegel cannot change the system, and in the end he agreed to have Debbie go for her court-ordered psychological evaluation. The day before it was scheduled, Siegel warned his client that these "psych evals," as they are known, can be traps. The client may think that she and the psychologist are getting along fine. She may think that she is answering every question as honestly and as straightforwardly as possible. But everything the person says or does—even the most innocent remark or action—can be twisted to take on deep psychological meaning. "Bam!" Siegel told Debbie, slapping the top of his hand against the opposite palm. "All this winds up in a report telling the judge you are Attila the Mom."

Debbie got one more warning: The psychologist she would see had a reputation as being biased against parents. Her reports are exceedingly well written and convincing, so social workers often request her services when they are trying to remove a child from a home.

"Good luck," the public defender told Debbie with an ironic lift of his eyebrow. "And just be yourself."

Debbie was understandably jittery when she arrived exactly on time at the therapist's office. She went to great pains to be neither too dressed up ("It might look like I was trying to hide something") or not dressed up enough. ("I didn't want to look like a slob"). She finally settled on crisply ironed jeans, a spotless white shirt, and cowboy boots. The therapist, too, was dressed casually in a loosely cut flowered dress, and her long gray hair was tied back with a brightly colored scarf. Debbie immediately felt more relaxed, since the therapist looked so benign and friendly, even motherly.

After Debbie was seated, the therapist explained that she would be asking questions and administering some psychological tests. There would be plenty of opportunities for Debbie to talk about herself and her life. "I know you didn't choose to come here, and I'm sorry you have to go through this," the therapist said. "I want you to understand that I don't work for the Department. I am independent and objective. I want to understand you and your son. I'll do my best to be as thorough as I can be."

The therapist obviously knew a secret about human nature that attorneys, journalists, and con men have all discovered independently: people in crisis are often desperate to tell the most intimate details of their lives. All the therapist had to do was to ask Debbie a simple question—"Why do you think the court sent you here to be evaluated?"—and then let her talk without interruption, nodding on occasion as encouragement.

"Why am I here?" Debbie began, glad for the opportunity to tell her story to someone in power. "I'm here because Brian is having problems and my ex-husband Dennis is crazy." Debbie, who is naturally talkative, slid into a breezy and rambling conversation about her childhood ("My father drank a real lot, but that was the thing to do in the military"), her marriage to Dennis, her breakup with Wade, her work as a bookkeeper, and her relationship with her son.

"We have always been very close," Debbie told the therapist. "I have had boyfriends and husbands, but Brian has always been, you know, the man of the house."

Debbie had been most worried about the tests. She knew that she had a good brain, but in school she always blew exams and struggled through with mostly Cs and Ds. The therapist assured her that this was a different kind of test. There were no right and wrong answers, nothing to blow.

In one test, Debbie was asked to draw a scene with a house, a tree, and people. She set to work with the brightly colored markers and drew a pleasant house with windows and a chimney. Standing close to the house and next to each other were Debbie, her daughter, and Brian. "I love flowers, so I also drew a garden and surrounded the house with flowers," Debbie recalls. "I guess it was a storybook kind of setting."

Another test resembled the kind of multiple-choice exams Debbie took in school, only, instead of math, the questions asked, "Which would you rather do: stay home and read a book or go to a costume party?" There must have been five hundred questions like that. At first, Debbie worried that she was missing some trick, but she quickly decided to just have fun. Of course, she would rather go to a party. Who wouldn't?

By the end of all the tests and all the talking, Debbie was exhausted, but she also felt confident. She had told the truth. She presented herself as a calm and intelligent person who had friends and a supportive family. The therapist could obviously see that she was trying hard to be a good mother.

• • •

Sitting in the courtroom, waiting for Judge Edwards to take the bench, Debbie was bent over her copy of the psych eval. She squeezed her hand on her temples and shook her head. "This is not who I am," Debbie said.

Debbie had not expected the therapist to give her the Mother of the Year Award. ("I know I'm not perfect. I know that Brian has been through a lot because of mistakes I made," she had confessed to the therapist.) But Debbie was completely unprepared for the derogatory eight-page, single-spaced report in front of her. She felt angry and betrayed, but she was also struck by the cleverness of the therapist. Nothing in the report was wrong exactly. Almost everything was correct in a vague kind of way. Yes, she had told the therapist that she was "feeling futile and was having trouble meeting her own goals." But who wouldn't feel futile in her situation? And yes, her emotions were often "angry and bitter toward Dennis." But what normal woman would not feel angry and bitter after what he had done?

The problem was the tone of the report and the way it twisted some things and overemphasized other things, until Debbie appeared to be a woman who could not be trusted with a dog, let alone a child. The sketch of the house that Debbie had drawn nonchalantly "indicated a remarkable immaturity, inaccessibility and mood change." How could one picture tell anyone that much about her? The report was filled with "these big old medical terms" that Debbie could hardly understand: "Lack of egocentrence with poor integration . . . borderline aspects to Debbie's personality. . . . She perceives Brian as an extension of herself." The therapist even managed to make Debbie's appearance—"No make-up, but long, long fingernails"—seem like a point against her. What did her fingernails have to do with her ability to be a decent mother?

Like anyone who has just gotten a devastating medical report, Debbie scrambled to find some reprieve, some proof that the prognosis was not as bad as it seemed. Debbie latched onto some glimmers of hope. She was described as "flexible and obliging. . . . She can be well-behaved and cautious. . . . She is energetic, courageous and goes along with the rules, especially in a work environment."

But the bottom line—a sentence that appeared near the end of the evaluation—was the one that really mattered: "Therefore it must be stated that her capacity to parent is minimal, even with an emotionally healthy child."

Debbie wanted to scream. She wanted to bring into court a parade of friends to testify that she was a good person, a mother who would die for Brian. This report was sick. There was only one consolation: Dennis's evaluation was even worse.

Sitting across the table from Debbie, Dennis was reading his evaluation. It was the story of his life ever since Debbie had set out to ruin it: an honest man goes forth into the world to perform one simple, well-meaning deed, and the world winds up crucifying him for it.

The house that Dennis had drawn "indicated a high level of insecurity and anxiety." His interpretation of the inkblots "strongly suggested an organic disorder with associated paranoid and depressive features." The therapist had even twisted the results of the one test in which Dennis came out looking like a somewhat decent human being: Dennis may have "distorted his answers in the direction of looking good and therefore may be more depressed and suspicious than his answers indicated."

The therapist concluded that "Dennis does not have adequate parenting capacity to meet the needs of his son on an extended basis. He has little insight and is not a candidate for intensive psychotherapy of the type that aims itself for understanding. Modification of his behavior will be difficult."

Dennis might have shrugged the whole thing off as psychological gobbledygook, another example of the system wasting money. But the therapist basically said that he was a bad father and would always be a bad father. Dennis could not live with that.

Earlier that morning, Judge Edwards had read the evaluations in his chambers. They were longer than the typical reports, and the therapist clearly did not have much hope for either of these parents. There was another report in the file that concerned the judge even more. A separate therapist had interviewed Brian and described him as "being one of the most disturbed children that I have evaluated in many months." Brian's drawings were chilling and lifeless. His house—which, in the most simple psychological terms, expressed his sense of security—was a hastily drawn square with no windows and no doors. His tree, the symbol of his sense of self, was a leafless, branchless line. Next to it stood two roughly sketched stick figures who were not touching. There were no eyes, no hair.

"That is me and my mom," Brian had told the therapist, and when she pointed to a mark in the corner so tiny that it looked like a slip of the pen, Brian had said flatly, "That's my dad."

While Judge Edwards considers these evaluations to be an excellent tool, he has read such alarming portraits a thousand times before. "Over and over, I have seen parents whom therapists describe as having 'no capacity to change' turn their lives around. I have seen many children come into court as 'hopeless cases' and leave twelve months later, happy, secure, and thriving children."

That was the message the judge wanted to get across to Debbie and Dennis. If they did the necessary work, "if, in this emergency, they can pull themselves out of their power struggle and focus on their son, there is hope."

Judge Edwards took the bench and was about to go through the preliminaries when Dennis sprang to his feet, waving a copy of the psych eval over his head. "Your Honor! Pardon the expression, but this is all such bullshit!"

"Mr. Wright. I warned you at the previous hearing. If you keep this up, you will have to leave the courtroom."

"But, Judge, I have the right to clear my name."

"Sit down, Mr. Wright," Judge Edwards ordered. "I understand that you are upset by some of the things in the psychological report. You could decide to take this to trial, and we could spend a lot of everyone's time and energy going back and forth arguing over every point in this petition.

"But I have also read Brian's report, and it is a disturbing one. Placing Brian with his grandmother has not worked out. She reports that Brian is out of control, either cowering in fear behind chairs or charging through the house. He has even been denying that he knows who his mother and grandmother are.

"Mr. Wright, I think we should use our energy to concentrate on the one thing that everyone in this courtroom agrees upon. Brian needs help, and we should get him the help he needs."

For a brief moment, Dennis thought about arguing. Then he nodded and slowly sat down. "It was the first time that anyone connected with this mess said anything that made any sense to me," he said later.

22

BRIAN: RESIDENTIAL PLACEMENT

AMERICA'S FIRST ORPHANAGE WAS OPENED IN NEW ORLEANS IN 1729 by Ursuline nuns to care for children left poor and parentless after an Indian massacre in Natchez, Mississippi. But in the New World, as in the Old, this was an exception. In general, abandoned and destitute children were treated no differently than their adult counterparts. Orphans and poverty-stricken adults and the mentally ill of all ages were either left to the streets or packed into abysmal almshouses, workhouses that were neither warmed nor ventilated, or jails that were swarming with vermin.

In the mid-nineteenth century, this treatment of children became a scandal, and intense debates raged in progressive parlors and legislative cloakrooms. The New York state legislature was among the first to respond to calls for reform by recommending that children be placed in private, subsidized asylums intended solely for youth.

The era of child saving took hold, and the righteous set out en masse to rescue the "deserving" children of the "undeserving" poor from their miserable lives on the streets. The federal government took a firm hands-off stance and refused to establish any national child welfare guidelines, licensing, or monitoring procedures. It was left to local jurisdictions, individual church groups, charities, and individuals to "save" children in any way they saw fit. Soon, redbrick institutions, large enough to contain hundreds of poor children and orphans at any one time, were constructed and proudly pointed out as monuments of significant social reform. With each ensuing epidemic of cholera and tuberculosis, each war, each wave of poverty and immigrants, the number of orphanages continued to grow well into the twentieth century.

But clearly, the reformers had not learned their history. They had not learned what happens when children are herded into large buildings and abandoned to the whims of their adult keepers. In these new institutions, children fared no better than their counterparts had fared in the almshouses of London or in the grim foundling hospitals of Florence, where children died by the thousands from communicable diseases during the Renaissance. In the New York House of Refuge, boys were beaten into submission and worked to exhaustion. New York City's Hebrew Jewish orphanage so underfed its wards that when the children were released at age fourteen it was noted that the boys consistently had a "weirdly short stature."

Brian was placed in a facility called Eastfield Ming Quong, which traces its roots, as well as its unusual name, back to the era of institution builders. In the second half of the nineteenth century, the Ming Quong Society of San Francisco devoted itself to rescuing Chinese immigrant girls from slavery and forced prostitution. Later, this group merged with the women of the San Jose Benevolent Society, whose cause was orphaned children. Using money donated by a "quiet bachelor," they built a small-scale institution for children just south of the downtown business area.

Over the next half century, institutions around the country began closing, the result of significant changes in social and economic policy. Children were no longer supposed to be sent to orphanages simply because their families were poor; instead, their mothers, often widows, were to receive adequate financial assistance so that they could remain at home. In 1935, to alleviate the crisis of the Depression, the first federal Mothers' Pension Act (Aid to Dependent Children, the precursor to today's Aid to Families with Dependent Children [AFDC]), was enacted and reduced the number of poor children needing out-of-home care.

In the late 1950s, scandals closed more institutions, including many in California's once model state hospital system. While bureaucrats were being paid handsome salaries, walls were crumbling and children were being underfed, overdrugged, and deprived of education and basic human contact. As California had once led the way with the creation of impressive institutions, it now led the nation in another direction. Across the country, community-based care, either in the home or in small, privately run facilities, became the ideal, and a twenty-two letter word was coined to describe the shift: "deinstitutionalization."

By the late 1970s, most of the nation's large institutions for children had been shuttered. The few that remain today—places like the legendary Boys Town in Omaha and Eastfield Ming Quong (EMQ) in Santa Clara County—have shed their Victorian images by moving children into new, smaller buildings and offering a wide variety of psychological services. In the vernacular of child welfare, they are called residential treatment centers. Like their predecessors, which took in victims of war and disease, residential treatment centers bill themselves as refuges, in this case for children who are victims of modern-day epidemics like drug addiction and broken homes.

In the continuum of out-of-home placement, residential treatment centers have the most restrictive setting, so few children come to a facility like EMQ as their first placement, and when they do, it is only because, like Brian, everyone is certain that no other place can or will handle them. Most of the children have lived for years in what social workers call "the black hole of placement failure." They have been removed from foster homes and group homes because they have attacked and molested other children. They have been in and out of psychiatric emergency clinics, where they stayed a day or two and were stabilized with tranquilizers and then sent on to yet another placement. They have been dropped off at the Children's Shelter by frustrated and terrified parents who did not know what else to do with them.

Unlike the orphanages of old, residential treatment centers do not keep children for the length of their childhood. A typical stay lasts between a few months and two years. "According to the law, we have a very specific, very practical goal," explains Jan Marx, who worked as a therapist at EMQ for sixteen years and is now its clinical program manager for the residential program. "Our job is to reduce the child's assaultive, violent behavior and stabilize the child enough to be able to move him to a less restrictive setting."

There are critics who say that this noble goal is totally unrealistic for many of the children who wind up in residential treatment. Why patch them up and return them to their parents when they are just going to "fail" again? Many of the proponents of long-term psychiatric care are operators of privately run centers and may be biased, but they also understand severely disturbed children as well as anyone. Says one, "You've got to ask, after the second or third or fourth foster care failure, when the child has set a fire, cut the cat's tail off, and attempted suicide, how come nobody has said, 'This kid needs psychological treatment and not just another foster home'?"

Money, as usual, is cited as the reason. Residential treatment is extremely expensive, especially when compared to the average $39 a day for "regular" family foster care. Room, board, clothing, medical care, special education, and round-the-clock therapy cost the same for a poor dependent child at EMQ as they do for a rich child whose family has hustled him off to a private lockup school in Utah that advertises in the backs of magazines like *Sunset* that it "effectively treats social withdrawal, noncompliance and self-destructive behaviors." To keep a child like Brian in residential treatment, the state, the county, and endowments by private charities combine to spend upward of $7,000 a month.

But money aside, there are other reasons residential treatment remains the refuge of last resort. Even a long-established and generally well regarded center like EMQ has been criticized again and again for what goes on behind its locked doors. Several years ago, state regulators threatened to revoke its license. In 1993, the California Department of Social Services issued a seventeen-page report enumerating "more than 200 runaways over a 3-year period, 14 sexual incidents among youngsters, and four incidents of theft from stores or residences. . . ." The report also listed "more than 200 incidents of excessive physical restraint, where counselors held children on the floor on their stomachs with hands behind their back for more than 20 minutes. One prone restraint lasted four hours."

An EMQ spokesman calls the charges overblown. Properly restraining a child is "legal and humane . . . and used only when a child becomes so enraged or uncontrollable that he puts himself or others in danger." So many of the residents have been sexually molested that it is impossible to wipe out all sexualized behavior without putting children in twenty-four-hour isolation. The spokesman emphasized that EMQ moves "quickly and efficiently to remedy problems." Its staff has extensive training. No child has ever been sexually or physically abused by a staff member.

"For many children, this is their last chance," the official told a newspaper reporter. "If EMQ were closed, these children would have to be moved to places like Napa State Hospital, to out-of-state facilities where they wouldn't be monitored, or to group homes that offer no therapy."

But in trying to defend its good name, EMQ bears the burden of history. The record we have accumulated for treating children in facilities with locked doors is not much better than it was in the days of foundling hospitals or almshouses. As social and medical historian David Rothman says, "When custody meets care, custody always wins."

. . .

"I was really nervous," Brian says, recalling the day when his social worker drove him to his new home, which resembles a suburban complex of doctors' offices. "But I had this friend at the shelter who said that, if you have to get locked up with all the other bad kids, Eastfield isn't so bad. It was the best place he ever lived, except that the food sucks."

They gave Brian a bedroom he shared with one other boy, "who played with Legos [building blocks] too much, but otherwise seemed OK." Brian even had his own dresser—"It was hands off to everyone else!"—where he could put his comics and other valuables. There were five bedrooms in Brian's unit and a common area with a couch, chairs, and a TV set. To Brian, the place seemed like the home of a big family, "except for the big glass cage where counselors lock their purses and spy on the kids."

On Brian's first day, the counselors explained that he could watch a few television shows in the evening if he earned enough points during the day. Points could also earn him a Friday night trip to Mountain Mike's Pizza or the chance to pick something out of the collection of plastic toys that were kept locked in the "reward closet." The young man who introduced himself as Brian's "one-on-one counselor" led the boy over to a wall and showed him that his name had been added to a behavior chart that was decorated with gold stars. "See," the counselor said. "You can earn points for just about everything."

At EMQ, there are points for getting out of bed when it is time and points for not getting back into bed until it is time. There are points for going to school and points for staying in school and points for coming right back to the unit after school. There are points for taking "meds" without throwing a tantrum—most of the children at EMQ are on one medication or another for depression, anxiety, or aggression.

"All kids need structure in their lives. But SED children [severely emotionally disturbed] thrive on it," says a counselor, explaining the philosophy behind the point system and the almost military precision in which every day on the unit unfolds. "Their inner self is so chaotic that having a life where they always get up at a certain time, then always brush their teeth, then always put on their shoes . . . well, it's a relief to them. They know exactly what to expect. They know exactly what to do to get a star on their chart. For maybe the first time in their lives, they can predict what is going to happen at noon, at dinner, at bedtime. It makes them feel safe, and a lot of them have never felt safe before."

Along with the general rules, each resident has a set of personalized rules. For instance, many of the children at EMQ have been sexually abused, and as a result, even though they are still in the latency period, they "act out like crazy." To earn points, these boys and girls are required to go a certain number of hours with no "overt sexualized behavior," which, a counselor explains, means no propositioning the adults, no humping other kids, no French-kissing their roommates, no masturbating. There are other children who, no matter how often they are checked, always manage to find minuscule pieces of glass, which they hoard like jewels. These children earn points for turning in the glass and not using the sharp slivers to draw blood on the insides of their wrists and elbows. This behavior is so prevalent among abused kids that counselors refer to them as "the cutters."

Brian's counselor told him that he would get a star if he went an entire morning without threatening or attacking anyone. Brian was also required to respect the boundaries of other people, just as everyone was required to respect his personal space. Many of the children in residential care have a terrible fear of intimacy and cannot tolerate normal physical proximity. One child on the unit would go off if someone looked him in the eyes for more than a few seconds. When counselors addressed him, they used only sideways glances.

To demonstrate the appropriate distance between children, the counselor held out his arm and stood that distance away from Brian. Brian was also told that if he wanted a hug from a counselor, he needed to "be appropriate" and ask first, rather than throwing his arms around the counselor and jumping up and down like a little monkey.

The counselor's official title was a mouthful—milieu-activity therapist—and he was taking a sabbatical after three years as a college psychology major, so "therapist," in any official sense, was a flattering exaggeration. His previous experience with children had been babysitting, working as a camp counselor, and doing volunteer work in a school for children with physical disabilities. This was his first real job, and it certainly paid like a starting position.

Milieu-activity therapists at EMQ spend eight hours a day, five days a week being emotionally bombed, cursed, spit at, and kicked. They are supposed to enforce strict rules without making the children feel like failures. They are supposed to develop a thick skin, yet they are also supposed to model warm and caring behavior, all the while being careful not to create an intimacy that these children cannot handle. Most of the staff are young and find it natural to be on the side of children who have been abused by their parents. "It's not so easy to put on a smiling face and feel compassion for the parents when they come visiting," says one counselor, "especially after they start criticizing me for the way I've been treating their child."

For all this, milieu-activity therapists earn not much more than they would make working full-time at McDonald's. There is an irony to the acronym for their job title—MAT, as in "doormat"—which does not escape them. "It's a totally crazy job. You have to really care about these kids," Brian's counselor says. "I myself love it. I have plans to become a therapist and work with children. Being with them all day . . . you can't beat this kind of experience. But a lot of people start out all enthused, then drop out. The emotional drain isn't worth it."

At the most, Brian and the other children see a psychologist or psychiatrist one hour a day. They might have an hour of group therapy. For the other twenty-three hours, it falls to the MATs "to give the child the opportunity to experiment and integrate normal developmental tasks," according to an EMQ training brochure. In effect, MATs are supposed to do what parents are supposed to do: use "teachable moments" to turn everyday behavior into learning experiences. Children in residential treatment have not developed the internal voice that enables most three-year-olds to distinguish "good" behavior from "bad" behavior. The MATs therefore provide a running commentary, a steady stream of microbehavioral analysis. "I like the way you walked across the room without spitting at someone." "It was good the way you said, 'You're welcome,' after I said, 'Thank you.' " "Good job putting on both of your shoes."

"Basically, our job is to help these kids experience a second childhood so they can become the children that they never had the opportunity to be," Brian's counselor explains.

Brian's honeymoon period at EMQ did not last twenty-four hours. At 7 A.M. he woke up charged with energy and cursed and clung to the sheets as the morning MAT tried to roust him. Brian's roommate, whose behavior chart was full of stars, suddenly became agitated and goaded Brian into throwing his Legos up in the air as if they were confetti. Both boys wound up being restrained.

At 10 A.M., when Brian was supposed to be sitting at his desk in class, he was storming around the room, huffing and puffing like a little steam engine. The other children took their cue and "started bouncing off the walls."

At noon, Brian slammed his forehead on the lunch table, upsetting four glasses of milk and causing three girls to start crying. At 3 P.M. he was rolling on the grass, pounding on a boy who had called him a name, and trying to fight off a counselor who was pulling them apart. At 3:30, Brian overturned a table full of sugar-free after-school snacks. Despite Brian's tearful promises to control his temper, despite his insistence that he really wanted to be at EMQ, he got into so many fights that he had to be restrained almost daily. He wet the bed almost every night and attacked any kid who teased him. He stole things out of his roommate's dresser. One afternoon, Brian ran out into the courtyard, a lush carpet of grass and willow trees. He grabbed a low-hanging branch and wrapped it around his neck, tighter and tighter. The other kids started screaming. The MATs started running.

Years after the incident, Brian remembers almost nothing of that day. He cannot say why he did it or what he was feeling or if he had really been trying to kill himself. For Brian, that entire period is mostly a blur, except for one memory that stands out with exceptional clarity. During his early days in residential treatment, he would pretend to be asleep whenever the counselor stuck his head in the doorway to check. Late at night, in the dark, Brian would tell himself that, finally, this day was done, day number one or day number two or day number eight. The days were bad, but the nights were even worse.

"At night, I felt so lonely and mad at stuff. I would do all these bad things all day long, and then in my bed I would just keep thinking about a certain song and how badly I treated my mom and how I missed everyone and how everyone here hated me. I can't remember the name of the song or anything. All I can remember is that it was a slow song, a really sad song."

23

BRIAN:
SCENES FROM THERAPY

THERAPY CAN BE DESCRIBED AS A MYTH. A HERO (THE CLIENT) SETS out from his comfortable home on a journey, guided by a wise man or woman (the therapist) who offers enigmatic and often scary counsel. During his adventure, the hero climbs mountains, battles demons, wins honors—each of these representing a life lesson that needs to be learned before the next step can be taken. In the end, the hero returns home, where everything has essentially remained the same. It is the hero who, having been scarred by his trials, is reborn and sees life anew, as it really is.

Jan Marx, the therapist assigned to guide Brian and his parents, is a middle-aged woman whose face is free of makeup and whose salt-and-pepper hair is cut into a no-nonsense bob. As the most experienced therapist at Eastfield Ming Quong, a large part of her job is to train, supervise, and "hold the hands" of the newer therapists, most of whom tend to be stylishly dressed, ebullient, and just a few years out of college. Compared with Marx, who has the slightly world-weary demeanor befitting somebody who has been through a divorce and raised three children, the younger therapists seem to have a lot to learn.

"Beginning therapists so often make the mistake of thinking that things are simple," Marx says. "They look at these children and feel their pain and feel so sorry for them. It's natural to want to blame the parents, to try to get the parents to change while seeing the child as an innocent party, a total victim, who needs to be rescued. That viewpoint might seem compassionate, but it does not do a thing to help."

What Marx has ascertained from her training, from the ups and downs of her own life, and, most of all, from sixteen years of sitting in the same room with some of the most twisted families on earth is this: in a family, no one is an innocent bystander. Every family is a system, and like all systems, from amoebas to societies to galaxies, the family has its "own rules, structure, leadership, language, style of living, and zeitgeist." As planets move through the solar system, pulled by the gravity of the sun and, at the same time, pulling other celestial bodies in complex orbits, so it is with families, happy as well as troubled. Each person influences and, in turn, is influenced by the others. Each member functions as a delicate counterbalance that keeps the family in harmony.

In troubled families, individuals behave in ways that seem bizarre and weirdly distorted but that make sense within the family orbit. They are making a desperate attempt to seek equilibrium, to keep the family from spinning off into an ever widening gyre.

On the surface, Brian appeared to be a pawn trapped between two powers. But, in truth, Brian's "craziness" served an extremely useful purpose: being out of control, he controlled his parents.

"Look at what his behavior actually managed to accomplish in his family system," Marx explains. "Now, I'm not saying that he was not treated horribly or that he did these things consciously. It was all unconscious, but he somehow kept his parents from killing each other. He kept them from killing *him*. And the way he played one parent off the other? That kept his parents in a very intense relationship with each other. As long as they were so involved, Brian could keep alive the fantasy that there would be a reconciliation—which is what most children of divorce want.

"Brian's 'crazy' behavior even managed to get him into the child welfare system, where he could get some help," Marx continues. "Innocent? This is very sophisticated, manipulative behavior. That boy had everything balanced just right, and children like Brian see their balancing act as being a matter of life and death. They will do anything to keep it going. The problem is that there was no way for Brian to live a normal life—to be a kid—while he was doing all that complicated emotional juggling."

So how could the system help Brian learn to live a "normal" life? The answer would seem to be, Cradle him in the protective arms of an institution. Don't subject him to any more of his parents' emotional upheaval. Don't waste thousands and thousands of dollars on therapy for parents who seem "incapable of ever making a meaningful psychological insight."

This would appear to make sense, but plucking the child out of the family system is not a psychologically sound solution. According to Marx, no matter how deplorably a child has been treated by his family, he remains enmeshed in that family. "There is a fantasy—and it is a huge, persistent fantasy—that if we can isolate the 'innocent' child and keep him emotionally safe, then we can fix him," she says. "But you can do all the goal setting you want. You can run residential treatment like it is a boot camp and do behavior modification twenty-four hours a day. But nothing is really going to happen until you connect with the whole family system in a truly meaningful way. That is the only way the child is going to be able to see his parents for who they truly are. And until he sees them, he really can't begin to disengage from them."

Marx gathers her thoughts for a moment, then continues: "This holds true for children who will eventually go home with their families and children who will remain in some kind of placement for their entire childhood. I have worked with children who have been able to go home and emotionally survive with horrible parents because they have managed to make an internal shift. I have also seen kids who have not seen their parents for ten years, but they blow out of one foster home after another. They can't settle in anywhere. That is because they are still emotionally all tied up with their family system."

When Brian entered EMQ, Marx began working with him, Debbie, and Dennis in individual fifty-minute-long sessions. After a few months, it became clear to the therapist that everyone in the family was feeling safer and less in crisis. However, in therapy, as in myth, nothing happens when the hero stays securely at home, so it was time for Marx "to make everyone less safe again." She scheduled a joint therapy session for Brian and his father, which would mark their first time together since the court hearing and since, what Dennis referred to as, the "accusation."

"In therapy, the idea is to create an emotional crisis in a physically safe environment, something that makes the parent say, 'I had better change or else,'" Marx explains. "In some ways, the way the dependency court system is set up—the fact that it creates the pressure of having twelve months to change or you lose your child—can be very beneficial. The idea is for the therapist to take advantage of that crisis, to intensify it. Fear can be a great motivator."

• • •

On the day of the father and son reunion, Dennis was waiting nervously in the therapy room and Marx was holding open the door for Brian. "Let's give it a try, Brian. I'll be in there with you the whole time." "But I can't go in!" Brian was shouting. "I'm afraid of my dad." He inched a step closer to the door, then stood there, not moving forward, but not stepping back either. "Brian," Marx said, softly but firmly, "you can always leave the room if you want."

That was all the encouragement Brian needed. He rushed through the door and flung himself on his father's lap, hugging and kissing him with the joy of a puppy. "Whoa, son!" Dennis said, startled but deeply pleased. Father and son were laughing with relief, and Marx allowed herself a knowing smile. The reunion was going much as she had predicted. Terrified of his father? Didn't want anything to do with him? That version of the story of Dennis and Brian had come from somebody else's myth—Debbie's myth—and had changed as soon as Brian was under no pressure to live it.

"I was never convinced that Dennis actually pointed a gun at Brian's head, as Brian claimed," Marx said later. "The timing of the accusation was too perfect. Very likely, it was Brian's desperate way of keeping things even between his parents. If he hurt one parent, he needed to even the score and hurt the other."

Real life, of course—even the rarefied real life of a therapy session—is never so literary as a myth. A lesson learned one day is forgotten the next. A dragon slain reappears in another form, fresh and revived. Therapists who work with severely emotionally disturbed (SED) children and their families cannot cling to the fantasy of magical transformations. They know that genuine change—if it ever does happen—is truly mysterious and often excruciatingly slow.

One of the most difficult things about working with a family is getting everyone involved to agree upon what the goal is. "You make what you think is some progress, but then the court system does something that sabotages it," Marx says. "A social worker gives a parent visitation when the therapist doesn't think that is the best idea at the time. The father wants the MAT [milieu-activity therapist] to do something one way and the mother wants the MAT to do something another way. There is a child advocate who thinks that she has the answer."

If Brian's "progress" during his stay at EMQ were charted on graph paper, it would look something like this: long flat lines, followed by sudden peaks and equally dramatic plunges. "Weeks and weeks can go by when nobody seems to be getting anything, no insight at all," Marx explains. "I can spend forty minutes out of every fifty-minute session just getting through the barriers, just getting everyone to stop blaming their ex-husband, their social worker, the judge. All I can hope for is that every once in awhile, somebody has a flash of insight, a breakthrough, a moment of aha!"

• • •

In the therapy room were balls, blocks, and a big basin filled with sand and plastic figurines—men, women, children, animals, furniture—and Jan Marx encouraged Brian to do what he liked with them. The theory behind play therapy is that a child learns best through play; he is his own best teacher. To learn a cartwheel, a child will try again and again, making minor and subtle adjustments to his body until he can finally flip. Gymnastics teachers don't lecture about physiology and the physics of a body in motion. The teacher may offer a tip or two, but she is basically there to keep the child from breaking his neck. Play therapy works much the same way: with minimal interference from the therapist, the child is free to experiment with his own emotions, to play out his inner battles over and over again in an environment that is physically and emotionally safe.

Brian began the session by staging a battle between two Lego men, and Marx immediately noticed what she always notices in the war games of children in residential care: in Brian's battle, there were no clear-cut good guys and no clear-cut bad guys. "Most boys in this age group set up one side that's good and one that's bad, and they play until one side wins. But with SED children, the battle quickly becomes impossible to follow. You can't tell who is on which side or who is winning or even when the game is over. There is always something muddling it up."

After Brian's war fell apart, he turned to a pile of stuffed animals. With a fastidiousness unusual for him, Brian lined them up, then pointed his index finger at Marx's face. "You are the director of the animals and I am the doctor," he said with authority. "Bring these sick animals to me."

"OK, Doctor." Dutifully, Marx picked out a brown bear with a perky red bow. "H'm," Brian the doctor said, peering into the bear's ear. "Take this medicine and you'll be OK soon." He put the bear aside and called for the next patient, a rabbit with soft white fur.

"Does this hurt?" Brian said, pulling the tail. "I thought so." He turned his finger into a hypodermic needle and gave the rabbit an injection in the bottom. "Ouch!" the rabbit said in a squeaky voice. "Don't be a crybaby!" the doctor scolded. "Next patient."

The next sick animal was a kitty. Brian the doctor slammed the kitty on the floor several times. "You go to the hospital!" The next patient, a giraffe, had a stomachache that the doctor "cured" by punching him hard in the gut. For extra measure, he twisted the legs until the giraffe "begged" the doctor to stop.

Marx could not resist stepping in and "heating things up just a little more." When the doctor commanded "Next!" Marx pointed to a duck. "What do you imagine that this duck is thinking?" she said nonchalantly.

"He's thinking that he's going to be cured."

"And is he?"

The doctor hesitated. "Maybe he is." The doctor took the giraffe and again slammed it hard on the floor. "And maybe he isn't."

"And how do you think the duck is feeling?" Marx asked.

"Scared!" Brian said boldly. "Because I'm a scary doctor."

For several weeks, Scary Doctor remained one of Brian's favorite games. He played it obsessively, almost verbatim, starting out as the kindly physician and deteriorating into a demented doctor of doom. Eventually, Brian's infatuation waned, and the doctor became less diabolic and less enthusiastic about his tortures. Finally, one day, the game just stopped.

"I never said to him, 'Brian, you are really working through this idea that good people can suddenly and without any reason turn bad,' " Marx explains. "But through this game of his own invention, he began to understand that. And he was probably beginning to understand something about himself as well: like most of the adults in his life, Brian, too, can't always be trusted."

·   ·   ·

For months, Marx had been holding joint sessions with Brian and his father and with Brian and his mother, and they were going reasonably well. Debbie was showing signs of understanding what Marx meant when the therapist explained that her "closeness with Brian" was much too intense. Dennis was not automatically flaring up when Marx suggested that his fathering style confused the boy because it bounced from rigidity to indulgence. Now that progress was being made, it was time "to heat things up again."

"I knew I was going to have to get everyone in the same room at the same time," Marx explains. "It's a big step because some of these families . . . well, they can't be in the same room without violence erupting."

Tension was high when Marx lead all three to a room furnished with a sofa, chairs, and tables. Across one wall was a one-way mirror, and Marx explained that a second therapist, who would be talking to her via a headset, was sitting behind the mirror. This way, there were two sets of eyes to see and two brains to help direct what was going on. Brian stuck out his tongue at the mirror, and Debbie and Dennis shifted uncomfortably. "The rule is that, if it gets too uncomfortable in here for anyone, it is OK to leave and go sit behind the mirror and watch," Marx began. "You can come back in once, but then if you leave again, that's it for the session."

After a few more preliminaries, Marx made a suggestion: "I want to go back to an incident that seems really pivotal to this family." During their individual sessions, both Dennis and Debbie had talked about a night when Brian was still an infant. Dennis had been watching the baby while Debbie went to a party, "one of those all-gal deals where they sell lingerie and makeup," Dennis had told Marx. In Dennis's version of the night, he had taken baby Brian over to a friend's house, and when it got late and all the kids were asleep, the dads decided to have a few beers. In Dennis's version, Debbie came bursting through the front door, "drunk and screaming like a raving lunatic."

In the version Debbie told Marx, it was Dennis who was drunk and who had behaved like a lunatic. Dennis had slapped her. To protect Brian, she had grabbed the baby and run out to the car. Dennis had chased them down the highway at ninety miles an hour.

"Today, I want to go through that night, step by step," Marx explained. "Dennis, you said you were at your friend's house baby-sitting. Brian, I believe you were asleep in a corner."

"First of all, he's a goddamn liar," Debbie broke in. "He wasn't at his friend's house; I had to track him all over town until I found him at a bar. Wouldn't you be mad? Taking an infant to a bar! He was supposed to be baby-sitting, not out getting drunk."

"Tell him, not me," Marx suggested and nodded in Dennis's direction. Debbie swung around and shouted in Dennis's face: "You were a fucking asshole to take a baby to a bar."

"Keep it in the present," Marx ordered. "You *are* a. . . ." The wounds from that night had been festering for years, and Dennis and Debbie immediately became the Dennis and Debbie they had always been.

"What's your problem?" Dennis came back at Debbie. "The baby's OK. There's a bunch of us here watching him. And where the hell were you? You're the one who's drunk."

"I'm taking my kid out of here, and you'll never see him again." Debbie started walking toward the baby; Dennis put out his arm to block her. "You're not driving anywhere drunk with my kid."

Debbie flinched. "Don't you hit me."

"I didn't touch you!"

As the scene gathered force, the "baby" in the corner grew more and more agitated. Brian flipped over a chair. He started bouncing on the couch. He ran up to his mother and pulled on her arm, demanding that she stop playing this stupid game. Finally, Marx halted the action: "Brian, do you want to stay in here or do you need to go behind the glass?"

"He's going to hurt her!" Brian shouted.

"I'm here. Nobody will hurt anybody," Marx assured him. Looking doubtful, Brian allowed Marx to lead him out of the room and into the smaller, darkened room behind the mirror. The second therapist placed a headset over his ears so that he could hear everything going on. "You can come back in anytime you're ready," Marx said and walked out the door.

Back in the therapy room, the scene had shifted from the bar to the home they once shared. Dennis was standing on the doorstep, pounding and pounding on the door with the butt of his shotgun. "Let me the fuck in," he was demanding. Debbie whipped open the door and stood there, a terrified look on her face. She turned, "ran" down the hall to the baby's room, picked up Brian, and cradled him in her arms. Dennis was right behind her, carrying the shotgun, poking it at her behind. When Debbie turned toward him, he lifted the gun and pointed it at her face.

In the therapy room, as she had done in baby Brian's room that night, Debbie let out a piercing scream. Her entire body was shaking, and she was suddenly drenched in a layer of sweat. "I can't take it anymore," she started to sob and rushed past Marx through the door and out into the hallway. "I can't live this way!"

Marx took off after her and reached her just as Brian came tearing out of the back room. "Tell him that you are OK!" Marx urged Debbie. "Tell him that he doesn't have to take care of you just because you feel terrible."

"Mom! Mom! I'll kill him!" Brian kept shouting.

"Tell him!" Marx insisted.

Between gulps of air, Debbie got out the words. "I'm OK, Brian. I'm OK."

After everyone calmed down, Debbie and Dennis walked out of the therapy room with a much different demeanor than when they had walked in. "They seemed more at peace somehow," Marx recalls. "They were not friends—probably they would never be friends—but they no longer seemed to be enemies. There was a sense that they were in this together. In the mirrored room that afternoon, they saw a new reflection of themselves: Both were responsible for the violence that night and for the violence of their marriage; both had been victims and both had been victimizers."

Brian had glimpsed something as well. He saw how his mother, even sobbing hysterically, could find the inner strength to take care of herself, that he did not need to do it. He saw how one story could take on so many different shapes; there was no reason for him to figure out which was the truth about that night, because, in fact, neither of his parents' versions alone was the truth. In the "real" world behind the mirror, there existed a bigger truth that encompassed both.

"You know something," Brian told Marx later. "Neither of them gave a damn that I was just a little kid. My father could have killed us. My mother put me in a lot of danger. That used to happen a lot. They'd be screaming at each other, and I'd get in the middle and she would just hold me there, hugging me. He wouldn't even see me. They were both assholes that night. They were both assholes a lot."

• • •

During Brian's almost two years in residential treatment, the insights were followed by setbacks that were just as dramatic. When his parents showed signs of making progress and becoming united in their approach, Brian, feeling that he was losing control of the only universe he knew, would "blow out to the point of needing constraints."

"The whole court system plays into this," Marx explains. "The family starts looking better, and social workers get excited and decide to increase the amount of time parents can spend with their child or they start talking about sending the child home again. Everyone is all optimistic, but as the time gets closer, the child starts feeling nervous and unsafe. Suddenly, this child who is so 'improved' tries to commit suicide or runs away or attacks another kid."

• • •

That was clearly Brian's pattern. One report would say that Brian had made "significant progress"; sure enough, the next report would describe him as having "dramatically regressed," saying that he had "managed to lose all of his friends. . . . He lies compulsively and has three to four nocturnal diuretic episodes per week."

All the while, Dennis and Debbie were whizzing through their reunification obligations. The social worker assigned to Brian's case was extremely optimistic about this family, more so than many on her caseload. It was not that Debbie and Dennis were easy to get along with—the social worker's phone sometimes rang ten times a day with one parent or the other calling to berate her or to report some infraction. "Oh, they were totally out of control and a real headache," recalls the worker, Gayleen Williamson. "The reason I was so optimistic is kind of ironic: these parents were so competitive, so at war, that they did not dare do anything wrong for fear of making the other parent look good in comparison. Whether they were genuinely determined to face the truth of their lives or whether they were just competing with each other for the perfect attendance report did not really matter at this point. What mattered was that they were putting out tremendous effort."

Debbie was diligent in attending twice-weekly AA meetings and her parent education classes. Not to be outdone, Dennis shined as one of the stars in his parenting class. His hand was always among the first to shoot up when the instructor asked for volunteers to play "the difficult son" or "the indulgent dad." At graduation, a letter of commendation was placed in Dennis's social service file that called him "a skilled problem solver. . . . He is respectful and seeks fair solutions. He struggles to understand his feelings and the feelings of others."

In court, at both the twelve-month and eighteen-month review hearings, there were kudos as well. Judge Edwards congratulated Debbie and Dennis for having completed their reunification plans. But Brian was not yet ready to go home. He spent six more months in EMQ, going to his mother's or father's home every other weekend, then every weekend, and then every day to his mother's home, until, finally, he was ready to say good-bye to the MATs and Jan Marx and to live with his mother.

When Debbie moved back to Modesto, Brian's dependency case was transferred to that county. Several months later, the court declared the reunification successful and the case was closed. The original divorce court order kicked in, giving the mother custody and the father visitation rights.

Several times, Dennis made the familiar Saturday morning drive through the fog and over the Altamont Pass. Then, one day, Dennis made a momentous decision: "I could feel the whole thing starting again. All the anger, all the games," he says. "Debbie was supposed to be taking him to therapy, and I felt strongly about that. I didn't want the time he spent at Eastfield to be wasted. But she stopped taking him, and I started in on her and she started in on me and there we were again.

"It finally came down to what I could do. I had learned something in therapy: a lot of times, my trying to come to Brian's defense just made things worse for him."

Dennis stopped his Saturday visits. When Christmas arrived—*his* Christmas, according to the custody order—Dennis called Debbie to say that Brian would be better off spending it with her.

"Maybe in the future, Brian will want to see me," Dennis says, pain in his voice. "But I need to wait until he makes the call."

24

THE THROWAWAY

BEHIND HIS PATERNAL GRANDPARENTS' HOUSE IN THE MOJAVE DESERT outside the town of Barstow, where Jesse Montgomery* went to live after his mother had kicked him out, there was a rickety old toolshed, too hot to enter in summer, cold and damp in winter. One spring afternoon, the fifteen-year-old in the tie-dyed T-shirt sneaked out to the shed and smoked a joint as he fashioned a noose. Jesse threw the rope over a beam and made sure the length was right. Then he stepped up on a chair, pulled his long sandy brown hair off his shoulders, and placed the noose around his neck.

It was the latest in a series of rendezvous with suicide that would have been comic had Jesse been a character in an existential novel. For months, Jesse had been sneaking a knife out of his grandmother's kitchen and going into the bathroom and sitting on the edge of the tub. He would stare at the knife and eventually begin running the blade over his wrist, gently at first, then harder, but never hard enough to open a vein. He always ended up sneaking back into the kitchen and slipping the knife back into the wooden block, deeply disappointed in his lack of courage.

There was also the time Jesse sneaked into the den and took one of the .22 pistols out of the glass cabinet that held his grandfather's gun collection. Jesse loaded the weapon and was holding it to his temple when a cousin burst in. His grandmother dismissed the event as idiotic and accused Jesse of staging it to drive her crazy. His grandfather screamed that Jesse was "weak, miserable, disgusting." "I'll fix you," Jesse thought. "Next time, I'll use your favorite gun."

The favorite gun was a little Baretta his grandfather had a license to carry in an armpit holster. (The grandfather owned a coin-operated car wash that was always being robbed; sometimes he would drive past in the middle of the night, hoping to catch thieves in the act.) Jesse waited until he was sure that his grandparents were sound asleep, then tiptoed down the hall to their bedroom and slipped the Baretta out of its holster. He returned to his room, shut the door, put the pistol to his head, and, without any thought, pulled the trigger.

Or tried to pull it. The gun would not fire, no matter how hard Jesse jerked the trigger. The Baretta had jammed. Jesse had to sneak back into his grandparents' bedroom and put the pistol back in its holster. Now, in the intense heat of the old shed, Jesse was giving suicide yet another try. He took a last long hit off his joint and jumped off the chair as he was exhaling.

Jesse found himself in a rainbow-colored heap on the floor, mumbling "What the fuck?" as he looked up at the dirt and dust and wood fibers that were drifting down on him. Dry-rotted through and through, the old beam had snapped.

That was Jesse's final attempt at suicide. On that afternoon, he decided to live with the problems that had defined his life, as formidable as they were. "If I had tried so many times and failed miserably every time, I figured I must be here for a reason," Jesse says.

• • •

As complex as it is, human behavior is in the end understandable. Human beings do things for a reason; those reasons may be largely unconscious or seemingly quite crazy, but they are there. Jesse's evolution from a bright little boy into a suicidal, sad-eyed, slow-talking teen (Jesse hangs onto vowels, rolls them out slowly—"I saaaid, Duuude, dooon't tell me that. . . .") is not much different from the thousands of "throwaway" kids who have nasty-looking scars running across their wrists and who end up pregnant or permanently stoned or making headlines with a weapon.

In the past, the law labeled a boy like Jesse a "status offender." Status offenders did things that were illegal only if done by minors—running away, not going to school, drinking alcohol, being beyond the control of their parents. The system sometimes responded by locking kids up for doing these things, sometimes for long periods of time. Children's rights advocates argued that status offenders were being treated as criminals when they had in fact committed no crime, and the category was finally removed from the law books in California in 1978. Many states followed suit.

Since then, the debate over whether this was the right thing to do has been ongoing. On one side are probation officers and district attorneys who believe that runaways and truants are budding juvenile delinquents. The sooner the system locates and begins working with them, the less likely they will develop into full-blown juvenile delinquents. On the other side of the argument are those who believe that children who have not committed a crime have no business being in a system that deals with minors who have.

The argument is somewhat academic. What both sides will agree to is that, since status offenders were removed from juvenile court, services designed specifically for truants and runaways have not been created. As a result, the category of status offenders was replaced by a new group that does not appear in law books: throwaway children.

Throwaway kids like Jesse grow up knowing that they come first with no one. Or second. Or third. Jesse loves his mom and dad and won't let go of them. But throughout his life, they have let go of him, time and time again. In his dress and in his eagerness to be kind and to believe that the world is essentially benign, Jesse resembles the hippies of thirty years ago. But long hair and tie-dyes do not mean he is trying to re-create The Furry Freak Brothers. These things are Jesse's way of expressing a connection to his father.

Jesse was born in the late 1970s to Danny, an acid-using musician and a career Deadhead, and Tracy, his wife. Jesse has always found it strange that for all of his father's pilgrimages to Grateful Dead concerts and all the hours of tape in his private collection, America's gypsy band appears to have had no influence on his music. Danny has always written songs with titles like "Wiggly Titties," songs with lyrics like "People always ask me but no one really cares / Why do fat people always stick to vinyl chairs?"

It is only after considerable thought—and with a marked sense of relief—that Jesse comes up with a job his father held when the son was little. What does come quickly to mind are his parents' favorite drugs. "My mom never got into the heavy stuff," Jesse says. "Her forte was wine and marijuana." Tracy, slender and pretty, a redhead with green eyes and freckles and a piercing, head-turning laugh, was, like her husband, a small-time dealer. The couple bought a kilo of grass, sold dime bags to their friends, and plowed the profits into another kilo. By the time Jesse was a toddler, Danny had escalated to cocaine. He would come roaring into their apartment at 2 A.M., coked-up friends in tow, and crank up the stereo.

Jesse was five when his mother packed their bags and left a coke-using acidhead to marry a methamphetamine freak. Earl, Jesse's new stepdad, had grown up in Hollister, a small farming town south of San Jose. From the time Earl was little, he identified with the motorcycle gangs that took over the town one weekend. (*The Wild One*, the film in which a woman asks a young Marlon Brando, "What are you rebelling against?" and Brando replies, "Whaddya got?" was based on the event.) Earl's fondest memories are the street rods he put together as a kid, the nights he and his buddies outran the cops.

Earl ran a small auto body shop in south San Jose. At home, he snorted crank and mellowed his jags by smoking grass and drinking wine with Jesse's mom. They were, in their way, a happy family. Earl loved Jesse's mom and called home three or four times a day just to talk. Tracy had always dreamed of going back to school, getting a GED, and then earning a degree in practical nursing. Earl not only made sure she went, but he also bought her a new car to drive back and forth.

Little Jesse became so much like Earl that his stepdad jokingly called him "Little Earl." Jesse insisted on wearing a black baseball hat with "NAPA Auto Parts" on the front, just like the man he called "Dad." When Earl had an errand to run, Jesse beat him to the 1954 Chevy pickup. Jesse says, "I loved hanging around the auto body shop, loved to have Earl tell me to go get a ⁹/₁₆ socket wrench and then hear him tell an employee, 'That little guy knows this shop as good as we do!' "

As a rule, it takes time for a family to fall apart. Drugs and alcohol, affairs, debts, and fights erode the foundation, and then one day an event occurs that brings everything tumbling down. Jesse remembers the day his life began "turning to crap" with the vividness that people recall what they were doing when an earthquake hit.

He was ten when his mother told him that his biological father was going to be checking into the motel down the street and spending three or four days visiting. Jesse could not sort out his own memories of his father from the bad things his mother had told him. He shrugged at the news of a visit. But inside "I was excited about meeting the man who was probably more like me than anyone in the world, except for my mom."

From their first dinner together, Jesse felt badly confused. Earl was acting really weird, not looking up from his plate, leaving the table to bang pots around in the kitchen, jumping up again to smoke a cigarette on the porch. Jesse was sitting there with his own problem: what to call this cheerful guy with the long hair and turquoise bracelets? "Danny," like his mother did? Or "Dad"? Something told him that calling this new guy "Dad" would be telling Earl that he was not his real dad. But how could he call his real dad anything but "Dad"?

For a day or two, Jesse mulled his dilemma over and avoided calling his father anything but "hey." Finally, he made his decision: His dad would be "Dad"; Earl would be "Earl." It was the wrong move. "Ever since then, Earl and I have never been able to get along," Jesse says, his voice flat and matter-of-fact.

Some kind of break had occurred. It wasn't that Earl had ever been overtly affectionate; he wasn't the type to put an arm around Jesse and say, "You're my son, I love you." But there had been an unspoken bond there—Jesse was an extension of the woman Earl loved. Now, overnight, that bond vanished. "I wasn't 'Little Earl' anymore," Jesse says. "Now, I was that 'little fuckup,' 'that ungrateful little asshole,' that 'wiseass little punk.' "

Jesse stopped hanging around the auto body shop and stopped knocking around in Earl's Chevy pickup. If Jesse spilled a glass of milk, it was never an accident in Earl's mind; it was because the twelve-year-old didn't give a fuck. If Jesse complained that Kathy, his four-year-old half sister, had taken something from his room or wouldn't stop tormenting him, the fault was always Jesse's.

One day, Earl crossed the line from verbal to physical abuse, slapping Jesse hard enough to cause a nosebleed. "From that day on, if I gave Earl a dirty look or mouthed off to my mother, if I didn't answer a question right away or my room wasn't clean, Earl would fly into a rage, pull off this wide leather belt he always wore, double it up, and give me a whipping." There came a time when Earl didn't just use his belt on Jesse, he used his brass belt buckle; when he didn't just slap the boy, he punched him with his fists. There were days when Jesse showed up at school "with cauliflower ears, two black eyes, and a limp from where Earl had kicked me in the leg." His friends knew what was happening, but if a teacher or school official ever noticed, they did not mention it.

Earl's poundings turned Jesse into a miniguerrilla warrior who used the weapon the weak always use against the strong: the brain. Jesse knew exactly what buttons to push: "You can't do that. You're not my *real* dad."

And he became adept at arranging fights between Earl and his mother. He would tell Tracy that Earl said one thing and tell Earl that Tracy said another. It worked like magic: the fight would start, and Jesse would step back and watch. "They were just stupid little arguments that got bigger and bigger," Jesse says in hindsight. "I was pretty good at starting them. It got to a point they were going to divorce. That's how good I was."

Jesse's mother tried to ignore the war between her husband and son until there was no living with them. They could not have a meal together without going at each other. At night, instead of getting a nice buzz on and enjoying whatever was on television, Earl ranted about how the kid was ruining their lives. When Tracy finally had to choose, she chose the man who bought her the new cars and sent her to school, the man who let her smoke her grass and drink her wine. She told Jesse, "I'm sorry, but you are only under my wing for eighteen years. I'm under Earl's for life."

"My mother is real sweet, real caring. I love her to death, love her far too much to blame her for anything," Jesse says. "But I do feel that sending me away was unfair."

Tracy called Jesse's father and told Danny that she didn't care where he was living, what he was doing, what his problems were, he was getting Jesse. She drove her twelve-year-old son to the Greyhound bus station and bought him a one-way ticket to Los Angeles, where Jesse found his father sharing an apartment with a crank and cocaine dealer.

In the year that followed, Jesse lived in fear that at any minute the cops would come bursting in. Customers came and went around the clock, and when Jesse cleaned (cleaning was how he earned his keep), he found wads of cash and sandwich bags of white powder stashed under cushions. His father was like a compulsive eater with a five-pound box of chocolates, consuming all the drugs he could and then doing more.

Meanwhile, Jesse was developing a way of coping that therapists call "parentified behavior," a sad role reversal that happens when a parent acts so irresponsibly that a child is forced to behave as the adult. Jesse cleaned house and rustled up meals; he reminded his father when it was time to take a shower and did his best to get him out of the apartment, away from the drugs. One night, his father was in his usual place on the couch, chopping up lines on the glass coffee table. Jesse was scrawny and shaggy and there was dirt under his nails, but he marched up to his father and said, "Dad, if you don't stop doing this, I am going to have to take drastic measures."

His father thought that it was hilarious, but Jesse was dead serious. While his middle school classmates were worrying about who liked whom and were struggling with schoolwork, Jesse was trying to figure out what he had meant by "drastic measures." Should he tell the principal about his father? The school nurse? One of his teachers? Should he go to the cops? What if he did and his father got sent to jail?

Jesse finally did what children who have too much responsibility thrust upon them often do: he sacrificed himself. "I didn't want to go back to live with Earl, but I was afraid if I stayed I'd tell somebody and my dad would get arrested. So I ended up calling my mom and telling her that I'd learned my lesson. Earl had been right about everything; I was a little asshole. If I could just come home, there wouldn't be any more problems."

Earl refused to consider it. Instead, Tracy talked Jesse's paternal grandparents into taking the boy. They were licensed foster parents, and they had cared for strangers' kids; surely they could take in their own grandson. Tracy went to court and signed the legal custody of Jesse over to his grandparents, and Jesse got another one-way bus ticket, this time to Barstow.

From the moment Jesse landed in the hot, bleak desert, he hated it, hated living with two old people and having no friends and nothing to do. His grandparents accepted him only after his father had promised to visit every weekend, and in the beginning Danny showed up almost every Friday. But he spent most of the weekend in the living room, telling Jesse's grandmother about his problems. After a couple of months, he stopped coming.

Saying the calls cost too much, Jesse's grandmother would not let him phone his mother. Jesse knew that she was lying and was trying to sever his relationship with his mother. That aggravated Jesse more than the fact that his mother never called him. His grandmother was smothering, always doing "really annoying little stuff."

"She was always power-tripping me, and when I didn't fall for that, she'd lay a guilt trip on me," Jesse recalls. "When I caught her at that and let her know about it, she started saying bad stuff to my grandfather, which put me on his bad side. I stopped getting attention altogether, so I resorted to doing bad things."

Smoking marijuana came first. Then Jesse began cutting class, sneaking back home when his grandparents were out, and rummaging through the house, looking for things to steal. His favorite target was two big jars that were full of the quarters his grandmother saved to play the slots in Las Vegas. Jesse skimmed a handful at a time, shaking the jars to make it look as if none were missing.

One afternoon, he just took both jars. He went out to the shed and also took the power mower. He called a guy he had met and traded the quarters and the lawn mower for a small go-kart. The guy drove him to an abandoned subdivision, and for one great evening "I felt free, buzzing over streets that had weeds growing in cracks. It was the first good time I'd had in years."

When Jesse got home that night, his grandparents were waiting in the kitchen. Their lips were pursed; their faces were blank. They told him to sit down. "Jesse, why do you think your mother doesn't want you?" his grandfather asked.

"Why doesn't your father visit anymore?" his grandmother asked before he could answer.

Jesse shrugged. "We'll tell you why: because you are no good, that's why!" his grandfather yelled, leaning across the table to look Jesse in the eye. "We take you in; we give you a roof over your head. All we ask in return is a little consideration, a little human decency. And what do we get? A thief! A thief who doesn't even have the gumption to go out and steal from others. This thief steals from his own blood!"

Jesse bowed his head and focused on the red Formica. There was a long silence. "Well, what do you have to say for yourself?" his grandmother finally asked.

Jesse said, "Nothing." His grandparents fell back in their chairs and looked at each other in disgust. Had he been able to, Jesse would have told his grandparents that they were absolutely right: he was definitely no good. His mother had chosen a jerk like Earl over him; what did that make him? Had his father liked him half as much as he did drugs, they could have made it together in Los Angeles.

It was after that night in his grandparents' kitchen that Jesse began experimenting with suicide. "I felt about as bad as a fifteen-year-old possibly can," he says. "My life was just crap."

25

JESSE: "I'VE LEARNED TO CALL EVERYTHING TEMPORARY"

THE TEENAGE YEARS ARE DIFFICULT IN LARGE PART BECAUSE IT IS then that a child tries to break away from parents who are not ready to let him or her go. Jesse would have loved that kind of problem; the people he was closest to had always pushed him away. The latest were his grandparents. After the suicide attempt in his grandfather's toolshed, his grandmother called his mother and suggested that she take Jesse over the summer. It could get up to 120 degrees in the Mojave Desert, and there wasn't much for a boy to do in that kind of heat. Besides, they needed a break; they were not getting any younger. Tracy agreed, as long as it was only for the summer. Jesse's grandparents put him on a bus to San Jose, and Jesse found himself back home, trying to pick up the threads of his old life.

A few days after he arrived, Jesse happened to look out the front window just as his grandparents' new Buick was pulling to the curb. He called his mother, and they met Jesse's grandparents at the door. "We brought Jesse's stuff!" his grandmother said cheerfully.

"But why?" asked Tracy. "He has enough things to get through the summer. It's not like we don't have a washing machine."

"He's not coming back," Jesse's grandmother said, as if she was announcing a pleasant surprise. "We've had enough. We can't handle him."

"But he lives with you! You have legal custody!"

"Not anymore," his grandmother said. "He's your kid. You take him." Jesse's grandfather walked back to the Buick, opened the trunk, and waited while Jesse unloaded his things. When his grandmother said good-bye, she gave Jesse a hug and a kiss and told him she loved him. "I vowed right then that my grandmother would never touch me again," Jesse says.

It was only a matter of days until Earl and Jesse were again locked in their Oedipal battle. He was only home two weeks when Jesse's mother told him, "Sorry, this isn't working out. You are going to have to leave." Jesse moved in with the family of a close friend, carrying his belongings an armload at a time the few blocks to his new house. It was the beginning of his "couch-surfing" period. Jesse stayed with one friend until the parents asked him to leave, then moved in with another friend until those parents kicked him out. Finally, when there was no place else to go, he wound up back home with Earl and his mother. The fighting and the beatings began again.

Night after night, Jesse sat in his room, waiting until Earl "got so fucked up, he'd pass out." Then he slipped into the kitchen and got a knife out of the butcher block. This time, he did not intend to use the knife on his own wrists. He was going to use it on Earl. "I would creep into the room where Earl had been watching TV and was now snoozing, and I'd place the knife up against his neck. I would sit there contemplating if I was going to do it. Then Earl would flinch, and that would scare the shit out of me and I'd run and put the knife away and go back to my room."

Jesse wandered around his high school in a daze, wondering if he was going to kill his stepfather. The thought terrified him. He wasn't a murderer; he didn't want to kill anybody, even Earl. He had walked by the social worker's office in his school hundreds of times and never before considered going through the door. His father and Earl both hated the cops, hated any kind of authority. Both of them had impressed upon Jesse that the only way to get by in life was to keep people out of your business. It took everything Jesse had to turn the doorknob.

Jesse told the social worker that if he stayed at home he was afraid he would wind up killing his stepfather. Or his stepfather was going to kill him. The social worker got Jesse's permission to call his mother and check into what was going on. Two days later, Jesse was daydreaming through a fifth-period class when a student proctor walked in and handed a note to the teacher: Jesse Montgomery was wanted in the office. When he got there, a police officer was waiting for him.

"Jesse, you cannot go home," the social worker informed him. "You are going to the shelter." She explained that he had done nothing wrong. Indeed, he was to be commended for coming to her before something really terrible happened. Jesse listened carefully and seemed so reasonable that, when he asked to go to the bathroom, the social worker and the police officer let him go alone. Jesse took off and ran through the halls, crying and screaming, "I'm out of here! They're taking me to the shelter! I'm gone! It's over."

An old friend Jesse had gone through grade school with recognized his voice and came running out of a classroom. She yelled, "Jesse!" and they ran toward each other and embraced in the hall. "I'm going to miss you," Jesse said. It was all he could think of to say.

· · ·

A Section 300(b) petition was filed in Jesse's case, alleging that Jesse should be made a dependent child because, first, his legal guardians, his grandparents, had sent the minor home to his mother and stepfather and they had refused to take him back and, second, his natural mother could not or would not protect him from the conduct of his stepfather.

Under Section 300(c) of the California Welfare and Institutions Code, the petition alleged that Jesse was suffering "serious emotional damage" because of feelings of abandonment and rejection by his mother and severe mood swings from "compliance to violence" and that, in moments of rage, he had made threats to murder his grandfather and stepfather.

At a dispositional hearing before Judge Edwards, a reunification plan was established: Jesse's mother, father, and stepfather were ordered to attend parenting classes. They were also ordered to get three months of counseling. Jesse was to get intensive psychological counseling. His natural parents and stepfather were ordered to participate in Jesse's treatment, at the discretion of the treating psychologist.

Jesse's mother agreed to the plan and kissed Jesse when the hearing was over. It was a good-bye kiss, literally, a kiss-off. Tracy ignored the court order, did not go to counseling, did not even visit Jesse in the shelter. Neither, of course, did Danny, his father, or Earl, his stepfather. Jesse was going to need a long-term placement.

In the shelter, Jesse lived in fear, not so much of the swaggering gang members or the huge seventeen-year-old a couple of beds down who was docile when he took his psychotropic medication but went on a rampage when he forgot or refused to take his pills. Jesse was afraid of his own anger that made him want to strike out at somebody, the pain that had led him to attempt suicide.

He dealt with these demons by becoming what counselors call a "caretaker." He listened as other teenagers spilled out their problems, made thoughtful suggestions, and tried to help in any way he could. It seemed to work: it is difficult to get angry with someone who really listens—and, after his years with Earl, the last thing Jesse wanted was someone angry with him. At night after the lights went out, Jesse could lie in his bed making plans to help the boy in the next bed instead of making plans to help himself.

Most of the time, the shelter felt like a jail. Before taking a shower, Jesse had to stand in line, file past a counselor who handed out soap, a washcloth and towel, underwear, socks, a shirt, and pajamas. A counselor patrolled the showers to make sure that all the boys did was take a shower, and Jesse had to yell at him if he wanted shampoo. He had to stand in line to eat. He had to stand in line to go to bed. "I didn't feel rescued; I felt lonely," Jesse says. "I missed my school and my friends, my mom, and my little sister—but not Earl, of course. I guess you could say I missed my life."

Months passed as Jesse's social worker tried to find a placement. Every time John Jackson, the counselor in the senior boys unit, saw Jesse moping around the shelter, he got angry. "Jesse was exactly the kind of kid the system should fall all over itself to help. He was obviously bright; he never caused problems. He had never done anything wrong. Why couldn't the system offer him something more than dead time in the shelter?" Jackson asks rhetorically.

On his own, there wasn't much Jackson could do, except to cut Jesse as much slack as he could. He let Jesse sit in the main room and play his guitar. One evening, a new teenager came to the shelter, and she sat apart from the group that had clustered around Jesse. She had long, silken black hair flowing down her back, bangs cut just over her eyes, and a face that tapered to a delicately pointed chin. She was wearing a tie-dyed dress with the Grateful Dead symbol, a skull with roses.

About the only thing his father had given Jesse was a thorough knowledge of The Dead's music. He went into "Truckin'" and, to show the new girl that he was on top of things, did The Dead's surprise hit

"Touch of Gray." When he finished, Jesse got up and walked over to the young woman.

"Have you ever seen The Dead?" the girl asked without looking up.

"A bunch of times. My dad's really into them."

"Me too. I'm Delia."

"OK, Delia," Jesse smiled. "I'm Jesse. I'm not glad I'm here and I'll bet you're not glad you're here, but I'm glad you're here."

There is sadness and suffering wherever one turns in the shelter, but the place also has the feel of a summer camp where children create their own impermanent little world. They pour their hearts out to each other and form friendships very quickly. They know that their time together is limited; children are forever returning from a day in court to find that a best friend's bed has been stripped and that he has moved on. For these reasons, relationships among shelter kids have all the intensity of a summer love.

At first, Delia was "really quiet, really unsure of herself, very afraid of everything." As she and Jesse grew "closer than any brother or sister," Delia shared with Jesse the only thing she had to share, the diary in which she had recorded her heartbreaking past. Delia's father had beaten her, and she hinted that he had raped her. By age sixteen, she had had three boyfriends; every one had beaten her up. "I'm nothing. I'll never be anybody special," she kept telling Jesse. "I'm ugly. I'm overweight. I've got a shitty personality."

"You're the foxiest, most interesting girl I've ever met," replied Jesse. "To be able to look at you, to talk to you, to hold you, it's like this great privilege."

Their relationship fell into a cycle that seemed as fixed as the seasons. They would sink into a world all their own and take comfort in one another's presence, and then Delia would start chanting her incessant "I'm ugly, I'm nothing" mantra. She would call the boyfriend she had sworn never to see again and run from the shelter to meet him. When Delia returned, she was inevitably covered with bruises. "I can't deal with this!" Jesse would explode. "I can't keep us both afloat; it's all I can do to keep myself from sinking. I really, really love you, but you've got to help me!"

Finally, Jesse figured out how to break the cycle. The next time Delia needed to run, they would run together. Jesse had $154 in a savings account he had started when he was a little kid. They would use it to visit his dad, who was running a shop in Venice, near Los Angeles, with his girlfriend. It would be their great adventure.

• • •

Jesse and Delia were on a Greyhound bus, in the seat directly behind the driver. Delia had a brand new diary on her lap and was dutifully copying down the names of the crops that are grown along Interstate 5 in California's vast Central Valley. The diary was not the only symbol of her "new start" in life. "She wanted everything to be new," Jesse says. "That's why, when she started her diary, she changed her name to 'Lynn.'"

The business Danny and his girlfriend ran turned out to be a posthippie head shop, full of handmade jewelry, shirts, pipes, and rings, "all that cool stuff." Jesse, who "just loves the surprise factor," strolled into his father's shop, walked up to him, and said, "Pardon me, sir, do you have any Grey Poupon?"

"He didn't know who I was until I pulled my glasses down," Jesse recalls. "Then he fell back against the wall and said, 'Jesse?' It was great!"

But the great moment passed, and over the next few weeks it became clear that, once again, Danny was not going to change his life to include his son. His girlfriend's apartment was much too crowded for four. Jesse and Lynn tried their best to help in the store, but all they did was get on the girlfriend's nerves. Danny finally told Jesse, "Look, I'd love to have you stay, but right now we're going through some pretty rough times and—"

"It's OK," Jesse said, cutting off his father. "No need to explain. We'll go back to San Jose."

Jesse and Lynn were broke. There were warrants out to pick them up as runaways, but Danny said that he couldn't afford to give them bus fare or even a few dollars for food. He dropped them off at a Highway 101 on-ramp. Jesse and Lynn watched him drive away, and then Lynn stuck out her thumb and Jesse held up a sign he had made that said "San Jose."

Tired and hungry and with nowhere to go, they walked up to the first police car they saw in San Jose; the officer returned them to the shelter. They were there for only a few days before Lynn was placed in a foster home. Depressed and feeling isolated, she slashed her wrists. After her wounds healed, Lynn was placed in residential treatment. Jesse spent a total of five months in the shelter before a slot finally opened in a group home and he left for good.

"We called each other a lot, and then her ex-boyfriend popped his nose back into the picture and I started hearing stuff like 'I can't talk to you anymore. You're no good for me,'" Jesse recalls. "Then she'd call again and say, 'I had to say that; he was standing right there, and he would have kicked my ass if I didn't.'

"We talked a couple of times after that, and then we sort of lost touch. The last time we talked, she goes, 'Don't give up on me.' And I said, 'You best not give up on me.'"

26

JESSE:
THE GROUP HOME

BEING REUNIFIED WITH THEIR FAMILIES WAS NOT AN OPTION FOR JESSE
and Lynn; nor, at their age, was there any realistic chance of being
adopted. The next alternative offered by the system was a foster home,
but there are never enough available and they are especially scarce for
adolescents. But placing every child who can't return home into a foster
home—even a good one—may be too simplistic an answer. Teenagers
like Jesse and Lynn raise serious questions about whether foster homes
are the best environment for every child. A "nice, well-meaning" family
may not be able to deal with such children. And the teenagers may not
be able to deal with a nice, well-meaning family.

A teenager who is filled with rage at his own father is not going to
trust an adult who says, "I want to be your father." A child who has been
abused most of her life is often not emotionally equipped to deal with
the intimacy, the conflicting roles, and the emotional intensity that come
with family life. This is one of the theories behind the establishment of
what are commonly called group homes. In social services circles, they
are given fancier titles—"community care facilities"—and they vary in
size, physical amenities, and the degree of care they offer.

The story of group homes in California began in the early 1970s
when the state hospitals and large child welfare facilities were being
emptied. Under the doctrine of deinstitutionalization, community-based
care became the goal for the mentally ill, developmentally disabled, and
older dependent children who were no longer cute and cuddly. Counties
subcontracted the care of these "clients" to privately run nonprofit facilities.

The first choice of social workers was to place the children on their
caseload into established, reputable facilities like Eastfield Ming Quong.

But it was definitely a seller's market, and the most popular group homes and treatment centers had their pick of the clientele. They began screening out the toughest children, the children who had no family support at all. Often, they accepted only those children who had a good chance of succeeding and therefore of enhancing the status of their program.

What was to be done with the "leftovers"? As demand for what is known in the social work world as "bed space" exceeded supply, entrepreneurs stepped in. They purchased old motels, ramshackle ranches in the middle of nowhere, and large, rambling mansions that had once been the pride of downtowns and were now boarded up, covered with graffiti and selling for a song. In the 1970s, real estate speculators bought up entire downtown blocks. After a few coats of paint and some wallboard were slapped up, the houses were given bucolic- or inspirational-sounding names like "Green Pastures" or "Excell Center" and found new life as group homes.

Some of the early group home operators were truly remarkable individuals. There were former social workers who were fed up with the bureaucracy and wanted to get back into the daily business of caring for people. Others, affiliated with church and charity groups, had few credentials but large hearts, and they devoted themselves to providing the kind of guidance and programs that truly turned the lives of children around.

There were also many group home operators who saw what adults have always seen in children: a way to wield power. The new, booming group home industry "called" many piously religious, strong-willed, and charismatic figures who set out to rescue children from their own internal demons. Often untrained and without credentials, these group home operators applied their own brand of "behavior modification" therapy, which could mean slaps across the face, long periods of isolation, and, in one recorded case of "adverse therapy," the electronic stinging of autistic children with a cattle prod. Child welfare workers, some incompetent, all overwhelmed, were often under such pressure to find bed space that they looked the other way. The rationalization born out of desperation went like this: it may not be the best place in the world, but at least the child has a roof over her head.

With little licensing and accountability, with no uniform regulation and review procedures, these group homes became worlds unto themselves. Physical and sexual abuse flourished, as did financial scams. With no one looking, it was easy to cut back on food, clothing, building repairs, education, and programs that had been promised and were being paid for. Every month, the county and state sent the agreed-upon reimbursement rate. Every month, many group home owners skimmed off what they could. As children languished, group home owners grew fat and prosperous on tax dollars.

For these reasons, group homes in California are now among the most closely regulated businesses—and are subject to some of the most arcane and complex regulations—in the state. The state ranks group homes on a scale from one to fourteen. The levels—and therefore the reimbursement rate charged to place a child there—are determined by, among other things, the amount of supervision and the degree of restriction in a facility, by the staff's level of education, and by the amount of therapy a facility offers. Eastfield Ming Quong is a level fourteen.

Star House No. 3, the small group home where Jesse ended up, is a level seven, right in the middle of the group home continuum. Critics of these smaller, less restrictive group homes consider them hothouses where the antisocial side of troubled teenagers grows like a vine in the tropics. Put six troubled boys together and they are bound to play off each other, to do crazy things to establish who is the baddest, who is the wildest. And, as always when it comes to children, there is a controversy over money.

At first glance, the $2,800 a month it takes to keep a boy like Jesse in a level seven group home seems outrageous, especially in light of the fact that most of the time the house is staffed by one or two counselors earning close to the minimum wage. Six boys means $16,800 a month. What family couldn't raise six boys on way less than $16,800 a month?

Steuart Samuels, the executive director of the Star House Group Homes in Santa Clara County, has been listening to such criticism for twenty years. He knows about the rip-off artists who have opened group homes and starved the kids so that they could plow the money into the mortgage. When the market was right, they folded the homes overnight and make a quick killing selling the houses. He knows about the time a social worker called a sixteen-year-old boy she had placed in a group home and noticed an unusual amount of noise in the background. The social worker asked the teenager what was going on, and the boy said,

"Well, the staff took the money and split for The Bahamas. We've been kind of running this place ourselves."

To Samuels, though, money is not what group homes are about. The $2,800 a month it costs to keep Jesse in Star House No. 3 pays for room, board, clothes, transportation, medical and dental care, a counselor on duty around the clock, a clinical supervisor, a case manager, a house supervisor, therapy sessions with a psychologist, and an array of recreational programs. To Samuels, group homes are about providing the best living environment possible for kids who cannot make it anywhere else in society. That is what has kept him going for twenty years. "Where else are these kids going to live?" Samuels asks. "Don't tell me foster homes. Most of them have already bombed out of four or five!"

The headquarters of the Star House Group Homes are located in a cramped, nondescript building near Valley Medical Center. Sitting behind his desk, Samuels looks like John Newcombe, one of the Australians who dominated tennis in the 1970s. In his mid-forties, he is powerfully built, has sandy hair that is thinning and a bushy mustache that is not, and dresses in sport shirts, shorts, and running shoes.

In the mid-1970s, Samuels was working as a resource counselor for a large mental institution, which meant that his job was to find housing, therapy, and schooling for patients when they were released. All sixty women in his unit received Social Security checks, which more than covered their monthly needs. Samuels helped them open a group bank account, and before long the women had saved enough to fulfill their dream: they hired escorts and went to Florida to visit Walt Disney World. "My wife, Shannon, and I were amazed that mentally disturbed adults could organize and do all that complex planning," Samuels says. "We said to ourselves, 'Imagine what teenagers in a small group home with the right counselors—people like us—could do.'"

The Samuelses were young and idealistic, and they looked around and found a church that wanted to sponsor a group home as part of its charity work. The church hired the energetic couple to start the home and run it. The Samuelses located a rambling old house in a quiet residential area, perfect for kids. "Living together, going to a school, or working in a pizza place gives teenagers who feel like aliens an opportunity to integrate into the larger community," Samuels explains. "You can get a kid to act a certain way in an authoritarian regime like a reform school or a boot camp, but the minute he comes back to the community, he is again faced with all the problems he was removed from, and he has not been given the skills or training to deal with them."

The Samuelses filed the necessary use permits, and they went door to door handing out pamphlets to neighbors and explaining what they wanted to do. The day the zoning board took up their request, the hearing room was packed with neighbors who offered every excuse under the sun. It wasn't that they had anything against children; it wasn't that they didn't think that unfortunate children should be helped. They just didn't think that their particular neighborhood was the right place. One neighbor said that the noise the boys were making when they played basketball in the backyard was terrible and that he couldn't live with it. ("Amazingly," Samuels recalls, "the house was still empty.") A woman in a tube top and incredibly short shorts stood up to say that she sunbathed in her backyard and was afraid that, once the boys spotted her, they would try to rape her.

Samuels gave an impassioned speech: These kids may have long hair and wear funky clothes, but they are not delinquents! They have never been convicted of breaking the law! Please, don't push them away! People have been doing that all their lives! They have as much right to live in society as any of us do! Give them a chance!

The zoning board had no interest in swatting away a swarm of angry neighbors. The request was denied.

A few months later in 1975, the Samuelses found an abandoned house on a vacant lot next to an apricot drying yard. The place had been gutted and the walls were black from Sterno fires lit by squatters, but there were no neighbors around to be scared of kids with long, scraggly hair. The zoning board issued a permit, and teams of volunteers from the church refurbished the house.

That was Star House No. 1, an upbeat acronym for St. Andrew's Residential Program, which over the next few years was followed by Star House No. 2, No. 3, and No. 4. While other group homes were falling to scandals and the state licensing agency was closing their doors, the Star Houses maintained a reputation for excellence. According to social workers in the Department's placement unit, the four homes are among the best facilities available. The staff is well trained, and the Star Houses deliver an impressive array of services.

"When we started, we tried to re-create the family," Samuels says.

"We'd tell boys that we loved them and that this was their home now. Was that unrealistic!"

Samuels had made an assumption common to people who do not know teenagers like Jesse or Lynn. He assumed that they were like him and would automatically respond in the same ways he does. "If somebody shows me kindness, I feel warm inside," Samuels says. "When we showed a kid kindness, he showed us suspicion. That's because the last time somebody was nice, he wanted to fuck the kid in the ass."

What Samuels has learned in his two decades is this: "If you try to re-create the family, the kids will rebel. They are angry that their own families failed; they are not about to accept a 'phony' family. These kids are not about to play the role of the happy son, the grateful daughter, the caring sibling. They are not about to reward a well-meaning couple for their altruism. They are not about to give love just because two strangers want to try to love them."

The philosophy of the Star Houses is to create an environment that provides the boys with some of the same benefits of a family but, at the same time, to remain emotionally neutral. It is one thing for a foster mother with her own emotional agenda to tell a boy, "We took you in and made you part of this family, and when you try to run away, you hurt me very badly," and quite another for a counselor in a group home to start a meeting with, "OK, two guys tried to run this week. Which one wants to be the first to talk about it?" The idea in a group home is to "seize the moment," to use incidents like running away to help a boy examine destructive behavior, to try to teach change while an incident "is happening and a child's feelings are still fresh."

This was the environment that Jesse moved into. Star House No. 3 is a dark gray house that from the outside appears to be just another home in a pleasant residential section of San Jose called Willow Glen. At the time, Jesse says, "I was a bottle of soda water waiting to explode. The next person to shake me might get hurt."

• • •

Among the five boys, all dependents of the court, who were living in Star House No. 3 when Jesse arrived was a sixteen-year-old African-American whose parents were in prison, a Vietnamese boy whose parents were boat people, and a Hispanic boy who was running with a gang.

They were from vastly different cultures, but in family backgrounds and temperament they were brothers. Like Jesse, they were all "mad at the world, stuck somewhere [they] did not want to be."

The conclusions a psychologist reached about Jesse could just as easily have described the other five boys. They were calm and reasonable one moment, in a rage and near tears the next. "Jesse sees himself as a victim, as someone who is always in danger of assault," the psychologist wrote. "He is extremely sensitive to perceived slights or insults from others. This, coupled with a great deal of pent-up rage, makes a very combustible mixture."

At Star House No. 3, the six "combustible mixtures" living under the same roof were always testing each other, constantly jockeying for position, always probing for a hot button that would set somebody off. In Washington, D.C., or inside a large corporation, these kinds of power games pass for politics. In the Star House, the game has a more accurate description: "intimidation." Not long after Jesse arrived, the residents decided to play a "sick joke" on a counselor named Julie. Sick jokes are a particularly creative, particularly malevolent form of intimidation.

Jesse happened to like Julie. She was motherly, and he sensed that she really cared about him and the other boys. That, of course, was why several of the others didn't like her. "Some of the kids had bad problems with their mothers," Jesse says. "They just couldn't handle authority figures, especially female authority figures."

Jesse wanted no part of the sick joke, but he was new and was coming in for his share of intimidation. The other residents accused Jesse of being a momma's boy. Momma's boys have to watch out, the boys warned. Things happen to momma's boys, sometimes when they are asleep. So Jesse ended up watching while the other boys wrapped a pillowcase around the working end of a mop and soaked the pillowcase in ketchup. They hung the mop from the ceiling outside the counselor's office. A sign taped to the handle read "Julie hangs tonight." Julie quit after the incident.

But the Star House wasn't all intimidation and sick jokes. As weeks turned into months, Jesse settled in in the same way he had settled in at the shelter. He learned to avoid trouble, to stop attacking anyone he thought might be "trying to put a move" on him. He took up his old role of caregiver and made friends with boys who had survived homes that were much worse than his. He became particularly tight with a

"Gothic punk" named Paul who wore his blond hair in dreadlocks and always dressed in the same clothes: black boots that laced to the knees, tight black pants, a white knit caftan over a black shirt. Paul's father used to tie him up and lock him in a closet and had left him without food or water for days at a time. "Paul gave me perspective," Jesse says.

Slowly, Jesse began gaining a measure of control over his life. In the previous semester at his old high school, his grades had been four Fs and one A (the A was in guitar). In his new school, he was earning Cs and the occasional B. Working with his psychologist and the Star House counselors, Jesse, for the first time, was taking a look at who his parents really were. He was slowly beginning to accept that they were not going to change. They were never going to make a place for him in their lives.

"I could deal with that because I was starting to make a life for myself that did not include my parents," Jesse says. "Things were starting to work out. The better I did, the more passes I got. The counselors seemed to like me, and the other residents seemed to like me. I was beginning to think of myself as an OK guy. I was beginning to think that life wasn't all that bad."

As his anger began to wane, Jesse was able to put a little distance between himself and his rage. When he felt himself losing it, he learned to tell a counselor that he was going to take an "anger walk." When he returned, Jesse and the counselor immediately sat down together. Instead of telling the counselor to fuck off, Jesse was beginning to find words for his feelings. Of course, he still got angry, tongue-lashed other residents, and had to be told to pick up after himself; there were still times when he fell into a depression and isolated himself from others to mourn his parents. Every now and then, he signed out and met some old friends and smoked a joint or two.

But Jesse's life was definitely on the right track. Within the Star House, he was regarded as "a relatively model resident who follows rules and attends school. . . . Unlike many of our boys, he has the ability to bond." Jesse not only had the ability to bond, but he was eager to bond. Residents came and went; some ran away, some went back home, and a few committed crimes that sent them to Juvenile Hall. Jesse stayed and became a kind of elder, a bridge between the staff and the residents, the old-timer who clued in the newcomers.

It was a role he delighted in. The Star House No. 3 was his fraternity.

He wanted it to do for every resident what it had done for him. So when a fifteen-year-old named Corey arrived from the shelter, it was Jesse who showed the sullen teenager around the four-bedroom house, Jesse who pointed to the Little Caesar's Pizza across the street where he worked, Jesse who told Corey the best thing he could do was take things easy. "I told him things are always tough at first, but they always get better. I wanted to help him out, make him feel welcome," Jesse recalls.

27

COREY:
THE WANNA-BE

To venture a few blocks east of downtown San Jose's main re-development area, past the renovated courthouse and cafés and restaurants with brick walls and white linen on the tables, is to leave one America and enter another. On West Santa Clara Street, visitors from the suburbs revive their health at a new juice bar, drinking wheat grass at a dollar a shot; on leisurely Sundays, they leave behind career concerns by listening to live jazz at a microbrewery. But a few blocks east, outside a liquor store, broken bottles litter the sidewalk. One shop sells "Black Water" to ward off enemies and herbs guaranteed to cure cancer. In this section of downtown, many storefronts are vacant, and in one doorway, a regular sleeping spot for the homeless, there are half-full cups of 7-Eleven coffee, grown cold and filmy. This is where Corey McKenzie grew up, in the shadow of urban renovation.

When compared to the ghettos in the East or in, say, Chicago, Corey's neighborhood feels less segregated, the poverty less crushing, the violence less omnipresent. San Jose is a Sunbelt city, and even the smallest house in the worst neighborhood is likely to have an orange tree perfuming the air. The weather is almost always pleasant, so children—mostly black, Hispanic, and Vietnamese—are inevitably jumping rope and chasing each other up and down the streets. But in Corey's neighborhood, there is poverty and despair all the same. The house with the juicy oranges on the lawn can easily be a crack house. (When the San Jose police targeted this area in an operation called Project Crackdown, they arrested thirty-three drug dealers and issued warrants for seven more.)

Some of the homes appear to need only a sagging front porch fixed and the front lawn mowed; the house where Corey lived with his two older brothers, his father, his father's girlfriend, and her children was such a house. Juvenile probation officer Cleveland Prince, who had Corey's brothers on his caseload, remembers it well.

Prince is one of the county's leading authorities on gangs, has great charisma, and is funny and highly outspoken. He has big arms and a huge chest—"Prince is buffed, man!" the kids say—and was an all-American sprinter at San Jose State University. He grew up in East Palo Alto, the town with the highest murder rate in California, and knows despair when he sees it. But Prince had never seen a house as "filthy, rotten dirty" as Corey's. "I was supposed to do a search, but the house was so bad, I wouldn't do it," Prince recalls. "The Health Department finally came in and made the family move. Then they closed that house down."

Corey was fifteen when he came to the senior boys unit at the Children's Shelter, a handsome young man about five feet ten inches tall and weighing 160 pounds, with dark brown skin, short black hair, a perpetually furrowed brow, and the hint of a mustache. Though different in its details, Corey's story is much like Jesse's, with a trajectory that seems to have been set at birth.

The rap sheet on Corey's mother says that she was a prostitute with arrests for robbery, forgery, and the sale and possession of cocaine. She walked out on the family when Corey was thirteen months old. For awhile, Corey's father, Dafford, a Navy veteran who had served in Vietnam, supported his family by working as a sous-chef in a number of hotels. But he, too, had his own past and deteriorated, by way of alcohol and drugs, into a distant and abusive father. One day, when Corey was thirteen years old, Dafford simply left without saying good-bye, abandoning his youngest son to Frances Crawley, the woman he had lived with for many years. "Corey had never been a particularly good student, but he had never caused problems, either," she recalls. "But after that he went wild. That boy was never the same."

Anyone who has attended a men's movement meeting or seen one televised knows that this mostly white, mostly middle-class phenomenon exists to explore and share the pain created by fathers who were physically present but spiritually and emotionally distant. The pain felt by men who have never bonded with their fathers, but who have therapists, careers, and wives and children of their own to diffuse it, nonetheless runs very deep. Corey had nothing and no one, and his pain ultimately went in one direction.

Someone from his high school was calling Crawley almost every day: Corey was suspended for threatening to hit a teacher, for running in and out of class, for stealing things from a teacher's desk. At home, Corey was flying into rage after rage. When Crawley's nineteen-year-old daughter forgot to return some music tapes she had borrowed from him, he threatened, "If I don't get them back, I'll stab you through your damn heart!" A few days later, the nineteen-year-old heard screams in the living room and came running to find Corey straddling her twelve-year-old brother, "punching him over and over again, like a man gone crazy." The sister pulled Corey off her brother, and he spun and punched her in the face.

"I kept asking him, 'Corey, why are you being so mean? I know you're mad about your dad leaving, but he didn't just leave you, he left all of us,' " Crawley says. "Corey kept promising me that he would stop doing all this bad stuff. And I know he wanted to, but the rage in him was terrible."

Corey's two older brothers had been arrested on drug and burglary charges and were serving time in juvenile facilities. Now, Corey was hanging on the corner of Seventh and Santa Clara with their friends, "Fake Crips [Family Crip Gangsters], Wanna-be Crips," Cleveland Prince calls them. When Corey was caught stealing a movie from a video store, the police did not file charges, but the officer who took Corey home warned Crawley, "If this kid of yours doesn't go through some heavy changes, he is going to be a statistic, or he is going to cause a statistic."

Crawley was having health problems and could not handle a boy who was running wild. She called the Department and begged a social worker for help. Aside from recommending counseling, the worker explained that there was nothing she could do. Corey was not a dependent child. If Crawley really couldn't handle him, she had the option of taking him to the Children's Shelter, which would instigate the filing of a dependency petition. "I felt like I had no other choice but to take him there," Crawley recalls. "The way he had been behaving, I couldn't have him at home."

Crawley parked in the shelter lot and left Corey, silent and slumped against a door, in the backseat of the car. After filling out the paperwork, Crawley knew that she needed a way to lure Corey into the building. So she said what she herself did not really believe: "Corey, come on. This is what we have to do to get your dad out of hiding." Corey followed Crawley into the shelter, and when it was time to say good-bye, she broke into tears and threw her arms around the boy. "If Dafford hadn't left, I would never have had to do this," she said later. "He wasn't no Christmas puppy I was dropping off at the pound. Corey is my son."

Corey saw things differently. Crawley had gone through terrible times with her own children—her oldest boy, a chronic thief, was in jail right now. But she had always stuck by her own children, never even threatening to take them to the shelter. When Crawley took a half step back to look at Corey, he was "staring at me so hard, it was like he wanted to stare right through me." Crawley turned and started for the door. Still crying, she stopped and turned around: "I guess now, Corey, I'm the bad one."

●   ●   ●

A dependency petition was filed alleging that, under Section 300(c) of the California Welfare and Institutions Code, fifteen-year-old Corey had suffered serious emotional damage; under Section 300(c), the petition stated that the adults in Corey's life had left him, making no provisions for his support. Corey's father did not appear at any of the hearings, but a social worker went through the motions and produced a reunification plan that, considering the reality of Corey's life, approached the surreal—"Issues of an individual and family nature need to be addressed by Corey and his father. . . . The reasons why Mr. McKenzie has neglected his responsibility and his relationship with his son should be explored in family therapy." The social worker scheduled a therapy session: Frances Crawley and Corey showed up; Corey's father did not.

His mother, his brothers, Crawley—they had all deserted him, but as is common among children who have been abandoned, Corey chose to glorify the person who really and truly broke his heart—his father. The Children's Shelter is full of kids who do the same thing: The daughter of a street dealer claims that the only reason her father does not visit her is because he is a high-ranking member of a Colombian cartel; a boy whose father is serving time for armed robbery brags about the family's Mafia connections. Corey gave his father a more down-to-earth résumé, one befitting a Silicon Valley parent: Corey turned Dafford McKenzie into a mover and shaker of the computer industry.

"Corey was loud and boisterous, bragging to everyone how rich his father was and how his being in the shelter was all a mistake," John Jackson, the senior boys' counselor, remembers. "He used to go around saying, 'My dad is in Asia on a business trip. When he gets back and finds out I'm in here, I'll be out of this place so fast, heads will be spinning.'"

But for all the big talk and all the noise Corey generated, he did not cause Jackson many problems, at least in the beginning. Corey got along with the other boys and followed the rules, and when he played basketball on the court behind the shelter, "he played with the fierceness of a warrior. We have a point system, and Corey reached one of the highest levels," Jackson says. "He made his bed, brushed his teeth, pretty much did everything that was expected of him."

Corey's behavior did not start slipping until he made friends with one of the "bad apples." Among counselors in the shelter, conversations eventually lead to the bad apples, and during this period they led to one boy in particular, a tall, wiry seventeen-year-old named James Nitta*. "This kid kept me up nights," Jackson says. "He had never been arrested on a delinquency charge, but he was a longtime member of the Nortenos [one of the two major Hispanic street gangs]. Nitta is exactly the kind of kid who I think should never, ever be allowed in the shelter."

Jackson has been a counselor at the Children's Shelter for three years, and he looks something of a sad sack, going to work in loose-fitting sweatshirts and wearing a baseball cap with his ponytail sticking through the opening in the back. The skin under his beard is pallid, and lately he has been putting on weight; only five feet ten inches tall, he is up to 230 pounds. Like many adults who work with troubled children, Jackson was one growing up. In high school, Jackson had been caught joyriding in a stolen car; his father had ended up shipping him to a military school in Virginia. "I know what it's like to be branded as a kid," Jackson says.

Yet all he could feel for James Nitta was fear. "All I could think about was how James was going to kill someone—if somebody didn't kill him first. The Surenos [the Nortenos's rivals] already had a death warrant out on James for supposedly pulling one of their 'homies' out of a car and beating him and raping his girlfriend. James thrived on the danger. He ran almost every night and then came running back, as if the shelter was a safe house."

Jackson felt that his hands were tied. If the incident reports, the IRs

Jackson and the other counselors filed meant something, if James Nitta knew that running from the shelter and running wild in the streets would land him behind bars in juvenile hall, maybe he would respect the shelter and its rules. But a kid like Nitta was a street lawyer who knew the routine at least as well as Jackson did, maybe better. A counselor filed an IR, the police came and took the troublemaker to Juvenile Hall, where he got a lecture and a return trip to the shelter. DA's are reluctant to file a petition that will turn a dependent child into a delinquent. And, as every kid in the system knew, juvenile hall was bursting at the seams with minors who had been charged with serious, violent crimes. There was no room for youths charged with nonviolent crimes like burglary or possession of drugs, no room for runaways who were already in the system.

Like everyone in the shelter, Corey was wary of Nitta at first. He kept a careful distance until the day they happened to discover that they were distant cousins. In a world where families have been shattered, establishing any kind of kinship, no matter how tenuous, is a major event. Corey became James's shadow. He tried to walk like James, talk like James, fly gang colors—a carefully folded red bandanna, hanging halfway out of a pants pocket—just like James. From then on, all Jackson heard out of Corey was "my gang, my crew, my set."

During the next two months, Corey ran from the shelter more than a dozen times with Nitta. "How could I keep him in the shelter? He was a dependent, not a delinquent; legally there was no way that I could physically restrain him," Jackson says. "What did I have to offer that would keep him there? The shelter is mostly deadtime. I would say, 'Hey, stay here tonight. We'll hang out and talk or watch TV, but I knew how lame that sounded."

Kids want excitement, adventure, a challenge, all things that Corey found on the street. Nitta took him to an abandoned house where the Nortenos partied, showed him the neighborhoods they controlled, took him along when they went looking for Surenos to jump. In the shelter, Corey began acting as if he were on the streets. One night, he sneaked in a can of spray paint and "tagged" walls and doors with gang signs. He raced in and out of the other units, stealing blankets and anything else he could grab. He climbed up on the roof and ran around up there.

"We filed the usual IRs, incident reports, about Corey 'being out of control,'" Jackson recalls. "As usual, nothing was done. Corey continued to run wild, and I got more and more frustrated. It is my deepest belief that it is not enough simply to provide children with a place that is cleaner than home, where the food is better and no adults are beating or sexually assaulting children. The system has to do what the parents have never done: hold kids responsible for their behavior. If they never learn that basic lesson, they will never fit into society.

"When we let kids run the streets and use the shelter as a motel, like James Nitta and Corey did, we are failing to hold them responsible for their actions and failing to teach them respect. That is a form of abuse," Jackson says.

Corey had been in the shelter for three months the night pandemonium broke out in the senior boys' unit. Jackson raced in to find him ripping up beds and chasing boys around with a hairbrush he was pretending was a knife. "Corey, that's enough!" Jackson yelled. Corey ignored him and jumped over a bed and started to chase another boy. "Corey, I said cool it!" Jackson screamed. Corey brought the hairbrush up and was about to bring it down on a new resident, who was cowering against the wall. "Corey, you are getting a zero for this!" Jackson yelled. "No points for this shift!"

Instead of smirking at Jackson or completely ignoring him, as he had on other occasions, Corey became enraged. "I'll kill you motherfucker!" Corey screamed.

"How will you do that?" Jackson asked.

"My gang will pass me a gun through the fence," Corey screamed. "Then I'll shoot you dead."

Kids "talk shit"—make threats—all the time, especially in a place like the Children's Shelter. It is an adolescent version of a tantrum, a way to exercise the only power they have. So threats were nothing new to Jackson, and he usually shrugged them off. But not this time. "The way his eyes were locked on me, I just knew that if that hairbrush had been a knife he would have used it."

Immediately after, a shaken Jackson recorded the incident, word for word, in an IR. The report fell into the usual black hole. Corey did not even get a trip to Juvenile Hall for a perfunctory questioning. Several weeks later, Star House No. 3 accepted Corey into its program. He left without saying good-bye, and Jackson never saw him again.

28

COREY AND JESSE: THE STAR HOUSE

"COREY DEFINITELY HAD THAT 'I'M-BETTER-THAN-EVERYONE, I-CAN-do-anything-I-want,' attitude," Jesse Montgomery recalls. "He definitely tried to mess with me. Made little comments about my music, my taste in clothing. If I didn't retaliate, he thought something was wrong and he'd get frustrated and keep making remarks. He wanted to get you as worked up as he possibly could.

"I think he was searching for attention, I really do," Jesse concludes. "But Corey seemed alright. He really did."

By the time Corey moved into Star House No. 3, Jesse had been there for almost two years and had emerged as a success story. He peaked in the point system and could receive a pass to leave the premises almost anytime he wanted. He joined the Independent Living Program (ILP), which prepares teens without families to live on their own, teaching them basic life skills like how to open a bank account and balance a checkbook, how to do taxes, how to pursue a trade, how to enroll in a community college. Jesse did so well in the program that a counselor asked him to lead a communication skills workshop at a statewide ILP conference being held at a hotel in San Jose. "I not only led the workshop, I played my guitar after the big dinner before the whole assembly and I got a standing ovation. There was a thousand people there," Jesse says with a sense of wonder. "It was a real big moment for me."

Every now and then, Jesse signed out and would meet with a group of friends to smoke a few joints and drink some wine. One night, Jesse returned to Star House too loaded to hide it. There was a new counselor on duty named John De Caprio, whom none of the kids liked because he took his job way too seriously, always doing things by the book, always ready to deliver a lecture. In his mid-twenties, soft-spoken and small boned, standing five feet seven inches and weighing 125 pounds, De Caprio had recently moved to San Jose from Southern California with his wife, Brenda. "He wore glasses, and you would prejudge him by the way he looked as a quote, unquote geek," Jesse says.

Star House counselors with no experience are paid $6.18 an hour, and they work a two-day, forty-eight–hour shift. That would have been tough for a couple with a baby, but it worked for John and Brenda. The two had been inseparable since the day they had met in San Bernardino seven years earlier, when Brenda was fourteen. Both were committed to working with children and had agreed to postpone starting their own family while building their careers. Their dream was to open a counseling practice together. In preparation, Brenda was working as a receptionist and had enrolled in San Jose State University, where she was studying psychology. John had an application in for a graduate program that awarded a master's degree in counseling.

Jesse figured that De Caprio was going to write him up for coming into Star House loaded and that he would lose his hard-earned freedom. Instead, the counselor told him to go sit down in the living room. "You're underage; you know you shouldn't be drinking," De Caprio began. "Were you in a car? Was the guy who was driving as messed up as you?"

"No, we were just walking around. I thought I'd be able to walk it off before I got back, but I guess I didn't. I know I'm wrong."

"This isn't like you, Jesse," De Caprio said.

"I know. It's just that I'm about to graduate. You know how that is," Jesse replied.

They talked for about fifteen minutes, and then De Caprio said, "Look, you've done really well here. I'll let this one slide because I think you have enough sense not to pull something like this again."

The way De Caprio handled that incident made Jesse realize that he and the other residents had been wrong about the counselor. "I realized that night that he was a really good guy, one of those guys that you felt you could trust if you talked to him for ten minutes," Jesse says. "He really did care."

The boys in Star House had misjudged De Caprio in other ways as well. He was an adopted child who considered himself fortunate to have parents who loved him as much as they loved their biological children, and he wanted to give something back to teenagers who were not as lucky as he had been. The "geek" was tightly muscled and had earned a black belt in karate. If De Caprio was a "hard ass," it was because he wanted to pass along his sense of discipline, his belief that there was a right way and a wrong way to do things.

But working at Star House had brought De Caprio face to face with the painful limits of idealism. Talks like the one he had with Jesse—a talk in which one of the boys actually admitted responsibility for his actions, in which De Caprio did not feel as if he was wasting his breath— were rare. Mostly, De Caprio came home exhausted and bewildered after his two-day shift and quizzed Brenda, "Why don't these guys like me? They are so volatile, always on the edge of exploding, always testing. Why won't they listen to me? What am I doing wrong?"

• • •

It was a Wednesday in April, and school was out for spring break. Jesse had been going to a continuation school, a kind of holding tank for students who, for academic reasons or because of disruptive behavior, cannot make it in mainstream classrooms. Continuation schools are usually located off campus, which is where the high schools that run them want to keep these kinds of students. But Jesse had worked hard and was about to graduate, a triumph and a cause for celebration. "Graduating was a goal my mother set for me," Jesse says. "She'd moved up to Oregon and wasn't going to be there to see it, but I promised her I'd graduate and I kept that promise."

Early that evening, Jesse signed out and took a bus to meet a new girl-friend, the first girl he had really liked since Delia/Lynn. They hooked up with a couple of other friends, smoked a couple of joints, and hung around a shopping mall. At 10 P.M., curfew time at Star House, Jesse found himself a mile from home. He called and told John De Caprio that he was going to be late. There was noise in the background, and the counselor sounded stressed as usual. "Jesse, this means a late mark," De Caprio said.

"I know; I'll get there as soon as I can," Jesse replied. Jesse's friends walked him home. He looked at his watch and saw that it was 10:35. It wasn't *that* late. Maybe he could convince De Caprio not to write him up. When Jesse opened the front door, he saw Karl Foster, a sixteen-year-old, one of the few residents who was in Star House on a delinquency petition for a nonviolent crime, "looking grim and scared and very serious." Karl had a dollar bill in one hand and a plastic water pitcher in the other. "Don't go in there!" Karl yelled as he blew past Jesse and ran out the front door.

"What's up, man?" Jesse asked, following as Karl sprinted across Meridian Avenue. Karl did not reply, but raced into an Arco AM/PM gas station and convenience store. Karl spotted a police officer and slowed down, approached the counter, and calmly bought two Reese's Peanut Butter Cups. As soon as they were out of the store, Karl sprinted toward a Shell station two blocks up the street. "Dude, what's up?" Jesse kept asking. At the Shell station, Karl pumped thirty-one cents worth of gas into the plastic pitcher. "You are not going to believe this. He's dead," Karl said.

"Who's dead?"

"John, the counselor! This is for real!"

Karl walked through a nearly empty parking lot, carefully balancing the full pitcher. Jesse followed him to the end of a strip mall, telling himself that this had to be one of the residents' sick jokes. They went around a Thrifty Drug Store to the small field in back that was waist high with weeds. Corey was at the far end of the field, throwing something up on a pitched tile roof. Whatever it was kept sliding down. Finally, he gave up and threw it into the field. Philip*, another boy from Star House, was standing in the shadows. "This isn't right; this isn't right," he kept saying.

Corey took the pitcher from Karl and poured gasoline on a pile of clothes in the weeds. "I'm getting out of here; I don't need this shit," Jesse said and began backing away. The gasoline ignited with a whoosh! Orange flames leaped over the clothes and set the dry brush on fire. Corey, Karl, and Philip stomped out the flames, and Karl picked up a pair of black leather gloves that were still on fire and threw them over a retaining wall. He jumped over the wall, stomped on the gloves, and threw them into a dumpster.

Corey wanted to go into the pizza place where Jesse worked and wash up, but Jesse said that the store was closed and led them to a nearby water faucet. Karl and Corey washed their hands, and as the boys walked back across Meridian Avenue, Corey slowed up to walk with Jesse. "Jesse, what happened here tonight didn't really happen," Corey said.

"Huh?" Jesse asked.

"It happened, but nobody knows who did it," Corey said.

As soon as Jesse entered Star House, he headed up the hallway to the counselors' office. He was still clinging to the hope that John De Caprio would be sitting there behind the desk. He was about to open the door when Karl burst out. "Don't go in there!" Karl warned, stepping in front of Jesse.

"I have to," Jesse replied. "If this is real, I have to see it for myself." Karl kicked open the door. John De Caprio was on his back, his body soaked with blood and his eyes open. "I remember thinking, 'His eyes are open. Maybe he doesn't realize he is dead.' That's when Corey yelled, 'Okay, everybody in the living room, now!' "

When the residents had gathered, Corey announced the plan: "Everyone is going to say some guy came charging in. He was dressed all in black and had a knife. He just barged in. We know he's white because just as we opened the door he was pulling the mask down. That's it."

"Nobody will believe that," Jesse said. Corey gave Jesse a chilling look, and for a moment Jesse thought that "he was going to kill me if I didn't go along." Then another resident said to Jesse, "Dude, you just go to your room and grab some of your shit and get out of here. We'll tell them you ran away."

Jesse was on his way out the door when Corey stepped in front of him. "Well, it's been fun," he said, and gave Jesse a hug. It was eleven o'clock, an hour after Jesse had talked to John De Caprio on the phone.

• • •

At 11:06, Karl dialed 911 from a pay phone across Meridian Avenue. "A man just came in our group home with a knife and chased our counselor into the office, and I don't know what happened then," Karl told a dispatcher. "He had a knife, a long knife. He chased my counselor, and I don't know after that. We ran out of the house."

"Stay on the line. We'll have someone there in a few minutes."

At the same time, Jesse was wandering down Meridian in a daze, trying to decide what to do. "One of the things that my father and stepfather have in common is, neither of them like cops in any way, shape, or form," Jesse says. "I was thinking that if I called the cops they could charge me as an accessory just because I was there. Just because I was a group home kid. But if I didn't call, they were sure to charge me as an accessory." Jesse's new girlfriend lived only ten minutes away. He walked to her house, and when she opened the door, he blurted out, "They killed my counselor."

After Jesse told the story, his girlfriend's mother handed him a phone. Jesse hesitated, but then he heard the police helicopter hovering nearby. He ran to a window and saw the searchlight moving up and down between buildings. Jesse dialed 911. "I'm reporting a murder," he told the dispatcher. "I called because I don't want to have anything to do with it."

When the sheriff's deputy arrived, Jesse told him the story in exacting detail, and at daybreak there was a search of the field behind the Thrifty Drug Store. The police found what Corey McKenzie had been trying to throw onto the roof: a bloody eight-inch butcher knife.

• • •

The sergeant was sitting in a semicircle with two other police officers and a deputy district attorney. A video camera was focused on Corey, who was leaning forward, resting his chin on the palm of his hand, looking blank. "Corey? Do you want to talk to us now?"

"Yes," Corey said slowly.

"Corey, I know you're tired. We are too," the sergeant said. "But there must be some justification for what happened. We can't figure out what he did to provoke you."

"He just got on everybody's nerves," Corey said. "He was trying to keep me from doing everything."

It was the middle of the night, and the police had already called the residents of Star House No. 3 into an interview room one at a time, asking each to tell what had happened. Each boy had started with the story of the masked intruder, and each time the sergeant, armed with the arsenal of information Jesse had given them, said, "That's bullshit." Immediately, the boys had caved in and told the truth. Teenagers can commit acts as brutal as hardened criminals, but they are not hardened criminals. They do not have the sophistication to plan crimes or to cover them up.

The longer the questioning went on, the more meaningless Corey's explanations became, even to himself. "John said he treats everybody equal and he cuts everybody slack, but he doesn't. . . . John said we had to have a study period, but I said we didn't because it's Easter break." Finally, Corey quit trying to explain and simply described what happened that night, step-by-step.

First, he had gone into the counselors' office and used the phone without permission. Second, De Caprio caught him and asked whom he was talking to. Corey lied; he said that he was talking to Frances Crawley, trying to locate his father. De Caprio took the phone, and when Corey's girlfriend identified herself, the counselor hung up. Corey had just committed a major infraction. Two majors and a boy is removed from the Star House and taken back to the Children's Shelter.

Furious, Corey went outside and smoked a cigarette. Karl Foster fueled his rage, asking, "Why don't you just get this over with?" The knife they used to make tacos for dinner was still drying in the kitchen; De Caprio hadn't had time to lock it up with the other knives in the cabinet in the counselors' office. If Corey had the balls to do it, Karl would lend him his black leather gloves.

"So, you just went into the counselors' office with the knife?" the sergeant asked.

"That's right," Corey answered.

"And how did you grab John?"

"By the neck. With my right hand."

"Did John ever fall to the ground?"

"Yes," Corey said, "he did."

"So you got him once in the back when he was on the ground?"

"I stabbed him in the back," Corey agreed.

"Did John say anything?"

"He said, 'No! I'm sorry for everything I did!' "

The sergeant then asked, "And what was Karl doing?"

Corey's expression did not change. "Karl said that I needed to finish him now."

"So you did?"

Corey nodded. "Karl said, 'That's the way you do it. Just like an OG [Original Gangster].' "

There was a pause; then the sergeant asked, "How do you feel about this now?"

"Just, you know, I took a person's life. I don't think that's right," Corey answered.

• • •

A ringing phone woke Steuart Samuels at 1:30 in the morning. A sergeant identified himself, and Samuels thought, "Oh no, a kid got hurt. Or maybe a kid hurt another kid." When the sergeant gave him the news, Samuels "felt like a linebacker hit me in the stomach. I dropped to my knees. For a moment, I thought I was going to faint." Later, driving up an empty interstate to Star House No. 3, he started crying.

In the two decades Samuels had managed group homes, not one resident had ever struck a counselor. For twenty years, Samuels had fought the public's fears and its desire to lock up as many children as possible. "I had staked my career on the belief that locking up kids solves nothing in the long run. Kids need a sense that they belong to the larger community. They need a living condition that is as normal as possible; they need a shove in the right direction. And now this."

The yellow plastic tape marking a crime scene surrounded the Star House, and high-powered portable lights were shining down on it when Samuels arrived. The neighbors were awake and clustered on the sidewalk. As Samuels walked by, one of them was saying that he just knew something like this was going to happen. The other neighbors nodded their heads in agreement.

Samuels gave a deputy all the information he could about John De Caprio and the boys in the home, then got back in his car and drove to his office. He called several key staffers and members of his board of directors, and they joined him for a vigil that lasted all night. Adrift in a sea of questions, Samuels searched for answers: Was he too willing to take a risk on kids? Had he overlooked something about Corey, something that should have alerted him that this boy, among the hundreds of boys who had passed through Star House, was capable of murder? Should he have had two counselors on duty? "Twenty years and it's not worth it," Samuels kept repeating. "Not after this."

Sometime before dawn, Samuels's mind shifted to practicalities. He called the sergeant who was handling the case to remind him that someone must tell Brenda, John's widow. "I really think it should be me," Samuels volunteered. The sergeant said, "No! Under no circumstances." He was concerned that Brenda would rush to the house while the body was still there and an investigation was ongoing. The sergeant assured Samuels that the sheriff's office had a special team for contacting relatives; they would handle it.

Soon after, by 7 A.M., reporters began calling Samuels. In all the time Samuels had been running group homes, no journalist had ever interviewed him. No one in the press had ever been curious about what happens to boys whose families fall apart. No one had ever asked him about the boys who left the Star Houses and went on to college. Now so many reporters wanted to interview him that Samuels had to schedule appointments at fifteen-minute intervals. He tried to be as professional as possible and tell them all he could about what had happened. But when each interview ended, Samuels went into the bathroom and broke down. Then he washed his face, composed himself, went back to his desk, and asked his secretary to send in the next reporter.

Between interviews, he managed to call the sheriff's office to see if Brenda had been notified. The team had missed her at home; Brenda had already left for school. "She brings John's lunch every day," Samuels told the officer. "What if she gets to the house before someone tells her what's happened?"

"Don't worry, we've got people on this. They'll get to her before noon," the officer assured Samuels, but Samuels was worried. He called San Jose State, but the school refused to give him Brenda's class schedule.

At noon, Brenda De Caprio came walking toward the Star House, carrying John's lunch in a brown paper sack. She paused when she saw the yellow crime scene tape. Then she approached a television reporter who was standing on the sidewalk. "Please, can you tell me what happened?" she asked. "My husband works here."

29

CHILDREN, CRIME, AND THE MEDIA

THE *SAN JOSE MERCURY NEWS* RAN THE STAR HOUSE MURDER ON page one, quoting angry neighbors who said that in the five years the house had been open they had called the police at least twenty-five times to report residents loitering, littering, or jeering. "It's been a terrible house to have in the neighborhood," one person said, who claimed that the boys had hidden wine on his property. "That house should be closed!" A few months after the murder of John De Caprio, it was.

The *Mercury News* also did what the media so often does when covering a sensational crime involving a minor. It took a specific incident and drew a dramatic general conclusion: the Star House murder became emblematic of what the newspaper called in an accompanying article "the alarming rise of juvenile violence." According to the article, the number of boys and girls arrested in Santa Clara County "for murder, attempted murder, manslaughter and accessory to murder" had doubled in the previous year and the "figures show little sign of declining." To further illustrate "the alarming rise of juvenile violence," the article rehashed an equally shocking San Jose murder, one that had received national attention two years previously, "the savage slaying of eight-year-old Melvin Ancheta, who was bound, gagged and stabbed to death in his San Jose home by three teenagers."

Packaged together, these tragic murders of an innocent third-grader and a humble young man cut down by the very boys he was trying to help could not have more perfectly confirmed the public's gut instinct: teenagers today are without a conscience and out of control.

This thesis is hardly new. Each generation tends to think that the younger generation is the worst ever. At best, they are presumed lazy and good-for-nothing; at worst, they are presumed murderous. "Our country has always had ambivalent feelings about children," explains Mark Soler, the former executive director of the Youth Law Center, a nonprofit public interest law firm that does advocacy work in juvenile justice, child welfare, education, and health care. "When a child is young—from infancy to a couple of years of age—everybody loves them. Politicians love them. Voters love them. But once they get to be nine and ten, once they start to misbehave, become truants, once they stop obeying their parents so easily, people don't love kids anymore. The American public, as well as many parents, have very ambivalent feelings, and when those kids commit crimes? Right away, we stop thinking of them as being children of our family or children of our community. Automatically, they become somebody else's children."

Looking back over a hundred years of headlines in major newspapers, one comes upon "juvenile crime waves" at regular intervals. A century ago, newspapers were railing about street urchins who were as dangerous as wolf packs. In 1924, the Leopold-Loeb murder case in Chicago sparked outrage across the country as hand-wringing editorial writers held up the two teenage "thrill" killers as symbols of an entire generation that was spoiled, lost, and depraved. Such a crime never would have happened, it was said, if America were still rural and children were still working ten hours a day.

In the late 1950s, one generation denouncing the next reached a fever pitch when rock and roll hit. Mayors canceled performances by Jackie Wilson and Little Richard because, according to a 1958 article in the *Christian Science Monitor*, "the savage beat of the music incites some teenagers to misdeeds and acts of violence." The headlines continued throughout the 1960s and 1970s, when the fear and anger that one generation harbors for the next was given a name suitable for sound bites—the "generation gap."

"Some blame a growing permissiveness in the nature of the young with a concurrent decline in respect for constituted authority," said a massive report by the National Advisory Committee on Criminal Justice Standards and Goals, published in 1976. "Liberals tend to point to the omnipresence of poverty in a generally affluent society and to the country's failure to meet increasing and legitimate expectations of the poor and minorities. The general dissidence of youth, highlighted by the generation gap of the sixties, and its accompanying and untraditional behavior modes and lifestyles sometimes are viewed as further evidence of the decline of conformity-producing social controls."

Thus, adults have long asked the same question about children going wrong: why? But in our current era, the dismay over youth has taken on unprecedented pessimism and outrage. The image of a juvenile delinquent as someone who skips school to smoke cigarettes and put a hot rod together has become as antiquated as Marlon Brando in *The Wild One* wearing a sneer and a silly hat. Teenagers hanging on a street corner are no longer seen as complex human beings, perhaps "misguided" but, with the right help, capable of learning and maturing; now they are often viewed as potential cold-blooded murderers, immune to rehabilitation. This gloomy outlook is what lurks behind the clamor to establish such "solutions" as evening curfews for teenagers, to "criminalize" juvenile court by making it more about punishment than rehabilitation, to lower the age at which a child can be tried as an adult, to build more boot camps and prisons.

The media that has always been instrumental in shaping the public's perception of youth is now lightning quick and has the world wired, giving rise to "global tragedies." When "wilding" teenagers in New York's Central Park attack a female jogger, when black teenagers in Florida murder German and British tourists, when two eleven-year-olds in England perform a brutal murder, when Corey McKenzie kills a counselor, it is reported around the world, leaving the distinct impression that teenagers everywhere are beyond control in the streets and that no one is safe.

On the same week, August 2, 1993, two national U.S. news magazines ran essentially the same cover story, giving birth to the era of teenage terror. The *Time* article opened with a meticulously detailed description of a boy firing a gun that becomes "the sound of a growing national tragedy." *Newsweek*'s "Wild in the Streets" called "today's violent teenagers a new and dangerous breed." The article pulled together a collection of particularly grisly murders that occurred across the country as proof of a "virtual epidemic of youth violence. . . . Violence is devastating this generation as surely as polio cut down young people 40 years ago."

Meanwhile, on prime-time TV, voyeuristic, "reality-based" television shows like *Hard Copy* and *Inside Edition* pump up the drama by "investigating" such crimes. On "real-life" shows like *Cops*, squad cars roll by teenagers of color on city streets, leaving the distinct impression that as soon as the cops leave the juveniles are going to mug an old lady for her Social Security check.

"If all the public reads and sees are these very dramatic crimes, they think that is all that is happening out there," Soler explains. "The public gets no sense that these crimes happen very, very rarely. They get no sense that we are not talking about all teenagers."

And by and large, this is what the public does read and see about children. In 1994, Children Now, a nonpartisan policy and advocacy group, published a study by a professor of communications on how five major newspapers and three television networks create and perpetuate the public's fear of children. During the month of the study, almost half the stories about children on television (48 percent) and 40 percent of the stories in newspapers equated children with crime and violence. In a country where 25 percent of children under age six live in poverty, a country where fewer than 50 percent of the two-year-olds are immunized against preventable diseases, topics like child poverty, welfare, and child care accounted for only 4 percent of all newspaper and television stories about children. A meager 2 percent of the coverage focused on public policy attempting to develop ways to deal with children who are not getting immunized, fourteen-year-olds who are getting pregnant, or fifteen-year-olds who are carrying guns.

Two reasons suggest why the media presents such a one-sided picture of youth. First, the media is obsessed with crime. "News coverage of crime, especially on TV, really didn't take off until after the fall of the Soviet bloc," Soler says. "There are no more headlines about the bomb scare, and we need something to occupy people's attention. Crime fills that vacuum."

Second, and more significantly, public policy is complex and often turgid. Policy and statistics make for dull television and back-page newspaper stories. The media focuses instead on what is known as "anecdotal" information, which is often presented from the viewpoint of terrified adults. The problem with anecdotal information is that it can be terribly misleading.

For example, elderly citizens in a retirement community interviewed on the evening news talk about their fears of being mugged by the ominous-looking teenagers hanging out at shopping centers. What the newscast doesn't explain is that, statistically, retirees have little to fear from the purple-haired kids mouthing off at the mall. Fewer than 1 percent of crime victims over age sixty-four are reportedly raped, robbed, or assaulted by minors. The people most likely to be victimized by kids are other kids. In violent crimes against twelve-to-nineteen-year-olds, the offender is a juvenile in nearly half the cases.

Here is another case in point. In the article accompanying the story of the Star House murder, the *San Jose Mercury News* emphasized that forty juveniles had been arrested for murder, attempted murder, manslaughter, and accessory to murder in the previous seven months and that the "figures show little sign of declining." Yet, that is exactly what the figures did: the very next year in Santa Clara County, not a single juvenile was charged with murder until the first week in October. There were, of course, no headlines announcing this decline.

So, beyond the terrifying headlines and personal anecdotes, what is the truth about juvenile crime in the U.S.?

Crime statistics, especially juvenile crime statistics, are notoriously difficult to collect. Many crimes are never reported, offenders are often not arrested, and many who are arrested are sent home or diverted into programs that do not add to the official counts. Compounding the problem is that even the most carefully compiled statistics are tricky to interpret. For example, the country's arrest rate can increase for a number of reasons. Maybe the actual number of crimes went up, or maybe the police just started cracking down harder. Further, more often than adults, juveniles commit crimes in groups. Let's say that there was an aggravated assault and that five young men were arrested. The crime rate for juveniles is going to appear to be different depending on what is being measured: the number of juveniles arrested for assault (five), or the number of assaults for which juveniles were arrested (one).

Since statistics are open to multiple interpretations, they are easy to manipulate to promote a point of view. Similar sets of crime figures have been used both by proponents of "get-tough" legislation to prove that juveniles are out of control and by progressives to prove that "juvenile crime rates have actually declined over the last decade."

Among juvenile justice professionals, the most widely respected and least-biased "truth" comes from the Office of Juvenile Justice and Delinquency Prevention of the U.S. Department of Justice. *Juvenile Offenders and Victims: A National Report*, prepared by Howard N. Snyder and Melissa Sickmund, is a 1995–96 publication that brings together information from a variety of sources, and the picture of crime and youth it paints is much more honest than the impressions left by splashy stories about wilding teenagers.

The United States is not going through a general epidemic of teenage crime in the 1990s. It should go without saying that the vast majority of teenagers are never arrested. In 1992, only 5 percent of the country's minors were arrested for "index" crimes (violent crimes and property crimes like burglary and car theft). Less than one-half of 1 percent of the juvenile population was arrested for a violent offense. That same year, minors, who make up 25 percent of the population, accounted for 16 percent of all arrests recorded by the FBI's Uniform Crime Reporting Program. Most minors who are arrested are never arrested again.

There is an area—and it is a deeply disturbing one—where the media's portrayal, the public perception, and the statistics do agree. After more than a decade of relative stability, the juvenile rate of arrest for violent crimes increased by 38 percent between 1988 and 1992. If this trend continues, juvenile arrests for violent crime could double by the year 2010. Another scary statistic is that between 1984 and 1994, the number of juvenile murderers tripled.

Part of the explanation, often overlooked by the media, is simple demographics. Since 1984, the population under eighteen has been steadily increasing, and this alone accounts for some of the increase in the number of violent juvenile offenders, as well as an increase in the number of juvenile victims. Another point often ignored or downplayed by the media is that youth violence rates are only slightly more horrendous than the rates for adult violence. According to the FBI, the Violent Crime Index for 1983–92 for juveniles increased 57 percent, while the adult index increased 50 percent. According to 1991 statistics, adults are responsible for 92 percent of the country's murders, 87 percent of the rapes and robberies, and 77 percent of the motor vehicle thefts.

What this all boils down to is that the U.S. does not have just a youth problem, it has a violence problem. And if we are ever going to deal with it, we need to face just what the problem is.

This generation of "troubled" youth has what previous generations did not have: easy access to guns. A 1993 study of incarcerated juvenile offenders and students in inner-city schools found that 83 percent of the inmates and 22 percent of the students possessed guns. "Only 35 percent of the students agreed with the statement 'It would be a lot of trouble or nearly impossible to acquire one.' "

The old "jacket gangs" romantically immortalized in *West Side Story* waded into battle with baseball bats; today, a young man has no trouble "borrowing a firearm from family or friends" or buying a semiautomatic 9-mm or an assault rifle from the trunk of a dealer's car. In states that have strict gun laws, dealers buy weapons in neighboring states where the laws are lax, drive the weapons across state lines, and sell them at stiff markups.

Statistically, Corey McKenzie is an anomaly. He used a knife. In 1994, eight out of ten minors who committed murder used a firearm. According to figures from the Department of Justice, the number of juvenile murderers using guns quadrupled between 1984 and 1994, while the number of juveniles using other weapons to kill remained the same.

Guns are not only tied to increases in killings by youth, but also in youth being killed. The number of juveniles murdered with a firearm nearly tripled in the same time period, while the number of juveniles killed with other weapons remained constant. Today, "teenage boys in all racial groups are more likely to die from gunshot wounds than from all natural causes combined."

Figures from the National Council on Crime and Delinquency, a think tank and research and advocacy group, are equally alarming: between 1986 and 1992, the total number of children killed by firearms (in the hands of both adults and juveniles) rose by 144 percent. Fifty-nine percent of homicide victims under age ten are killed by their parents, 18 percent of the time using a firearm. And for every two minors who are murdered, one commits suicide, using a gun 62 percent of the time. (Between 1979 and 1991, the suicide rate for ten- to-fourteen-year-olds increased 76 percent.)

America's problem is not teenagers who are wild in the streets, teenagers who can't be rehabilitated, teenagers who are lost causes. What's changed over the past hundred years is that kids today can settle their disputes and personal problems in a permanent way, with guns.

30

COREY: THE HALL

THE SANTA CLARA COUNTY JUVENILE HALL IS PART OF JUVENILE
center, a complex that encompasses the delinquency courts, juvenile traffic court, and the probation department. The center is located a couple
of miles north of downtown San Jose on the Guadalupe Freeway. The
freeway is built along the Guadalupe River, a polluted, sluggish stream
that barely moves in the dry months; when the rains come, it overflows
its banks, flooding neighborhoods and downtown businesses. Immediately to the east of Juvenile Center is the brand-new county jail and a
new courts building with impressive glassed-in hallways. No building in
this civic center is so lackluster as Juvenile Hall, which is three stories of
cinder block painted pale yellow and light olive. Thousands of drivers
pass by on the freeway everyday, oblivious to the building that incarcerates as many as 329 minors.

The hall serves several purposes: to hold minors between the time
they are arrested, tried and released, placed on probation, or sent to one
of the county's detention ranches or to one of the California Youth Authority institutions. Sometimes, a minor serves his entire term here. The
hall has been operating close to capacity and, at times, above capacity for
years, but inside, surprisingly, it does not feel overcrowded. The corridors
are mopped a couple of times a day and have the unmistakable institutional smell of Pinesol mingling with cooked food. When the minors
leave their living units, they follow a colored line on the floor to their
destination—the blue stripe leads to a small visiting area, the green to an
interview room where they meet with their attorneys, the white to a
small, crowded clinic, and so on. Guards in a high-tech control booth
watch everything on a bank of television monitors. They can open a
door or seal off a hallway with the flip of a switch.

There are many white faces in Juvenile Hall, but the majority of the minors in custody are black, Hispanic, and Asian. Many people attribute the overrepresentation of minorities to sociology and economics: children of color tend to be poor and live in crime-ridden urban centers. The harshest line of reasoning is that vast numbers of kids of color are committing the most brutal crimes and are therefore locked up more often and for longer periods than white kids. (In 1994, 39 percent of juveniles arrested for murder were "white," according to FBI statistics.)

But many studies indicate that "offending rates" alone cannot account for the large number of minority arrests and for the disparity in treatment once kids of color enter the system. The Office of Juvenile Justice and Delinquency Prevention reviewed three decades of literature on the system, conducted its own studies in several states, and came to the dramatic conclusion that the juvenile justice system discriminates on the basis of race. "Studies of the adult criminal justice system do not indicate that race effects are common . . . but clearly this is not the case in the juvenile justice system. . . . The processing decisions in many state and local juvenile justice systems are not racially neutral: The effects of race may be felt at various decision points, they may be direct or indirect, and they may accumulate as youth continue through the system . . . with a relatively large net effect." The federal report also concluded that, throughout the country, there are very few programs or specific policies designed to address this inequity of treatment.

Cleveland Prince, the probation officer, is quick to come up with examples of how subtle racism can be: "I had a black kid whose mother and daddy were calling me all the time, and the attitude around the office was 'They got to be crazy because they're making all this noise.' But when a white kid's mother and father keep calling, they're not crazy, they're trying to protect their kid.

"Not too long ago, we had two kids in court for doing the same thing: a drive-by with a paint gun," Prince continues. "It was basically a prank, but the Hispanic kid from East San Jose went down on assault with a deadly weapon and was sent to the ranch. The other kid was from Palo Alto. Both his parents came to court, and he ended up with six months probation on a misdemeanor.

"In a lot of cases, the judge will release a kid to parents who show up in court. In a lot of cases, the parents of a minority kid won't show up and the kid gets held in custody. It's not that the mom has fewer or lesser feelings for her kid than the white, middle-class mom. It's often because she's a single parent and cannot miss work because she will get fired."

Black, white, Hispanic, or "other," the minors in the hall have, for the most part, been charged with serious crimes. Gone is the era when habitual truants and repeat shoplifters were taken to Juvenile Hall and locked up overnight to teach them that such actions can have severe consequences. California law is one reason: since status offenders were removed from the jurisdiction of the juvenile court, probation officers and police can no longer lock up a kid just "to scare some sense into him."

But even if the law allowed, Juvenile Hall for years has been too crowded to use valuable bed space to teach truants—or even burglars—"a lesson," much to the frustration of police, prosecutors, and probation officers, who want the hall to be a tool to "scare kids straight" and to hold them immediately accountable for their behavior. "What we're saying to kids," says Kurt Kumli, a deputy district attorney in the juvenile division, "is you have to stay crime-free and drug-free and gang-free, and if you don't, you know what's going to happen to you? Nothing."

One of the only ways that the hall is able to stay under or at capacity is by severely restricting admittance to those who have committed the most serious crimes—murder, attempted murder, rape, robbery, possession of a firearm, the sale of large quantities of drugs. In Santa Clara County, as around the country, half of all delinquency cases are handled informally, without filing a California Welfare and Institutions Code 602 deliquency petition. Probation officials have also come up with ways of monitoring minors so that they can be quickly moved out of the hall. Many are phoned at home and identified by their voiceprints. Others wear electronic anklets to ensure house arrest.

But even among those charged with serious crimes, there is a hierarchy. When Corey McKenzie entered the hall, he was placed in B-1, one of the two secure units that hold fifty teenagers in twenty-five small cells, each with an over-under bunk and a steel shelf for holding personal belongings like magazines, pictures of girlfriends, and letters from mothers. In this unit, every action is performed in full view of the counselors, who sit at a desk in the common area. During the day, young men and women in the less secure units go to the Osborne School, a county-run program that operates inside the hall. For security reasons, B-1 has its own school, located in a long, narrow space behind a glass partition.

There are desks and bookshelves and San Francisco 49er posters on the wall. The recreation area, where the boys play volleyball and basketball and the classic penal institution game, handball, is on the other side of a sliding glass door.

The minors on B-1 may have committed the most serious crimes, but they are, ironically, the easiest juveniles to manage. The younger boys in the less secure units, many of whom are in custody for the first time, are scared and far more volatile. They challenge authority and, to prove themselves, fight each other at any opportunity. They strut their gang affiliations and, just to raise hell, scream gang challenges after the lights go out.

An eerie calm pervades B-1. Many of the boys here have been locked up before or have lived in other institutional settings like group homes or the Children's Shelter. By now, they know how to follow the colored lines on the floor, and they know that "flipping off" a counselor is not worth it. They know that the more serious the charges, the more slowly the legal system moves, so they have settled in for the long haul. There is a predictable rhythm to the hall that young men who have lived for years in homes where chaos reigns find satisfying.

Corey had been living on B-1 for two weeks when the door to the unit buzzed open one morning and Prince came striding in. Corey spotted him and ran up the narrow corridor. "Mr. Prince! It's me! Corey! Don't you remember? You had my big brothers on probation! Don't you remember?" Corey was wearing the hall's standard issue: cheap black tennis shoes with Velcro straps, loose-fitting dark brown pants with an elastic waistband, a white T-shirt. His eyes searched Prince's for a sign of recognition. Prince knew who Corey was, but the boy had grown so much in the three years since the probation officer had his brothers on his caseload that he would not have recognized him.

"Hey, Corey, why you accusing me like that?" Prince asked. "Think I'd forget you?" Corey beamed, delighted.

"How you doin' in here?" Prince asked.

Corey frowned. "I'm doin' OK, I guess."

"OK? What's that mean, OK?"

"Just OK. It ain't so bad," Corey replied.

As usual, Prince was dressed much like the boys on his caseload: a black baseball cap pulled low over his short hair; black nylon sweatpants, black sweatshirt with black Nike high-tops completing the outfit. To some police officers, Prince's style of dress is an outward manifestation of his true sympathies: they think that Prince identifies with the gang-bangers he knows so well and gets much too close to them. The cops say that sometimes they don't know which side Prince is on.

"Too many cops think that this work is all about us versus them," Prince says, responding to the criticism. "But to me, it's really about having a heart for kids. I'm not saying that loving kids means you let them go free after they say, 'I'm sorry.' Kids still need to be held accountable. Some of them need to do life in prison. But I see hope, I see a future, even for the kids who are going to do life. All of them have the ability to change. The kids who are going to spend most of their lives in prison can still educate themselves and still be an asset to the community, even if that community is a prison community."

It would seem only logical that probation officers need to be connected to the families and the community they serve. Hauling a teenager who has violated the terms of his probation back into court and making sure a judge holds him accountable is the routine part of the job. The challenging part is helping kids straighten out their lives. If the probation officer can take a kid to a recreation center and get him into a karate class, if he can arrange after-school tutoring and help him find a part-time job, he can have a major impact on a young person's life.

Critics of probation departments—which have some of the strongest unions in any branch of the justice system—say they have abandoned the role that Prince describes as primary. Says one critic, Barry Krisberg of the National Council on Crime and Delinquency: "Instead of fighting for rehabilitation, probation departments have caved in and become junior G-men. We spend a lot of money on people who sit and drink coffee and eat doughnuts and travel around to conferences and we get nothing out of them."

More minors are arrested and placed on probation in Santa Clara County than in most urban counties in California. In 1994, nearly one in ten youths were arrested, the vast majority for misdemeanors. The reason usually given is that the county is "prevention-oriented." But, as in other counties in the state and around the country, programs that could make "prevention-oriented" a meaningful phrase have become scarce. Mental health services have been slashed and the only residential drug treatment program for youths was eliminated in 1990. After-school programs have vanished.

Youth advocates argue that locking a kid up in a juvenile hall overnight and placing him on probation is not going to turn that kid's life around. Instead, the system should be investing its time and money in programs that prevent kids from getting into trouble. Says one youth advocate who was struggling to organize a midnight basketball league, "People like myself have to beg, borrow, and steal in order to get money for programs, while money for prison beds seems to fall out of the sky."

Adds Krisberg, "My goal would be to abolish probation, get rid of their union, and spend money on community-based programs."

Prince is as hard on some of his "sorry-ass" colleagues as Krisberg is. "Scheduling an appointment in your office, having a kid come in at a set time, and saying, 'How you doin'? You keepin' your nose clean? OK, glad to hear it. Keep it up, and I'll see you here next month'—that's nothing but theater," Prince says. "All that does is teach kids to manipulate the system. And if there's one thing they already know, it's how to manipulate."

Statements like this have done nothing to add to Prince's popularity among his supervisors, which is another reason he is often on the streets and in the hall, why he likes to get out of the office, away from "the bullshit and the politics," as much as possible. But Prince is popular with kids, who respond to his easygoing friendliness and sense of humor. The minors on B-1 all knew him, or they knew who he was, and they began approaching, one at a time.

"Mr. Prince, can you fix it so my girlfriend can visit?" asked a boy who had been charged with a drive-by shooting. Prince was convinced that, like many youths who come from solid homes with loving parents, this boy ran with a gang because "right now, gang activity is socially acceptable. Rap artists have taken gang values mainstream. Kids emulate what they hear on CDs and what they see on TV and in the movies. Violence, hate, they're cool." Prince smiled at the teenager and shook his head. "I don't believe in doing girlfriend visits," he said matter-of-factly. "I want you to miss her. I want you to think about what you have done. That way, maybe you'll think twice before doing something that'll get you locked up again."

Corey listened closely as one boy after another approached Prince, until finally it was his turn. "So, Corey, you been here what, two weeks? Three weeks?" Prince asked when they were finally alone. "Your father been by to see you? Miss Crawley?" Corey shook his head no.

"Anybody been by?" Again, Corey shook his head.

"How you feelin' about what you did?" Prince asked.

Corey ran a finger over the ripples in the waistband of his pants. "It happened," he muttered.

"It what?" Prince asked.

"It happened. It's done," Corey said sullenly.

"Acting tough got you here. It gets you nowhere with me," Prince said, leaning across the table.

"What you want me to say?" Corey asked.

"Say anything you want, long as you tell me what you're feeling."

Corey looked at the probation officer. "I'm sorry I did what I did," he said, and his eyes filled with tears.

"Anything else? Might as well let it out. You got nothing to lose now," Prince said. Corey shook his head. "It was stupid. I took somebody's life. I . . ." Prince waited for Corey to continue, and when he did not, the probation officer said, "OK, Corey, that's a start."

Prince let a moment pass, then told Corey that he had been in San Quentin recently and was walking through the yard when Corey's oldest brother spotted him and came running up to say hello and that "I should have listened to what you were trying to tell me." For about ten minutes, Corey peppered the probation officer with questions about his brother, and then Prince stood to leave.

"Will you be comin' by to see me?" Corey asked. He had turned halfway around in his chair. If the answer was no, he could at least duck his head quickly and hide his disappointment.

"I'll make it a point to," Prince promised.

Later, Prince recalled the meeting. "People were describing Corey as a psychopath who decided he was going to kill someone, and John De Caprio just happened to be that person for no reason other than the fact that the opportunity was there. But talking to Corey that day, I knew they were wrong. He was hurting. I've worked with a lot of teenagers who have killed, and I am as sickened by those crimes as anyone. But I believe that very few of the teenagers who are written off as cold-blooded sociopaths truly lack remorse.

"After that day, every time I went on B-1, Corey came running. His eyes would follow me everywhere. It was like I was his daddy."

• • •

Time dragged on B-1, as it does in all penal institutions. Corey picked his way through three meals a day and went to the B-1 school and spaced out while a teacher did her best to teach history and the fundamentals of reading and writing. The Corey who was once a fiery basketball player disappeared. In the exercise yard, he played a halfhearted game of volleyball, threw a few shots up at the basket, and retreated to the shade.

The sessions Corey had with a court-appointed psychologist did not go well at first. Corey acted tough and was very guarded, responding to questions with a yes, no, or maybe. But during the fourth session, he suddenly opened up and told a secret that he had been keeping since he was a little boy: his father had beaten him at regular intervals, often with an extension cord. "That took four sessions to come out because Corey did not want to admit his father had beaten him," says Richard Roggia, Corey's court-appointed attorney. "To have to tell the psychologist, that was very hard for Corey."

Over the next three months, Corey's lethargy deepened into depression. Unable to sleep most nights, he stared at the ceiling. One night, he buried his face deep in his pillow and tried to suffocate himself. It didn't work, of course, any more than holding his breath would. Corey ended up pulling his head out of the pillow and gasping for air.

In preparation for his trial, which was three months away, a psychologist did an evaluation and described Corey's mental state in his final report: "Corey is experiencing intense feelings of rejection and abandonment. The utter lack of stable, caring adult role models has left him paranoid with regard to the adult world and authority figures. He feels he has lost everything already . . . any action he takes to improve his life will be ineffectual."

Corey said it better in his own straightforward way. During one session, he blurted out to the psychologist, "Nobody cares if I live or die. People think I'd be better off dead."

31

COREY: THE TRIAL

THE THREE COURTROOMS IN THE DELINQUENCY BRANCH OF THE SANTA Clara County Juvenile Court are small and cramped, with battered furniture and ersatz wood paneling. Since proceedings are routinely closed to all but family, clergy, and youth workers, the spectator sections are small. There is a run-by-the-seat-of-the-pants feel as officers and bailiffs scurry about the waiting room calling cases and searching for people to shepherd into one of the courtrooms. Deputy district attorneys, who may be involved in a dozen or more cases on any given day, stop to huddle with public defenders, who carry caseloads that are even heavier. Together, they hammer out the last-minute deals they will present to a judge.

On a hazy morning in September, five months after Corey McKenzie killed John De Caprio, Jesse Montgomery and Steuart Samuels were standing outside the courtroom of Judge Richard C. Turrone, waiting for Corey's trial to begin. Jesse, his long hair hanging straight down his back, peered through a small oval window in the door and saw Marc Buller, the district attorney who had interviewed him earlier and would be prosecuting Corey. Buller leaned over a balustrade to explain to members of De Caprio's family how the trial would unfold. Looking pale and obviously in agony, Brenda, John's widow, was seated in the middle of the first row, flanked by her mother on one side and by John's mother and father on the other.

Jesse turned his gaze to the two figures sitting on the defense side of the courtroom. One was a reporter from the *San Jose Mercury News*, who was allowed entry because confidentiality is removed when a juvenile is accused of a serious crime like murder and because the De Caprio slaying was a high-profile case. The other person was Dafford McKenzie.

"Corey's father doesn't look rich," Jesse said, then stepped aside to allow Samuels to peer through the window. Corey's father was wearing blue slacks, a butterscotch-colored windbreaker, and an oil-stained baseball hat with the words "Mac Tools" on the front. "Rich? Why would you say rich?" Samuels asked.

"Corey told us he was worth a million dollars," Jesse replied. "He said his dad had bought him seven guitars."

A door to the right of the judge's bench opened, and a bailiff led in Corey, who was handcuffed and wearing regulation loose-fitting pants and a white T-shirt. Brenda took one look at him, and her head collapsed on her mother's shoulder. A bailiff unlocked Corey's handcuffs, and he sat down, faced the bench for a split second, and then spun around to look at his father. Dafford McKenzie lifted a hand and let it drop on an armrest. Corey shot his father a look that mixed anger, contempt, and pain and quickly spun around.

A few minutes later, Judge Turrone, a slightly built, energetic man with a carefully trimmed mustache, entered the courtroom. The judge established the gravity of what lay ahead in his opening remarks: This was a murder trial. One life had been taken; the future of another life would be determined here.

With that, Judge Turrone turned to Buller, the supervising DA in delinquency court, who cut the classic figure of a young, aggressive prosecutor. A jogger who appeared trim in a light gray suit, Buller is half-Irish and half-Hispanic, with coal black eyes, a somber voice, and a direct manner. Politically ambitious and widely respected, Buller considers young murderers like Corey to be products of a society that has lost its sense of direction. Inside his home, Corey had been neglected, possibly abused. Outside, he had been allowed to flounder. No one—no neighbors who regard the community's children as their children, no teachers or counselors in the schools, no cop walking a beat, no one in a church or a boys club—had cared enough to reach out to Corey. No one had established any boundaries. No one had done anything to put an end to the cycle of violence that defined the young man's life. John De Caprio had tried, but by then it was too late.

There are any number of studies that show how childhood abuse increases the odds of future delinquency and adult criminality. In one survey that is following a thousand seventh- and eighth-graders, children who are victims of maltreatment or who are being raised by parents who abuse each other are more likely to commit violent acts than children who are growing up in "happier environments."

Buller understood that Corey's childhood had been surrounded by violence. He knew that Corey's life was indeed tragic, but Buller also believed that the murder Corey committed placed him beyond compassion. Juvenile law prohibited Buller from locking up Corey for the rest of his life, so he was intent upon putting Corey behind bars for as long as the law allowed. "Not all victims of a violent past turn into murderers," Buller told the court in his opening statement. "Those that do must be held accountable and not be allowed to use the past as an excuse. Nothing can ever justify the killing of John De Caprio. He was in the Star House working to help this young man and others like him. At no time did he present a threat to the accused. John De Caprio was murdered by a sociopath for whom we should have no pity."

Next, Judge Turrone turned to Richard Roggia, Corey's court-appointed attorney, for his opening statement. Roggia, a bear of a man in a rumpled blue suit, reminiscent of the way Orson Welles portrayed Clarence Darrow in *Compulsion*, fit the model of the defense attorney as closely as Buller looked the part of the DA. Good criminal defense attorneys believe that they are all that stands between a defendant and a cruel, impersonal leviathan, a Siva that devours human beings. Defense attorneys also see themselves as defenders of the Constitution. If the rights of a defendant are not vigorously asserted, especially in a case in which the crime is odious, those constitutional rights will slowly erode away.

Criminal defense attorneys tend to be good actors. Not only because of their ability to play a particular role in the courtroom, but also because they learn to see the world though a client's eyes, in much the same way that an actor must get inside a character. They also pride themselves on having a view of humanity that is more compassionate and hopeful than that of a prosecutor. Buller looked at Corey and mentally calculated the number of years he should spend behind bars. Roggia looked at the same boy and thought, "With a few breaks, he can still have a life."

"Corey's case was far from routine. That case got to me," Roggia explained later. "When I first met Corey, he was wary, but when that dissolved, I discovered that he was basically honest and quick-witted. I remember one morning dropping my own son off at his private school, and I happened to glance across the campus and see a young man who looked exactly like Corey walking between two white boys. In that moment, I realized that if life had led Corey to a prep school he would have made it through and would be on his way to college instead of prison. I looked at that kid and thought, 'That boy could be Corey; Corey could be that boy!' It hit me so hard, I almost started to cry."

Roggia's task in his opening statement was not to convince the judge that Corey was innocent of killing John De Caprio. He wanted to get Judge Turrone to make the same trip Roggia had made into Corey's psyche, to show the judge what was going on in Corey's mind the night of the murder. If Roggia could get the judge to understand Corey, perhaps the judge would mitigate the boy's sentence.

As Roggia presented Corey's history, Corey kept turning his head and sneaking glances at his father. Roggia claimed that Corey had endured a lifetime of neglect and abuse, that he had been dumped in the Children's Shelter, that he was placed in the Star House with robbers and burglars, that on the very few occasions his father had come to visit he was either high on drugs or intoxicated by alcohol. "As is common with abused and neglected kids who have been robbed of their childhood, Corey built himself a rich fantasy life," Roggia told the judge. "Central to that fantasy was his father, who was rich and would do anything for him."

Roggia moved to the night of the murder, when John De Caprio had hung up on Corey's girlfriend. Corey had screamed that the girl knew where his father was, that going through her was the only way to reach him. "At that point, John unwittingly dismantled Corey's fantasy," Roggia stated, throwing open his arms to illustrate the magnitude of the point. "John essentially said to this boy, 'Corey, listen to me: Your father has abandoned you. You are going to be an adult soon. You have got to stand on your own two feet.' "

At that, Brenda De Caprio sprang to her feet and strode swiftly up the aisle and out of the courtroom, followed closely by her mother. Ignoring or oblivious to the sobs that were echoing outside the door, Roggia continued. "John had unwittingly stumbled on the fantasies that are the essence of this young man's being, of his survival," Roggia said, laying a hand on his client's shoulder. "He had unwittingly taken the stopper out of the bottle. It was then that Corey went outside to brood. It was then that Corey, a boy with no juvenile record, fell prey to Karl Foster, a boy who does have a criminal past. It was then that Karl began working on Corey's anger, began egging him on."

When Roggia finished, Buller, the prosecutor, waited a few moments to allow the emotional impact of Roggia's speech to dissipate in the stillness. He was about to get to his feet when Brenda and her mother came back into the courtroom, their arms around each other as they walked up the aisle. Buller paused until they were seated and then began to speak: "Your honor, the People will not rely on psychobabble to explain what happened that night Star House No. 3. The People will use the physical evidence and eyewitness testimony to show that what took place that night was cold-blooded murder."

Buller played a tape of the 911 call that Karl Foster had made from a phone booth. While Karl's voice was heard telling a dispatcher about "a white man dressed in black," Corey sneaked another look at his father. Dafford McKenzie's head was resting on the back of his chair. His eyes were closed, his mouth was open, and he was snoring softly. Corey shook his head slowly and turned back to the trial.

Dafford McKenzie slept through both the morning and afternoon sessions on the first day of his son's murder trial. He missed hearing Jesse Montgomery meticulously detail the events that had occurred when he returned home the night of the murder. On the second day, Dafford fell asleep soon after sitting down and slept through both the morning and afternoon sessions. Among other things, he missed the testimony of the boys who were in the Star House when the murder occurred. On the third day of his son's trial, Dafford did not appear. He missed seeing Corey take the stand to testify that, when he was little, his father had whipped him with an extension cord. He missed hearing an affectless Corey connect his childhood beatings to the murder of John De Caprio. "Every time my dad hit me, I stabbed him," Corey testified in a flat voice, apparently saying that he was having a flashback as he was committing the murder.

"Did John say anything that angered you that night?" Roggia asked.

"He said, 'No wonder you are in a group home. No wonder your family doesn't care about you. You're pathetic,'" Corey replied.

In the spectator section, Jesse Montgomery and a supervising counselor from the Star House were shaking their heads back and forth, as if to say, "That never happened." In the row ahead of them, Brenda was trembling with anger. "That wasn't John," she would later tell a reporter. "He would never say anything like that about anybody."

In his cross-examination, Buller went on the attack. If Corey was having flashbacks when he murdered John De Caprio, why had he not told the police about them when they questioned him in the hours after the murder? Corey had no answer to that question.

"When Mr. Roggia asked if you had planned to kill your counselor, you denied that you had," Buller continued. "But the whole time you were walking down that hallway, you were thinking, 'I'm going to kill John.' Isn't that right?"

"I guess," Corey said slowly.

On the final day of his son's trial for murder, Dafford McKenzie did not appear. He missed seeing Corey stand and face the judge, his face empty of expression. He missed hearing Judge Turrone convict Corey of murdering John De Caprio. Corey did not flinch. Brenda buried her face in her hands and whispered, "Yes. Yes."

"There is no question that Corey suffered tragic events in his life," Judge Turrone said in passing sentence. "But that, while tragic and unfortunate, does not lead one to conclude that Corey suffers some abnormal mental condition that negates premeditation or malice aforethought." The judge imposed the longest sentence possible for a minor. Like his older brother before him, Corey was going to the California Youth Authority. He was almost sixteen; he would remain there until he was twenty-five.

That was not long enough for the De Caprio family. "I think his crime deserved more," Rita De Caprio, John's mother, said outside the courtroom. "I, personally, don't think he will ever be rehabilitated."

"He will be free in nine years," Brenda said. "I will never be free of losing John."

Roggia also made a statement to the press. He described Corey's case as a tragic example of the social system's failure to properly help abused and unwanted children. "How many more Coreys are out there? And John De Caprios too?"

Frances Crawley did not come to court because "I couldn't bear to see it. It would have killed me." A reporter had to phone her to get her reaction to the sentencing: "I'm sorry for the man's wife; God in heaven knows it shouldn't have happened. But I feel sorry for Corey, too. He is just like a son to me."

32

CHILDREN, CRIME,
AND POLITICS

"WHEN COREY MCKENZIE KILLED MY HUSBAND, HE TOOK A PART OF my life, too."

Soon after the murder of John De Caprio, Brenda appeared before a meeting of the Judiciary Committee in the California State Capitol building in Sacramento. She was there to lobby for tougher penalties for juveniles convicted of murder. Under California law in 1994, youths under the age of sixteen had to be tried in juvenile court, no matter how heinous their crimes. They served sentences in a juvenile penal system that—in theory—was designed to rehabilitate as well as to protect the public. In California, the maximum sentence the juvenile justice system could render for the ultimate crime—murder—was the sentence Corey received: confinement in the California Youth Authority until age twenty-five.

The Judiciary Committee was holding hearings on Assembly Bill 136, a bill aiming to drop the threshold to the adult courts to age fourteen. Throughout the 1990s, similar get-tough measures were topping the agendas of many state legislatures as politicians scrambled to respond to public sentiment that the juvenile justice system was too soft. If AB 136 had been law, Corey's case could have been transferred from juvenile court to the adult criminal courts, where the maximum sentence for a person under eighteen is life without parole. Adult prisons offer little in the way of rehabilitation. Prisons are about punishment.

"Corey killed that part of me that loves life, that part that believes that good necessarily triumphs over evil and that true happiness can be achieved if one is committed to achieving it," Brenda testified. "I have received a life sentence, a life sentence of pain."

The hearing room was hushed when Brenda finished. It was powerful, moving testimony, exactly the kind that Chuck Quackenbush, a Republican assemblyman representing parts of Santa Clara County, was looking for. Quackenbush, the author of AB 136, is an astute politician and knew that the media would cover the hearings because Brenda's testimony was so poignant. As a result, his name would also be in the newspapers and his face on television, all of which would convince his constituents that he was as tough on crime as conservatives traditionally were on Communism.

But experts like Barry Krisberg, who has been studying and working to improve the juvenile justice system for more than twenty years, insist that high-profile hearings featuring heartbreaking testimony like Brenda's present the public with a distorted picture of youth crime and blind the public to genuine solutions—solutions that must go to the very heart of who we are as a society.

"There is no such thing as a decent society held together by cops and prisons. Ultimately, societies are kept together by vibrant communities and social institutions that work," Krisberg says. "The privileged in this country need to understand that. They may send their kids to private schools and move out to the suburbs, but they won't be able to live a tranquil, happy life by bailing out. They need to understand that being involved, having a stake in the kids who live on the other side of town, is really in their own self-interest."

Krisberg and other reform-minded criminologists see bills like AB 136 as cynical attempts to gain political ground at the expense of children. "AB 136 is a quack bill by a quack politician that offers a quack's solution," Krisberg charges, stooping to play off Quackenbush's name.

The two opponents could be poster boys for their positions. Krisberg is ethnic and lives in Berkeley, where his children attend public schools. Quackenbush is tall and chiseled, a student leader when he attended Notre Dame, and an ex-air force fighter pilot. A successful businessman who lives in suburban Cupertino, Quackenbush emphasizes that the United States was built by people who "believed in personal responsibility." He opposes most social welfare programs for the standard conservative reasons: "Once you bring the government into the family, you really are zapping the energy of society. People think, 'Why should I bust my tail to raise a family? Government will take care of all that for us.'"

It was Quackenbush's belief in "personal responsibility," in the idea that "a society cannot function unless individuals know they will be held accountable for their actions," that led him to file AB 136. When he read the story of Melvin Ancheta in the newspapers, Quackenbush was sickened to learn that the teenager who had tortured and stabbed the eight-year-old was only a month shy of his sixteenth birthday. He was disgusted that Corey McKenzie was only six months away from being sixteen when he murdered John De Caprio. Both would be back on the streets at age twenty-five. To Quackenbush, it means that they got away with murder.

"The juvenile justice system is antiquated. It was not designed to handle the murderers we have now," says the assemblyman. "It was designed to handle the wayward youth who shoplifted something or stole a bicycle or maybe got into petty drugs. The little monsters we have today who murder in cold blood are very dangerous individuals. They have to be punished and walled off from society for a very long period of time, if not forever."

Quackenbush argues that "progressives"—those who persist in thinking that the goal of juvenile justice should be prevention and rehabilitation—have the crime issue backward. Progressives wring their hands over Corey McKenzie's terrible childhood. They talk about how horrible it is to "lose" a boy like Corey at age fifteen and how important it is to invest in treatment programs. By doing that, Quackenbush says, progressives ignore the life-shattering pain of victims like Brenda De Caprio. They ignore the fact that thousands of children come out of homes that are as bad—if not a whole lot worse—than Corey's and somehow manage to live dignified, productive lives. Progressives ignore the risk that Corey may come out of the juvenile penal system "rehabilitated" and kill again.

"Are you willing to bet your life he's rehabilitated? Your daughter's life?" Quackenbush asks rhetorically. "That's what we're talking about here: life. I may be willing to bet my bicycle or my car, but not my life, my wife's life."

To Quackenbush, the issue is very basic, "very primitive." The first duty of the state is to protect its citizens. To do that, the state must do what the parents who have produced "these little monsters" failed to do: punish them so severely that they will never commit another crime. "The criminal life is deceptively easy for kids to get into," Quackenbush explains. "You want to steal cars? Someone will teach you the rudiments. You want to sell drugs? Give so much back to the main guy, and you get all this cash. You want to kill somebody? Go ahead; among your peers it's a cool thing to do, cool because you can get away with it.

"The way you turn things around is to make crime hurt. If you hurt a person in this society, society has to hurt you back. It's very primitive, but people understand it."

Quackenbush's arguments are compelling because they are so primitive. They tap into humanity's craving for vengeance, an urge that was the foundation of the earliest legal systems, the Hammurabi Code and *lex talionis*, the law of an eye for an eye.

Barry Krisberg has set himself a formidable task: to counter the human urge for revenge. He spends much of his time flying around the country to oppose bills that are carbon copies of Quackenbush's or even harsher. "The conservatives want to blame and punish people," Krisberg says with disgust. "As if that would work! It makes absolutely no sense to use the prison system to try to solve complex social problems. It's a costly lesson that we should have learned by now."

Progressives rely on statistics to make their points: If stern punishment were the deterrent some insist it is, if locking up more criminals at younger ages for longer periods of time were effective, the United States would have one of the lowest crime rates in the industrialized world. The United States locks up more of its citizens (517 per 100,000) than any country in the world. California locks up more people (626 per 100,000) than any other state. "Even though California's general population is 27 times smaller than India's, California keeps about 3,000 more people behind bars [than India]," says a report issued by the Center on Juvenile and Criminal Justice, a public policy center in San Francisco. (The center earns its funding in large part by developing plans for alternative sentences for juveniles and adult criminal defendants.) By comparison, the incarceration rate in South Africa is 355 per 100,000; in Japan, 35 per 100,000; and in repressive Singapore, only 221 per 100,000.

And yet, despite these astronomical incarceration figures, the United States also has the highest rate of violent crime of any industrial society—732 crimes per 100,000. The rate in California is much higher—1,059 per 100,000. By comparison, the violent crime rate in France is 205 per 100,000; in Sweden, 129 per 100,000; and in Japan, an amazingly low 19 per 100,000. "Japan incarcerates its citizens at one eighteenth the rate of California, yet California's violent crime rate is nearly 56 times Japan's," says the center.

What these numbers suggest is precisely the opposite of what the get-tough politicians claim: the higher the rate of incarceration, the higher the rate of violent crime. That holds as true for juveniles as it does for adults.

Yet, since the 1970s, an increasing number of states have done what Quackenbush drafted AB 136 to do in California: take more youths out of juvenile court and sentence them as adults in criminal courts.

In 1978, legislators in Albany passed a bill that made New York one of the first states to give the criminal courts "original jurisdiction" over thirteen-year-olds charged with murder and over fourteen-year-olds charged with serious crimes like rape and assault with a deadly weapon. ("Original jurisdiction" means that for a youthful offender who has committed one of these crimes the juvenile justice system does not exist. His case goes directly to the adult criminal courts.)

What has been the result? Certainly not the strict punishment striking fear into the hearts of young hoodlums that lawmakers had in mind. In 75 percent of the cases involving juveniles, judges in New York criminal courts did not hand out harsher punishment than judges in juvenile court. In fact, in many cases, they did not convict the kids at all.

The reasons? The dockets in the New York criminal courts, like criminal courts everywhere, are clogged with cases. Youthful offenders do months of "dead time" in jail awaiting trial. When they finally get to court, a judge who is used to staring down at hard-core adult criminals sees a juvenile standing before him. The judge thinks, "This kid doesn't belong in my courtroom. I can't sentence him as I would an adult. I'm sending this case back to the juvenile court, where it belongs."

Those juveniles who do stand trial in criminal courts often do not get the harsh punishment they are supposedly there to receive. A national survey found that "the majority of transferred cases . . . received probation, fines or other alternatives to incarceration." Another study, conducted in New York between 1986–87, found that "robbery cases were more likely to receive incarceration in juvenile court (57 percent vs. 27 percent)." The young age of a client makes it easy for criminal defense attorneys to do for juveniles as they do for adults: plea-bargain. The attorney argues that his client is young and malleable and capable of change. Because this is the first time his client has appeared in adult court, the crime he is charged with is "a first offense."

"There have been three separate evaluations of New York's juvenile offender law," the National Council of Juvenile and Family Court Judges reported in 1994. "All three have concluded that the statute does not offer more public protection, more punishment of juveniles, more protection for juveniles, or better rehabilitation of juveniles. The state of New York is second only to Florida in the number of violent crimes per 100,000, with a rate of 1,207."

It is telling that Florida is another get-tough pioneer. Using the "mandatory waiver," Florida has sent thousands of juveniles directly into the adult system over the past thirteen years, and the state still has the highest violent crime rate in the country—1,222 per 100,000.

Yet, despite these results, state after state has followed the lead of New York and Florida. Between 1988 and 1992, the number of cases judicially waived to criminal court increased by 68 percent.

The politicians who want to lock up juveniles at a younger age for longer periods of time always focus on the "little monsters," like Corey McKenzie. They have a legitimate argument here; as probation officer Cleveland Prince says, there are kids who "need to do life in prison." But it is not just "cold-blooded teenage murderers" who are being swept into the adult criminal courts. Across the country, the vast majority of teenagers entering the adult criminal system have *not* been charged with a violent crime.

Criminologists have pointed out that violent repeat offenders constitute only a small fraction of the minors who wind up in the adult system. A study done by the Florida legislature's Commission on Juvenile Justice revealed that during a nine-month period only 23 percent of the cases transferred to the adult criminal courts were violent offenders. Nationally, only 38 percent of the juveniles whose cases get kicked up to adult courts are charged with committing a violent crime. The others are crimes against property, like setting fire to a building (41 percent), or drug charges, like selling crack cocaine to an undercover agent (15 percent).

Even more troubling are signs that transferring a juvenile to adult court does not "teach him a tough lesson" but can actually increase his chance of recidivism. One study found that "The probability of rearrest and reincarceration was no different for youth charged with burglary, regardless of which court handled their case. Offenders charged with robbery, on the other hand, were significantly less likely to be rearrested and reincarcerated if they were handled as juveniles."

Do politicians like Quackenbush know all this and ignore the facts for political gain? "Yes," says Krisberg. "Everything I know about politicians leads me to be very cynical. It's hard for me to imagine that someone could be so naive to believe that any of these repressive things work. I've got to believe at some level they know what's going on, but they just don't see it."

What is going on is that the juvenile justice system does not now—nor has it ever—let youthful offenders "get away with murder." It is anything but "soft." Between 1983 and 1991, the number of juveniles locked up in correctional facilities increased by 10 percent. The Office of Juvenile Justice and Delinquency Prevention conducted a study of the juvenile courts in ten states and found that in all ten there was a higher rate of conviction for the crimes of sexual assault, aggravated assault, and robbery in the juvenile courts than there was in the adult courts.

Get-tough politicians score politically when they point out that there is no life sentence in the juvenile justice system. But in California, juveniles sentenced for homicide tend to serve more time behind bars than adults who are convicted of the same crime. Figures for 1992 show that youths incarcerated in the California Youth Authority served an average of sixty months for homicide. Adults incarcerated in the California Department of Corrections served an average of forty-one months for the same crime.

But facts and figures don't count for much when the American public is angry, frustrated, and afraid and wants the "teenage crime problem" solved once and for all. Nowhere is this hysteria more apparent than in California. In 1985, the state was still spending two and a half times as much on education as it was on prisons. But after 1985, funding for the penal system began to increase, and money flowing into higher education began to plummet. California is now building new prisons the way it once built universities. Between 1989 and 1994, employment in the state's Department of Corrections increased by 9,032. In the state colleges and universities, the number of faculty, staff, and administrative positions dropped by 10,790.

For fiscal year 1996, the governor of California submitted a budget that earmarks more money for prisons—$3.7 billion—than for higher education—$3.5 billion—the first time in the state's history that this has happened. The Department of Corrections plans to build six new prisons in 1996 and a total of fifteen new prisons by the year 2000 "to handle the flood of inmates from the 'Three-Strikes-and-You're-Out' bill. The additional prison capacity is critically needed to avoid court-ordered releases of dangerous felons due to overcrowding," says a department spokesman.

Given this climate, it came as no surprise that AB 136 passed in November 1994 and was signed into law by the governor, along with three other bills that added rape, kidnapping, robbery, and armed burglary to offenses that would send juveniles fourteen or older to adult criminal courts.

This has not been enough for the get-tough school of politicians. In 1996, more than 70 bills designed to crack down further on juvenile offenders were introduced in the California legislature. Plans for prevention and rehabilitation were an after-thought, if they were present at all.

33

COREY:
THE CYA

Corey McKenzie was taken to the California Youth Authority (CYA) Northern Reception Center and Clinic in Sacramento, where he joined nearly five hundred other wards who had recently been committed to the CYA. In the twenty-eight days he spent in the center, a cluster of eerily quiet, aging brick buildings in an industrial zone, Corey got more attention than he had ever gotten in his life. The casework specialist assigned to Corey put him through a series of diagnostic tests and did a psychosocial workup that probed his past. Corey got a thorough medical and dental exam and completed a battery of educational tests designed to determine his grade level in reading and mathematics, as well as his vocational aptitude and manual dexterity.

The caseworker summarized the results in a lengthy report that went to the Youthful Offender Parole Board. In theory, the board could release Corey before he had served the nine years that Judge Turrone gave him. It is the parole board, not the judge, that ultimately determines how much time a ward serves in the CYA. But members of the board are tough-on-crime types, appointed by conservative Republican governors. Wards are serving longer sentences in the CYA than ever before.

Corey's report was also sent to an administrative board that determined where he would begin serving his sentence. From the eleven CYA institutions and four youth conservation camps that are scattered throughout the state, the board chose the Preston School of Industry. "School of Industry" has an archaic ring because Preston, which opened in 1894, is the oldest—and still one of the toughest—institutions in the CYA.

• • •

"They send kids to us saying they need rehabilitation," says Al Picucci, a health and safety manager who has worked at Preston for twenty-two years. "Hell, most of the kids we get have never been habilitated."

Preston is located in the sleepy gold rush town of Ione, in the Mother Load, and is the town's main industry, employing hundreds of locals. The original building, a Victorian monstrosity with a tower and turrets and with wide, winding porches, is known locally as "the Castle." It is still standing but has been boarded up since 1960. Until then, Preston functioned as an old-fashioned reform school, where wards were taught a trade and put to work on a farm. Things are not much different now.

"Today, we've got more programs than any place in CYA," Picucci said proudly as he drove slowly around the hilly fifty-six–acre campus, pointing out buildings that housed the auto mechanics program, print shop, restaurant services, computers, masonry, refrigeration and air-conditioning, and landscape gardening. "Wards are either going to school, or they are in a program all day long," Picucci said. "To not go is a lockup offense."

But Preston is not the topflight trade school that Picucci seemed to be describing. It is, at heart, a prison surrounded by a fence topped with razor wire that glistens in the sun. "Kick the fence and it sets off an electronic signal. Someone will come in a truck real fast," Picucci said. The only difference between the guards in the CYA and those in, say, San Quentin is that the CYA staff does not carry firearms. If they spot a ward trying to go over the wall or a riot breaks out, the "correctional peace officers" respond with clubs and tear gas.

Up and down the fence, there were places where hardware cloth had been used to patch holes wards had cut in escape attempts. "Hardware cloth has such a tight mesh, kids can't get a grip in it," Picucci explained, amusement and a certain respect mingling in his voice. "So they steal forks and use them to climb the fence. They get to the top and throw a blanket over the razor wire. Pretty damn ingenious."

A squad of teenage boys wearing brown pants and white T-shirts marched by in a tight formation, eyes straight ahead, faces fixed and grim. They were in LEAD—for Leadership, Esteem, Ability, Discipline—the first boot camp program for delinquents in California. "It's too early to tell how LEAD graduates are doing recidivism-wise; the program's only three years old, but the wards love it. The spirit is great," Picucci said.

Picucci continued driving past rows of long, low redbrick lodges, or dormitories. "This is where Corey McKenzie is housed," he said, coming to a stop in front of one of the dorms. It was empty, and the doors at both ends were open. Inside, the bunk beds were crisply made and the floor was spotless. "Corey hasn't caused us any headaches," Picucci said as he drove away. "He's getting with the program."

Down the road from what was Corey's dorm is Oak Lodge, a single-story brick building that is the home of the Oak Specialized Counseling Program, one of the most intensive programs in the CYA and one of the few long-term, in-depth programs offered. "Oak," Picucci said succinctly, "is for 'predators.' "

The childhood atrocities done to the wards living in Oak Lodge are beyond imagining. Genitals have been slashed with razor blades; hot irons have been stuck into rectums. One boy came home from elementary school every day knowing that his stepfather was going to take him into the basement, fasten his arms and legs in leather straps, and sodomize him. He did not run away because his mother was ill.

The wards, in turn, have done things that are unfathomable. After his mother died, this same boy killed a five-year-old. Another boy who was beaten and sexually abused by his alcoholic mother and a series of her boyfriends broke into the home of an elderly lady, intending to steal her car. When she caught him rummaging for her keys, he went into a rage and raped and stabbed the woman, over and over. She was eighty-eight years old.

The Oak program is twenty-four hours a day of therapy, both group and individual, seven days a week. Wards may spend three years here or longer. Their two-man rooms are tiny and the lodge has a spartan feel, but for a vast majority this is as good as life has ever been. For the first time, the wards are living in a safe environment. For the first time, there are people who care about them. For the first time, they are taking the arduous emotional, journey that in the juvenile justice system gets lumped under the rubric of "change."

"The judge had a choice of sending me to state prison or CYA, and when he said, 'I'm going to give you another chance,' I said to myself, 'I got over on you, sucker.' He was a preppie-looking motherfucker," sixteen-year-old Johnny was saying in the main room in Oak Lodge. The forty other wards sitting on metal folding chairs in a big circle nodded and laughed knowingly. "I didn't really care where he sent me 'cuz my goal was the penitentiary," Johnny continued. "All my family's locked up. But when I got here they put me in 'mainline' [the general population], and it was just a big waste of time. I got real suicidal. I kept telling myself, 'I ain't nuthin.'

"They put me in Oak and I been here two years now, and it's taken me that long to learn how to feel," Johnny continued. "I never felt nothing for my victims 'cuz I didn't feel nothing for myself. I was never able to cry or to tell people how I felt. I'm learning to do that here. I'm working on controlling my anger, and I've learned how to read. Now, in the back of my mind, I'm telling myself, 'I want to do something. I want to do something right.'"

The task in Oak Lodge is to break the victim-victimizer cycle that is at the heart of violent crime. These boys have been prisoners at home and have had their spirits imprisoned. Living together, listening to each other, they learn what most people learn by having a family, friends, and a community: others have suffered as they have. Gradually, a thread of compassion begins to emerge.

In the end, though, it all comes down to the individual. To "break the cycle," each ward must do what it has taken Johnny two years to begin doing. They must find their own humanity and discover it in others. They must also take responsibility for what they have done in the past. Those are extraordinarily difficult tasks for youths who have had such terrible experiences with authority figures, who have been so brutally dehumanized.

"Our wards come here seeing their victims as objects," says Peter Shumsky, a clinical psychologist who has worked in Oak Lodge since 1980. "The only way they know to gain respect, the only way to get power and a sense of worth, is to victimize. If you molest or rape or attack someone, then you are no longer weak, you are in control. We try to teach them that you and another person can have a relationship where you are neither victim nor victimizer.

"Our wards have gone through life feeling only hurt and anger," Shumsky continues. "Guys who thought, 'If you are caring, you are weak,' learn to take risks and share. A sense of courage and pride comes out of that. They begin to regain the 'soft' emotions, care and compassion."

As often as not, the moment when a ward, in Shumsky's phrase, "reclaims his humanity," occurs during a marathon group therapy session. Marathon sessions are held once a month, usually beginning around midnight and sometimes continuing until noon the next day. "Typically, what happens is, I'll be sitting on the floor during a marathon, and a boy will come over and start whispering in my ear, telling me all about his committing offense," says Gail Steinkamp, a counselor in the Oak Program for many years. "He'll say, 'I don't deserve to live; I should be dead,' and then there will come a wail of pain, like a dog in terror.

"These kids need to be touched. So many were touched in violent ways, raped by their fathers, beaten by their mothers. I'll hold him and rock him in my arms, sometimes for hours. When the time is right, I'll tell him how much I respect him for the human being he is right now. I never minimize the committing offense. I always tell them that nothing will ever make up for what they did to their victims, that there is nothing they can ever do for their victims' families. But they can make sure it doesn't happen again."

After working in the CYA for twenty years, Steinkamp believes that the humanitarian way is the only way. If an institution does nothing but incarcerate, it does nothing but turn young criminals into older, more sophisticated criminals. If an institution does not offer programs designed to break the victim-victimizer cycle, the institution itself becomes part of that vicious cycle.

"We had a sixteen-year-old come in who had torn a six-month-old baby to shreds," Steinkamp recalls. "Other staff [at Preston] said, 'How can you be civil to him? How can you touch him? These kids are here to be punished; they don't deserve anything.' My answer is always the same: 'Maybe if somebody had been "civil" to him earlier, that baby would be alive.' If nobody gets to these kids, someone will pay for what's been done to them. If nobody helps these kids deal with their pain and humiliation, we will never be able to reduce the number of victimizers in our society."

Corey McKenzie—a victim who turned into a victimizer—would seem the perfect candidate for the Oak Specialized Counseling Program. But it is reserved for "the neediest of the needy," and, in the world of the CYA, Corey was deemed not needy enough. He was not suicidal enough; he was not cutting or mutilating himself; the results of his tests were not alarming enough. There was a long list of boys who were in much worse psychological shape. "Ideally, we'd have 100 percent of our wards in programs like Oak Lodge," says a CYA spokesman at the Northern Reception Center. "As it is, only 2.5 percent of our wards are in special programs."

The reason is money. In 1996, it cost $30,100 to keep a ward in the CYA for a year. It costs $52,000 a year to keep a ward in the Oak Program. As a result, Corey McKenzie, like the vast majority of the 9,968 wards who were incarcerated in the CYA in 1996, did his time in "mainline," which Johnny, in the Oak program, accurately described as "a big waste of time."

During the 1980s, the Commonweal Research Institute published three studies that denounced the CYA. Overcrowding has increased since then, causing conditions to get even worse. Commonweal's conclusion is that for the wards in the mainline population the CYA is "criminogenic"—it creates criminals. For years, the CYA—like so many long-term juvenile institutions throughout the country—has been operating way over capacity. In 1996, it was 148 percent of capacity. This overcrowding affects every aspect of a ward's life, from "the violent, gang-oriented atmosphere that prevails in the overcrowded dayrooms and dormitories [to] . . . the frequency with which Youth Authority inmates assault each other [which] should be appalling to any reasonable observer.

"The tragedy of the Youth Authority today is that a young man convicted of a crime cannot pay his debt to society safely," writes Steve Lerner, the author of the Commonweal reports. "The hard truth is that CYA staff cannot protect its inmates from being beaten or intimidated by other prisoners."

The reality is that the CYA staff does not control events in the institutions' dormitories and dayrooms; gangs do. Wards who come to the CYA caught in the deadly victim-victimizer cycle find that they have only two options: "being an agent of the gang's violence or its victim."

"Those inmates who seek protection by joining a gang are often ordered by its leaders to assault someone as part of the price of admission—a proposition that is hard to refuse when they realize that their choice is beating someone up or becoming the target of a group attack," Lerner writes. "Either way they lose."

Many states operate similar large-scale institutions that hearken back to the 1850s. Up until the 1970s, Massachusetts was among them. For more than a hundred years, the Massachusetts Department of Youth Services (DYS) did what the CYA does today: lock up 100 percent of the wards in its custody. In the early 1970s, Jerome Miller was appointed to head the department. Miller turned out to be an iconoclastic reformer who outraged politicians and terrified the public by closing that state's decrepit reform schools. However, the public's fears turned out to be as empty as the politicians' rhetoric. Miller did not send the wards over the wall, even though he somewhat ruefully titled the book he wrote about his experience in Massachusetts *Last One over the Wall*. Miller placed the wards in a new system that turned conventional thinking on its ear.

In Miller's new system, only 15 percent of the wards, the most violent and the most disturbed, were kept under lock and key. The other 85 percent were placed in group homes and in small residential programs that had varying levels of security. A boy who killed a stepfather who was beating his mother might end up in a "staff-secure" group home (the doors were not locked). A repeat rapist whose attacks showed a pattern of increasing violence might be locked in a cell. Delinquents "failed toward incarceration." For example, if the minor ran away from a staff-secure group home, he was transferred to a program that had locks on the doors. If he kept running, he eventually ended up in a cell in an institution.

Despite the common perception that large institutions holding hundreds of wards are cost-efficient, the opposite is true. Big buildings are notoriously expensive to maintain, and they require a large staff that is on duty twenty-four hours a day. The money that Miller saved shutting the institutions was spent on independent contractors who offered intensive small-group therapy programs similar to the one that operates in Oak Lodge. ("I've never been able to understand why conservatives hate what I did in Massachusetts," Miller says. "Basically, all I did was introduce free enterprise into the juvenile justice system. Aren't they the champions of free enterprise?")

The cost Miller paid for fighting the political battles required to get his program up and running was his job. ("I knew I'd get fired; you couldn't do what I did and not get fired," he says.) The remarkable thing is that his successors were able to keep his reforms in place and, in some cases, to expand upon them. Every time public figures in Massachusetts talk about the need "to lock up more kids," they are attacked by a powerful new lobbying group—the providers of small, intensive programs for youthful offenders.

The Massachusetts model has become a bellwether for other states and is the most discussed, most frequently studied juvenile justice system in the United States. "Over the last two decades, the new system of juvenile justice in Massachusetts has performed remarkably well," Steve Lerner writes in *The Good News About Juvenile Justice*. Lerner cites a study that tracked eight hundred youths who served time in Massachusetts after Miller had made his reforms. The study found that "The rearrest rate of young people leaving DYS is considerably lower than the national average. . . . In 1972, 35 percent of the adult prisoners in Massachusetts prisons had been through DYS facilities; by 1985 [after the Miller reforms], that percentage had dropped to 15 percent."

The Massachusetts model has been implemented in other states, most notably Pennsylvania and Utah. The results there are as encouraging as they have been in Massachusetts. So, why haven't more states followed Massachusetts's lead? Two reasons—both political.

"There's no question that the humane approach to juvenile incarceration works, and is much more cost-effective in the long run," says Alan Breed, who was director of the CYA from 1967 to 1977, when it was one of the most progressive institutions in the nation. "But marketing that idea is quite another question.

"Back in the '60s, the idea took hold that the only way we were ever going to do anything about crime is to lock more people up for longer periods, and it has just grown and grown. Crime rates continue to increase, and the only answer the political world has is to get tougher and get tougher. I've been in corrections more than forty years, and I've never seen a time when policy making has been more politicized and ideologically based. And there doesn't seem to be any end in sight."

The second problem is inherent in any large public bureaucracy: over time, the task it was created to address becomes secondary to jobs. As California metamorphoses from the "Golden State" into the "Lock-Em-Up State," the 23,000-member California Correctional Peace Officers Association is becoming one of the most powerful unions in Sacramento. The association already has a political action committee that "is now second in the state only to the American Medical Association in political contributions."

No political figure in California, on the scene or on the horizon, has the political or personal strength to do what Miller did in Massachusetts twenty years ago. No governor in California is going to take on the Correctional Peace Officers Association by closing all but a few of the institutions and putting guards—most of whom do not have a college degree, most of whom do little more than turn keys, but whose average salary is $53,000 a year—out of work.

The end result is this: For thousands of wards serving time, the primary influences are not professionals dedicated to breaking the victim-victimizer chain. The primary influences are gang leaders dedicated to preserving that chain. As Corey's "stepmother," Frances Crawley, says, "Every time Corey calls, he says, 'YA ain't so bad. I'm up here, hanging with my homies.' "

34

DELINQUENCY COURT, 8:30 A.M.

A FIFTEEN-YEAR-OLD BOY WHO WAS CAUGHT MAKING OBSCENE PHONE calls in Arizona thirty years earlier was, in part, the reason Deputy District Attorney Kurt Kumli was walking into the Santa Clara County Delinquency Court on a brilliant spring morning. The original juvenile court was founded on a premise that was closer to the New Testament than the Old and had no role for a district attorney. The special court for children was to be less punitive and less formal than the adult courts. There would be "hearings" instead of trials; youths would be "adjudicated as delinquents" instead of being sentenced as criminals; they would be sent to reform or training schools instead of prisons. The DA, whose traditional role is to see that the letter of the law is upheld and a pound of flesh is extracted, rarely if ever appeared in juvenile court.

All that began to change the day an Arizona judge held a cursory hearing and summarily remanded fifteen-year-old Gerald Gault to the state industrial school, where he was to remain until age twenty-one. Gault's parents filed a suit claiming that their son's right to due process had been violated. The Arizona Supreme Court ruled against the parents, but the case went all the way to the U.S. Supreme Court, which overturned the Arizona court's decision in 1967. Justice Abe Fortas noted in a majority opinion that if Gault had been eighteen or older when he made the obscene phone calls "the maximum punishment would have been a fine of $5 to $50, or imprisonment in jail for not more than two months." Justice Hugo Black concurred, adding, "Where a person, infant or adult can be seized by the State, charged, and convicted for violating a state criminal law, and then ordered by the State to be confined for six years, I think the Constitution requires that he be tried in accordance with the guarantees of all the provisions of the Bill of Rights made applicable to the States by the Fourteenth Amendment."

The decision the Supreme Court reached in *In re Gault* was in large part meant to correct a sorry state of affairs the court had discovered a year earlier when it considered *Kent v. United States*, the first case from juvenile court ever to reach the high court. In this case the court had declared that "there may be grounds for concern that the child [in juvenile court] receives the worst of both worlds: that he gets neither the protection accorded to adults nor the solicitous care and regenerative treatment postulated for children."

From *In re Gault* on, minors have been accorded many of the same legal rights enjoyed by adults who are charged in criminal cases: the right to be represented by an attorney, protection against self-incrimination, the right to confront witnesses. (Minors still do not have a Constitutional right to a jury trial, and there is no right to bail in delinquency court.) Without a right to trial, minors were routinely locked up and held for long periods before delinquency petitions were filed and they appeared before a judge. The reforms that followed *In re Gault* established, among other things, strict limits on the time a minor could be held before appearing in court. Those veterans who lament the passing of the informal system say that when we gave children more legal rights and attorneys to shield them, we gave up the chance to reach status offenders and incipient delinquents early on, when they were more malleable, more amenable to change.

Intended or unintended, *In re Gault* also helped to criminalize proceedings in juvenile court. In California, for instance, the word "punishment" was added to the section on purpose in the juvenile court code. Punishment now receives equal weight with the court's original purpose, rehabilitation. And district attorneys like Kumli, "once unwanted and unnecessary in the juvenile court, have now become an integral part of its operation."

When Kumli walked into the delinquency court's central waiting room, a dark and shabby space with fraying gray carpet and cheap plastic chairs, it was already full of minors, their parents, and attorneys. It is this way five days a week, and Kumli is quick to say that get-tough legislation will do nothing to stanch the flow of cases into delinquency court. Threats of dire punishment do not work with kids who are full of anger and hurt. They are too caught up in the drama of their lives, and there is more noise in their heads than in a recording by Nine Inch Nails. They do not think about the consequences of their actions or what the law will do until after the fact, when it is too late.

When Kumli passed by, three Asian girls dressed in green sweatsuits that indicated they were being held in Juvenile Hall nudged each other and looked his way. For six years, Kumli has been the so-called gang DA in delinquency court, handling gang-related cases exclusively. Later that morning, he would appear at a hearing where the three Asian girls faced a petition charging them with a premeditated assault. The teenagers were members of a female gang called True Blue Crips, and they had tracked down and brutally attacked a girl who had spurned the advances of their bisexual leader. The cop investigating the case discovered that the True Blue Crips had beepers and an 800 number, and when he called the number, he heard the three girls who were now in custody bragging about "Fucking up that fuckin' ass chick we jumped today."

"Kurt, can I have a minute?" asked a young private attorney who was representing a member of a Hispanic gang whom Kumli had prosecuted twice before on assault charges. Previously, the boy had been represented by public defenders and had ended up in one of the county's youth ranches. This time around, because the minor was facing an indefinite sentence in the California Youth Authority (CYA), his parents had dug up the money to pay for private counsel.

The attorney wanted Kumli to dismiss one of the two assault charges against his client, hoping that one charge would not be enough for a judge to send his client to the CYA. Kumli explained that, to recommend a commitment to the CYA, all he had to do was prove one of the assault charges and then walk the judge through the minor's record. The defense attorney had not done his homework and clearly had no interest in learning how the law operated in juvenile court. He simply wanted to cut a deal so that he could tell his clients he had fought for their son.

"Kurt, you're the man in juvenile court," the attorney said after Kumli had finished his lecture. "Everybody knows the judge will go along with what you recommend. This family is finally making an investment in their son, Kurt. I'm living proof of that. They are paying thousands of dollars for my time—probably 20 percent of their gross income."

To be "the man" in delinquency court is, by Kumli's own estimate, to spend 25 to 30 percent of his time explaining the system to private attorneys, who seldom step inside the court because the families of minors charged with crimes seldom have the money to pay for private counsel. Kumli does not mind explaining the facts of life. In this case, as in hundreds of others that have preceded it, the defense attorney ended up ceding the case to the district attorney. That is also what it means to be "the man." When a DA works as closely with probation officers as Kumli does, he walks into court knowing more about the minor and his family than the defense attorney does. When judges who are overwhelmed by heavy caseloads look up and see the same DA in their courtrooms every time there is an especially tough case, they grow to rely on his judgment. Inevitably, it is Kumli who ends up calling the shots.

"The job's an addiction, a wonderful addiction," says the thirty-two-year-old DA, who handles four hundred to five hundred cases a year. "I work ten-hour days, six days a week. I've taken two three-day vacations in the last five years. And I love it!"

Before joining the DA's office, Kumli was a staff attorney for Honda, where he plotted strategy against plaintiffs in liability lawsuits. He had a big office with a plush carpet and a nice view, and he hated every minute of it. Using his talent to protect a giant corporation turned out to be worse than meaningless. To Kumli, it seemed evil. Now he has an office the size of a storage closet; the window has not been washed in years and the coffee is industrial strength, but every morning driving to work Kumli finds himself repeating, "This stuff matters, this stuff matters," like a mantra.

"Actually, I consider the work I do in court the minor part of my job," Kumli says. "If I just went to court and sat in my office, I'd simply be a cog in the machine. For me, the job means getting out into the community and doing something to stem the flow of cases coming into the system."

His time spent in delinquency court has turned Kumli into a "sheep in wolf's clothing." He sees his task as "getting the system's hooks in a kid to teach him that behavior has consequences." If he thinks the system has done that and a youth is not an immediate danger to the community or to himself, if he has a choice between sending a juvenile to CYA or placing the youth in a program that offers minors a chance to turn their lives around, Kumli will opt for the program.

"We can keep the community safe for three or four years by locking a kid up, but what happens when he gets back out?" Kumli asks rhetorically. "If the system can teach kids to act responsibly, they'll learn to take care of themselves and we won't have to worry about them reoffending."

Unlike politicians who believe that the answer is to get tough, Kumli insists that more cops, more probation officers, more judges, more district attorneys, more jails, and more prisons are not the answer to youth crime. The answers rest with the community. "It's no longer a law enforcement versus gangs thing," Kumli says. "Gangs grow out of the community. They are a community problem, and the community has to work together to solve it."

To that end, Kumli works closely with a staffer at a neighborhood center who has become a role model for kids who would otherwise have none. He belongs to a neighborhood coalition that has put an end to graffiti in an eight-block area by inviting "taggers" to become "mural artists." He stages mock trials for grade school classes and delineates the consequences of gang activity for high school students. He goes on ridealongs with cops and probation officers so that he knows what is happening on the streets.

"Year after year, 30 percent of the violent crimes in Santa Clara County are committed by juveniles," Kumli says. "We have a big-time gang problem here, but it's not Los Angeles, Chicago, or New York City, where the system is in a state of virtual collapse and things seem hopeless. Our task is to make sure that this place never becomes Los Angeles, Chicago, or New York."

Back in his office during the noon recess, Kumli took off his suit coat, turned on a rock and roll station with the volume down, and went through a big stack of fresh cases that had just arrived on his desk. The cases all had the green folders used to designate gang cases, and the minors had all been charged with assaults. As Kumli made his way through the stack, the difference between big, violent cities like Los Angeles and Santa Clara County appeared to be only a matter of degree. Santa Clara County has hundreds of different ethnic gangs. Over the years, Kumli has prosecuted Skinheads, Sons of Samoa, Nip Boys, Hopsing Tong Boys, Killer Boys, Eternity Boys, Junior Outlaw Brothers, Eastside Gangsters, Eastside Terminators, Southside Crips, Southside Posse, Northside Posse. What Kumli has learned doing this work is that different ethnic groups form gangs for different reasons. They have different internal structures, and they indulge in violence for different reasons.

For instance, the Southeast Asian gangs, Vietnamese and Cambodian—in particular, a gang called Cambodians with an Attitude—tend to be among the most violent. The reasons became clear to Kumli when, years earlier, he prosecuted three young Cambodians for murder. They tried to extort money from a Vietnamese family who had just opened a video store. The Vietnamese father was proud of his new store and was not about to be pushed around by three punks. He laughed at them and told them to get out. One of the young men went out to the car, grabbed a sawed-off shotgun, came back in, shot the owner in the face, and pumped two rounds into his body after he was dead. The Cambodians left without bothering to rob the store.

"The confessions in this case were so cold and chilling they were absolutely shocking," Kumli recalls. "The shooter was seventeen. It turned out that, fourteen years earlier, the Khmer Rouge had come into his village, taken him and his father and his brothers and all the other males in the village, and herded them into a field. They killed all of them and dumped them in a mass grave. A few days later, this boy's mother and the other women from the village went through the mass grave looking for the bodies of their loved ones, and they found this kid alive. He'd been hit over the head with a shovel and left for dead.

"To the extent that you can explain a psychopathic personality, this is a pretty good start," Kumli observes.

Hispanic youth gangs, like black gangs, are an outgrowth of prison gangs and tend to be less violent than Southeast Asian gangs. Hispanic inmates formed the Nuestra Familia to protect themselves against the Mexican Mafia. Blacks founded the Crips to protect themselves against the Bloods, on the street and in penitentiaries. Over the years, the black gangs have evolved into criminal enterprises. Crips and Bloods form allegiances with other gangs, white, Asian, or Hispanic—or, secretly, with each other—in the interest of controlling the supply and distribution of drugs, in particular, crack cocaine.

The Nortenos and the Surenos, the Hispanic street gangs that grew out of the Nuestra Familia and the Mexican Mafia prison gangs, are separated by an imaginary line that runs through the state of California in the Bakersfield area. Gangsters from the south generally claim Sureno and the color blue. Gangsters in the north generally claim Norteno and the color red. Both Hispanic gangs claim turf, which their "taggers" mark off with spray paint. The x-ing out or painting over of a rival gang's insignia happens incessantly, much to the annoyance of businessmen and city workers, who themselves are continually painting over cryptic-looking insignia. In effect, "taggers" from rival gangs are performing the same functions the cavalry did during the Civil War. They patrol the boundaries of a territory their troops control, feeling out the other side and fighting skirmishes that often lead to major battles.

"The most distressing thing to me about the Hispanic gangs is that Norteno-Sureno fighting boils down to self-inflicted genocide," Kumli says. "Basically, Nortenos are American-born kids of Hispanic ancestry. Surenos are, by and large, Mexican nationals who came up here with their parents. I've had cases where kids claiming Norteno will walk up to someone who appears to be a Mexican National and they'll say, 'What do you claim?' If the response is in Spanish, they'll shoot him, they'll stab him. The racists must love it. It's incredible."

Despite these significant differences in gangs, Kumli has discovered patterns that cut across ethnic lines, patterns that are deeply distressing. "More girls are joining gangs," Kumli says. "It's a fad, a trend, like gangsta rap. Those three True Blue Crips who were in court this morning consciously created an exact replica of a male gang, right down to getting the tattoos and carrying the beepers. That assault they did was done for no other reason than to gain status, to prove their prowess.

"The age of kids coming into gangs is becoming lower, which means that the age of kids who are committing serious violent offenses is also getting lower," Kumli continues. "We used to have sixteen- and seventeen-year-olds shooting each other; now it's thirteen- and fourteen-year-olds."

Kumli has also noticed that kids who end up flying colors share other fundamental similarities that are independent of their ethnic backgrounds. "The breakdown of the traditional family and the loss of community; the fact that we're seeing more and more single mothers who are younger and younger; the economic pressures that keep both parents working; the sex, violence, and valueless materialism that get portrayed in film and on television—there's a cluster of reasons why we're seeing so many kids ending up in gangs," Kumli says. "The bottom line is, as a result of poverty and the breakdown of communities and traditional values, these kids are completely without a moral compass.

"All this is aggravated by the fact that when a family fell apart in the past kids fell into safety nets. Families could rely on extended families, the extended family could rely on the community, and the community could rely on traditional institutions like churches and schools. For a variety of reasons, that support system is no longer in place, and as a result everyone is looking to us—'the System'—to be the new safety net. But we're not a net. We're the cold, hard floor."

Kumli continued thumbing through the stack of new cases until he arrived at a thick folder that was near the bottom of the pile. "Here's exactly what I'm talking about. It looks to me like time might be running out for this kid," he said.

The name running down the side of the file was "Soto, Luis."*

35

LUIS: THE HALL

"Mija! I didn't do it!"

"Luis! Where are you?"

"Juvenile Hall, Mija! But I didn't do it!"

"What did you do?"

"I didn't do nothing! They say I was with some homies that attacked a guy, but I wasn't. I was waitin' at the bus stop, and they came along and asked if I wanted a ride. I got in and we only went a little way, and then the cops swarmed us. The homies in the car, they had just been in a fight, Mija! They used The Club on somebody, that thing that locks the steering wheel. They cracked his skull. The cops found it under the front seat, and they found coke on one of the homies! They arrested us and locked us up. Mija, I swear, I'm innocent!"

There was a silence that made Luis uncomfortable. "Mija?" he asked.

"You know what, Luis?" Claudia, the mother of Luis's two little girls, said finally. "I don't even care."

"Don't care if I'm innocent?" Luis asked, perplexed.

"Don't care that you're back in the hall," Claudia said.

"But Mija, I need you to care!"

"You want to know what I care about, Luis? I care that you didn't come home today and I had a doctor's appointment and you were supposed to watch the girls. I care that I've been up with them since 5:30 this morning and they're in the bath right now and they're fussy and you aren't here to help get them to bed. I care that tomorrow we are supposed to go shopping. You know how heavy the girls are in the double stroller. How am I going to push them all the way to the Safeway and get the groceries back here without you?"

"But Mija—"

"You think one of your homeboys will come around and help me go to the Safeway, Luis? You think the homies will put food on the table? If you get sent away, they'll find someone to replace you. But where are your babies going to find another daddy?"

"I know, Mija! I been trying; you know I been trying."

"That's what I mean. Trying isn't enough. I want a life, Luis. I want my babies to have a life. This isn't a life; this is bullshit. It's stupid and going nowhere."

"You're stupid; you don't know nothing," Luis snapped.

"You're right, Luis. If I did, I wouldn't be with you."

When no reply came, Claudia said quickly, "The babies are yelling. I've got to go."

She hung up before Luis could say, "Kiss them for me."

• • •

Part suburb, part barrio, East San Jose sprawls across the valley and climbs into the foothills of the Diablo Range before giving way to ranch land that seems a world away from the congested Bay Area. Ask police, kids on the street and pastors who work the streets, probation officers, the staff at recreation and community centers, or anyone else on top of the scene in East San Jo, if they know the Soto brothers; chances are that they will say, "Since they were kids. They're notorious."

Luis, "Little Sleepy," is the youngest Soto, a handsome, compactly built seventeen-year-old with rich black hair he keeps oiled, dark eyes, the famous Soto smile, and a disarming laugh. In Luis's case, a street name is well chosen. He often appears lethargic, half asleep, and bored with what is taking place, until a squad car turns onto his block. Then, quick as a cat, he is up and off the couch and moving to a corner, where he drops to his knees, peeps through the blinds, and, completely focused, eyeballs the patrol car until it turns off his street.

Javier, "Fat Sleepy," one of Luis's older brothers, is also well named; nearly 300 pounds, he is garrulous and sweet natured—until something triggers his temper. Santos, "Big Sleepy," Luis's oldest brother, looks enough like Luis to be his twin. "Sometimes, I get in trouble because my brother did something and they come after me," Luis says. Santos is the mysterious Soto, a young man with dark good looks who often disappears for weeks at a time and then comes walking in the front door of the Soto home as if he had just gone around the corner to the 7-Eleven.

After years of asking, "Santos! Where have you been?" and receiving only a scowl in return, his mother has quit asking.

The boys' mother, Eloisa Soto, was fourteen and still living in Mexico when she gave birth to a daughter named Isabel. Santos was born two years later, followed quickly by the other two boys. When Luis was a few months old, his father left, never to return, and Eloisa took her four children to California to join her brother and mother. "Santos, my oldest brother, he's real curious about our father," Luis says. "He even went back to Mexico and tried to look him up, but he never found him."

The maternal grandmother wound up taking care of the Soto children while their mother rode the bus across San Jose to the Willow Glen area, where she cleaned houses. As the oldest in the family, it was Isabel's job to help her grandmother care for her little brothers. The boys were in elementary school when Eloisa met Julian, a man in his early thirties, at a Sunday afternoon dance. Julian was respectful and polite and had a steady job installing and refinishing hardwood floors. After a proper courtship, he and Eloisa married and Julian made a down payment on a small three-bedroom house near the intersection of King and Story roads, the heart of the Eastside.

"Julian? My stepdad? He's all right," Luis says. "He's always working, not around much. When he is, he just minds his own business and works on cars and everything. He gets mad if we tell him things."

Gilbert Chaidez, a probation officer who has had the Soto brothers on his caseload and has come to know the family well, describes Julian much the same way: "The stepfather's out of the picture, always working, trying to make ends meet. He figures supporting the family is enough. When the boys get into trouble, he always says, 'I don't have time for this.' He puts the problems on the mother.

"Eloisa is very nice; I like her very much," Chaidez continues. "She's respectful, she's caring and very protective. That's part of the problem. In her eyes, the boys have never done anything wrong. She minimizes everything."

It is difficult to say who raised the Soto brothers, Eloisa or Varrio Locos Trece, a street gang affiliated with the Surenos. By the time the boys had turned ten, home was not much more than a place to eat and sleep and watch television. They were never much interested in what their mother and stepfather were doing or in anything either had to say. They were, however, fascinated by what was happening in the barrio.

The Soto brothers were full-blooded Mexicans in a sea of Chicanos (Mexican-Americans), and they were thrilled when they became old enough to join the Surenos. Luis was eleven when he was "jumped in" and began whizzing around the neighborhood on his bike, a blue bandanna flying out of a back pocket. (Gang members jump a recruit and beat and kick him until someone in authority says that he has had enough; then they pick him up off the ground, and it's handshakes all around as he or she is welcomed into the gang. "My jump-in lasted thirteen seconds," Luis says. "Thirteen for *M*, the thirteenth letter of the alphabet, for Mexican Mafia.")

For some boys on the Eastside, being jumped in is a family tradition. A father who has spent years in prison teaches a four-year-old son how to shoot a .22 pistol and how to file a butter knife into a shank. At the start of the holiday season, he dresses the boy in baggy jeans and wraps a blue bandanna around his head and takes him to Sears, where he tells a photographer to take the boy's portrait when the little fellow flashes a gang sign.

The conventional wisdom is that other youths, Hispanic as well as white and black, join gangs because gangs give them a cause that is bigger than themselves, a social system that gives shape to reality by dividing the world into homies and enemies, a ritualized system of behavior that rewards courage and severely punishes perceived acts of cowardice, an arena where inner-city youths, who have not had much fun and have little sense of a future, can find intensity and feel truly alive. "Gangs," says Cleveland Prince, the probation officer, "are all the right instincts—loyalty, commitment, self-preservation, the drive to be someone—going in all the wrong directions."

Claudia, the mother of Luis's two little girls, has never been a gang member, but she is an uncommonly perceptive observer. She worries that one of these nights the Norteno who lives next door is going to make good on his promise to jump Luis and lives in fear that somebody is going to do a drive-by on them for something Luis did but did not tell her about. Taking her two babies out for walks, she has had young women in a rival gang come up and "dog me and kick me in the butt. I hate it; I feel stupid and look stupid and everybody is laughing at me, but I don't say nothing because, if I get in a fight, she's in a gang, she's got a homeboy, and the next thing I know there's some big incident and a social worker is coming to get my girls." After living like that, Claudia has developed her own take on gangs.

"The whole idea that the gang is just like a family that sticks by you is bullshit," she says. "It's not about loyalty or commitment. It's not about deprived kids. It's about immaturity.

"Luis and his brothers were never neglected; they were fuckin' spoiled. Their mom never really treated those boys bad. She loves her kids. Growing up, they did anything they wanted. If their mother told them not to do something, they'd swear at her and do it anyway. They don't respect her or their stepfather; they don't respect authority; they don't respect nobody. That's why they like gangs so much. Gangs give them limits and boundaries they don't get anywhere else."

Among themselves, Santos, Javier, and Luis fought incessantly, pounding on each other and on any member of the family who tried to break them up. When Santos was sixteen, his uncle and his mother, feeling spent and powerless, reported him to the police for abusing the family pet. He was admitted into Juvenile Hall, and a psychologist who performed a court-ordered evaluation noted, "At home, Santos continues to abuse his brothers and sister and to defy his mother. . . . He indicates that his mother often gets angry with him for fighting with his two brothers and states, 'My mother and grandmother tell me I'm making her [his mother] sick, it's my fault she goes to the hospital . . . they say I'm killing her.' "

The Soto brothers only beat on each other at home; in the streets, they were a united force, which is how Luis first came to the attention of the juvenile justice system. He was thirteen years old when he and his brothers jumped two boys who were affiliated with a Norteno gang and who, Luis says, had been "talking shit. Plus, they stole my bike." The Sotos went after the Nortenos with homemade whips—TV cable cord with AA batteries taped to the ends—and proceeded to flog their enemies. One boy suffered "a seven-inch lash mark from forehead to ear"; the other had "good-sized welts across his back."

"In a situation like this, it is often difficult for the police to make an arrest; and if they do, these cases are notoriously difficult to prosecute because the victims are members of a rival gang," Kurt Kumli explains. "Part of the gang ethic is to refuse to cooperate with the authorities. Like cabals in the Balkans, they prefer to keep the violence alive by nursing their wounds and plotting revenge. That is why for every incident that results in a minor's arrest there are usually a number of others that were never reported, or that were reported and the police were unable to make arrests because they got no cooperation from victims and witnesses."

In this case, the Norteno victims cooperated with the police, and Luis was arrested and taken to police admissions at Juvenile Hall, where a screening officer from the probation department asked questions and added up the point values assigned to each answer: Is the minor a threat to a person or the property of others? Is the minor a danger to himself? Does the minor have a place to go? Is he at risk to flee? Has the minor violated a previous court order—i.e., was he on probation when he committed this new offense? Scoring above a certain number of points means that a minor is automatically held in the hall.

Although this was Luis's first arrest, he scored enough points to warrant holding him in custody. His case was passed on to an investigation and intake probation officer, who had forty-eight hours to put together a "detention packet." Essentially a miniature probation report, the packet detailed the nature of Luis's offense and his past record; it examined his behavior in school and in the community and took statements from Luis and his parents.

The probation officer quickly uncovered a pattern of denial that would resurface every time Luis was arrested. Luis "denied using the whips and denied having any gang affiliations." He told the officer that he "would very much like to be released from Juvenile Hall as soon as possible, as he misses his mother very much." Eloisa backed up her son's story, saying that she "does not believe Luis is gang affiliated and has never known Luis to own any kind of weapon . . . he almost always completes his chores around the home and she never allows Luis and his siblings to remain unsupervised." Eloisa tried to convince the probation officer that she did "not want Luis to be influenced in a negative manner by his peers in Juvenile Hall and does not want him to miss further days of school as he is very enthusiastic about school."

This all rang hollow to the probation officer. There were numerous eyewitnesses who had seen Luis, whip in hand, attacking the Nortenos. The vice principal at his school said that Luis was far from being an enthusiastic student; he had, in fact, been put on a restricted schedule because of fighting and generally poor behavior. With a touch of irony, the probation officer concluded that "It is very likely Luis's involvement in this incident appears to be greater than he cares to admit."

The DA who reviewed the detention packet had seventy-two hours after Luis was brought into custody to file a delinquency petition, which he did. At a detention hearing, Luis appeared before a judge, who followed the probation officer's recommendation to keep him in custody. At an adjudication hearing several weeks later, a judge found the allegations in the petition (assault upon a person by means of force likely to produce great bodily injury) to be true and, following the language of juvenile court, declared Luis a delinquent.

For his first offense, Luis got a standard "sentence" of sixty days in Juvenile Hall. But many veteran probation officers say that locking up a minor loses its effectiveness as a "teaching tool" after the first twenty-four or forty-eight hours. Kids who are scared and open to change during the first day or two begin to adjust after that, and their vulnerability evaporates. That was certainly true of Luis.

"That first time I got locked up, I cried and cried," he recalls. "The second time, I cried a lot less. The third time, I wasn't scared anymore. It was like I was back in Hotel California."

Over the next couple of years, Luis was arrested several more times on assault charges. He always claimed that he had been provoked, and probation officers always came to the same conclusion in their reports: "The minor's involvement in this matter was impulsive and appears to have been motivated by not wanting to back down or appear weak." Luis puts it another way: "The ones who join [gangs] are the ones that have the pride to walk the streets and show their colors, no matter where they are. If you have to fight, then you fight."

Most often, Luis served his time in Juvenile Hall. Once, a judge sentenced him to a term in one of the county's youth ranches. A throwback to the days when the West was open and land was cheap, the ranches are in bucolic settings and are clean and well run and staffed by counselors and teachers who attempt to instill discipline and respect. The ranches are not locked facilities surrounded by fences topped with razor wire. The minimum security is intentional. It keeps pressure from building up inside, reducing the stress on staff. And it helps teach the wards that staying and completing their obligation to the court is a responsibility they must fulfill.

The downside is that if a minor really wants to escape he can without much trouble. Luis says that he ran from the ranch for the same reasons his brothers did: "The ranch was full of Nortenos. They called me a 'Scrap'—that's what they call Surenos; it's like saying you are garbage—and they spit at me and kicked me under the table. When we ate, a guy held his fork to his throat, like he was going to stab me. I told a counselor and got a bed by the guard station, but they were still harassing me. I ran for my own protection."

Like all young gangsters, Luis was not a sophisticated criminal. The cops quickly tracked him down, and Luis was taken back to the "Hotel California," where he spent another ninety days. It was right after this stay in Juvenile Hall that Luis, and Claudia, both age fourteen, became a couple.

36

CLAUDIA:
THE GOOD GIRL

WHEN LUIS CAME INTO HER LIFE, CLAUDIA WAS AN EIGHTH-GRADER with dark hair and high cheekbones, which she inherited along with the Cherokee blood that runs in her mother's side of the family. An honor student and the vice president of her class, an editor on the school paper, and a member of the volleyball team, Claudia "was into everything. Mostly, I joined because I would do anything so I had an excuse not to go home."

Home was, and had always been, a nightmare. The oldest of four siblings from three different fathers, Claudia had bounced from her mother—"My mother was sexually abused by her brothers and everything, and she got into drugs and sex early. I feel bad for her because she grew up with real low self-esteem"—to the Children's Shelter, to her father—"He had his own business, and he made a lot of money. He started doing drugs, and he lost it all. Now, he's homeless"—back to the shelter and back to her mother and a new stepfather—"He's a real-life monster. He was on PCP and he was a heavy drug addict, and he hit my mother all the time. He molested my sister, and I was terrified he was going to molest me. He'd do things like come into the bathroom when I was taking a shower and tell me I looked sexy with my hair wet.

"There were so many times when I was going to run away, but didn't because I was scared of leaving my little sister and brothers alone with him."

At home, Claudia survived "by keeping my mouth shut a lot"; in school and among her friends, she created a persona of "the good girl, the little virgin." In the sixth and seventh grades, when other girls in the neighborhood started hanging out with gangs, Claudia stuck with the nerds, the A students, "mostly Asian kids who didn't have a clue about what went on in my house."

Luis, of course, ran with a different crowd. He lived around the corner and had never taken any notice of nice little Claudia, but she had noticed him. "I remember the first time I saw him, riding around on that bike of his. Even though my friends were nerds, I never wanted a nerd for a boyfriend. I was attracted to the bad boys, which is something I got from my mother, I guess. Luis was definitely a bad boy, a little tough guy. I was, 'Wow! That guy is hot! He's really sexy.' I decided, 'I want that.'"

The class vice president and the bad boy started going together, and before long Claudia was pregnant. "What upset me the most was, I had a lot of plans. I always wanted to be a reporter, but, being pregnant, I had to drop out of school. I remember bumping into another girl on the street, and she took a look at my big belly and said, 'I never thought I'd see you like this!' Her mother had always thrown me in her face— 'Why can't you be more like Claudia? Claudia gets good grades.' That girl acted really smug."

It was not only acquaintances who looked down on Claudia because of her "condition." It used to be that pregnant teens were generally viewed with a complicated mixture of scorn, sympathy, and embarrassment. But whether she stayed home to raise the baby or entered a Florence Crittenden Home and surrendered the newborn for adoption, a pregnant teen inspired at least a measure of pity. Claudia had the misfortune to become pregnant in an era when teen moms are now widely viewed as irresponsible leeches who expect taxpayers to pay for their babies. It is assumed that they get pregnant so that they can coast on Aid to Families with Dependent Children (AFDC) and have a real-life doll to fill up their empty lives. They make such lousy parents, some claim, that if their children do not come into the system as dependents they surely will as delinquents.

"It was horrible. Total strangers came up to me on the bus and demanded to know how old I was," Claudia recalls. "In the doctor's office, this woman just marched up and started shouting, 'What makes you think you have a right to have a baby?' Because I'm young, people acted like they had the right to say any mean thing they wanted."

The pregnancy, however, turned out to be the easy part. When Claudia gave birth to a six-pound thirteen-ounce girl they named Elena, the couple moved into the Soto home. "I was tripping; I didn't know what was going through my head when the baby arrived," Luis recalls. "I wanted a baby, but it was too soon." Luis's allegiance was to Varrio Locos Trece, his gang, not his new family. He stayed away for days at a time, and when he did come home, he and Claudia got into screaming matches that ended with doors slamming and Claudia sobbing.

Adding to the rancor was Isabel, Luis's nineteen-year-old sister, who also had a new baby. Resentful of having to raise her younger brothers, she had little interest in raising her own son or in supporting Claudia's efforts with Elena. "Isabel still wanted to party and everything," Claudia says. "She would be there with her baby, but she would not feed him or change him—Luis's mother did all that. She got jealous because I was taking care of my baby. I said right in front of her, 'I'm not going to let anyone else take care of my baby because I'm her mother.' Isabel got offended by that."

Worn down by the never ending strife, worried about her three Sureno sons, frazzled by the cries of two newborns, and exhausted by getting up in the middle of the night to take care of her grandson, Eloisa took out her frustrations on the one member of the household who was not a blood relative. In a fit of anger, she informed Claudia that Elena did not look anything like Luis and must not be Luis's child. Claudia's response to all this acrimony was to get pregnant again—"by mistake," she says with some embarrassment.

"Luis went really crazy when he found out, doing stupid, dangerous things on the street and getting locked up all the time," Claudia says. "Everyone told me it was because he felt all this pressure and didn't want a second child, but I just couldn't have an abortion. I loved Elena so much, all I could think about was that this new baby was just like her and deserved to be alive. How could I just get rid of it?"

Six months into her second pregnancy, Claudia's rows with Luis escalated into what police and social workers and talk show hosts refer to as "domestic violence," an abstract phrase that does little to reveal the reality of the slaps and scratches and punches and of Claudia's feelings of remorse and humiliation. "The first time he actually hit me, we were arguing because a friend of Luis kept saying that he was doing things with this girl and she was rich and on and on," Claudia remembers. "Luis kept saying, 'I'm not doing anything with her; why don't you believe me?' and I said, 'You are just a liar!' He slapped me in the face, and that shut me up pretty quick. I started to cry because I was shocked.

Here I was, just like my mother, and I had vowed never to become like her.

"After that, Luis tried not to hit me. He would hit the walls and stuff and make big holes and make big scenes. But he still kept hitting me while I was pregnant, and I hit him back. I hear a lot of people saying, 'Oh, the poor woman, the man's beating her.' It wasn't really like that. It was both of us making this bad cycle. I was hitting him, too."

By Claudia's due date, she had just about counted Luis out, vowing that somehow she would raise her children on her own. But when their second daughter was born, Luis reacted in the way Claudia had hoped he would when their first daughter had arrived. They named her Eloisa in honor of Luis's mother, and Luis was suddenly full of promises about getting out of the gang and being a good father. Words can be just words, but when Luis agreed that they had to leave his mother's house, Claudia began to believe that he was serious. She found a young couple with a young son who was renting out a garage they had converted into sleeping quarters; both young families would share the kitchen, the living room, and a bathroom.

In the months that followed, Luis developed into a doting father. He hated changing diapers, but he really got a kick out of the babies. Elena, petite and wiry, had black eyes that peeked out naughtily from under her straight black bangs. She was always into something. Her sister could not have been more different. Placid and round faced like a Cabbage Patch doll, all chubby cheeks and smiles, Eloisa amused herself by playing with her own toes. Luis would hold the girls for hours, making faces and laughing when one of them made a face back. When they woke up crying in the middle of the night, Luis often dragged himself out of bed and warmed a bottle. When Claudia murmured thanks, he patted her on the shoulder and went back to sleep.

Luis's behavior at home may have changed, but on the streets he was still the same Luis. He returned to school but was expelled twice, once from a neighborhood high school for gang-related fighting and once from a continuation school for truancy. His probation officer ended up pulling some strings and got Luis one of the "precious" spots in an alternative school that has a national reputation in educational circles. "I wanted Luis to have the chance, not so much for him but for his kids and his girlfriend," the officer explains. "I saw that Luis really did care about his family, and it was worth a shot to see if he could make them the center of his life instead of just one part of it. And if any place could help him do that, it was the Foundry."

The Foundry, which takes its rather Dickensian name from a mill where scrap metal is melted down and poured into new forms, has had enormous success doing what parents, teachers and vice principals, therapists, judges, probation officers, and all the rest of the king's men have not been able to do: teaching teenagers like Luis how to learn so that they can return to public schools and succeed and helping them to get off drugs and work through the personal problems that have determined the course of their lives.

On the first day of school, Luis found himself sitting in a circle along with fifty other delinquents and chronic truants. They were told that they had two weeks to earn their way into the school by completing their assignments, by shedding their insularity, and by showing that they were willing to become part of a community. "Most of you are here because you have not been held responsible," a counselor said, explaining why they had to punch a time clock. "Here, we will hold you responsible."

Over 90 percent of the students who spend a year at the Foundry return to public schools, graduate, and do not get arrested again. Luis did not turn out to be one of them. He did not do his homework, and he contributed almost nothing to the group. In the middle of the second week, when the alarm went off, Luis rolled over and went back to sleep. He told Claudia that taking care of the girls and going to school were too much. People change when they are ready to change, and Luis, for whatever reason—lack of character, laziness, immaturity, an inability to focus—was not ready. "Sometimes, the system fails kids," explains one of the Foundry teachers. "But sometimes, kids fail the system."

For Claudia and Luis, the honeymoon period was definitely over. Sleep deprivation and the constant demands of two kids in diapers took their toll. Luis got a job working as a roofer and came home tired, resentful, and stinking of tar, only to find Claudia even more tired and at least as resentful. Elena had driven her crazy all day, never sitting still for a minute. She wouldn't listen to Claudia, and now she was starting to bite. "She's spoiled," Luis insisted. "You should spank her more. Bite her back and she'll see what it feels like and won't do it again."

"Bite her back?" Claudia countered. "That's the stupidest thing I ever heard."

"That's what my family did to me, and I turned out OK."

"Yeah, that's what I want, Luis. I want the girls to grow up just like you and your brothers."

It was not long before Luis and Claudia were back slapping and scratching each other. Every time it happened, Claudia was haunted by the feeling that she was reliving her mother's life. The social workers had finally investigated her stepfather and had ended up taking her little sister away and putting her in long-term foster care. After her fights with Luis, Claudia, scared and depressed, often picked up the phone to call a battered women's shelter or a social worker to ask for help. But what if they decided to take away the girls? With that question hanging over her, Claudia always put down the phone and vowed not to get into another battle with Luis.

"For me, the isolation was as bad as the fights," Claudia recalls. "I didn't know anything about raising kids; I was scared all the time. The only parents I was ever around were always screaming and smacking their kids, and I knew that wasn't right. Babies don't know they are doing something wrong, so why hit them? But who was going to show us what to do? His mother? My mother? I kept thinking, 'If only I could sneak into the pocket of a good mother and watch how she does things.'"

Claudia discovered a way out of the house and into the world when she enrolled in a parenting class for teenagers at a community center the Department runs on the Eastside. She was too young to drive, so the center sent a van to pick up her, Elena, and Eloisa and provided child care while Claudia took the ten-session class.

So much of raising a child is trying one thing after another until something finally works or until the child simply passes onto the next developmental stage and the next set of problems. But the young mothers in the class had only a few techniques—threatening, yelling, spanking—at their disposal and were frustrated by their ineffectiveness. It was liberating to talk about problems that had been gnawing at her and to go home with fresh ways of dealing with them. "Even if the ideas didn't work right away, I felt like I was doing something new instead of the same things over and over," Claudia says.

For instance, the teacher suggested that Elena was probably biting out of stress, the way grown-ups bite their nails, and Claudia's instincts had been right: biting back would only stress her out more. The teacher and other members of the class came up with some suggestions: give Elena more "positive" attention, like hugging her or praising her when she does something right, rather than just going off at her when she does something wrong; keep reminding her that it hurts when she bites people, but get her a special doll so that she can still bite when she gets the urge.

"I was really concerned that Elena was hyper because of all the fighting she had seen between me and Luis," Claudia says. "I never told the ladies at the child care about the fights, but I asked them questions about why she never minded me. They said I should look on the bright side. Elena is just so smart that she's always one step ahead of me. When the lady told me, 'That will serve her well in life,' you can't believe how good that made me feel."

When the parenting class ended, Claudia immediately enrolled in courses on health care and nutrition, nurturing, family communications, and legal rights. She completed them all—and then took them all again. "Those classes and talk shows on TV, that's where I get the vocabulary to figure out what is going on in my life," Claudia says. When the center offered a course in domestic violence, Claudia was one of the first to enroll. She was still too ashamed and scared of the social workers' power to talk about herself; she always asked questions about "a friend who comes from a dysfunctional family and fights with her husband." After the first few sessions, Claudia insisted that Luis attend the classes too, because "if somebody found out what was going on with us and reported it, they'd take the babies." He was the only guy in the room and was embarrassed, but, much to his surprise, Luis ended up getting something out of the course.

"They taught you stuff; it wasn't like school," he says. "They told us that when you fight you should use 'I phrases,' like 'I feel this and I feel that.' Like when Claudia would go, 'You are a fucking shithead,' I would go, 'You are supposed to say, "I think you are a fucking shithead." ' It sounded so stupid, we'd both start laughing. It wasn't nothin' special, but we stopped hitting each other."

For awhile, their lives seemed to go well. Claudia decided to return to school in pursuit of a high school diploma. Luckily, there was an opening in a program for teen parents that offered child care and a flexible schedule of English, math, and history classes. When the rainy season arrived and the roofing company laid off Luis, he found a job as a stock boy at Ross, a large clothing discounter. "Mija," he asked Claudia one day after work. "Can you teach me to read better? I want to read what's in those big boxes I move around." Every morning, Luis put on a white shirt and tie, and he had to admit that, after years of wearing jeans that were four sizes too big and extra-large plaid shirts, he liked the feeling of putting on a clean white shirt.

Until he ran into his homeboys. The way they looked at him "made me feel like, you know, a geek or something." It was a feeling the homeboys rubbed in. "Little Sleepy, what's happening? Why you not 'down' anymore, man?"

"Sleepy, you never come by Poco no more. Sleepy, you never party-down no more."

"Sleepy's in a new clicka. His old lady's clicka."

It never took more than a few minutes of this to put Claudia, the girls, and learning to read out of Luis's mind. "I'm down, let's go see what's up," he'd say, and Luis and the homies would wander over to Poco Way, a ramshackle apartment complex that is a nexus for the drug trade on the Eastside. Poco is Varrio Locos Trece turf, ground zero for Luis's gang, where "partying-down" means hanging out and consuming whatever drugs and alcohol happen to be available. Luis would spend three or four hours getting loaded, then he would walk the two miles home at a brisk pace, hoping to burn off his high. He always told Claudia that he had worked overtime or had been over at his mother's and had a beer or two with one of his brothers.

Those were more or less the circumstances the night the homies "used The Club on somebody" and Luis ended up in Juvenile Hall. "I was disgusted with him, but I can't say I was totally surprised," Claudia said later. "I knew he was hanging around Poco, but I guess I just couldn't believe that he would choose Poco Way over his babies. It's so fuckin' stupid."

Luis's arrest put Claudia and a district attorney she had never met in the same position: both had to decide how many more chances to give Luis. For Claudia, the question was "Would my daughters and me be better off without their daddy?" For Kurt Kumli, the question was "Should I ask a judge to send this kid to CYA?"

"The Corey McKenzies are the easy cases to call," Kumli says. "CYA is the only option for a kid like that. But for every Corey, there are hundreds and hundreds of Luis Sotos out there. Kids who might make it, or they might not. At what point do you say, 'Enough is enough; you've burned up every chance we've given you. You need to go to CYA and do some serious time'?"

37

LUIS AND CLAUDIA: OUT OF THE SYSTEM

THE DISTRICT ATTORNEY DECIDED TO GIVE LUIS "ONE LAST BREAK." Instead of recommending that the judge send him to the California Youth Authority (CYA), where he conceivably could be held for five or six years, Kurt Kumli worked out a creative sentence: since Luis was only three months away from turning eighteen, he was to stay in Juvenile Hall, and, on his eighteenth birthday—"to give him a taste of adult incarceration and let him know what his future would hold if he didn't end his affiliation with the Surenos"—Luis was transferred to the county jail to serve a ninety-day sentence.

The decision that Claudia made—to tell Luis that she wasn't going to visit him and wasn't going to sit around moping because he got himself locked up—had enormous repercussions in her life. Luis's family, the only "family" she really had, turned on her. Claudia had never counted on them for much, but now Luis's mother would not give her own granddaughters a ride to the doctor's or invite them over for Thanksgiving dinner. As Claudia had predicted, not one of Luis's homies called to offer help, but they did call to threaten her. "They said they were going to come over and beat me up and beat up the people I lived with because I wasn't standing by Luis when he was in jail," Claudia says. "I was terrified. I called the police, but there was nothing they would do because it was just threats. But I knew what those guys were capable of, and I was freaked."

During the day at school, Claudia kept this all to herself and slipped back into her old persona: "When anyone asked about Luis, I just did my 'perky, Miss Perfect' routine and said, 'He's great.' I didn't want anyone to know he was in jail." But at night, after the girls fell asleep, the converted garage that seemed so crowded when Luis was there now seemed big and empty. Claudia worried constantly about money and about being alone. "I started having the same nightmares I did when I was a kid," she says. "A big hand would come up from under the bed and grab me." One morning, she woke up with a piercing headache and saw everything blurred. When she felt a huge lump on the back of her head, she panicked, thinking that she had a brain tumor. The doctor said that Claudia was so tense her neck muscles had tightened into knots. He sent her home with a muscle relaxer and impossible advice: "Don't stress so much."

"I had always threatened to leave Luis and to do everything on my own," she says. "But I didn't know it would be so hard. I had to keep fighting the urge to call him and beg, 'OK, I've changed my mind. We're still together.' "

But Claudia did not give in, and from this show of strength she began learning other things about her own tenacity. Somehow, she managed to get herself and the girls to school almost every morning. Even when it meant studying late into the night, she finished most of her assignments on time and got excellent grades. In her classes, Claudia made new friends, and it was a revelation to discover that without Luis it did not matter if her friends were Sureno or Norteno or neither; she could pick them just because she liked them. Without Luis at home, she found that she was more consistent in her discipline of Elena and watched, in relief, as the little girl's tantrums began to diminish. Money remained a problem, but Claudia began sticking closely to a budget, and at the end of one month she had a few dollars to put aside for Christmas. Claudia even went on a diet and lost the weight she had gained during pregnancy.

By the time Luis was released, Claudia saw the possibility of living her life without him. "I told him that, if he was really serious about changing, we could try again, but not with him living here. I owed him that much," she says. "But Luis was not going to stop me from getting on with my life."

•   •   •

During Luis's "trial period," he officially lived at his mother's home, but he spent most evenings with Claudia and most days with Elena and Eloisa. Claudia counted on his baby-sitting because she had been accepted into "this dream program." City Year is a VISTA-like federal service project in which young people from a wide range of backgrounds work as aides in inner-city schools, on cleanup crews, and in antigraffiti task forces. Because Claudia was still in high school, she spent part of her work week studying for her GED. In return for putting in ten-hour days, City Year paid her a small salary and promised a college scholarship.

Almost every weekday for nearly two months, Luis showed up at 6:30 A.M. to begin his shift with his daughters. In the evenings, Claudia came home tired, but bursting with news about her day. She was working in an elementary school and would go on and on about teachers and other people he did not know. Luis could not understand her enthusiasm about being in a class of loud kids all day. But he was proud that he did not tell her to be quiet because he had a headache and he did not "go off" whenever she mentioned a friend who was dating a Norteno. Mostly, Luis paid attention for as long as he could; then he let his mind glaze over. "We were doing good," he says. "We weren't fighting or anything."

So, it came as a surprise when Claudia told Luis that she needed to talk: "Mijo, this isn't working for me."

"It's not working because they've changed your work schedule? You want me to watch the girls at a different time?" he asked.

"No, Luis, you know that isn't what I mean. I want us to be over."

"But Mija, since I got out, I've been doing so good!" Luis wailed.

"I know. You've been doing good for you, but not good enough for me," Claudia said. "I want someone to really listen to me, someone who has some goals in life. Half the time when you're here to watch the girls, you're drunk or all hung over 'cuz you've been up all night partying."

"But mija, I do better with the girls when I'm hung over; you know that. They don't make me so crazy. Anyway, I'm just partying till I get a job. I've got a lot of time on my hands."

"Luis, please listen. We got together when I was fourteen. I'm not fourteen anymore. I'm doing really good. I went through all that legal stuff to get myself emancipated so my mom doesn't have any say over my life anymore. I know I'm going to do great on my GED test, and I want to start college next year."

"But the babies—"

"You can still see the girls, I want you to see them. You'll always be their daddy. But I need my own life."

"There's another guy! Who is it?" Luis demanded. Claudia was waiting for that and was somewhat surprised it had not been the first thing
out of Luis's mouth. "There's no other guy; this is not about another guy.
I'm trying to tell you what I want. I want a future, Luis, for me and the
girls. With you, I'd never get off welfare. I've got two children, Luis. I
don't need you as the third."

"There's some guy! I know there's a guy!" Luis shouted. He jumped
off the edge of the bed and ran to the closet and rummaged around until
he found Claudia's journal. Her prized possession, where she recorded
her thoughts and wrote her poems, the journal had always been
off-limits to Luis. He had gone for it a time or two in the past, and
Claudia had shrieked and battered him with her fists. But this time,
she just watched as Luis opened it and began reading from the back.
"Read all you want. You won't find anything in there about a guy,"
Claudia said.

It was part truth, part bluff. There *was* a guy, but not in any way that
Luis would ever understand. At City Year, Claudia had become friends
with a young man who had taken a year off from Harvard to join the
program. He found Claudia funny, smart, and full of energy and was tutoring her in math prior to her GED. He was also pushing her to start
college. "Teachers and social workers had always told me I was smart,
but being smart compared to gang kids is one thing and fitting in with
regular people, you know, people who have been to college and everything, that's something else," Claudia said later. "It just blew me away
that somebody who wears shirts with little alligators thought I was special and that he and I could be so tight."

Claudia watched as Luis ran his finger up and down the pages, trying
to locate a male name. "This is ridiculous," she finally said. "Luis, I'm
going to say it: I don't love you anymore."

Luis looked up, surprised and bewildered. She had made such threats
before, but never so calmly, never when things were going OK. He
stared at Claudia for a long moment and knew that this time she meant
it. He closed her journal. "I'll come back for any of my stuff," he said,
and he walked past Claudia out of the converted garage and out the
front door.

For several days, Luis told no one about the breakup, partly out of
pride and partly because he knew what his friends would recommend:
Luis should beat up Claudia to teach her a lesson. "I didn't want to hurt

her or the babies no more," he says. "But I can't trust my own temper, so I figured I just better stay away for awhile."

To pass the time, Luis took solace in his usual ways. One night, he was at a Sureno party in Poco Way, drinking beer and passing a joint in the kitchen when two homies walked in and told Luis that "the Shot-Caller" wanted to see him in the backyard. "He's older, he's tough, he's done time in Soledad, everybody respects him," Luis says of the Shot-Caller. "I went back there, and he was sitting in a chair with a bunch of homeboys behind him. I knew it was going to be kind of a trial. I knew what it was about."

During Luis's time in the county jail, there had been a fight between a Norteno and a Sureno that was the product of a complex, convoluted incident that had occurred months earlier on the street. The fight was carefully staged in a corner of a recreation area, away from the surveillance cameras, at a time when the guards were occupied. The Sureno had asked Luis to "back him up," and Luis had declined. It was probably the first time in his life that he had backed away from a fight, and because of that, Luis had a problem with the Shot-Caller.

"I told him, 'I don't bang no more. Everybody knows that. I got two babies and a wife. A guy who has a family, he can get out,' " Luis recalls.

"The Shot-Caller looked at me for awhile, and then he goes, 'You didn't ask me to get out. You're not out until I say you're out.' He's quiet for awhile, then he goes, 'If you want out, you're gonna have to get jumped out. Think about that for a day or two. Call my beeper, and I'll get right back to you and you will let me know what you've decided. If I don't hear from you, I'm gonna send guys to find you.' "

After that, Luis "pretty much went underground." A half dozen of the homeboys stayed loyal, and he moved from one house to another, from one apartment to the next, sleeping on couches or in a sleeping bag on the floor. Claudia asked him to baby-sit every once in awhile, and while he was with the girls, Luis was especially jumpy, checking the street every few seconds and studying every car that passed. He was looking out the front window late one afternoon when a car stopped and Claudia got out of the backseat. There was a guy back there, and Luis erupted.

"I got jealous, I guess, 'cause I still love her," he says. Luis ran outside, pushed Claudia out of the way, reached in the car, and yanked the guy out and began slugging him. Claudia screamed and jumped on his back, and two City Year friends who were sitting in the front seat jumped out and wrestled Luis to the ground. "You blew it, Luis!" Claudia yelled, shepherding the girls back inside the house. "I don't want you around here at all."

Everything had changed for Luis. The streets he had rocketed down on his bike as a boy were not his anymore. He thought of calling his probation officer and asking if he could be locked up in Juvenile Hall in protective custody. Maybe a counselor or someone in the Gang Unit could help him get out of this mess. Then he remembered: he was eighteen, and he didn't have a probation officer anymore. "I decided that I should go to L.A., and my brother Santos would put me up," Luis says. "But the phone number we had just kept ringing and ringing, and I didn't have his address."

His other brother, Javier, had moved to Fresno, and he agreed to let Luis come and share his room for a while. On a bright day in November, Luis borrowed $60 from a friend and got a ride downtown to the Greyhound bus station. The next bus to the Central Valley did not leave for three hours, and for three hours Luis sat in the waiting area, a denim laundry bag with all his possessions across his lap. He looked stiff and almost formal. Several times, Luis got up to make phone calls. The first was to a homey. "Everything's cool now." The second was to "this girl I met."

The other calls were to Claudia's beeper. He kept paging and paging, but she decided that she was too busy with her job and her girls, "too fed up," to return the calls.

When it came time to board, Luis started for the bus and looked around hesitantly. He did not know whom to hand his ticket to. He did not know how to be sure when the bus reached Fresno. Where should he put his bag? Was the bus going to stop for food somewhere? Did he have to change buses? Entering the bus, the young man who had "the pride to walk the streets" looked lost and lonely. This was the first time he had ever been out of San Jose.

EPILOGUE

LUIS SOTO SETTLED TEMPORARILY IN FRESNO, WHERE HE WORKED part-time as a roofer. He met a woman and, "We were thinking of getting married, but I got into . . . 'stuff.' " "Stuff" meant drugs. Luis eventually returned to San Jose where he began harassing Claudia. She eventually went to court and got a restraining order. A year after his final arrest as a juvenile, Luis has been served for failure to pay child support and has been picked up for a gang-related assault. The district attorney is deciding whether there is enough evidence to file charges.

CLAUDIA continues working for City Year, which is paying for day care for ELENA and ELOISA. "They love it!" Claudia says. She scored high on her GED test and plans to attend a community college to pursue the goal she has had since she was twelve: becoming a journalist. "Some days, I get really mad at myself for wasting so many years and I think I'll never make it, that I should give up and do something more practical," she says. "But I'm just eighteen, and, even for someone who has kids and everything, I think that's too young to give up my dreams."

COREY MCKENZIE is still incarcerated in the California Youth Authority. A judge ruled that sixteen-year-old KARL FOSTER, who had urged Corey to stab John De Caprio like "an OG," was "unfit" for juvenile court. Foster was charged with first-degree murder and tried in adult court in December 1995. His attorney argued that he should be considered an accomplice to murder, but prosecutor Marc Buller convinced the jury that Foster was as responsible for this "senseless, brutal, and ruthless" crime as was Corey McKenzie. Karl Foster was convicted and is facing a sentence of twenty-five years to life.

BRENDA DE CAPRIO, the widow of John De Caprio, was satisfied with the verdict in the Foster trial. "I don't think there was anything that could have been done for Karl," she told a newspaper reporter after the trial. Brenda is a volunteer in a San Diego children's shelter and is a college student, majoring in psychology. "I'd like to be able to reach kids before they get into the criminal justice system—before they get to the point where Corey was," she says.

After turning eighteen and being released from the system, JESSE MONTGOMERY surfed from couch to couch, from minimum-wage job to minimum-wage job. Along the way, he began using drugs heavily, but he quit when he realized that "I could no longer play the guitar with subtlety." Steuart Samuels hired him as a maintenance worker at the Star Houses, and Jesse eventually became the maintenance crew chief. Samuels is now grooming Jesse to become a counselor.

BRIAN WRIGHT and his mother, DEBBIE, continue living together in Fresno. Technically, they are a success story because Brian has not come back into the dependency system. "But we have a lot of ups and downs," Debbie says. "Brian's still very domineering and pushy, and he's so big now that I can't restrain him. He threatens to kill me, to kill his sister, and he's always threatening suicide." Debbie says that she has seen some small improvement since Brian was admitted to an SED school, a school for severely emotionally disturbed children. Brian has been picked up twice by the police recently—once for shoplifting and once for mooning on a school bus.

DENNIS WRIGHT has continued in therapy, attempting to better understand his part in the family chaos. He sees Brian very rarely, and they talk on the phone only when Brian initiates the contact. "I don't see a lot of hope for my son," Dennis says, with sadness. "I won't be surprised when I get the call from Juvenile Hall saying that he's been arrested."

Almost two years after the BEYER FAMILY filed their lawsuit against the Department, they decided to drop it. "We found out that, if we were going to press it further, Kimberly might have to testify," Sandy Beyer says. "We weren't about to put her through that. Kimmy is doing just great; the boys are just fine; we're all doing great. We made our point by taking the case as far as we did. It was time to put this all behind us."

NICKY KENNEY is suffering very few seizures and is a cheerful four-year-old. "He's so enthusiastic and so cute, when psychologists test him, they end up thinking Nicky is less damaged than he is," says his mother, Claire. "But I know my son; I make them do the tests over, and that's when they finally acknowledge he has learning disabilities. But he's doing just great, and we couldn't love him more."

STEVEN DELGATO is doing time in a California state penitentiary on drug charges.

After being released from the system, JENNY LANDGON'S daughter, LISA, was taken to the Children's Shelter twice while the Department looked into charges of abandonment and neglect. "We found absolutely no evidence and returned the baby to her mother," says the social worker who handled the cases. After living with a roommate and then with an aunt, Jenny accepted an offer for her and Lisa to move to New York State and live with the woman who had once sought to adopt her. "She's really strict and is making me promise to go to school," Jenny told her former child advocate. "I hate it."

In December 1995, Santa Clara County opened a new $13.4 million Children's Shelter in a residential neighborhood. In an article in the *San Jose Mercury News*, the collection of eleven buildings on an eight-acre campus was described as "socially responsible architecture . . . looking more like a farm than a county institution." The run-down dorms are gone, and children live in small cottages with semiprivate bedrooms. Outside, there is a sunken amphitheater on one side of the lawn; there also is a playground with basketball, volleyball, and street hockey courts.

The new shelter was not built with public money alone. In an era of government budget slashing, when jails seem to be the only new buildings going up, more than half of the money came from private donors, as evidenced by the Jennifer and Joe Montana ball field and the William R. Hewlett (of Hewlett-Packard) courtyard.

• • •

And every weekday morning at 8:30 A.M., there is always a line of attorneys, social workers, advocates, and parents with squirming children snaking up the block in front of the boxy two-story building that is the home of the dependency court in Santa Clara County. "We will never 'cure' the juvenile problem the way we cured polio," says Judge Leonard P. Edwards. "We have to face that there will always be work to do because there will always be poverty and inadequate resources, abusive or unavailable families. Every morning, I arrive in court and there they are."

WHAT YOU CAN DO

JUDGE LEN EDWARDS IS AS FINE A JUVENILE COURT JUDGE AS THERE IS in America. Mary Agnes King was an excellent social worker, and Cleveland Prince is a great probation officer. We need more like them. But more judges, more social workers, and more probation officers are not the solution to complex social problems. We also need to use government in a more effective way to create better programs, but that too is only part of the answer. Our society needs to make a commitment to better the lives of families, to make somebody else's children all our children. That commitment can begin in your community, with you.

There are a thousand ways you can make a difference, in large and small ways, whether you have a little time or a lot. Each community has its own organizations and programs that work with families and children. Some have well-established volunteer programs where you can get involved in fund-raising or work directly with children and teenagers. Others may need you to be more creative and come up with a way to use your skills. Here is how you can get involved:

For information about volunteering at a children's shelter for abused and neglected children or at a residential care home for emotionally disturbed children, contact the facility directly or call the local department of family and children's services.

The National Court Appointed Special Advocate Association (CASA), 100 W. Harrison St., North Tower, Suite 500, Seattle, WA 98119, 800-628-3233, can put you in touch with the closest court-advocate and Guardian ad Litem program.

County hospitals sometimes run outpatient and residential drug treatment programs for women and children. Call the hospital volunteer department for information.

Teen parents can benefit greatly by having mentors and role models. Contact the local social service department or the school district to learn about programs.

School districts usually operate alternative schools for teenagers who are having trouble in regular school. There is much need here for volunteer tutors, teachers, and babysitters to watch toddlers while their mothers are in class.

Juvenile halls often have volunteer tutors, artists, and craftspeople working with inmates. Contact the hall directly or the probation department to see what other programs are in need of volunteer support.

Ask around. Call the presiding judge in the local juvenile court, the neighborhood recreation department, a church working with street kids, any agency involved with youth. Someone out there will be glad to hear from you.

AN UPDATE FOR THE PAPERBACK EDITION

In November 1997, President Bill Clinton signed legislation that again changes the emphasis of the nation's child welfare system. This time, it is a shift away from the idea that the system's chief consideration ought to be reuniting children with their biological parents. The new law mandates that the health and safety of the child must come first.

The new federal law is designed to speed up the adoption of abused and neglected children. States are now required to begin proceedings to terminate the birth parents' rights after a child has spent fifteen months in foster care. If a child is abandoned or tortured, if a child has been chronically physically or sexually abused, or if the parents have murdered or assaulted a sibling, termination proceedings are to begin immediately.

The new law also gives states a financial incentive to move children out of the foster care system and into adoptive homes.

But as anyone who works with abused and neglected children knows, federal laws are not silver bullets. They are merely guidelines. The real work is done at the grassroots level. And there, the big questions remain: How do we decide if a child is better off with his family or in out-of-home care? Where do we attract enough adoptive parents? How do we support families who can keep their children?

How do we do the best for each child at the crucial moment when a child needs our best?

NOTES

Prologue

ix *One eighth of the country's children*—*Kids Count Data Book 1996*, Annie E. Casey Foundation.

Chapter 1

1 Figures on San Jose's growth and population are from the U.S. Bureau of the Census and the San Jose Chamber of Commerce.

2 *a father who had lost custody* "Three Deputies Are Shot in San Jose, Suspect Also Wounded in Gun Battle," *San Jose Mercury News*, August 12, 1992.

3 Jenny Langdon's story is based on interviews with Jenny, her social workers, her child advocate, counselors at the Children's Shelter, relatives, and former roommates and on her case file and court reports.

4 "*California's strongest voice*" Press release from the national office of the Court Appointed Special Advocates (CASA) program, naming Judge Edwards the Juvenile Court Judge of the Year, and the *Los Angeles Daily Journal*, August 24, 1993.

5 *never been any political power or prestige* "The Juvenile Court and the Role of the Juvenile Court Judge," by Leonard P. Edwards, *The Juvenile and Family Court Journal*, 43 (1992): 34. "In many jurisdictions throughout the United States, the court system assigns the work of juvenile court to referees . . . because judges cannot or do not want to handle all the emotional and tiring work. . . . Moreover, the government saves money by hiring lesser-paid judicial officers."

5 "*social institution with legal trimmings*" and *juvenile law is rarely taught* Edwards, "The Juvenile Court," 34–35. "An astounding number [of law schools] don't even offer a course, and none of them require a course."

5 *Veteran child welfare workers talk* The Child Welfare League recommends a caseload of 28 cases per worker. In the Santa Clara County system—one of the best staffed in the country—workers often juggle 40 or more cases. In

Washington, D.C., caseloads are as high as 125 per caseworker. Stacy Robinson, "Remedying Our Foster Care System: Recognizing Children's Voices," *Family Law Quarterly*, 27: 395.

5 *Foster parents are dropping out* Gordon Evans, information director of the National Foster Parents Association, in "The Foster Care Crisis," *Parents Magazine*, January 1994.

6 *Edwards's role* The judge has helped establish Kids in Common, an inoculation program to ensure that children are vaccinated by the age of two; the Domestic Violence Coordinating Council, which brings together all parts of the system—including police and the courts—that deal with family violence; and the Zero Tolerance Program, to keep weapons off school campuses.

6 *With his wife—Child Abuse and the Legal System*, by Inger J. Sagatun and Leonard P. Edwards (Chicago: Nelson-Hall, 1994).

6 *There is a photograph of—Turning Point: The 1964 Mississippi Freedom Summer*, by Frank R. Parker (Washington, D.C.: Joint Center for Political and Economic Studies, 1994).

Chapter 2

10 *Public Law 96-272* "Too many children were removed from their parents' care, with little or no effort to keep families intact; children in foster care received few, if any, services to facilitate reunification with their families. Children in foster care were allowed to drift from one placement to another, with no long term plan for their future and little likelihood that they would ever enjoy a stable, family-like placement." Report of the Little Hoover Commission, "Mending Our Broken Children: Restructuring Foster Care in California," April 1992.

11 *"the most family-like"* "Child Abuse and Neglect in California—A Review of the Child Welfare Services Program," Legislative Analyst's Office, January 1991, 10.

12 *a lot of time in court* For a full explanation of California law regarding dependent children, see *West's Juvenile Laws and Court Rules, Welfare and Institutions Code*.

12 The Nicky Delgato case is based on interviews with Nicky's first foster mother, his social worker, his Fost-Adopt parents, his biological father's attorney, his case file, and his mother's file.

13 *reported the results of the drug scan* Throughout the 1980s, mandatory reporting of child abuse did not include the discovery of a drug-exposed infant as a
"reportable" event. "Since the abuse took place before birth and could not
take place in the same form after birth, it did not appear to be covered by the
law." But in the 1990s, many states, including California, specifically required
physicians to test newborns and immediately report the child and mother for
illicit substance abuse. California mandates that a further assessment by a
health practitioner or medical social worker be made before the infant is released from the hospital.

The law in California has been modified, however, to specify that a positive toxicology screen at the time of delivery is not in and of itself sufficient
basis for reporting child abuse and neglect. "In contrast to many laws passed
in other states, the law in California . . . emphasizes the desirability of treatment and medical services, rather than criminal prosecution or automatic referral to child protective services." Sagatun and Edwards, *Child Abuse and the
Legal System,* chapter 14.

14 *effects cocaine and alcohol have in the womb* Interviews with Ron Cohen; "Infant Mortality," *Congressional Quarterly Researcher,* July 31, 1992; "The Limit
of Viability: Neonatal Outcome of Infants Born at 22 to 25 Weeks' Gesta-
tion," *New England Journal of Medicine,* November 25, 1993; and "Fetal Alcohol Syndrome: Identification, Treatment, and Prevention for Mother and
Child," *Proceedings of the Indian Child Welfare Act Conference 3,* published by
the U.S. government, August 1990. See also *The Broken Cord* (New York:
HarperCollins 1989), Michael Dorris's moving account of raising his alcohol-exposed adopted son.

Chapter 3

19 *the kind of child needing long-term care has changed dramatically* "The population now consists of more severely disturbed children, including drug-
addicted, drug-exposed and HIV-infected children and children with AIDS.
The majority of these youth require some degree of specialized care and
the role of the foster parent has changed from one of providing a normal
family environment and basic board and care to one which requires specialized skill and training." Spokesman for the state Department of Social Services in the report of the Little Hoover Commission, "Mending Our Broken
Children," 36.

20 *there are more—not fewer—children needing substitute care* The substitute care population increased by more than two thirds between 1982 and 1992. It is estimated that 659,000 children experienced substitute care for some period of the year, according to *Juvenile Offenders and Victims: A National Report*, prepared by Howard N. Snyder and Melissa Sickmund for the National Center for Juvenile Justice, Washington, D.C., Department of Justice, Office of Juvenile Justice and Delinquency Prevention, August 1995, 40. In 1990, 75 percent of the children in substitute care lived in foster homes, 16 percent in group homes and emergency shelters, and 9 percent in hospitals, correctional institutions, and other facilities.

20 *the curious distinction* According to the state's Department of Social Services, foster parents in California are paid the same rates in 1996 as they were in 1990: $345 a month for a preschooler; $375 for a five- to eight-year-old; $400 for a nine- to eleven-year-old; $444 for a twelve- to fourteen-year-old; and $484 for a fifteen- to eighteen-year-old. There is an extra stipend, $100 to $200 a month, to care for a special needs child, one requiring "a high degree of attention." The Department sometimes pays "top dollar"— $741 a month—to a foster parent who takes in an adolescent like Jenny who has a history of acting out.

Even as far back as 1989, these rates fell far short of the cost of raising a child. A U.S. Department of Agriculture report estimates that the cost of raising urban primary-grade schoolchildren in the Western states in June 1989 was $496 per month (not including medical costs, which would be covered by a foster child's Medi-Cal). "Updated Estimates of the Cost of Raising a Child," U.S. Department of Agriculture, *Family Economics Review*, cited in "Tackling California's Demand for Foster Care," Senate Office of Research, December 1990, 6.

21 *Foster parents face any number of legal liabilities.* "Foster Parents' Strike? Insurance Crisis Resolution Sought," *San Jose Mercury News*, July 14, 1986.

21 *allegations of child abuse* Interviews with the Raaps and with representatives of the county and state Foster Parent Association. In its 1994 training conference, the California State Foster Parent Association held the workshop "Foster Parents and Their Rights with Complaints and Allegations" to help "foster parents know what to expect" when a grievance or allegation is filed against them.

Chapter 5

37 *the thirteenth assault* Other incidents included one child who was pinned down and beaten by seven shelter residents and a counselor who was assaulted and bitten by a resident of the unit for senior girls. From a shelter Incident Report.

Chapter 6

45 CASA was started by Juvenile Court Judge David Soukup. Today, there are more than 30,000 trained volunteers working in more than 500 programs in all fifty states. Santa Clara County has 500 child advocates.

48 At the 1997 meeting of the Society for Neuroscience in New Orleans, a range of new research was presented that verified the effects of early deprivation on the brains of maternally deprived animals. In one study, the neurons in the brains of the neglected animals died at twice the rate as those animals kept with their mothers. See, among others, the work of Mark Smith at the Du Pont Merck Research Labs in Wilmington, Delaware, and Michael Meaney at the Douglas Hospital Research Centre in Montreal.

Mary Carlson of Harvard Medical School, who studied Romanian infants raised in orphanages, reported that when lacking the attention and stimulation typical of family life, "the 2-to-3-year-old children developed abnormally high and lasting levels of the stress hormone cortisol, which can have serious long-range effects." *Los Angeles Times,* October 28, 1997.

49 *"these mute, solemn children"* *Every Child's Birthright: In Defense of Mothering,* by Selma Fraiberg (New York: Basic Books, 1977), 52. "What we see in the evolution of the human bond is a language between partners, a 'dialogue,' . . . in which messages from the infant are interpreted by his mother and messages from the mother are taken as signals by the baby. This early dialogue of 'need' and 'an answer to need' becomes a highly differentiated signal system in the early months of life; it is, properly speaking, the matrix of human language and of the human bond itself."

51 *"The cult of happy childbirth"* "Only Connect" by Alan Wolfe, *The New Republic,* Oct. 4, 1993.

51 *the first few minutes of life* A study by John Kennell and Marshall Klaus in the *New England Journal of Medicine* in 1972 indicated that as few as sixteen

hours of close contact between mother and infant immediately after birth produced better results on child development scales as late as five years after. See Wolfe, "Only Connect."

51 *if bonding goes poorly* "An unattached child, even at the age of three or four, cannot easily attach himself even when he is provided with the most favorable conditions for the formation of a human bond. The most expert clinical workers and foster parents can testify that to win such a child, to make him care, to become important to him, to be needed by him, and finally to be loved by him, is the work of months and years." Fraiberg, *Every Child's Birthright*, 50.

51 *Proponents of this theory* For an excellent overview of bonding history, studies, and criticism, see "Becoming Attached," by Robert Karen, *The Atlantic Monthly*, February 1990, 35–70. See also *High Risk: Children Without a Conscience*, by Ken Magid and Carole A. McKelvey (New York: Bantam Books, 1987), and *The Moral Sense*, by James Q. Wilson (New York: Free Press, 1993).

51 *attacked by feminists* See Diane Eyer, *Mother-Infant Bonding: A Scientific Fiction* (New Haven: Yale University Press, 1993).

52 *Common sense alone says* Harvard psychologist Jerome Kagan believes that too much attention has been paid to early experience, citing studies of teenagers who experienced deprivation when very young but rebounded handsomely in adolescence. See Karen, "Becoming Attached," 66.

Chapter 7

58 *a figure without equal* Interview with Richard O'Neil, director of Santa Clara County Social Services Agency.

58 *the image of social workers* For a discussion of the role social workers have historically played, their standing in academia, and the way they are perceived, see *Unfaithful Angels: How Social Work Has Abandoned Its Mission*, by Harry Specht and Mark E. Courtney (New York: Free Press, 1994).

59 *a 1992 grand jury report* "Final Report Investigation: The Department of Family and Children's Services," the 1992–93 Santa Clara Grand Jury, 29–44. "There is even controversy as to which children are selected for the [Fost-Adopt] program; these are children referred to as 'marketable children,' meaning they are young and cute. . . . The Department recognizes the unique

position of the fost-adopt parent and believes the fost-adopt parent is capable of handling the dual role; the grand jury disagrees." Putting a child in Fost-Adopt, the "case worker makes a judgment call, namely that reunification efforts will fail. This looks like a judgment call has been made before the natural parents have had a chance to prove their fitness or to show that they are not unfit."

59 *"withholding the psychosocial and medical history"* ". . . no agency shall place a child for adoption unless a written medical background, and if available, so far as ascertainable, the medical background of the child's biological parents, has been submitted to the prospective parents. . . ." *California Civil Code* 222.26. For more on adoption, see *Adoption Crisis: The Truth Behind Adoption and Foster Care*, by Carole A. McKelvey and JoEllen Stevens (Golden, Colorado: Fulcrum Publishing, 1994).

60 *adoption "disruptions"* An estimated 13 percent of all adoptions fail—12 percent before the process is final and another 1 percent afterward, often because the parents have not been fully informed of the child's past and often "because the parents and children aren't given the financial and mental health treatment they need. Each failure leaves the children a little more scarred. . . . Some children are adopted and given back as many as three times before the system stops trying to place them. Most people wouldn't think of divorcing their birth children, no matter how bad the problems are, but adopted children often are viewed differently. Some parents get so distraught that they give up, especially in the teenage years." McKelvey and Stevens, *Adoption Crisis*, 48.

60 *most families who have their children removed and undergo reunification are successful* The proportion of children leaving substitute care who were reunited with their families increased nationally from 50 percent in 1982 to 67 percent in 1990. There was a small decline in the number and proportion of children leaving substitute care who were adopted between 1982 (10 percent) and 1990 (8 percent). Snyder and Sickmund, *Juvenile Offenders and Victims*, 41.

61 *applauded reunification* "Research over the past 40 years says that if you remove the child from home, you often traumatize the child more than he is already hurt. You inflict a subsequent injury, especially on a young child who can't understand why he's been removed from his family. They feel they did something bad, and that it is their fault, or they view it as a kidnapping." Charles P. Gershenson, former chief of research and evaluation in the Children's Bureau of the U.S. Department of Health and Human Services,

quoted in "Saving Families Fosters Hope for America's Troubled Youth," by Daniel Kagan, *Insight*, April 29, 1991, 16.

61 *reunification enlightened* "Some professionals estimate that between 35 and 70 percent of children who end up in foster care should not be there and can be severely damaged psychologically by the experience." During 1991, only 19.9 percent of children were removed for reasons of physical or sexual abuse. The other 80 percent were removed because of general neglect, a violation of the law by a parent, or because the caretaker was "absent or incapacitated." Better in-home services "would allow children to remain in their homes under a placement prevention program." Report of the Little Hoover Commission, "Mending Our Broken Children," 12, 17.

61 *political and economic causes* The abuse rate was four times higher in lower-income families (an annual income of less than $15,000); the neglect rate was nearly eight times higher. Snyder and Sickmund, *Juvenile Offenders and Victims*, 34.

62 *cheaper than out-of-home care* Foster care costs an average of $6,483 per child per year in California. Report of the Little Hoover Commission, "Mending Our Broken Children," 26. According to "Keeping Families Together," a publication of the Edna McConnell Clark Foundation, the median cost of intensive family preservative services is $4,500 per family and $3,000 per child.

62 *did not stop the flow* Between 1985 and 1991, federal reimbursements to the states for foster care maintenance nearly quadrupled, to $1.8 billion, and it continues to grow. This is in addition to funds for family preservation and re-unification services. Edna McConnell Clark Foundation, "Keeping Families Together."

62 *by the "reunification" book* "In any case in which a child is removed from the physical custody of his or her parents pursuant to Section 361, preferential consideration shall be given to a request by a relative of the child for placement of the child with the relative. . . . The county social worker shall ask the parents if there are any relatives that should be considered for placement." *California Welfare and Institutions Code* 361.3.

62 *his body weighing nineteen pounds* The parents of Jory Daniels were charged with murder, torture, and felony child abuse and were taken into custody to await trial. Jory's grandparents were given three years' probation and ordered to perform fifty hours of community service each. "Starved Boy's Parents Face Murder Charges," *San Jose Mercury News*, June 25, 1994, and "Grandparents Spared Jail," April 11, 1995.

62 *Opponents of reunification cite* "Why Leave Children with Bad Parents," *Newsweek*, April 25, 1994. In Snyder and Sickmund, *Juvenile Offenders and Victims*, 39, it is explained that the exact number of children who die from maltreatment is difficult to determine and often misidentified. The National Child Abuse and Neglect Data System found that almost 1,100 children were known to have died as a result of neglect or abuse in 1992 in the forty-four states that routinely report such deaths. This translates into more than 1 death for every 1,000 substantiated victims. The U.S. Advisory Board on Child Abuse and Neglect estimates as many as 2,000 child maltreatment deaths per year. *A Nation's Shame: Fatal Child Abuse and Neglect in the United States*, Washington, D.C., xxiii.

62 *Even onetime proponents* Patrick Murphy argues that aggressive family reunification keeps children with parents who have no ability to raise their children or no intention of trying to raise them. He believes that child welfare agencies waste years trying to patch up dead-end families when they should be hurrying to free children for early adoption. *Newsweek*, April 25, 1995.

62 *As one social worker in the Santa Clara County Department puts it* Many workers complain that there is a financial incentive to leave children with their families. A finding by the juvenile court that "reasonable efforts" have been made in each case is required in order to qualify a child for Federal Foster Care Funds. These funds pay for 50 percent of the placement costs. Without such a finding, future placement costs for the child may become the sole responsibility of the county. See the Santa Clara County Child Abuse Prevention Coordinating Council, "Final Report by Reasonable Efforts Task Force," February 1990.

Others critics say that the goal of child welfare is no longer protecting children; it is making the system look good. And under the public policy of family reunification, the system looks good by keeping kids out of it—even if it means leaving them at risk. Patrick Murphy says, "Nobody said, 'Keep the fucking cases out of the system,' but that is the net effect." Adds Richard Gelles, director of the University of Rhode Island's Family Violence Research Program and once an ardent supporter of family preservation programs: "Family preservation programs operate under the naive philosophy that a mother who'd hurt her child is not much different from one who can't keep house—and that with enough supervision, both can be turned into good parents." *Newsweek*, April 25, 1994. See also *The Book of Davis: How Preserving Families Can Cost Children's Lives* by Richard Gelles (New York: Basic Books, 1996).

63 *risking the lives of children* "The most alarming trend in the decade of the 1980s has been the tendency of the courts to give the interests of society and the family precedence over the rights of women, children and the elderly. This is a regressive movement. . . . All too often children are left in homes where they have been abused in order to keep the family together." *Unequal Protection: Women, Children and the Elderly in Court*, by Lois Forer (New York: Norton, 1991), 41–42. Judge Forer has written several important books on the inequity of American law, including *No One Will Listen: How Our Legal System Brutalizes the Youthful Poor* (New York: John Day, 1970).

63 *postpone a child's being adopted* "It has become almost impossible to free children for adoption because of the emphasis on family preservation. I know people who have been trying for two years to adopt these crack babies that have been abandoned in hospitals, but . . . the state is not terminating parental rights even if there is no contact with the biological mother." Interview with Mary Beth Seader, vice president of the National Council for Adoption, in *Current Magazine*, October 1994.

Chapter 8

64 *The History of Childhood: The Untold Story of Child Abuse*, Lloyd de Mause, ed. (New York: Peter Bedrick Books, 1974).

64 For the Mary Ellen case and the founding of the SPCC, see *The Children's Rights Movement in the United States: A History of Advocacy and Protection*, by Joseph M. Hawes (Boston: Twayne Publishers, 1991), 20–21, and Sagatun and Edwards, *Child Abuse and the Legal System*, 7. For an alternative view of the Mary Ellen case, see *The Book of David—How Preserving Families Can Cost Children's Life* by Richard J. Gelles (New York: BasicBooks, 1996), 10–11.

65 *The organization only stepped in* For an account of child labor throughout history, see de Mause, *The History of Childhood*, chapter 1, "The Evolution of Childhood." Social work pioneer Homer Folks concluded that "the societies' greatest beneficence has been, not to the children who have come under their care, but to the vastly larger number whose parents have restrained angry tempers and vicious impulses through fear of the Cruelty." Hawes, *The Children's Rights Movement in the United States*, 23.

65 *the Constitution was a reflection* "The entire legal system in Great Britain and in the United States until the twentieth century was confined exclusively to

propertied adult males of sound mind. Consequently, all other human beings, who, of course, constituted the vast majority of the population, were largely excluded from legal rights and protections." Forer, *Unequal Protection*, 31–34.

65 For a historical view of how children were abandoned and maltreated from the Roman Empire to early Christian Europe, see *The Kindness of Strangers: The Abandonment of Children in Western Europe from Late Antiquity to the Renaissance*, by John Boswell (New York: Pantheon Books, 1988). A remarkable achievement, this book changes the way one views child rearing, historically as well as in our own era. Children have always been loved and cared for; they also have been treated as chattel, to be killed or abandoned when they were of no economic use.

66 *children remained valuable commodities* Baby "farming" was also a profitable family business. Women who advertised to adopt children were paid by parents who wanted to limit the size of their families to preserve their property. In some cases, the adoptive family pawned the baby's clothing and let the infants die of neglect. Forer, *Unequal Protection*, 195–96.

66 *The Puritans* See Hawes, *The Children's Rights Movement in the United States*, introduction and chapter 1, ix–10. In Puritan New England, there were few curtains drawn between family and community. Everyone had a duty that must be fulfilled. An individual who faltered weakened an entire village.

66 *the mother and father had a duty* Cotton Mather, the greatest of the Puritan ministers, advised parents to threaten children with eternal damnation to make them conform to God's—and their parents'—will. For a historical account of how children have been beaten, battered, and abused in the name of discipline, see Elizabeth Pleck, *Domestic Tyranny: The Making of Social Policy Against Family Violence from Colonial Times to the Present* (New York: Oxford University Press, 1987).

66 *the Body of Liberties*—In *The Children's Rights Movement in the United States*, Hawes says that this was the first set of laws "anywhere in the world to offer legal protection of any kind to children. . . ." But children whose families failed them fared no better in the New World than did children in the Old. Many Puritan children grew up in homes other than their own. Poor families had no choice but to place children in wealthy homes, where they became servants.

67 *Even Charles Dickehs* Hawes, *The Children's Rights Movement in the United States*, 17.

67 *A crime wave that had begun after the Civil War* See Otto Bettmann *The Good Old Days—They Were Terrible!* (New York: Random House, 1974), 89. "The

lawlessness of the 1860s through the 1890s," wrote criminologist Cesare Lombroso, "is an American phenomenon with no equal in the rest of the world." Daylight muggings in Chicago were so commonplace that one resident wrote that he always walked down the middle of the street "so that no hold-up man could step from an alley and salute us with a piece of lead—or an elongated canvas bag filled with sand." Nationally, according to the crudely formulated statistics of the time, the crime rate rose 445 percent while the population increased 170 percent in the decades after the Civil War.

67 *"the Perishing and Dangerous Classes"* Hawes, *The Children's Rights Movement in the United States*, 17–18.

68 *the Children's Aid Society* See Hawes, *The Children's Rights Movement in the United States*, 18–25, and Specht and Courtney, *Unfaithful Angels*, 66, 187.

68 *for the "crime" of being sexually active* Kristin Luker, *Dubious Conceptions: The Politics of Teen Pregnancy* (Cambridge: Harvard University Press, 1996), 29.

69 *Jane Addams* See Specht and Courtney, *Unfaithful Angels*, 80–84, and Hawes, *The Children's Rights Movement in the United States*, 40. For a comprehensive description of the Progressive Era, see *Rendezvous with Destiny: A History of Modern American Reform*, by Eric Goldman (New York: Alfred A. Knopf, 1952), and Page Smith, *The Rise of Industrial America: A People's History of the Post-Reconstruction Era* (New York: McGraw-Hill, 1984).

69 For a detailed description of Benjamin Lindsey and the case that altered the course of his professional life, see Goldman, *Rendezvous with Destiny*, 121–23. See also Lindsey's autobiography, *The Beast*, written with Harvey J. O'Higgins (New York: Doubleday, 1917).

69 *except for the occasional kind word* This was the brutal reality for the thousands upon thousands of children who were hauled into criminal courts and then sent off to adult prisons. On the police treatment of youthful offenders, see Bettmann, *The Good Old Days*, 91. Children were locked up on the slightest suspicion of a misdeed. "In Chicago, upwards of 10,000 young persons were arrested, clubbed, handcuffed and jostled around . . . without having committed any crime." However, dating back to English common law, there had been some legal recognition that younger children were not as responsible for their actions as were adults. William Blackstone's *Commentaries* acknowledged that "Under seven years of age indeed an infant cannot be guilty of felony; for then a felonious discretion was almost an impossibility in nature."

But it was the rare nineteenth-century judge who gave special consideration to children. For an account of these few cases, see the appendix in *The Child Savers: The Invention of Delinquency*, by Anthony M. Platt (Chicago:

University of Chicago Press, 1969). Platt points out that black children were not granted the same immunities as white children. Between 1806 and 1882, two American children under age fourteen were executed; both were slaves.

69 *The new courts were the first in the world* For a description of the early juvenile courts, see Sagatun and Edwards, *Child Abuse and the Legal System*, 8, and Goldman, *Rendezvous with Destiny*, 121–23.

70 *a lousy parent* On page 4 of *The Child Savers*, Platt sums up the criticism: Although the progressives who founded the juvenile court were "rhetorically concerned with protecting children from the physical and moral dangers of an increasingly industrialized and urban society, their remedies seemed to aggravate the problem." Since its inception, there have been almost constant calls to reform the system—especially the delinquency branch—and some critics have suggested that it be abolished. "Conservatives and liberals may disagree on the policies that ought to be implemented to deal with youthful criminal offenders, but both ends of the political spectrum agree that the child-adult distinction is a false dichotomy that can no longer support disparate justice systems." Janet E. Ainsworth, "Re-Imagining Childhood and Reconstructing the Legal Order: The Case for Abolishing the Juvenile Court," 1083–133 and 1103–4, as noted in Edwards, "The Juvenile Court."

70 *"the worst of both worlds"* "There is evidence, in fact, that there may be grounds for concern that the child receives the worst of both worlds: That he gets neither the protection accorded to adults nor the solicitous care and regenerative treatment postulated for children." *United States v. Kent*, 383 U.S. 541, 566 (1966). This was the first case from juvenile court to reach the U.S. Supreme Court. "Most Supreme Court decisions involve issues of great importance to the public as a whole. Many are concerned with clarifying, expanding or revising prior decisions involving the same issue. For example, in the years following the landmark libel decision New York Times v. Sullivan, the court has written multiple opinions in more than 80 cases involving libel. During the same period the court has considered very few cases involving the rights of children." Forer, *Unequal Protection*, 21.

70 *A child who had loving parents* The idea of a child's psychological well-being and the concept of a psychological parent are presented in *Beyond the Best Interests of the Child*, by Joseph Goldstein, Anna Freud, and Albert J. Solnit (New York: Free Press, 1973).

71 *Reform began in a most unlikely place* See Hawes, *The Children's Rights Movement in the United States*, 99–100. See also the "Saving Our Children" series

from the *Chicago Tribune*, Aug. 21–24, 1994, and Edwards, "The Juvenile Court," 14–15.

71 *In a civil case—Landeros v. Flood* (1976).

72 *Civil libertarians and others* See Richard Wexler, *Wounded Innocents: The Real Victims of the War Against Child Abuse* (Buffalo: Prometheus Books, 1990).

72 *The levels of abuse and neglect* See *A Nation's Shame: Fatal Child Abuse and Neglect in the United States*, Department of Health and Human Services, April 1995. Violence aimed at young children—the vast majority of them under four—claims the lives of at least 2,000 children annually and seriously injures 140,000 more, making abuse the leading cause of the deaths of young children. The study lambastes the system and its inadequately trained investigators, prosecutors, and medical professionals, its inadequate autopsy procedures, and its lack of adequate legal sanctions. (Only twenty-one states have laws that allow parents to be prosecuted for killing their child under "felony murder" or "homicide by child abuse" laws.) The study also criticizes the public for "responding to the deaths of infants and small children at the hands of parents or caretakers . . . in a strangely muffled, seemingly disinterested way.

"Little money has been spent to understand this tragic phenomenon. The true numbers and exact nature of the problem remain unknown, and the troubling fact of abuse or neglect often remains a terrible secret that is buried with the child."

73 *garden variety cases* While almost half of children in substitute care remained in one placement, the proportion of these children declined from 56 percent to 43 percent between 1982 and 1990. Snyder and Sickmund, *Juvenile Offenders and Victims*, 41.

73 *"We are not showering families with resources"* According to the Santa Clara County Child Abuse Prevention Coordinating Council's seventy-page task force report, quality subsidized child care is extremely limited. Only one third of those parents who are able to afford child care can locate it. Only one tenth of those who need subsidized care can find it. There are very few services available for teenage parents. Many children would remain at home with their families if homemaker services were available. Waiting lists for residential drug treatment programs are considerable. Low-income housing is wholly inadequate. The council's "Final Report by Reasonable Efforts Task Force" was prepared in 1990, and while some improvements have been made, things remain pretty much the same.

73–74 *"Currently, very few families"* *San Jose Mercury News*, Jan. 7, 1996. Also according to the Little Hoover Commission's report "Mending Our Broken Children," 18 "... placement prevention programs exist in California in only 13 counties. Moreover, the 13 counties in which the programs exist account for only 30.5 percent of all children placed in out-of-home care. It is safe to say that, at this point in time, family preservation programs are the exception rather than the norm."

Chapter 9

81 *started adoption proceedings* The adoption was held up by the possibility that Jenny's father was part Native American and that she therefore fell under the jurisdiction of the Indian Child Welfare Act. In 1979, "Congress expressed its clear preference for keeping Indian children with their families, deferring to tribal judgment on matters concerning the custody of tribal children, and placing Indian children who must be removed from their homes within their own families or Indian tribes." *Guidelines for State Court; Indian Child Custody Proceedings, Policy Section and Pretrial Requirements,* U.S. Department of the Interior, Bureau of Indian Affairs. The act was established to rectify an appalling situation in which Native American children were routinely removed from their families and tribes and either adopted or placed into foster care with white families, effectively erasing their cultural heritage. In Jenny's situation, however, a meaningful law was partly responsible for prolonging her "drift" in the system. After nearly a year of research, it was determined that Jenny was not eligible for tribal membership. By this time, Jenny had begun to act out seriously. The potential adoptive mother eventually decided to place her into residential care.

Chapter 10

82 *not a scientist* The long-term effects of in utero drug and alcohol exposure on the resulting premature births are still being studied. Some of the effects are obvious. For example, in the fetal alcohol syndrome population, there are usually physical characteristics that persist into adulthood: "the thin upper lip; long, smooth philtrum, and the small eyes remain constant." *Proceedings of the Indian Child Welfare Act Conference 3.* What Sharon Ruprecht was saying was that problems like delays in cognitive development, a tendency to-

ward oppositional defiance disorder, hyperactivity, and impulsivity are often hidden and not easy to measure and confirm.

84 *The early statistics and initial studies* For an excellent bibliography on studies of fetal alcohol syndrome and its effects, especially among Native Americans, see Dorris, *The Broken Cord*, 283–300.

84 *a "bio-underclass"* Charles Krauthammer, *San Jose Mercury News*, July 29, 1991. "We can either do nothing, or we can pass laws saying that any pregnant woman who takes cocaine during pregnancy will be sent until delivery to some not uncomfortable secure location (boot camp, county jail, house arrest—the details are purely technical) where she will be allowed everything except the liberty to take drugs."

85 *This "diagnosis" scared off countless* "These are children with serious problems," a speaker told the North American Council on Adoptable Children's Sixteenth Annual Conference in 1991, not "children for parents whose lifestyles are better suited to 'quality' versus 'quantity time' parenting." Quoted in *Adoption Crisis*, by McKelvey and Stevens, 104.

85 *The grim forecast* Ron Cohen believes that the argument to close NICUs is based on political, not medical, reasons. "When you want to cut money, you go after people who don't vote, and babies and poor women don't vote," the doctor says. "You can fund every NICU in this country for what roughly goes for one day of care for the elderly. And yet there are people out there saying we should close NICUs to balance the medical budget." For a full discussion of the shift in federal funding from children to the elderly, see *When the Bough Breaks: The Cost of Neglecting Our Children*, by Sylvia Ann Hewlett (New York: HarperCollins, 1991). Of particular interest is chapter 5, "Public Choices: Shortchanging the Future." The author contends that the "dirty secret" of contemporary social policy is that we are spending our collective resources on the wrong generation. During the 1980s, the government spent five times as much money on the old as on the young, and a significant proportion of these public funds went to the affluent elderly. An American citizen six years or younger is twice as likely to be poor as a citizen sixty-five or older.

Hostility to the health and welfare of children has a long history in this country. A particularly egregious example is the repeal in 1929 of the Sheppard-Towner Act. Passed in 1921, Sheppard-Towner was the first use of federal funds to promote the health of children. The act established "a bench mark for a number of issues—women's roles in health care, the use of the power of the state to improve children's rights, the role of education in issues like infant mortality rates and the role of physicians in the nation's health care system." The repeal of Sheppard-Towner, after intense lobbying by the American Medical Association, "was one of the most grievous blows American children have ever received." Hawes, *The Children's Rights Movement in the United States*, 65.

85 *"every child who has been exposed to drugs"* Ron Cohen's impressions are backed up by several studies. A research team at Emory University studied 107 full-term babies born to women who used cocaine along with alcohol and other drugs during their pregnancies and found that "though the coke babies were smaller than average, they were free of problems typically blamed on the drug, including gastrointestinal upsets, hyperactivity and tremors." Study by psychologist Claire D. Coles, cited in *Newsweek*, April 20, 1992.

Another study, at the University of Florida, compared children who started life in an NICU with children at the same school who were born without drug and medical complications. There were no significant differences in academic achievements, language problems, or learning disabilities. See *The Edell Health Letter*, August 1992.

Ira Chasnoff, onetime president of the National Association for Perinatal Addiction Research and Education, says that cocaine-exposed infants often catch up to children from similar (that is, deprived) backgrounds in weight, height, and language development and score in the normal range on scales of infant behavior. "These babies are not retarded; they are not brain damaged," Dr. Chasnoff says. However, the babies often do have more trouble concentrating and organizing their behavior, which is not surprising for children growing up in chaotic drug-damaged households. *San Jose Mercury News*, July 23, 1992.

85 *taxpayers will pay for all this* Twenty-five percent of all pregnant women in America do not receive prenatal care in the crucial first trimester of pregnancy, according to *Congressional Quarterly Researcher*, July 31, 1992. For black women, the figure is 40 percent, largely due to the fact that health insurance is provided by employers and minorities are more likely to be unemployed or working in jobs that do not offer health insurance. More than 13 percent of black babies are born underweight, double the rate for white babies. The infant mortality rate for black babies is 17.7 per 1,000, also double the rate for whites.

The infant mortality rate in America declined from 1965, the year Medicaid became law, to 1981, the year the Reagan administration's Omnibus Budget Reconciliation Act removed most of the working poor from the welfare roles, making thousands of poor pregnant women ineligible for prenatal care under Medicaid. Funding for Community and Migrant Health Centers was slashed by 33 percent. The Women, Infants and Children Program, or WIC, administered by the Department of Agriculture, distributes food to infants and low-income pregnant women. Few federal programs are as cost-effective as WIC—the Department of Agriculture estimates that every dollar spent on WIC saves three dollars in medical costs to keep low-birthweight babies alive. But WIC has never been fully funded and today serves only about half of the eligible pregnant women.

The irony is that cutting back federal programs delivering prenatal care to poor pregnant women does not save money; it costs taxpayers dearly. According to Ron Cohen, it costs a minimum of $2,000 a day to keep a newborn in the NICU. Across the nation in 1990, each low-birthweight baby typically costs taxpayers $21,000. That is nearly eight times as much as the $2,824 in hospital fees for a baby born at a normal weight.

Chapter 11

90 *faced criminal prosecution* No state has passed legislation that specifically makes it a crime to use a controlled substance during pregnancy. Instead, prosecutions have been based on existing criminal laws, such as drug sales, use, and possession. Attempts to prosecute women have usually failed because the criminal laws were not intended to cover the "provision" of drugs by a woman to her fetus. Sagatun and Edwards, *Child Abuse and the Legal System*, 238–43.

90 *More permanent and humane solutions* According to Finnegan, Connaughton, Emich, and Wieland, "Comprehensive Care of the Pregnant Addict and Its Effects on Maternal and Infant Outcome," pregnant addicts who receive proper prenatal care give birth to babies with significantly fewer neonatal problems. However, ". . . drug rehab programs would not admit [women who were] pregnant. . . ." A survey by W. Chavkin, "Drug Addiction and Pregnancy," revealed that 54 percent of treatment programs categorically excluded the pregnant. Both are cited in Sagatun and Edwards, *Child Abuse and the Legal System*, 242.

According to 1992 statistics from the California Department of Alcohol and Drug Programs, only a limited number of the 135 alcohol and 123 drug treatment programs around the state provide services to pregnant women or are characterized as women's and children's programs, those in which children are permitted to accompany their mother into treatment. Many addicted mothers are faced with the choice of forsaking treatment or placing their children into foster care. Waiting lists for programs that target pregnant and parenting women are often three to six months long.

91 *15 percent of women giving birth* California Department of Alcohol and Drug Programs, 1992. According to another 1992 study of women delivering babies in Santa Clara County hospitals, 9.8 percent had alcohol or other drugs in their systems at the time of delivery.

91 *Jailing these women* Anthony Puentes agreed with what the Florida Supreme Court recognized in *Johnson v. Florida* in 1992 when it reversed a mother's criminal conviction on two counts of delivering a controlled substance to another person, i.e., to her two newborns during a short interval after birth before the umbilical cords were clamped. The court acknowledged that drug abuse is a serious problem, but it pointed out that prosecuting drug-addicted mothers is "the least effective response to the crisis. Rather than face the possibility of prosecution, [they] may simply avoid prenatal or medical care for fear of being detected. . . . A decision to deliver these babies at home will have tragic and serious consequences."

101 *Over-the-fence gossip* Interview with Karen Kaho, Ombudsperson, Department of Family and Children's Services, Santa Clara County.

Chapter 13

109 *"They'll send it to me"* There are many codes governing contact between birth parents, adoptive parents, and the child. For instance, a birth parent signing a relinquishment may request from the Department all known information about the status of the child's adoption "except for personal, identifying information about the adoptive family." *California Civil Code* 222.13. Social workers act as intermediaries.

110 In June 1995, suddenly and unexpectedly, Mary Agnes King died of a heart attack. She was a great person, always truthful and always full of hope, and a wonderful social worker.

Chapter 14

114 *one incest victim* "When I started in 1971, it was supposed to be one case of incest in every one million people," says Henry Giaretto, a San Jose psychol-

ogist who founded one of the country's first incest victim treatment programs. "That year, I had twenty-six cases. Now, we're running more than a thousand new cases a year in a metropolitan area of a million people." See also "Incest Comes Out of the Dark," *Time*, Oct. 7, 1991, and *By Silence Betrayed: Sexual Abuse of Children in America*, by John Crewdson (Boston: Little Brown, 1988) 25, quoted in "Child Sexual Abuse," by Charles S. Clark, *Congressional Quarterly Researcher*, Jan. 15, 1993.

114 *Today, approximately 14 percent* The latest available figures come from *Child Maltreatment 1992: Reports from the States to the National Center on Child Abuse and Neglect*. The statistical breakdown is as follows: neglect—49 percent, physical abuse—23 percent, sexual abuse—14 percent, emotional maltreatment—5 percent, and other maltreatment—12 percent. The total is greater than 100 percent because victims can be included in more than one category. See Snyder and Sickmund, *Juvenile Offenders and Victims*, 38.

115 *Expert witnesses* To be admissible at trial, expert testimony must be relevant to the issues at hand, and it must be based upon scientifically valid reasoning properly applied to the facts of the case. Sagatun and Edwards, *Child Abuse and the Legal System*, chapter 13.

115 *taking children seriously as witnesses—Federal Rules of Evidence* 601 now dictates that every person is competent. This leaves to juries the responsibility for assessing the credibility of child witnesses. Many states have followed the federal lead. For a full discussion, see Sagatun and Edwards, *Child Abuse and the Legal System*, chapter 10, and Forer, *Unequal Protection*, 154–76.

116 *cases like that of Malinda S.* "The Relationship of Family and Juvenile Courts in Child Abuse Cases," by Leonard P. Edwards, *Santa Clara Law Review*, 27 (1987): 205.

116 *"start the nightmare"* Members of the grand jury looking into the Santa Clara County system reviewed a case in which a four-year-old child was removed from his home because a child care provider reported that he had "French-kissed" a playmate. On the theory that this behavior could only have been learned at home, an allegation of child abuse was lodged against the father. It was only after the father moved out that the child was returned to the mother. Later, the teacher who made the initial report said that the whole thing had been blown out of proportion, but nobody in the system would listen. "The parents have been financially ruined as all their assets have been funneled into efforts to end the nightmare."

116 *legal scholars like* Douglas J. Besharov, "Unfounded Allegations—A New

Child Abuse Problem," *Public Interest*, 83 (Spring 1986): 19, quoted in Hawes, *The Children's Rights Movement in the United States*, 101.

117 *Reports of children being sexually abused* Edwards, "The Relationship of Family and Juvenile Courts," 203, and "The Juvenile Court," 15.

117 *looking into every case* According to the National Center on Child Abuse and Neglect, child protective service agencies received an estimated two million reports of alleged abuse and neglect in 1993. Because many of these reports involved more than one child (siblings), it is difficult to determine how many individual children were involved. Child protective service agencies conducted about 1.6 million investigations. In 41 percent, the allegations were substantiated (i.e., the allegation was supported or founded on the basis of state law or policy) or was indicated (i.e., the allegation could not be substantiated, but there was reason to suspect its validity). In one study, only 5 percent of the unsubstantiated allegations were determined to be intentionally false. Three percent of all allegations were intentionally false. Cited in Snyder and Sickmund, *Juvenile Offenders and Victims*, 38, and the 1996 Update, 8.

117 *the Child Abuse and Neglect Center receives 120 to 140 calls every day* "Final Report Investigation: The Department of Family and Children's Services," the 1992–93 Santa Clara Grand Jury, 32–33.

118 The Kimberly Beyer case is based on information in her case file, along with interviews with her parents; attorney Albie Jachimowicz; Mike Clark, the county attorney who represented the Department in the case; and doctors David Safir and David Kerns, chairman of pediatrics at Valley Medical Center.

120 *a colposcopic examination* Interview with David Kerns and "Clinical Commentary: Accomplishing Atraumatic Child Sexual Abuse Medical Examinations: Pointers for the Clinician and Power for the Children," by Mary L. Ritter and David Kerns, Center for Child Protection, Department of Pediatrics, Santa Clara Valley Medical Center, San Jose, California, 1994.

Chapter 15

123 *Multi-Disciplinary Interview (MDI) Team* More and more municipalities across the country are forming these teams, but what seems to be a sensible solution to a big problem is often a tough task politically. The problem is turf.

In Santa Clara County, the first proposal to establish an MDI team in the late 1980s was shot down by the district attorney's office. The DA insisted on being the first to interview children in sexual abuse cases. Social workers could get their crack at them after he was done. The DA didn't want social workers, however unwittingly, trampling on evidence or making mistakes that would render evidence inadmissible in a criminal hearing. After months of haggling, it was finally agreed that social workers who had received special training could conduct interviews with children. But most of the time, they would be handled by police officers like Sergeant Marv Lewis.

125 *The MDI team unanimously agreed* Supplementary Offense Report by Sergeant Marv Lewis, San Jose Police Department (1993), 2.

130 *there is a grassroots movement* Most notable are VOCAL (Victims of Child Abuse Laws), headquartered in Sacramento, California, and the False Memory Syndrome Foundation in Philadelphia, consisting mostly of parents who feel wronged by the system. There are also many professionals who work in the system who agree that too many children are taken from their parents. In Santa Clara County, public defender Thomas Spielbauer has tried to initiate legislation that would bring jury trials to child welfare cases, rather than having all the decisions made by a judge who "has absolute power. It is very difficult for someone who has absolute power to believe that the system that gave him that power is improper, unfair or unjust.

"With jury trials, the Department would realize very quickly that a lot of the cases that it attempts to bring into dependency court are not going to hold up in front of citizens of the community."

Chapter 16

133 *The grand jury* "found that the bias touched those in the Department as well as others involved in the dependency process and that the bias was at times on a conscious level but at other times was automatic and ingrained. For example, a Hispanic father was told that he and 'his kind' are known for sexually abusing their children." "Final Report Investigation: The Department of Family and Children's Services," the 1992–93 Santa Clara Grand Jury, 41–42.

133 *"Grievances pour into my office"* Interview with Karen Kaho, Ombudsperson, Santa Clara County.

134 *there was a police investigation going on* Depending on the quality of evi-

dence, a decision can be made to press criminal charges in a child abuse case. Once rare, criminal prosecutions of child abuse have increased dramatically in the past ten years. Of child abuse cases that are closed by the police, nearly 40 percent of the sexual abuse cases and about a quarter of physical abuse and neglect cases result in the arrest of the suspected perpetrator. However, in spite of the increase in police investigations, many do not result in prosecution for a variety of reasons: inability to establish a crime, insufficient evidence, unwillingness to expose the child to additional trauma.

There is controversy over prosecuting these cases. Some believe that the benefits are nullified by the "blaming, punitive and accusatory approach of the criminal justice system." J. Meyers, "The Legal Response to Child Abuse: In the Best Interest of Children," and *Journal of Family Law* 24, 1985, 149–269. Sagatun and Edwards, *Child Abuse and the Legal System*, chapter 7.

Chapter 17

138 *Charlotte Ketterer had filed* Ketterer later filed an amended petition which alleged that Kimberly had suffered a torn hymen, "constituting definite evidence of prior penetrating vaginal trauma," and that her parents "were unable to offer a reasonable explanation for the injury."

140 *The easy way . . . the least intrusive form* If the Beyers decided not to take the case to trial and decided to submit to the petition, the court could place the family on what is called informal supervision. Ron and Sandy would agree to attend parenting classes and to get counseling for Kimberly and the boys. A social worker would make a phone call every now and then to check on how things were going. If all went well, the case would be dismissed at the end of six months. The parents would not even have to show up for the hearing.

Chapter 18

146 Brian's case is based on the family's files in divorce, or family, court and in dependency court and on paperwork compiled by his parents. It is also based on interviews with Brian; his mother and father; his aunt; his grandmother; his sister; his therapist and counselors; Gayleen Williamson, the social worker handling the case; and the therapist who prepared the parents' psychological evaluations for the court hearings.

153 *a case comes to them from Divorce Court* In California the official name for what is popularly called "divorce court" is family court, which handles legal issues surrounding divorce, child and spousal support, property division, child custody, and visitation. "No one denies that child molestation is widespread. But the rise of false allegations as a wedge in custody cases is an alarming modern development." Richard Gardner, *Congressional Quarterly Researcher*, Jan. 15, 1993. Gardner, a Columbia University professor, points out that such allegations are suspicious by their timing. It is one thing for a mother to uncover sexual abuse and then to confront her husband for a divorce. But "compare that to a situation where there . . . has been no evidence of abuse, and then there's a divorce. After unsuccessfully trying various exclusionary tactics, such as blocking visitation, suddenly a parent brings up allegations of child abuse."

Approximately 2 to 10 percent of all family court cases involving custody or visitation disputes involve a charge of sexual abuse, a sharp increase from the years before 1980. N. Thoennes and J. Pearson, *Summary of Findings from the Sexual Abuse Allegations Project*, Association of Family and Conciliation Court Research Unit, cited in Edwards, "The Relationship of Family and Juvenile Courts," 202.

Chapter 19

158 *Brian's dilemma* A much-publicized 1993 study by Child Trends, Inc., indicated that divorce takes a long-term toll on children. Children whose parents divorced were 73 percent more likely than the general population to suffer from depression when they grew up. Among 18- to 22-year-olds from divorced families, 65 percent had poor relationships with their fathers, 30 percent had poor relationships with their mothers, 27 percent had dropped out of high school, 41 percent had received psychological help at some point, and 19 percent had significant behavior problems.

The study has been used by "family values" proponents to prove that divorce is bad. What the study does not indicate is how much of the emotional damage was inflicted on the children while the battling parents were still married. Several studies downplay the relevance of divorce and single parenthood to behavior problems and emphasize marital discord as stronger in predicting delinquency. See the studies cited in *Family Life, Delinquency, and*

Crime: A Policymaker's Guide, Department of Justice, Office of Juvenile Justice and Delinquency Prevention, May 1994, 12–15.

Another factor is the economic stress caused by divorce. After a divorce or separation, children are almost twice as likely to be living in poverty as they were before. "Children and Divorce: The Damage Done," *San Jose Mercury News*, April 6, 1993.

159 *instance of emotional disturbance* Jay Haley, quoted in *The Family Crucible*, by Augustus Y. Napier with Carl Whitaker (New York: HarperCollins, 1978), 84. This book provides an excellent overview of family therapy history, theory, and practice by following one family through treatment. Other, more technical books include *Family Therapy Theory and Practice*, ed. Philip J. Guerin, Jr. (New York: Gardner Press, 1976), and *Foundations of Family Therapy*, by Lynn Hoffman (New York: Basic Books, 1981). For the child's perspective on divorce, see *Surviving the Breakup: How Children and Parents Cope with Divorce*, by Judith S. Wallerstein and Joan Berlin Kelly (New York: Basic Books, 1980).

159 *"going on the attack"* A clinical assessment of Brian from Eastfield Ming Quong and the court-appointed psychological evaluator.

Chapter 20

161 *Puritan society* According to the Puritan minister Samuel Willard, "If God in his Providence hath bestowed on them Children or Servants, they have each of them a share in the government of them; tho' there is an inequity in the degree of this authority over them by God; and the Husband is to be acknowledged to hold a Superiority, which the Wife is to allow." Even when there was no husband around, as in the case of a child born out of wedlock, economics ruled over the mother's custodial rights. In Colonial America, bastard children were routinely separated from their mothers upon weaning and "bound out" to a master. *From Father's Property to Children's Rights: The History of Child Custody in the United States*, by Mary Ann Mason (New York: Columbia University Press, 1994), chapter 1, 1–47.

161 *even a "prudent, discreet and virtuous woman"* The precedent was English common law. In *Rex v. DeManneville*, a mother had taken her child and run away from a brutal husband. But the King's Bench returned the child to her father, even though "she was an infant at the breast of her mother." In 1809, a

South Carolina court was one of the first to allow common sense to overrule common law. A husband, father, and notorious womanizer named William Prather threw his wife of ten years out of their home and, in a move that defied all moral standards of the time, lived with another woman in open adultery. The court awarded the couple's five-year-old daughter to the mother, but it was not a decision made lightly. The court noted that it is "apprised that it is treading on new and dangerous ground." Mason, *From Father's Property to Children's Rights*, 60.

161 *The courts of the time* The Talfourt Act of 1839 directed British courts to award the custody of children under seven to their mothers, since "Nature has devolved upon the mother the nurture and care of infants during their tender years, and in that period such care, for all practical purposes, in the absence of exceptional circumstances, is almost exclusively committed to her." This landmark legislation, known as the "Tender Years Doctrine," influenced child custody on both sides of the Atlantic for the next 125 years. It was written to focus on children in their early years, but it was quickly applied to children of any age.

Another significant social trend of the time was also dramatically redefining women's roles inside and outside the family. In the mid- to late 1800s, early feminists were calling for the right of married women to keep not only their gifts and wages but also to keep their children following divorce or separation. Thus, two views of womanhood that appear contradictory—women as politically assertive and women as innately nurturing—joined forces to turn the tide in the courtroom, where women were now awarded their children under "maternal presumption." Mason, *From Father's Property to Children's Rights*, chapter 2, 50–57, 60–65.

162 *as the twentieth century progressed* "By the last third of the century, law relating to child custody had permeated the casual discourse of everyday life; few households were untouched by a custody matter. The (high rate) of divorce once again rearranged the tentative symmetry between mother, father, and the state with regard to the custody of children." Mason, *From Father's Property to Children's Rights*, 121.

162 *As the legal system looked* Until the 1960s, family law "favored women by making divorce hard to obtain and by requiring extended support for the wife and the children in the event of divorce." This was justified under the conviction that wives were less able to take care of themselves economically than were husbands. Once again, feminists played a part, citing cross-cultural

studies by anthropologist Margaret Mead as evidence against the firmly entrenched philosophy of natural law. Mead wrote that the idea that women are innately better caregivers is a "subtle form of anti-feminism by which men— under the guise of exalting the importance of maternity—are tying women more tightly to their children than has been thought necessary since the invention of bottle feeding and baby carriages." Mason, *From Father's Property to Children's Rights*, 123–24.

162 *first joint custody statute—California Civil Code* 4600.5. "There shall be a presumption, affecting the burden of proof, that joint custody is in the best interest of a minor child. . . ." There are two basic types of joint custody. Under joint physical custody, parents share their time with the children as equally as possible. Joint legal custody gives parents equal input in all decisions affecting the children, such as choosing medical treatment and schools.

163 *These same laws can be manipulated* Court-ordered mediation is an example. Feminist critics say that mediators can often be swayed by an abusive husband who appears to be friendly and forthright; they believe that a formal legal setting provides more protection for an emotionally weak woman, who may agree to custody conditions merely out of fear of retaliation by her ex-husband. Studies also indicate that a child inevitably drifts toward spending more time with one parent, usually the mother. She winds up with essentially sole custody but with less economic support than she would have received without mediation. Randy Klaff, "The Tender Years Doctrine: A Defense," *California Law Review* (1982), cited in Mason, *From Father's Property to Children's Rights*, 183.

163 *All too often, the court misuses* "Of the 166 cases resulting in joint custody, 36 percent involved substantial or intense legal conflict," according to a study by social researchers Eleanor E. Maccoby and Robert H. Mnookin, then of Stanford University. They also noted that in about half of the high-conflict cases, the umbrella term of joint custody was misleading because the children actually lived with the mother. Cited in "Child Custody and Support," *Congressional Quarterly Researcher*, Jan. 13, 1995. See also "Bargaining in the Shadow of the Law," by Robert H. Mnookin and Lewis Kornhauser, *The Yale Law Review*, 88 (1979): 950.

163 *"Loyalty conflicts are common"* Goldstein, Freud, and Solnit, *Beyond the Best Interests of the Child*, 38. Researcher Frank Furstenberg, in a five-year study of children with a variety of parental arrangements, concluded that "on the basis of our study we see little strong evidence that children will benefit psycholog-

ically from the judicial or legislative interventions that have been designed to promote paternal participation." Mason, *From Father's Property to Children's Rights*, 172.

Chapter 21

170 *"marked intolerance for postponement"* For an explanation of a child's sense of time, see Goldstein, Freud, and Solnit, *Beyond the Best Interests of the Child*, 40–49.

171 *"emotionally unaware of the events"* and *"day-to-day interchanges"* Goldstein, Freud, and Solnit, *Beyond the Best Interests of the Child*, 12.

171 *The outsiders who do have standing* "The use of experts in child custody trials was gradually introduced in the 1940s and 1950s, reflecting the growth of the mental health profession itself. By the 1960s, almost 19 percent of the cases on appeal involved expert testimony. By 1990, more than one third of the cases on appeal had been tried with the aid of some sort of expert testimony." Mason, *From Father's Property to Children's Rights*, 175.

For case studies in the use of expert witnesses in child abuse cases, see Sagatun and Edwards, *Child Abuse and the Legal System*, chapter 13.

171 *reputation for being "psychologically oriented"* The Santa Clara County dependency court was labeled "clinically-oriented" in a comparative study of two California courts. H. Ted Rubin and Richard Gable, "Dependency Proceedings in California Juvenile Courts," Institute for Court Management, National Center for State Courts, Denver, March 1990, 60.

177 *"Brian needs help"* The social worker came up with the following reunification plan: Brian was to be placed in an institutional setting where the staff was trained to work with disturbed children. Dennis and Debbie would be given visitation rights with their son only as long as they did not interfere with his therapy and as long as they complied with their individual service plans. Each was to complete a parent education course and participate in family counseling. Since both had family histories of drug and alcohol use, both had to attend AA meetings. Both had to refrain from physically disciplining Brian or allowing anyone else to do so.

Chapter 22

179 Children raised in foundling hospitals in Renaissance Florence, the precursors of orphanages, had no adults to bond with, no family they could claim as

their own, and, in a class-bound society, were members of no class. They did not have fathers who could secure an apprenticeship; they were not eligible to join a guild. Like many of the kids roaming city streets in the United States today, they were "unconnected adolescents with no claim on the support or help of any persons or groups in the community."

That was the future they faced if they survived the foundling hospitals, which a majority did not. A parent who left a newborn in a foundling hospital "was consigning his child to death." Fifty percent of the children left at San Gallo in Florence were dead within a year. Only 32 percent of the children who had been left at La Scala in Florence lived to age five. Boswell, *The Kindness of Strangers*, 421–23.

179 For an overview of the history of orphanages, see Hawes, *The Children's Rights Movement in the United States*; "History of the Orphanage," *Newsweek*, Dec. 12, 1994; "The Storm over Orphanages," *Time*, Dec. 12, 1994; "When Parents Are Not in the Best Interests of the Child," by Mary-Lou Weisman, *The Atlantic Monthly*, July 1994, 43–63; "The New Orphanages," *U.S. News and World Report*, Oct. 8, 1990.

The grim truth about how children were being "saved" in turn-of-the-century orphanages was finally revealed by muckraking journalists and social reformers, but only after the childhoods of several generations had been shattered. In 1916, state inspectors and investigators put into words an image of New York City orphanages that still haunts us today: "little children with their hair cropped, sitting at wooden benches and eating out of tin plates . . . forced to do drudgery, working eight or nine hours a day, with only one hour for schooling, and that often at night . . . antiquated methods of punishment prevailed."

179 *Eastfield Ming Quong* "Half-Orphan Fondly Recalls S.J.'s Home of Benevolence," *San Jose Mercury News*, July 11, 1995. Volunteers and hired "parents" provided the children with all the tools considered necessary for a proper Victorian-era upbringing: rigid discipline, strong Christian values, and relentless work to prevent young, idle minds from becoming the devil's playground.

"The girls learned home-making skills and the boys got instruction—and experience—in farming the surrounding acreage," according to the 1995 article. No doubt, the "experience" amounted to free labor for the farmers.

179–180 *large institutions for children had been shuttered* For an account of institutional abuses, see *The Kid Business: How It Exploits the Children It Should Help*, by Ronald B. Taylor (Boston: Houghton Mifflin, 1981).

180 *"You've got to ask"* Nan Dale of The Children's Village, a residential treat-

ment center for boys in Dobbs Ferry, New York, quoted in Weisman, "When Parents Are Not in the Best Interests of the Child," 51.

181 *To keep a child like Brian* Interviews with residential placement social workers at the Department, and the "AFDC-FC Rate List for California Group Homes and Foster Family Agencies," 1994.

181 *charges overblown* EMQ director Jerry Doyle says that the four homes the agency runs are not as bad as the state has portrayed them to be. "Center for Troubled Kids Has Problems of Its Own—Runaways, Sex Abuses Imperil Eastfield's License," *San Jose Mercury News*, April 8, 1993.

181 For more on residential treatment, see *Love Is Not Enough* (New York: Free Press, 1950), Bruno Bettelheim's account of a year at his experimental school at the University of Chicago.

182 David Rothman, quoted in *Newsweek*, "History of the Orphanage," Dec. 12, 1994.

185 *"started bouncing off the walls"* Brian's progress report at EMQ.

Chapter 23

187 *"own rules, structure, leadership"* Napier and Whitaker, *The Family Crucible*, 79.

187 *"Brian's 'crazy' behavior"* Family therapists often talk about how one member of the family—the designated "sick" or "crazy" one—has taken on the role of the family scapegoat, openly suffering "the stress of the entire family." "Children who are hyperactive, have persistent sleep problems, are underachievers, wet their beds repeatedly, stutter, adamantly refuse to go to school . . . are probably suffering the stresses of their parents' marriages." Napier and Whitaker, *The Family Crucible*, 53, 149.

Chapter 24

197 The Jesse Montgomery case is based on Jesse's case file and on interviews with Jesse; Steuart Samuels, the director of the Star House Group Homes; Mary Rolison, Jesse's social worker; and Marc Buller, a deputy district attorney.

198 *status offenders* See Hawes, *The Children's Rights Movement in the United States*, 57, 107–9. The Juvenile Justice and Delinquency Prevention Act of

1974 provided federal funds to states that agreed to remove status offenders from secure confinement and to separate children from adults in jails.

Chapter 26

212 *Teenagers like Jesse and Lynn* "For at least the last decade, we in the field have been reporting, usually to each other, a worsening struggle to work with a much more damaged group of child and families. . . ." Richard Small, quoted in Weisman, "When Parents Are Not in the Best Interests of the Child," 46.

213 *"adverse therapy"* The Kate School was a private, nonprofit center located in the San Joaquin Valley that specialized in the "treatment" of autistic children. Along with the cattle prod, other therapy methods included hair pulling, slapping, spanking, and forcing children to eat regurgitated food. Taylor, *The Kid Business*, 225.

214 *financial scams* One typical story involved a corporation that bought houses and opened group homes. After operating for a year, the corporation folded the homes without notice and sold the real estate. It turned out that the corporation was a dummy set up by the four men who were running the homes. Money that was supposed to be paying for services for the children was being used to pay off mortgages. The partners sold the real estate at a profit and vanished.

For an account of deinstitutionalization and group home scandals, see Taylor, *The Kid Business*, chapter 6.

Chapter 27

221 The Corey McKenzie case is based on his case file; interviews with Frances Crawley, the woman who raised Corey; John Jackson, senior boys' counselor at the Children's Shelter; Cleveland Prince, Santa Clara County probation officer; Richard Roggia, Corey's attorney; Marc Buller, the district attorney; and Jesse Montgomery. Information was also taken from a videotape of Corey's interrogation by officers from the Santa Clara County sheriff's office and from testimony at Corey's trial.

221 *Project Crackdown* "Two-Day Drug Sweep Nets 33; Police Catch Dealers near S.J. Grade Schools," *San Jose Mercury News*, April 29, 1995.

Chapter 28

230 *in Star House on a delinquency petition* In group homes, minors who are in the system on a dependency petition are mixed with minors who are in the system on delinquency petitions. But, as Steuart Samuels is careful to point out, "none of the delinquents have committed a violent crime. We do not take kids who are violent."

Chapter 29

237 Coverage of the Star House murder, "Shock Waves from Slaying; Teen Held in Killing of S.J. Counselor" and "Number of Kids Tied to Killings in County Doubles," *San Jose Mercury News*, April 15, 1994.

237 *the public's gut instinct* "Bay Area residents say crime is the No. 1 problem facing the region, worse even than unemployment and the economy, which headed their 'worry list' in 1993 and 1992. That assessment comes as part of a survey of 600 households conducted periodically since 1980 for the not-for-profit Bay Area Council by Field Research Corp. in San Francisco." "Crime Edges Out Job Fears As Top Worry, Poll Finds," *San Jose Mercury News*, Dec. 16, 1994.

238 *"When a child is young"* In the 1990s even young children are no longer quite so beloved by politicians and the public. The Republican Party's "Contract with America" reflects the notion that Americans are fed up with caring for somebody else's children, even young ones. According to the Children's Defense Fund, it calls for drastic cuts in Medicaid, child support cases, food stamps, and nutrition assistance through the Women, Infants and Children and the school lunch programs, along with cuts in crime prevention programs targeted to children. Californians voted for Proposition 187, which promised to deny education and health services to children whose parents are in the country illegally.

Editorial columnist Joanne Jacobs made this point in a March 13, 1995, column in the *San Jose Mercury News*: "Increasingly, kids are seen not as bundles of joy but as burdens—and too often burdens borne by someone other than the parents. . . . The idea that society has a responsibility to care for 'our' children is losing support. We want parents to care for their own kids—or not have them in the first place."

238 For the media's reaction to street urchins of the late nineteenth century, see Bettmann, *The Good Old Days*, 87–89.

238 *Mayors canceled performances* "The Media's War on Kids," by Jon Katz, *Rolling Stone*, Nov. 25, 1993.

238 *"Some blame a growing permissiveness" Report of the Task Force on Juvenile Justice and Delinquency Prevention*, U.S. Department of Justice, 1976, 5.

239 *immune to rehabilitation* The most widely publicized study with this viewpoint says that with "few and isolated exceptions, the rehabilitative efforts that have been reported so far have no appreciable effect on recidivism." D. Lipton, R. Martinson, and J. Wilks, "The Effectiveness of Correctional Treatment," cited in "Reaffirming Rehabilitation in Juvenile Justice," by Dan Macallair, *Youth and Society* (Newbury Park, California: Sage Publications, 1993).

The study, however, was seriously flawed, and the media did not give equal attention to Martinson's attempt to rectify his earlier mistakes in a follow-up study, which saw signs of positive results from treatment. "New Findings, New Views," *Hofstra Law Review* (1979), cited in *The Limits of Punishment As Social Policy*, by Don Gibbons, National Council on Crime and Delinquency, January 1988.

239 *evening curfews* Like many urban areas, San Jose has established evening curfews for children. Yet, FBI statistics indicate that violent crimes committed by juveniles peak dramatically at the close of the school day and decline throughout the evening hours. This is also the time when juveniles are at greatest risk of being victimized. In contrast with juveniles, the number of violent crimes committed by adults increases from early morning through midnight. Statistics cited in Snyder and Sickmund, *Juvenile Offenders and Victims*, 30, 48.

"Maybe some of these communities with curfews at night will look at these numbers and realize that instead of having curfews starting at 11 P.M.—when juvenile crimes are dropping—they should put more resources into giving kids something to do when they're most in danger, after school," says Snyder. "Juvenile Crime Rate Rising Fast; Report Says Findings Indicate Violence Against Youth Peaks Right After School Lets Out," *San Jose Mercury News*, Sept. 8, 1995.

240 *published a study* Commissioned by Children Now and prepared by Dale Kunkel, associate professor of communications, University of California, Santa Barbara. Data was gathered during November 1993 from the *Atlanta Constitution, Chicago Tribune, Houston Chronicle, Los Angeles Times,*

and *New York Times*, as well as from the nightly newscasts of ABC, CBS, and NBC.

240 *children under age six live in poverty* Snyder and Sickmund, *Juvenile Offenders and Victims*, 7.

240 *two-year-olds are immunized* Interview with James P. Steyer, founder and president of Children Now.

241 *crime victims over age sixty-four* and *In violent crimes against twelve-to-nineteen-year-olds* Snyder and Sickmund, *Juvenile Offenders and Victims*, 47. See also *Teenage Victims: A National Crime Survey Report*, by Catherine J. Whitaker and Lisa D. Bastian, Bureau of Justice Statistics, May 1991.

241 *the very next year in Santa Clara County* Interview with Kurt Kumli, deputy district attorney in delinquency court.

241 *diverted into programs* In 1992, 30 percent of juveniles taken into custody by law enforcement officials were given a warning and then released to parents, other relatives, or friends. Snyder and Sickmund, *Juvenile Offenders and Victims*, 121.

241 *juveniles commit crimes in groups* One in seven serious violent crimes involves juveniles in groups. Multiple-offender killings have more than doubled since the mid-1980s. Snyder and Sickmund, *Juvenile Offenders and Victims*, 47, 99.

241 *"juvenile crime rates have actually declined over the last decade"* "Juvenile Crime, Youth Violence and Public Policy," by Michael A. Jones and Barry Krisberg, *Images and Reality*, National Council on Crime and Delinquency, 2.

241–242 *information from a variety of sources* In the sections on juvenile offenders, the report relies primarily on data developed by the Bureau of Justice Statistics's National Crime Victimization Survey and National Youth Survey, the FBI's National Incident-Based Reporting System, and the National Institute of Justice's Drug Use Forecasting Program and Monitoring the Future Study, as well as on published research studies.

242 *teenagers are never arrested* For statistics on juvenile crime rates and recidivism, see Snyder and Sickmund, *Juvenile Offenders and Victims*, 51 and chapters 3 and 5.

242 *"index" crimes* Since the 1930s, police agencies have reported crime incidents to the FBI Uniform Crime Program. The indexes are similar in concept to stock indexes, in that they are sensitive to changes in the nature and volume of crime. The Violent Crime Index includes murder and nonnegligent manslaughter, forcible rape, robbery, and aggravated assault. The Prop-

erty Crime Index includes burglary, larceny and theft, arson, and motor vehicle theft. For an excellent explanation of the indexes, see Snyder and Sickmund, *Juvenile Offenders and Victims*, 98–99.

242 *If this trend continues* Snyder and Sickmund, *Juvenile Offenders and Victims*, 111.

242 *Another scary statistic* Snyder and Sickmund, *Juvenile Offenders and Victims, 1996 Update on Violence*, 22.

242 *Since 1984, the population under eighteen* Snyder and Sickmund, *Juvenile Offenders and Victims*, 2.

242 *A 1993 study of incarcerated juvenile offenders* "Gun Acquisition and Possession in Selected Juvenile Samples," by Joseph F. Sheley and James D. Wright, *Research in Brief*, U.S. Department of Justice, December 1993.

243 *"borrowing a firearm from family or friends"* Sheley and Wright, "Gun Acquisition and Possession."

243 *Statistically, Corey McKenzie is an anomaly* Figures on gun use from Snyder and Sickmund, *Juvenile Offenders and Victims: 1996 Update on Violence*, fact sheet #35, Office of Juvenile Justice and Delinquency Prevention.

243 *"teenage boys in all racial groups"* According to the National Center for Health Statistics, quoted in Jones and Krisberg, *Images and Reality*, 15.

243 For statistics on young homicide and suicide victims, see Snyder and Sickmund, *Juvenile Offenders and Victims*, 24–27.

Chapter 30

245 *The harshest line of reasoning* Compared to their representation in the general population (15 percent), black juveniles make up 26 percent of all juvenile arrests and 49 percent of the juvenile arrests for offenses included in the Violent Crime Index. Snyder and Sickmund, *Juvenile Offenders and Victims*, 91.

245 *39 percent of juveniles* Snyder and Sickmund, *Juvenile Offenders and Victims*, 100.

245 *"offending rates" alone cannot account* Black juveniles are overrepresented at all stages of the juvenile justice system. They make up 41 percent of detained delinquency cases, 43 percent of out-of-home placements, 46 percent of the juveniles placed into public long-term institutions, and 52 percent of the cases judicially waived to criminal court. Snyder and Sickmund, *Juvenile Offenders and Victims*, 91.

Also, "while black youth made up 31% of delinquency cases processed in 1992, they were involved in 39% of detained delinquency cases," and "cases involving white youth were the least likely to be detained." "There were substantially more minorities (65%) held in public detention centers in 1991 than in 1983." See the charts on 142–44 of *Juvenile Offenders and Victims*.

245 *The Office of Juvenile Justice and Delinquency Prevention reviewed three decades—Minorities and the Juvenile Justice System*, December 1993.

The authors of *Juvenile Offenders and Victims* are more measured on the influence of race. "One possible explanation for disparity and overrepresentation is, of course, discrimination. . . . However [disparity and overrepresentation] can result from factors other than discrimination. This line of reasoning suggests that if minority youth are involved in more serious incidents and have more extensive criminal histories, they will be overrepresented in secure facilities. . . . Thus . . . the causes of observed disparity remain unanswered." Snyder and Sickmund, 92.

246 *Gone is the era* From 1975 to 1991, the number of status offenders and nonoffenders in secure facilities dropped 76 percent. Today, 95 percent of the juveniles in public detention centers are there for delinquency offenses. Office of Juvenile Justice and Delinquency Prevention, *Children in Custody Census*, 1993.

246 *Juvenile Hall for years has been too crowded* Nationwide, the population of detention centers grew 46 percent from 1983 to 1991. The crowded conditions in Santa Clara County are mirrored around the country. One study of a single day in February 1991 (cited on page 149 of Snyder and Sickmund, *Juvenile Offenders and Victims*) indicated that 53 percent of detention centers were operating above their design capacity. In 1991, one third of confined juveniles were in living units with twenty-six or more juveniles, and one third slept in rooms that were smaller than required by national standards. "Conditions of Confinement: Juvenile Detention and Corrections Facilities, Research Summary—February 1994" and "Conditions of Confinement," by Dale G. Parent, spring/summer 1993, both published by the Office of Juvenile Justice and Delinquency Prevention.

246 *half of all delinquency cases* Snyder and Sickmund, *Juvenile Offenders and Victims*, 131.

249 *says one youth advocate* Jeff Herd, quoted in *Metro*, the Santa Clara Valley's weekly newspaper, April 4, 11.

Chapter 31

252 *One was a reporter* Several U.S. Supreme Court cases have dealt with the issue of confidentiality and the press. In *Oklahoma Publishing Company v. District Court in and for Oklahoma City*, the court ruled in 1977 that an order prohibiting the press from reporting the name and publishing the legally obtained photograph of a youth involved in a juvenile court proceeding was an unconstitutional infringement on freedom of the press. In a 1979 case, *Smith v. Daily Mail Publishing Company*, it was held that state law cannot stop the press from publishing a juvenile's name obtained independently of the court. Snyder and Sickmund, *Juvenile Offenders and Victims*, 81–82. California code also waives confidentiality and allows public access to juvenile court proceedings under certain conditions: when the minor is in "violation of any one of the following offenses: murder, arson, robbery while armed with a dangerous or deadly weapon, rape. . . ." For the full code and list of offenses, see *California Welfare and Institutions Code* 676.

253 *There are any number of studies* "The 'cycle of violence' hypothesis suggests that . . . victims of neglect are also more likely to develop later criminal violent behavior as well." For an overview of studies, see *The Cycle of Violence*, by Cathy Spatz Widom, *Research in Brief*, U.S. Department of Justice, October 1992.

In the ongoing study of a thousand seventh- and eighth-graders, a greater proportion of children who were "substantiated victims of maltreatment before age 12" committed violent acts than did youth who had not been abused at home (70 percent versus 56 percent). Seventy percent of children exposed to spousal violence reported violent behavior (49 percent for children not exposed); 70 percent of children exposed to maltreatment reported violent behavior (53 percent for children not exposed); and 68 percent of children who grew up in a "family climate of hostility" reported violent behavior (43 percent for children growing up in happier homes). Seventy-nine percent of the children who suffered from all three negative factors at home reported violent behavior; 39 percent of the children who grew up in homes where none of the negative factors was present reported violent behavior. Snyder and Sickmund, *Juvenile Offenders and Victims*, 42.

254 *"Not all victims of a violent past"* There has been much speculation as to why one abused child grows up to be a murderer and why another lives a productive life. Research indicates there to be a "cumulative effect" with "different

combinations of life experiences" that produce different behaviors and degrees of delinquency. For instance, in a 1988 study, delinquents with parents who were not incarcerated, whose mothers expressed positive opinions of them during their childhood, and who did not spend their leisure time with their fathers were more successful in their adjustment to adult life. David P. Farrington, et al., "Are There Any Successful Men from Criminogenic Backgrounds?" This study and others are cited in *Family Life, Delinquency and Crime*, Office of Juvenile Justice and Delinquency Prevention, May 1994.

In *Within Our Reach: Breaking the Cycle of Disadvantage* (New York: Anchor Press, 1988), author Lisbeth B. Schorr describes how the piling up of "risk factors" increases a child's chance of a "rotten outcome." Along with childhood abuse, risk factors can include being born prematurely, living in poverty, suffering from physical defects, being born with a "difficult" personality, and having a depressed parent. "No one circumstance, no single event" is the "cause." Each risk factor that is "vanquished" by a healthy birth or a functioning parent "powerfully tips the scales toward favorable outcomes." See chapter 2, "The Risk Factors," 23–32.

256 *his father had whipped him* Frances Crawley, Corey's father's longtime companion, denies that Dafford McKenzie ever beat his son. "As far as him not being around and taking care of Corey, that kind of abuse, yes, he did that," Crawley says. "But beating him? Never! That was just something Corey and his lawyer made up."

256 *"That wasn't John"* "Boy Testifies Father's Abuse Drove Him to Stab Counselor," *San Jose Mercury News*, Sept. 15, 1994.

257 *A reporter had to phone her* "Judge Finds Boy, 15, Guilty of Murder," *San Jose Mercury News*, Sept. 16, 1994.

Chapter 32

258 *"When Corey McKenzie killed"* Brenda De Caprio's statement is taken from a letter she wrote to Judge Richard C. Turrone. Judges in California consider victims' statements at the sentencing phase of a trial.

258 *Throughout the 1990s, similar get-tough* "Some laws removed classes of offenders from the juvenile system and handled them as adult criminals in criminal court. Others required the juvenile system to be more like the criminal system and to treat certain classes of juvenile offenders as criminals in juvenile court." Snyder and Sickmund, *Juvenile Offenders and Victims*, 72.

Other get-tough measures were also gaining popularity. In 1983, Georgia and Oklahoma started a national trend by opening boot camps for young offenders, and ten years later the U.S. House and Senate passed crime bills expanding federal funding for boot camps, emphasizing "certainty of punishment" for young offenders. Federal penalties were also approved for possession of guns by minors, and the Senate passed legislation to subject gang participants to stiff federal sentences.

In Minnesota, a juvenile justice task force recommended that the state move away from its therapeutic orientation in cases of violent crime. Public safety, rather than the best interests of the child, would be the deciding fact in shifting a juvenile to adult court. Many states also added to their juvenile codes phrases such as "provide effective deterrents" and "protection of the public from criminal activity." "Juvenile Justice: Should Violent Youth Get Tougher Penalties?" *Congressional Quarterly Researcher*, Feb. 25, 1994.

In 1989, the U.S. Supreme Court, in *Stanford v. Kentucky*, decided that the Eighth Amendment (giving constitutional protection against cruel and unusual punishment) does not prohibit the death penalty for crimes committed at ages sixteen or seventeen. The minimum age authorized for the death penalty is now under eighteen in seventeen states. Between 1973 and 1993, 121 death sentences were handed down to juveniles, but a large percentage (66 percent) have been reversed. Since 1973, 7 percent have resulted in executions and 27 percent are still in force. Snyder and Sickmund, *Juvenile Offenders and Victims*, 179.

260 *the story of Melvin Ancheta* Melvin Ancheta's killer had two accomplices. They watched the stabbing but did not touch the knife. Both were over sixteen. Their cases were transferred to criminal court, where they were sentenced to life in prison.

261 *Progressives rely on statistics* The national and international statistics are taken from *Singapore West: The Incarceration of 200,000 Californians*, by Mark Koetting and Vincent Schiraldi, Center on Juvenile and Criminal Justice, July 1994, 7. The authors compiled them from a lengthy list of sources, including the Human Rights Watch/Prison Project, the National Criminal Justice Commission, the Council of Europe, and the California Department of Corrections.

261 *astronomical incarceration figures* The word "astronomical" also applies to the number of youths up to age seventeen who are incarcerated in California. Nearly half of all youth in detention centers in the United States on Feb. 15, 1991, were in four states—California, Florida, Michigan, and Ohio. Califor-

nia had 5,754 in detention centers, a detention rate of 178 per 100,000 juveniles. Florida was a distant second, with 1,289 youths in custody and a detention rate per 100,000 of 103. The District of Columbia had the highest
detention rate, 478 per 100,000. By comparison, North Dakota had 5 youths
in detention, a rate of 7 per 100,000. Snyder and Sickmund, *Juvenile Offenders and Victims*, 145.

262 *an increasing number of states* Some states, including California, have permitted juvenile offenders to be transferred to criminal courts since before the
1920s. "Traditionally, the decision to transfer was made by a juvenile court
judge and was based upon the individual circumstances. Beginning in the
1970s, state legislatures increasingly moved young offenders into criminal
court based on age and offense seriousness without the case specific assessment." Snyder and Sickmund, *Juvenile Offenders and Victims*, 85, 154.

262 *Certainly not the strict punishment* The New York study was conducted by
the American Institutes of Research and cited in "Where We Stand: An Action Plan for Dealing with Violent Juvenile Crime," National Council of Juvenile and Family Court Judges, University of Nevada, March 1994, 3. It also
found that, nationally, some criminal courts dismiss "50% or more of juvenile
complaints received on waiver, transfer, or certification."

Another study found that "only about 10 to 12 percent of juveniles transferred to criminal court do any time in California, which is an incredibly low
rate of incarceration for juveniles who are supposed to be treated more
harshly. . . . It does not appear that juveniles receive harsher penalties on the
average, when transferred to criminal court, for a broad range of offenses."
Dean J. Champion, chairman of the Criminal Justice Department at Minot
State University in North Dakota, quoted in *Congressional Quarterly Researcher*, Feb. 25, 1994. However, the authors of *Juvenile Offenders and Victims*
say that most research on the impact of transferring juveniles to criminal
court is ten years old and has "not yielded definitive conclusions." See Snyder
and Sickmund, 156.

262 *Another study, conducted in New York* "Where We Stand," National Council
of Juvenile and Family Court Judges, 4.

263 *violent repeat offenders* "Deep End Juvenile Justice Placements or Transfer to
Adult Court by Direct File?" by C.E. Frazier, reprinted in Jones and Krisberg, *Images and Reality*, 33.

263 *Nationally, only 38 percent of the juveniles* National Corrections Reporting
Program, Bureau of Justice Statistics, 1989.

263 *"probability of rearrest and reincarceration"* J. Fagan, "The Comparative Im-

pacts of Juvenile and Criminal Court Sanctions for Adolescent Felon Offenders," National Institute of Justice, 1991, cited in Snyder and Sickmund, *Juvenile Offenders and Victims*, 156, 161.

264 *anything but "soft"* "I think it's a myth that juveniles get treated leniently." Rand Corporation researcher Peter Greenwood, quoted in *Congressional Quarterly Researcher*, Feb. 25, 1994.

264 *Between 1983 and 1991* Snyder and Sickmund, *Juvenile Offenders and Victims*, 167.

264 *a study of the juvenile courts in ten states* J.A. Butts and D.J. Connors-Beatty, "The Juvenile Court's Responses to Violence: 1985–1989," U.S. Department of Justice, 1993, cited in Jones and Krisberg, *Images and Reality*, 24. Also cited in Snyder and Sickmund, *Juvenile Offenders and Victims*, 134. "Despite the fact that adult court defendants would be expected to have, on average, more lengthy criminal records, the study showed that violent juvenile offenders were more likely to receive sanctions in juvenile court than were adult violent offenders in criminal court."

264 *Figures for 1992 show that youths incarcerated* Cited in Jones and Krisberg, *Images and Reality*, 26. Another study of New York and New Jersey courts found that dispositions were no less severe in juvenile court compared to adult court. Fagan, Schiff, Brisben, and Orden, "The Comparative Impacts," 156.

264 *two and a half times as much on education* "'96 Budget Favors Prison over College; '3 Strikes' to Eat into Education Funds," *San Jose Mercury News*, July 8, 1995.

265 *"AB-136 passed"* "14-Year-Olds Can Be Tried as Adults," *San Jose Mercury News*, Sept. 10, 1994.

Chapter 33

270 *"These kids need to be touched"* Gail Steinkamp adds, "I always asked if I could touch a boy first. If I didn't, I could get hit. Even after asking and getting an OK, I'd sometimes feel a boy's muscles tighten. I could hear him asking himself, 'What's she going to do next?'"

270 *"the neediest of the needy"* Al Picucci, interview at Preston School of Industry.

271 *it costs $30,100 to keep a ward* "CYA Facts," February 1994, published by the California Youth Authority, and information from CYA public information officers in Sacramento.

271 *the Commonweal Research Institute published*—*The CYA Report: Conditions of Life in the California Youth Authority*, by Steve Lerner (Bolinas, California: Common Knowledge Press, 1982); *Bodily Harm: The Pattern of Fear and Violence at the California Youth Authority*, by Steve Lerner (Common Knowledge Press, 1986); and *Reforming the CYA: How to End Crowding, Diversify Treatment and Protect the Public Without Spending More Money*, by Paul DeMuro, Anne DeMuro, and Steve Lerner (Common Knowledge Press, 1988).

271 *148 percent of capacity* The CYA Information Office, Sacramento.

271 *"the violent, gang-oriented atmosphere"* Lerner, *Bodily Harm*, 11–12.

271 *"The tragedy of the Youth Authority today"* Lerner, *Bodily Harm*, 12.

271 *"an agent of the gang's violence or its victim"* Lerner, *Bodily Harm*, 14. The conditions at the CYA are also seen at juvenile institutions across the country. A 1991 study by Apt Associates, Inc., under contract with the Office of Juvenile Justice and Delinquency Prevention, found that "facilities had substantial and widespread deficiencies in the following areas: crowding, security, suicide prevention and health screenings and appraisals." *Juvenile Justice*, spring/summer 1993.

272 On Jerome Miller and the changes in the Massachusetts Department of Youth Services, see *Last One over the Wall: The Massachusetts Experiment in Closing Reform Schools*, by Jerome G. Miller (Columbus: Ohio State University Press, 1991), and *The Good News About Juvenile Justice: The Movement Away from Large Institutions and Toward Community-Based Services*, by Steve Lerner (Bolinas, California: Common Knowledge Press, 1991).

273 *"The rearrest rate of young people leaving DYS"* Some critics of the Massachusetts model contend that the lower rate merely reflects the demographics of the time. Criminal arrests everywhere were lower.

273 *"California Correctional Peace Officers Association"* See "Three Strikes, They're Rich," *Metro*, the Santa Clara Valley's weekly newspaper, Oct. 27 and Nov. 2, 1994. See also "The Undue Influence of California's Prison Guards' Union: California's Correctional-Industrial Complex," by Vincent Schiraldi, Center on Juvenile and Criminal Justice, October 1994.

Chapter 34

276 *In re Gault* Forer, *Unequal Protection*, 201. Justice Abe Fortas, in the majority decision, said, "The state of being a boy does not justify a kangaroo court." Several other U.S. Supreme Court decisions have made juvenile courts more like criminal courts, while maintaining differences. *Re Winship* (1970) found

that in delinquency matters the state must prove its case beyond a reasonable doubt. *McKeiver v. Pennsylvania* (1971) found that jury trials are not constitutionally required in juvenile court hearings. In *Eddings v. Oklahoma* (1982), it was found that a defendant's youthful age should be considered a mitigating factor in deciding whether to apply the death penalty. In *Schall v. Martin* (1984), the court ruled that preventive "pretrial" detention of juveniles was allowable under certain circumstances. See Snyder and Sickmund, *Juvenile Offenders and Victims*, 80–93, for details of *re Kent* and these other landmark cases.

276 *"the word 'punishment'"* Many states, including Pennsylvania and Wisconsin, still emphasize prevention, diversion, and treatment as the goals of their juvenile justice system. Other states, like Texas and Hawaii, emphasize punishment, while others have a mixed purpose. Survey by L. Szymanski, cited in Snyder and Sickmund, *Juvenile Offenders and Victims*, 71.

276 *"once unwanted and unnecessary"* Edwards, "The Juvenile Court," 7.

276 *it was already full of minors* Nationwide, U.S. courts handle four thousand delinquency cases each day, according to 1992 figures, the latest statistics available. Snyder and Sickmund, *Juvenile Offenders and Victims*, 126.

279 *Kumli works closely with a staffer* In a review of many studies and programs, the Office of Juvenile Justice and Delinquency Prevention concluded that juvenile delinquency efforts have been unsuccessful because of several weaknesses, including the "narrow scope, focusing on only one or two of society's institutions that have responsibility for the social development of children. Most programs have targeted either the school arena or the family. Communities are an often neglected area." "Comprehensive Strategy for Serious, Violent, and Chronic Juvenile Offenders: Program Summary," December 1993.

279 *delineates the consequences of gang activity* According to the 1991 school crime report from the *National Crime Victimization Survey Report*, 15 percent of students reported gangs at school. U.S. Department of Justice, Bureau of Justice Statistics. It is not at all conclusive that antigang, antidrug, and antisex school programs using scare tactics or strict messages like "don't join gangs," are particularly effective in combating problems that are sociologically complex. For instance, a three-year study of five thousand students in California's multimillion-dollar drug education program, conducted for the state's Department of Education, concluded that it was not stopping kids from trying drugs. Further, "its underlying message—all substance use is abuse—erodes the credibility of teachers, and alienates students most at risk of serious drug abuse." "Message Erodes Credibility of Teachers: Program

Fails to Stop Kids from Trying Drugs," *San Jose Mercury News*, Nov. 13, 1995.

279 *"a big-time gang problem"* A 1992 survey of metropolitan police departments in the seventy-nine largest U.S. cities and a sampling of forty-three smaller cities indicate that the "number of jurisdictions affected by gangs has increased substantially in the past 20 years."

In the early part of the twentieth century, gang members were most commonly second-generation white immigrants from eastern and southern Europe and African-Americans who had recently immigrated to Northern cities from the South. Today, the ethnicity of gang members is estimated to be 48 percent African-American; 43 percent Hispanic, 5 percent Asian, and 4 percent white. The proportions of white and Asian gang members appear to be increasing. Snyder and Sickmund, *Juvenile Offenders and Victims*, 54–55.

280 *Crips and Bloods form allegiances* Some gang experts claim that, contrary to media reports, the bulk of gang violence is not a cause or consequence of drug dealing. "Violence occurs independently and is more often related to status and territorial disputes directed at members of other gangs. . . . Individual gang members may be involved in [drug] distribution networks, but in most instances these networks are not gang-organized activities." Snyder and Sickmund, *Juvenile Offenders and Victims*, 55.

281 *"More girls are joining gangs"* Data from the 1992 survey of law enforcement agencies did not find a major involvement of girls in gangs. One reason may be that, as a matter of gang policy, females are not classified as "members." It was estimated that about 6 percent of gang members are female. Among gang members, a higher proportion of male crimes are violent, while a higher proportion of female crimes are property offenses. But this appears to be changing. Female juvenile violent crime arrests more than doubled between 1985 and 1994. Snyder and Sickmund, *Juvenile Offenders and Victims*, 55, and *1996 Update on Violence*, 11.

281 *"the age of kids who are committing serious violent offenses"* Between 1972 and 1992, the average age of the U.S. population increased by nearly three years. But even so, those arrested for murder and weapons violations in 1992 were, on average, nearly three years younger than those arrested for the same crimes in 1972. This, however, was not the case for lesser crimes. The average age of persons arrested for larceny and theft and burglary was nearly four years higher than for those arrested in 1972. Snyder and Sickmund, *Juvenile Offenders and Victims*, 109.

Chapter 35

283 The case of Luis Soto and his girlfriend Claudia is based on their case files from dependency and delinquency courts, along with interviews with Luis, Claudia, friends, probation officers, Kurt Kumli, Claudia's mother, social workers for Claudia and her mother and sister, attorneys for Claudia and her mother, and counselors at the Alum Rock Counseling Center and at Connections, a social service organization for pregnant teens.

Chapter 36

292 *It was not only acquaintances* "It is impossible to maintain civilization with 12-year-olds having babies. . . ." Newt Gingrich quoted in *The New Republic*, Nov. 7, 1994.

"Calling it nothing less than a national mobilization against teen-age pregnancy, President Clinton's assistants have drafted a plan that calls teen-age pregnancy 'a bedrock issue of character and personal responsibility . . . the spiraling number of births among unwed mothers is the driving force behind many of the nation's problems, including poverty, crime, drugs and educational failure.' " *New York Times*, March 21, 1994.

292 *viewed as irresponsible leeches* There is no denying that teenage pregnancy is costly. Between 1980 and 1991, the birthrate for unmarried women between the ages of fifteen and seventeen increased by 50 percent. In 1991, 200,000 babies were born to mothers under age eighteen; four out of five were unmarried. The costs start at birth. Infants born to teens have the greatest risk of low birth weight, 10 percent to mothers age seventeen and younger, as compared to 7 percent to mothers above age seventeen. See Snyder and Sickmund, *Juvenile Offenders and Victims*, 12. On average, only 5 percent of teen mothers get college degrees, and one third of the daughters of teenage mothers go on to become teen mothers themselves.

Politicians typically place the full brunt of the blame on rampant teenage sex, in particular the young women "who just can't say no." But this ignores the reality. Approximately two thirds of all teenage mothers are impregnated by men age twenty to fifty. Most of the young women are young, poor, and politically powerless; to demand responsibility only from them is inept public policy. For a fascinating look at how society's view of teenage mothers has changed see Kristin Luker, *Dubious Conceptions: The Politics of Teenage Pregnancy* (Cambridge: Harvard University Press, 1996).

293 *"domestic violence"* In 1994, 7,842 Santa Clara residents called police to report domestic assaults, and experts say that these numbers only hint at the amount of family violence. Of these, the county prosecuted eighty cases. For a view of how social policy has historically responded to the "war at home," see Elizabeth Pleck, *Domestic Tyranny: The Making of Social Policy Against Family Violence from Colonial Times to the Present* (New York: Oxford University Press, 1917). *Family Violence: A Guide to Research* lists publications and literature under headings such as "Children in Violent Homes," "The Dynamics of Domestic Violence," and "Batterer Treatment Programs." It is available from the National Criminal Justice Reference Service, Rockville, Maryland.

ACKNOWLEDGMENTS

WE BEGAN WITH THE IDEA OF STICKING CLOSE TO JUDGE LEONARD Edwards's courtroom, but, as the judge himself predicted, we quickly found ourselves carried off into a confusing, often depressing, often exhilarating world of agencies, prisons, shelters, and foster homes. With Judge Edwards, we could not have had a better, more enthusiastic starting place. His guidance along the way, his help at every obstacle was always encouraging and always instructive, without ever being intrusive. As the best teachers do, he pointed the way, then stepped back and allowed us to learn. We could not have done this book without him.

Deputy District Attorney Kurt Kumli escorted us through the intricacies of delinquency court. Through him, many doors were opened that otherwise would have remained closed. To this project he brought the same energy that he brings to his work with kids, day in and day out.

Many social workers, in addition to those mentioned in the book, patiently answered our most mundane questions about a system that at first seemed indecipherable. Our heartfelt thanks to them all. John Oppenheim, director of Family and Children's Services, encouraged us to accurately portray the department he oversees, warts and all.

Juvenile law is particularly challenging to understand. Mike Clark of the county counsel office, public defender Thomas Spielbauer, Judge Len Sprinkles, Guy Jinkerson, and district attorneys Bob Masterson and Marc Buller were outstanding teachers. To them and to all the "regulars" in courtroom 42, Earl, Carol, and Lance, we owe much gratitude.

Pam Clark and Kelly Robinson at the county Perinatal Substance Abuse Program were astute guides into the world of addicted mothers. Counselors John Jackson and Charlie Gebetsberger helped us interpret the reality of life for both residents and staff at the Santa Clara County Children's Shelter. John Malloy and Steve Schwimmer at The Foundry showed us that, naysayers to the contrary, troubled kids are not lost causes.

Howard Snyder, statistics "guru" for the National Center for Juvenile Justice, reviewed our figures and percentages with a meticulous and critical eye. Typist Shannon Watenpaugh listened to hundreds of hours of rambling taped interviews and transcribed them neatly and efficiently.

Our agent, our friend and all-around good guy, Joel E. Fishman, saw the potential for this book in our scattered stories about juvenile court. He helped us shape our thoughts into a coherent proposal and got it into the hands of the right editor. Ann Patty at Crown has been a real champion for us and, along the way, a lot of fun. Her editing has made it a much better book. Thanks also to Patrick Sheehan for stepping in and to copy editor Robert Rauch for catching about two hundred comma splices.

• • •

The impetus for this book began with an article that John wrote as a staff writer for *West Magazine* of the *San Jose Mercury News.* His editors there, Pat Dillon, Bob Ingle, Fran Smith, and Jerry Ceppos, approved a sabbatical. We are grateful for the time and freedom to do justice to the topic of children and families.

On a personal note, our children, Alex and Gwen, were eight and five respectively when we started this book. Over the past few years, they have met some of the characters and heard a lot of disturbing stories about children whose lives are much harder than theirs. The way in which they inevitably responded—with concern and compassion, with a desire to help—gives us faith in the future.

Many other family members and friends provided emotional and moral support. Thanks to our parents, Lillian and Gilbert Wolfson and John and Elaine Hubner. Also thanks to our friends at Horace Mann School and the sangha of Kannon-Do. For comic relief and last-minute child care, a tip of the hat to The Shoobies and their parents, in particular to Dan Mayfield for his numerous juvenile court contacts and for his superior baby-sitting.

And last, thank you to the dozens of children, teenagers, and parents who spoke with us and who do not find their stories in this book. Rest assured that your insights, suggestions, experiences, and honesty shaped this narrative in the most profound ways.

INDEX

CPSIA information can be obtained at www.ICGtesting.com
Printed in the USA
LVOW132109250812

295945LV00001B/64/A